I've always been an extreme shut-in by nature, so my lifestyle has not changed much recently, which is kind of shocking. I'm eternally grateful to the people who deliver food and other stuff to my home.

This is *World Trigger* volume 22.

—Daisuke Ashihara, 2020

Daisuke Ashihara began his manga career at the age of 27 when his manga *Room 303* won second place in the 75th Tezuka Awards. His first series, *Super Dog Rilienthal*, began serialization in *Weekly Shonen Jump* in 2009. *World Trigger* is his second serialized work in *Weekly Shonen Jump*. He is also the author of several shorter works, including the one-shots *Super Dog Rilienthal*, *Trigger Keeper* and *Elite Agent Jin*.

WORLD TRIGGER VOL. 22
SHONEN JUMP Manga Edition

STORY AND ART BY DAISUKE ASHIHARA

Translation/Caleb Cook
Touch-Up Art & Lettering/Annaliese "Ace" Christman
Design/Julian [JR] Robinson
Editor/Marlene First

WORLD TRIGGER © 2013 by Daisuke Ashihara/SHUEISHA Inc.
All rights reserved.
First published in Japan in 2013 by SHUEISHA Inc., Tokyo.
English translation rights arranged by SHUEISHA Inc.

The stories, characters and incidents mentioned
in this publication are entirely fictional.

Printed in the U.S.A.

Published by VIZ Media, LLC
P.O. Box 77010
San Francisco, CA 94107

10 9 8 7 6 5 4 3 2 1
First printing, May 2021

viz.com

WORLD TRIGGER 22

DAISUKE ASHIHARA

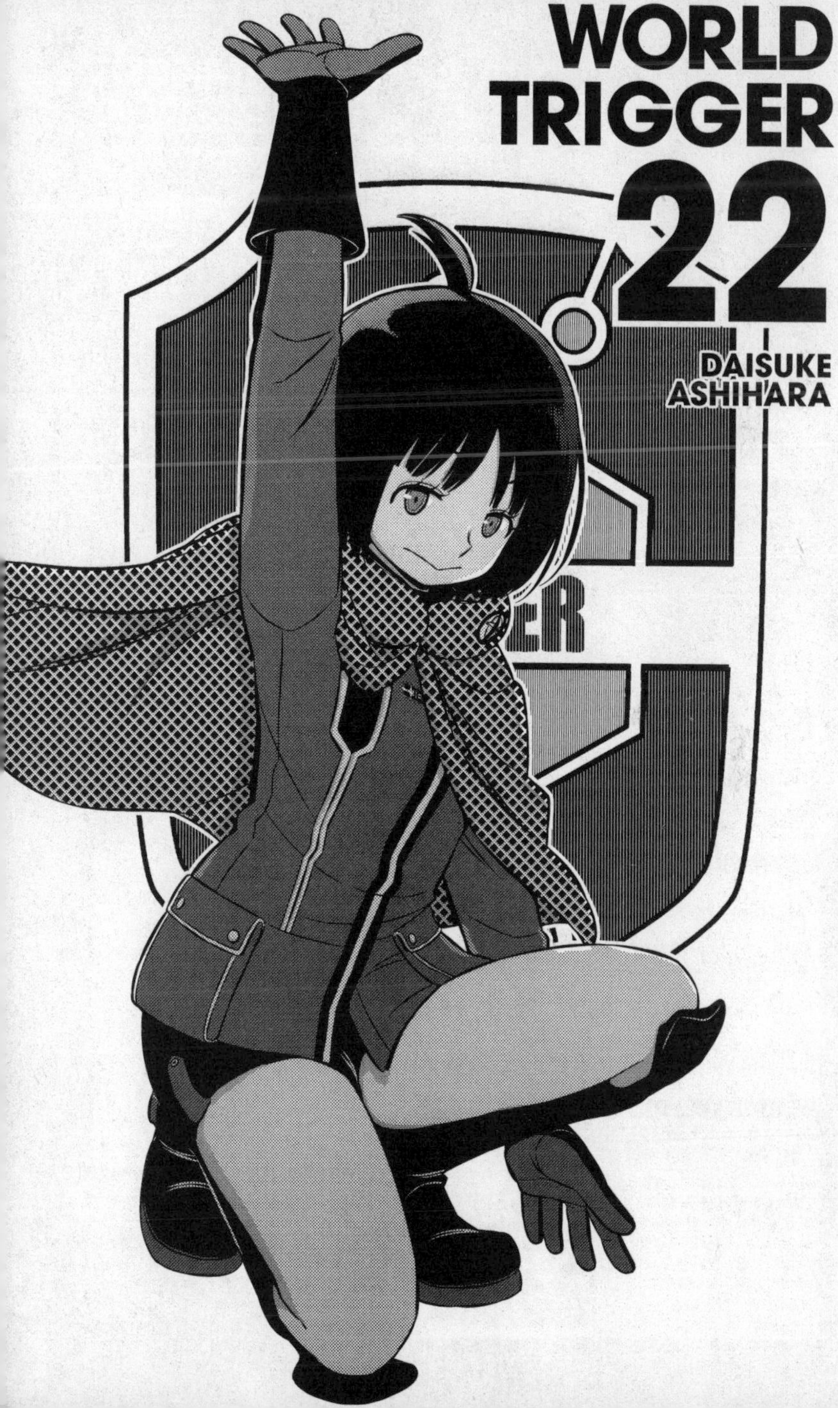

WORLD TRIGGER
DATA BASE

BORDER

An agency founded to protect the city's peace from Neighbors.

S-Rank Black Trigger Users (i.e. Tsukihiko Amo)

A-Rank (Elite) — Away teams selected from here (Arashiyama, Miwa squads)

Promoted in Rank Wars

B-Rank (Main force) — Agents on defense duty must be at least B-Rank (Tamakoma-2)

Promoted at 4,000 solo points

C-Rank (Trainees) — Use trainee Triggers only in emergencies (Izuho Natsume)

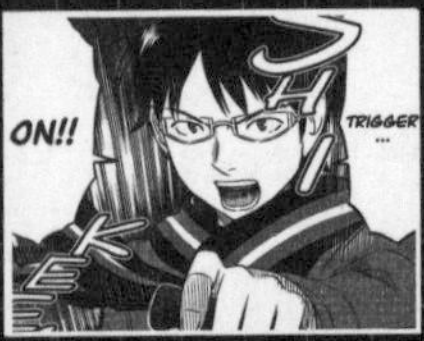
ON!!
TRIGGER...

TRIGGER

A technology created by Neighbors to manipulate Trion. Used mainly as weapons, Triggers come in various types.

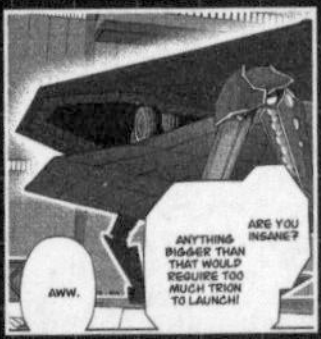
ARE YOU INSANE?
ANYTHING BIGGER THAN THAT WOULD REQUIRE TOO MUCH TRION TO LAUNCH!
AWW.

◀ Away mission ships also run on Trion.

POSITIONS

Border classifies them into three groups: Attacker, Gunner and Sniper.

Attacker

Close-range attacks. Weapons include: close-range Scorpions that are good for surprise attacks, the balanced Kogetsu sword, and the defense-heavy Raygust.

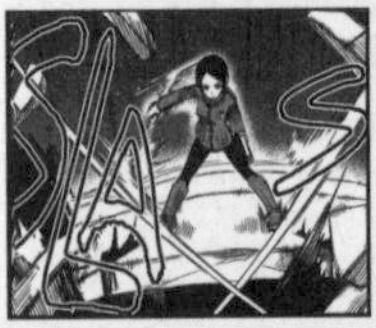

Gunner

Shoots from mid-range. There are several types of bullets, including multipurpose Asteroids, twisting Vipers, exploding Meteors, and tracking Hounds. People who don't use gun-shaped Triggers are called Shooters.

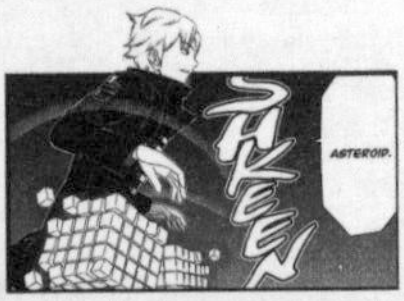
ASTEROID.

◀ Osamu and Izumi are Shooters.

Sniper

Fires from a long distance. There are three sniping rifles: the well-balanced Egret, the light and easy Lightning, and the powerful but unwieldy Ibis.

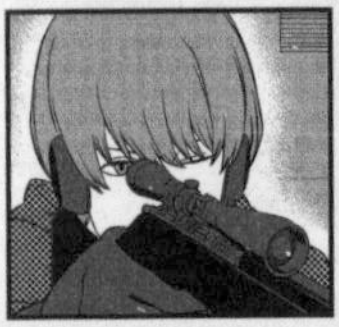

Operator

Supports combatants by relaying information such as enemy positions and abilities.

RANK WARS

Practice matches between Border agents. Promotions in Border are based on good results in the Rank Wars and defense duty achievements.

A-Rank

Top two B-Rank squads get to challenge A-Rank.

B-Rank

B-Rank agents are split into top, middle, and bottom groups. Three to four teams fight in a melee battle. Defeating an opposing squad member earns you one point and surviving to the end nets two points. Top teams from the previous season get a bonus.

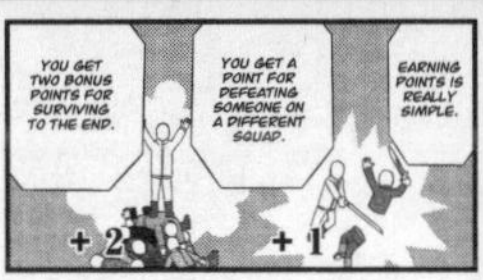
EARNING POINTS IS REALLY SIMPLE.
YOU GET A POINT FOR DEFEATING SOMEONE ON A DIFFERENT SQUAD.
YOU GET TWO BONUS POINTS FOR SURVIVING TO THE END.
+1
+2

B-Rank middle groups have set strategies. Top groups all have an A-Rank level ace.

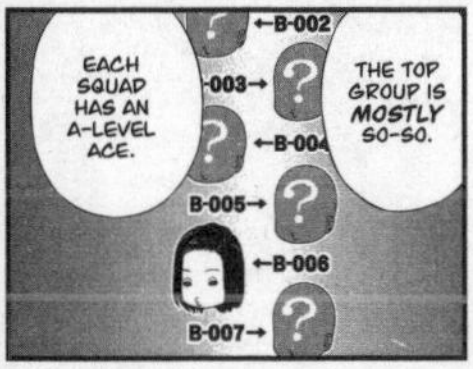
THE TOP GROUP IS MOSTLY SO-SO.
EACH SQUAD HAS AN A-LEVEL ACE.
←B-002
-003→
←B-004
B-005→
←B-006
B-007→

The lowest-ranked team in each match gets to pick the stage.

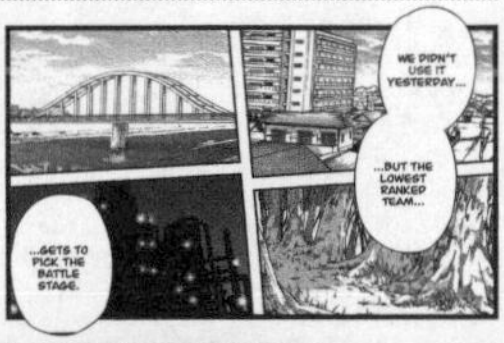
WE DIDN'T USE IT YESTERDAY...
...BUT THE LOWEST RANKED TEAM...
...GETS TO PICK THE BATTLE STAGE.

C-Rank

Agents (B-Rank and above) can't fight trainees (C-Rank) for points. ▶

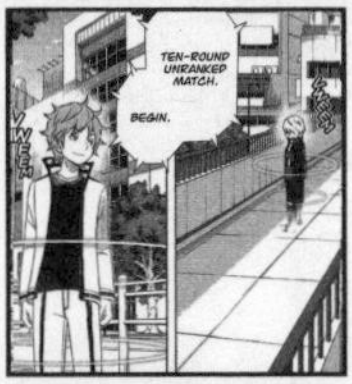
TEN-ROUND UNRANKED MATCH.
BEGIN.

C-Rank Wars are fought through solo matches. Beating someone with more points than you gets you a lot of points. On the other hand, beating someone with fewer points doesn't get you as many.

STORY

About four years ago, a Gate connecting to another dimension opened in Mikado City, leading to the appearance of invaders called Neighbors. After the establishment of the Border Defence Agency, people were able to return to their normal lives.

Osamu Mikumo is a junior high student who meets Yuma Kuga, a Neighbor. Yuma is targeted for capture by Border, but Tamakoma branch agent Yuichi Jin steps in to help. He convinces Yuma to join Border instead, then gives his Black Trigger to HQ in exchange for Yuma's enlistment. Now Osamu, Yuma and Osamu's friend Chika work toward making A-Rank together.

Hoping to be chosen for the away missions, Osamu and his squad are aiming for No. 2 or higher in B-rank. Plotting to give the squad more firepower, Osamu has added the captured Hyuse to the Tamakoma-2 roster, which helps the squad reach B-Rank No. 3. Now it's round 8, and the key to reaching No. 2 will be Tamakoma-2's strategy against Ninomiya Squad, along with the critical answer to the question, "Can Chika shoot people or not?"

WORLD TRIGGER CHARACTERS

TAMAKOMA BRANCH

Understanding toward Neighbors. Considered divergent from Border's main philosophy.

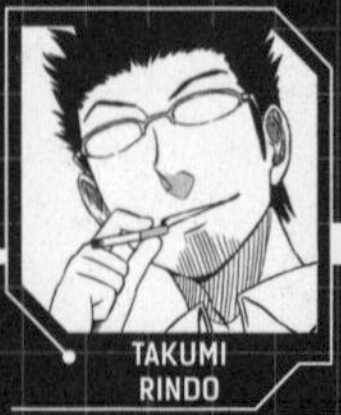

TAKUMI RINDO

Tamakoma Branch Director.

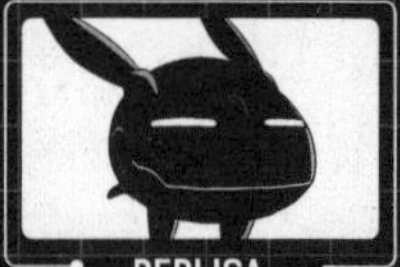

REPLICA

Yuma's chaperone. Missing after recent invasion.

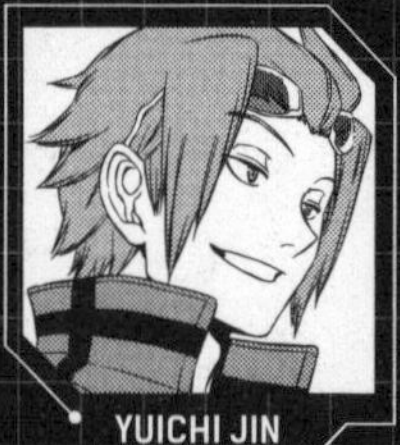

YUICHI JIN

Former S-Rank Black Trigger user. His Side Effect lets him see the future.

TAMAKOMA-2

Tamakoma's B-Rank squad, aiming to get promoted to A-Rank.

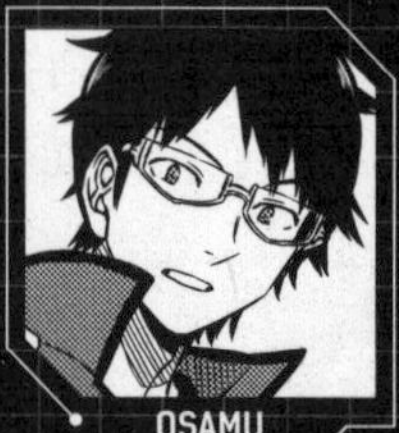

OSAMU MIKUMO

Ninth-grader who's compelled to help those in trouble. Captain of Tamakoma-2 (Mikumo squad).

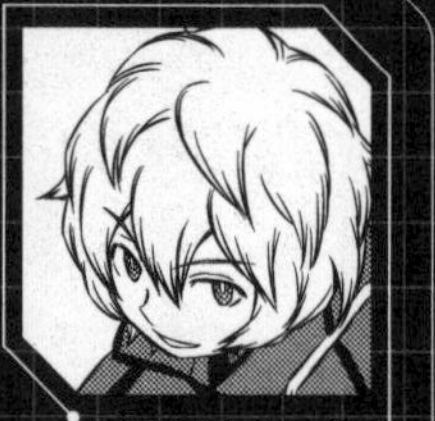

YUMA KUGA

A Neighbor who carries a Black Trigger.

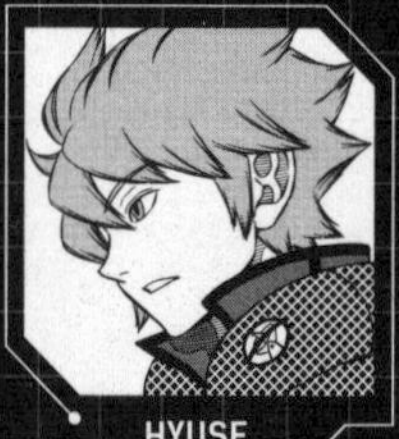

HYUSE

A Neighbor from Aftokrator captured during the large-scale invasion.

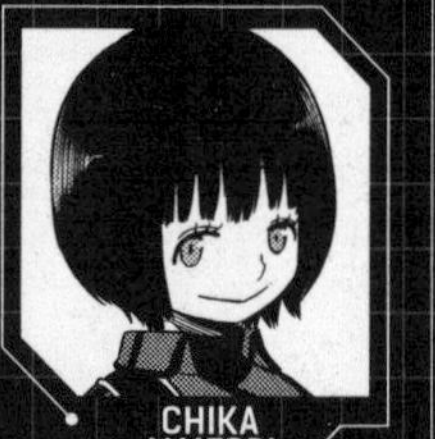

CHIKA AMATORI

Osamu's childhood friend. She has high Trion levels.

TAMAKOMA-1

Tamakoma's A-Rank squad.

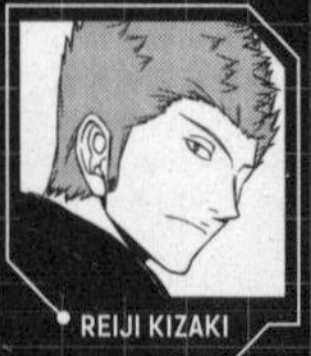

REIJI KIZAKI

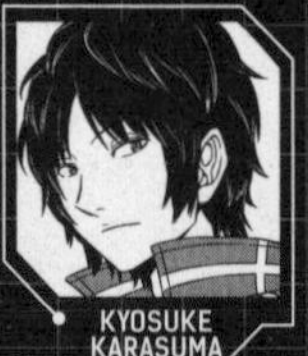

KYOSUKE KARASUMA

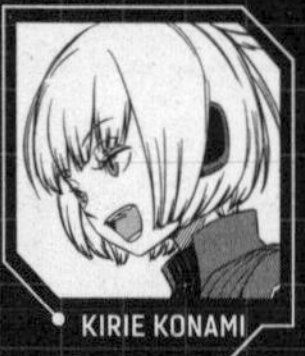

KIRIE KONAMI

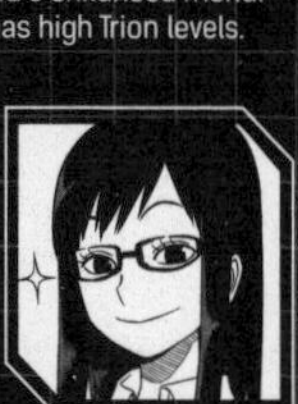

SHIORI USAMI

Famous operator now supporting Mikumo and pals.

YUBA SQUAD

Border HQ B-Rank #7

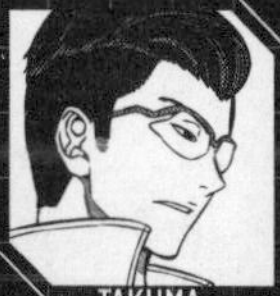
TAKUMA YUBA

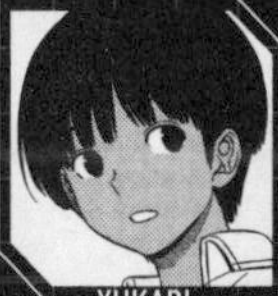
YUKARI OBISHIMA

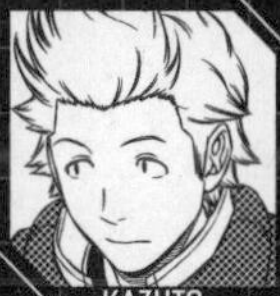
KAZUTO TONOOKA

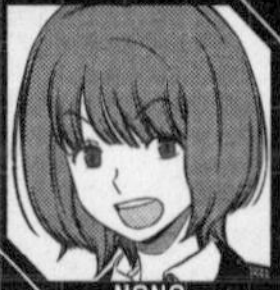
NONO FUJIMARU

NINOMIYA SQUAD

Border HQ B-Rank #1.

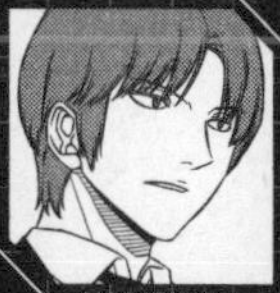
MASATAKA NINOMIYA

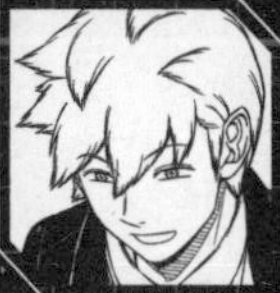
SUMIHARU INUKAI

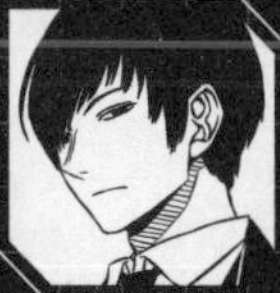
SHINNOSUKE TSUJI

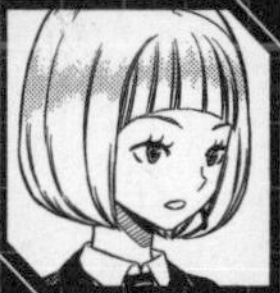
AKI HIYAMI

IKOMA SQUAD

Border HQ B-Rank #4, with five members.

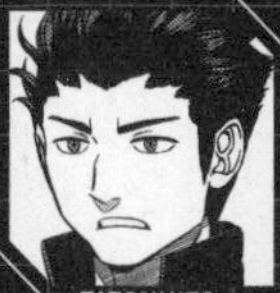
TATSUHITO IKOMA

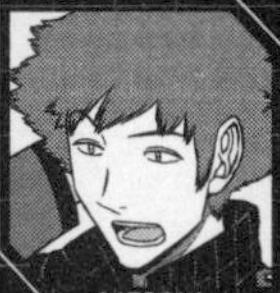
SATOSHI MIZUKAMI

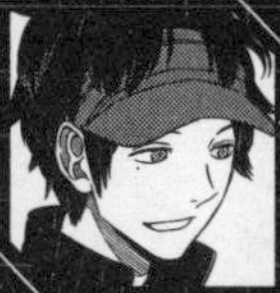
KOJI OKI

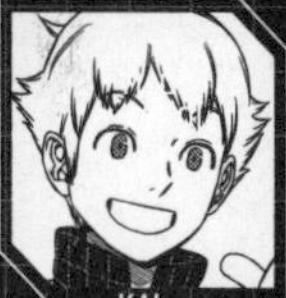
KAI MINAMISAWA

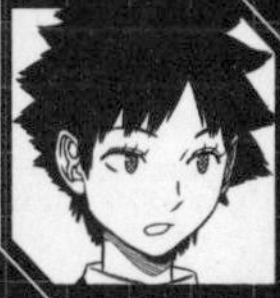
MAORI HOSOI

A-RANK AGENTS

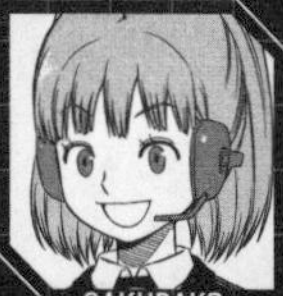
SAKURAKO TAKETOMI

Operator from B-Rank #15 Ebina Squad.

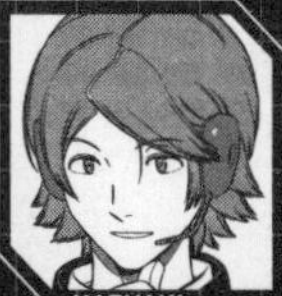
KAZUAKI OJI

Captain and attacker from B-Rank #5 Oji Squad.

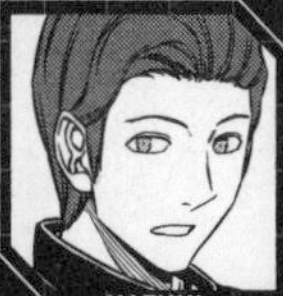
KAZUKI KURAUCHI

Shooter from B-Rank #5 Oji Squad.

WORLD TRIGGER

CONTENTS

22

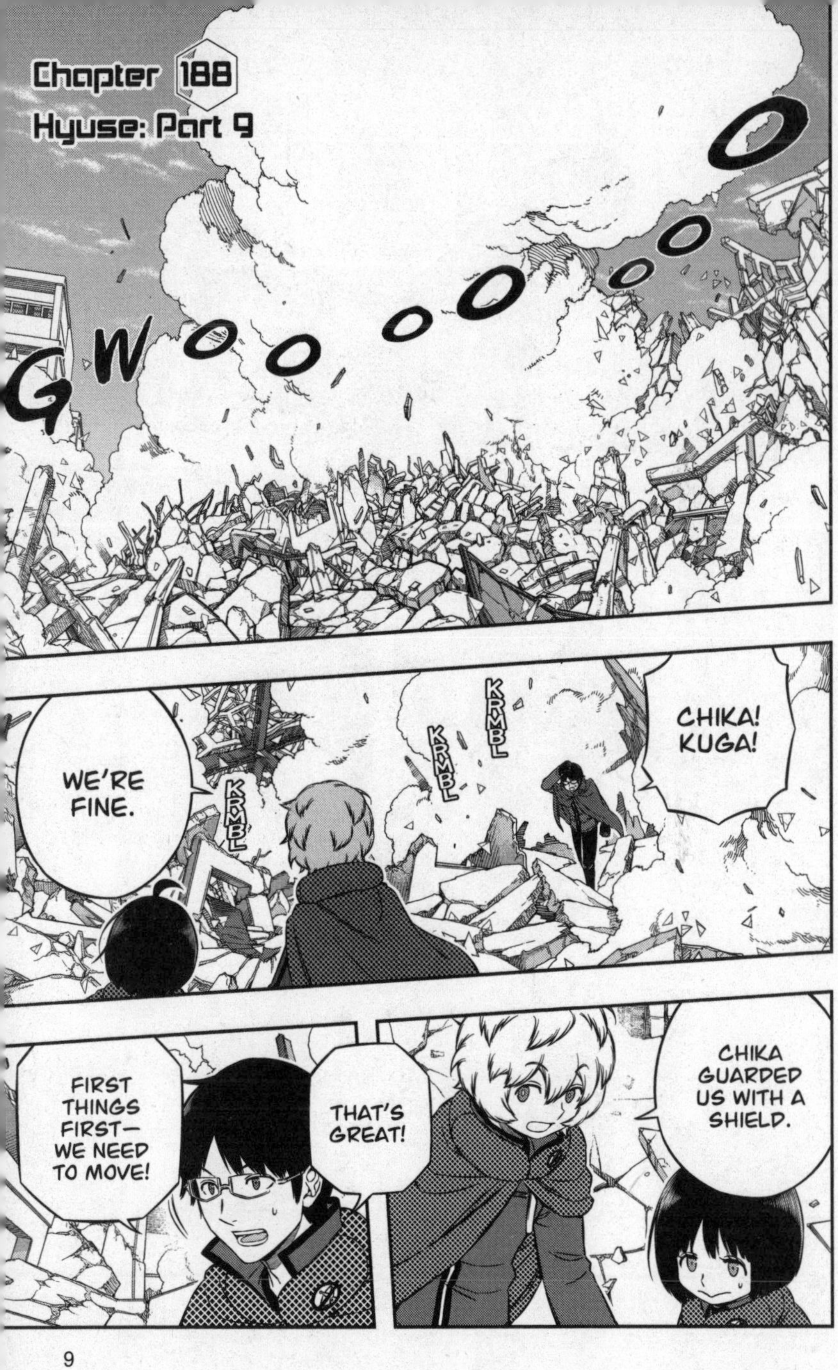
Chapter 188
Hyuse: Part 9
GWOOOOOOOOOO
CHIKA! KUGA!
KRMBL
KRMBL
KRMBL
WE'RE FINE.
CHIKA GUARDED US WITH A SHIELD.
THAT'S GREAT!
FIRST THINGS FIRST— WE NEED TO MOVE!

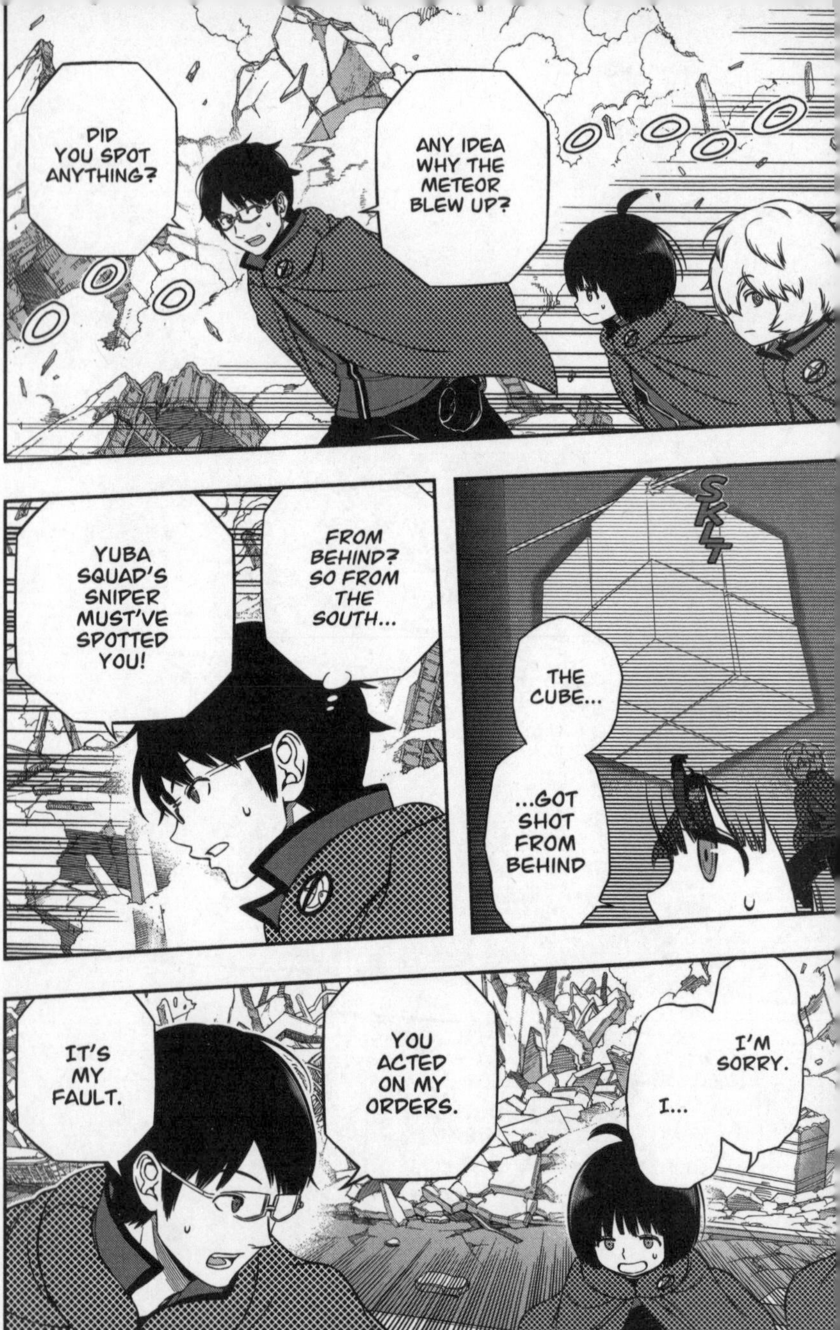
ANY IDEA WHY THE METEOR BLEW UP?
DID YOU SPOT ANYTHING?
SKLT
THE CUBE...
...GOT SHOT FROM BEHIND
FROM BEHIND? SO FROM THE SOUTH...
YUBA SQUAD'S SNIPER MUST'VE SPOTTED YOU!
I'M SORRY.
I...
YOU ACTED ON MY ORDERS.
IT'S MY FAULT.

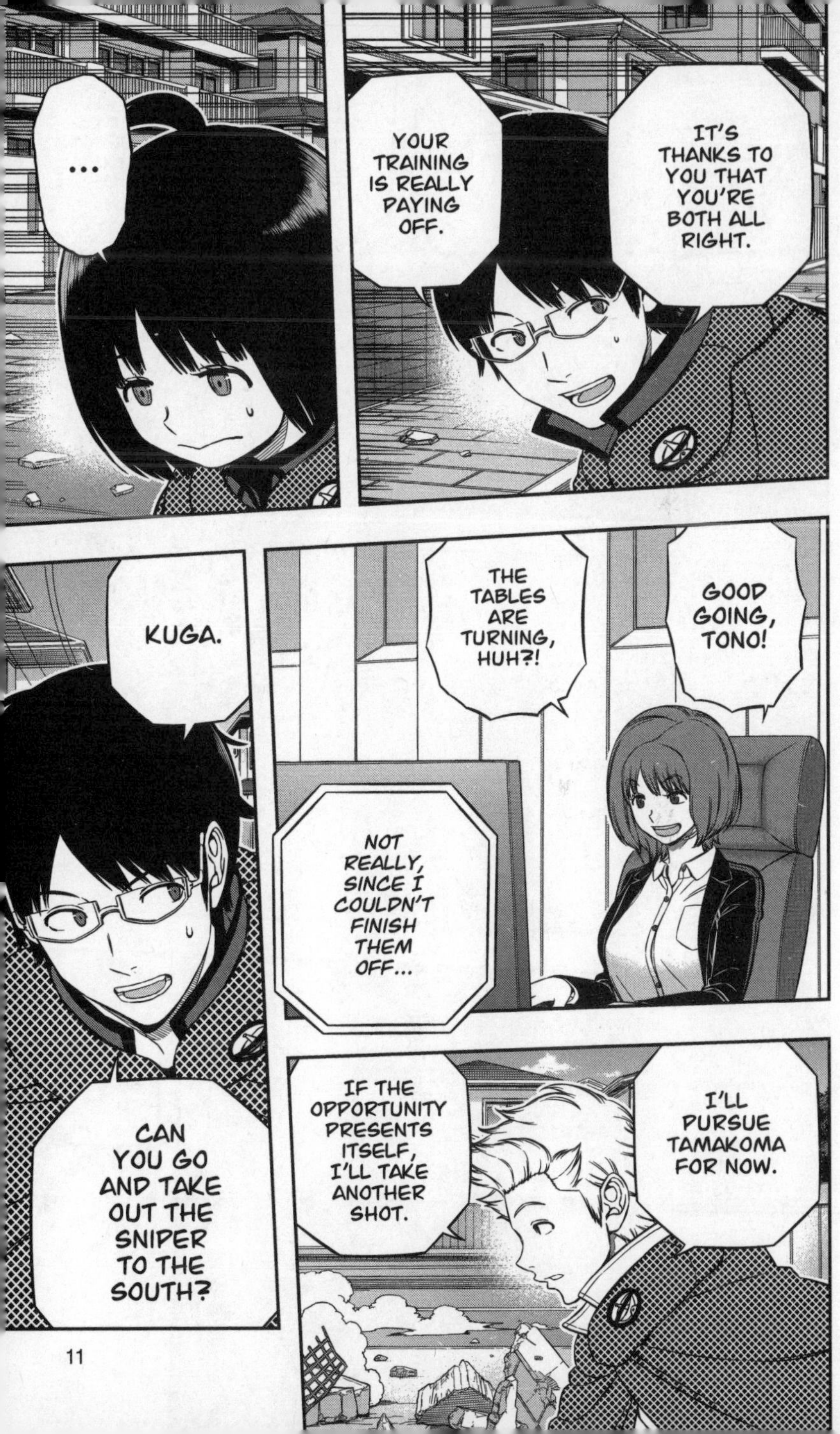

IT'S THANKS TO YOU THAT YOU'RE BOTH ALL RIGHT.
YOUR TRAINING IS REALLY PAYING OFF.
...
GOOD GOING, TONO!
THE TABLES ARE TURNING, HUH?!
NOT REALLY, SINCE I COULDN'T FINISH THEM OFF...
I'LL PURSUE TAMAKOMA FOR NOW.
IF THE OPPORTUNITY PRESENTS ITSELF, I'LL TAKE ANOTHER SHOT.
KUGA.
CAN YOU GO AND TAKE OUT THE SNIPER TO THE SOUTH?

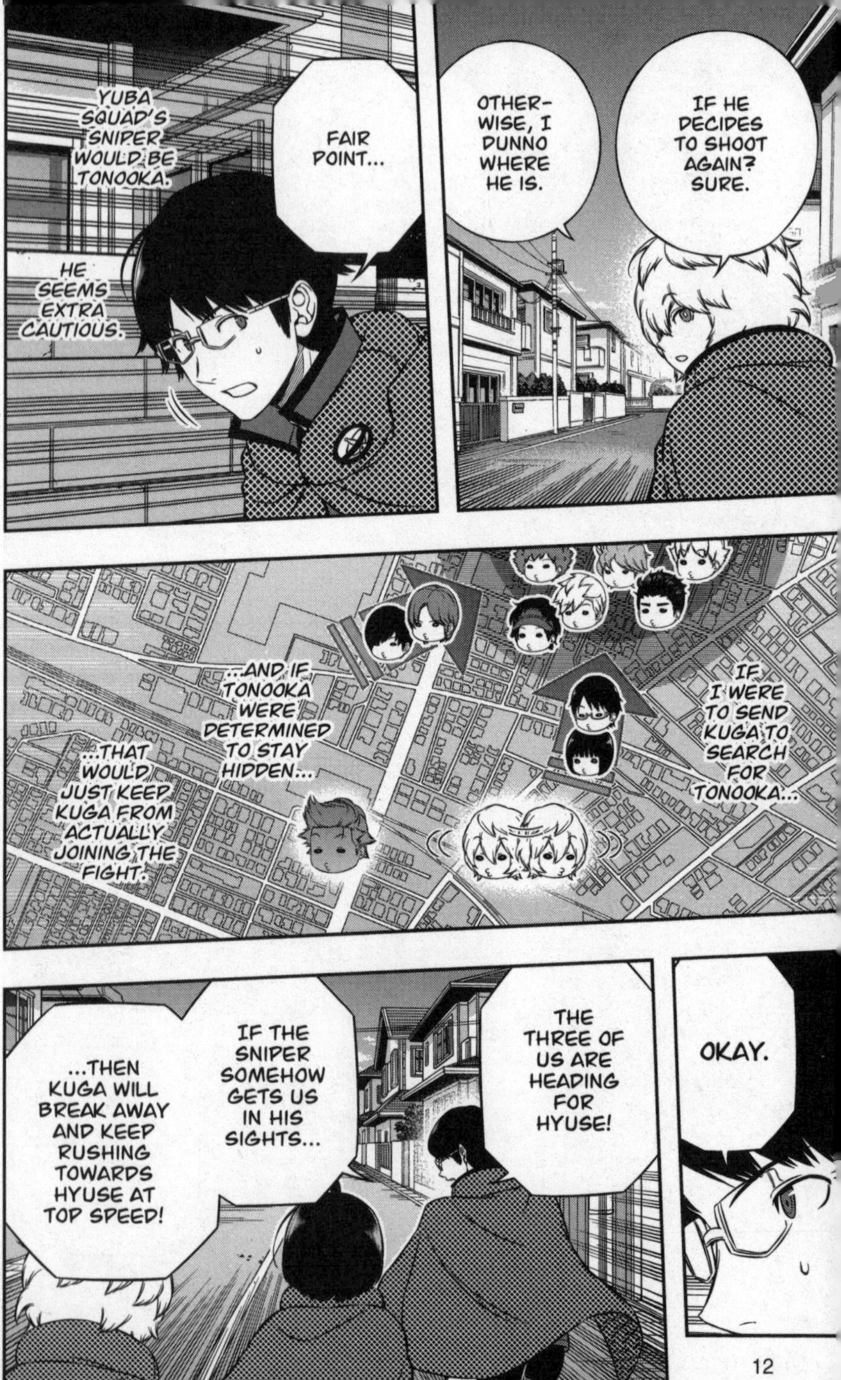
IF HE DECIDES TO SHOOT AGAIN? SURE.
OTHER-WISE, I DUNNO WHERE HE IS.
FAIR POINT...
YUBA SQUAD'S SNIPER WOULD BE TONOOKA.
HE SEEMS EXTRA CAUTIOUS.
IF I WERE TO SEND KUGA TO SEARCH FOR TONOOKA...
...AND IF TONOOKA WERE DETERMINED TO STAY HIDDEN...
...THAT WOULD JUST KEEP KUGA FROM ACTUALLY JOINING THE FIGHT.
OKAY.
THE THREE OF US ARE HEADING FOR HYUSE!
IF THE SNIPER SOMEHOW GETS US IN HIS SIGHTS...
...THEN KUGA WILL BREAK AWAY AND KEEP RUSHING TOWARDS HYUSE AT TOP SPEED!

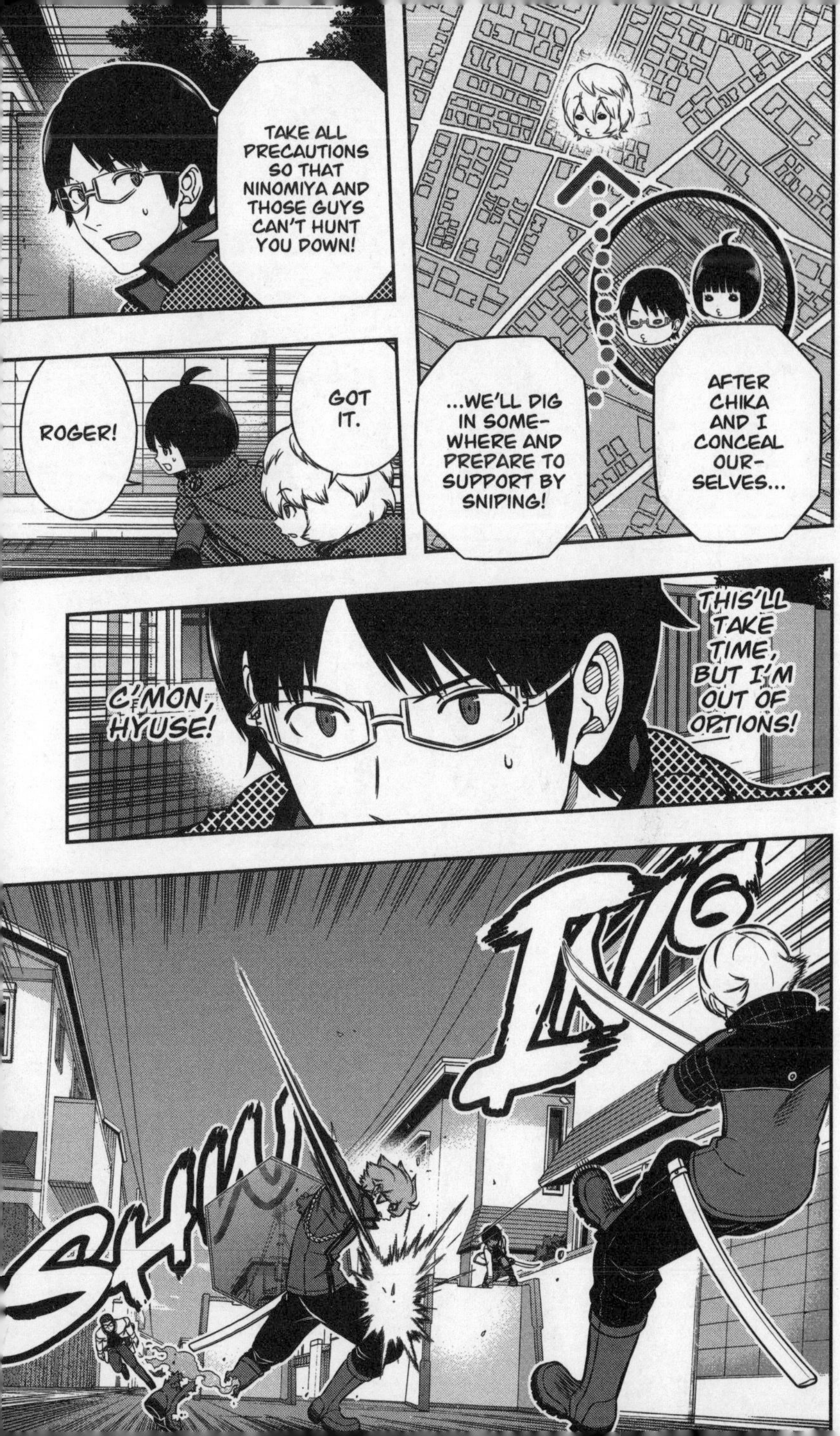
AFTER CHIKA AND I CONCEAL OUR-SELVES...
...WE'LL DIG IN SOME-WHERE AND PREPARE TO SUPPORT BY SNIPING!
TAKE ALL PRECAUTIONS SO THAT NINOMIYA AND THOSE GUYS CAN'T HUNT YOU DOWN!
GOT IT.
ROGER!
THIS'LL TAKE TIME, BUT I'M OUT OF OPTIONS!
C'MON, HYUSE!

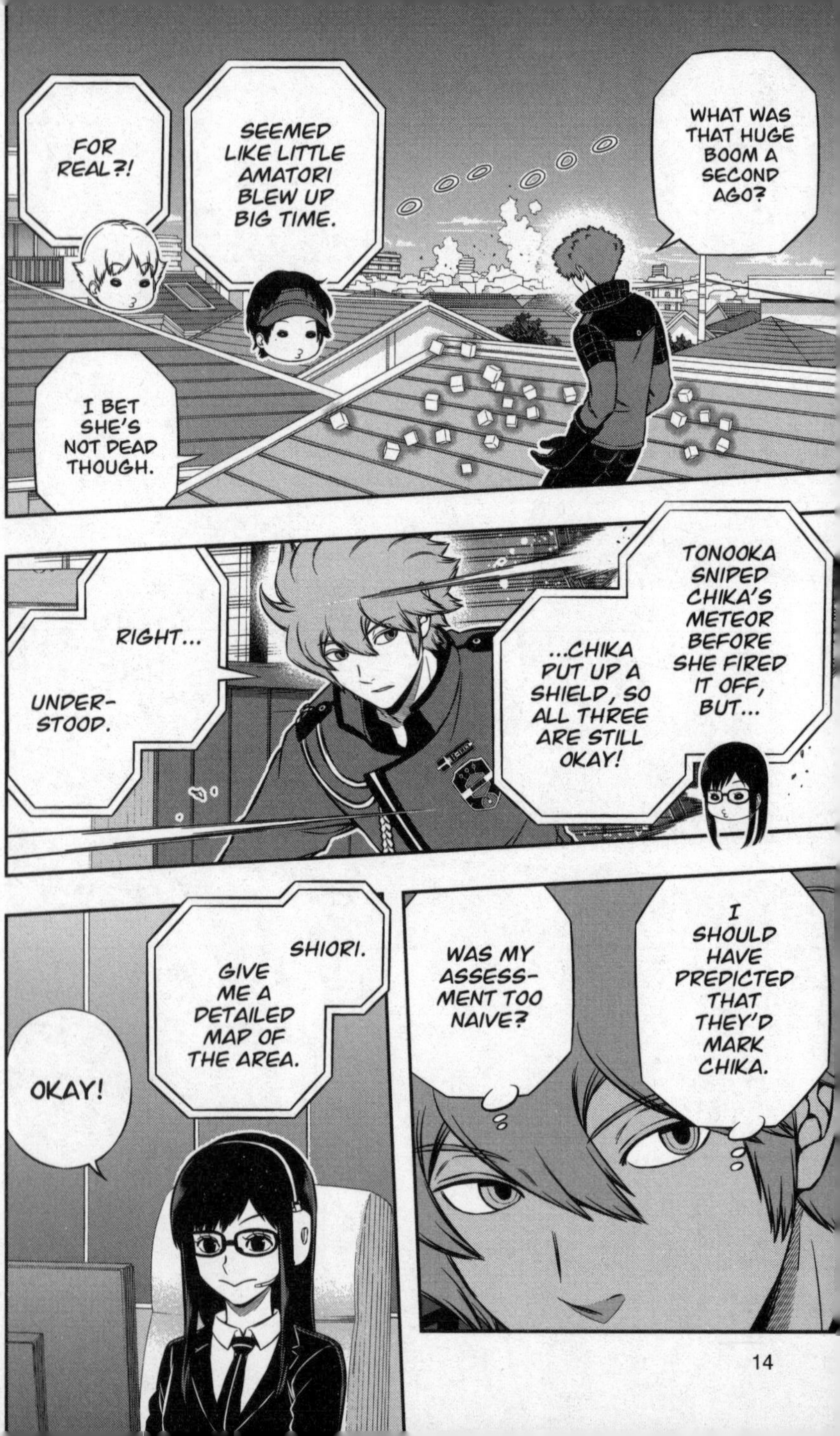
WHAT WAS THAT HUGE BOOM A SECOND AGO?
SEEMED LIKE LITTLE AMATORI BLEW UP BIG TIME.
FOR REAL?!
I BET SHE'S NOT DEAD THOUGH.
TONOOKA SNIPED CHIKA'S METEOR BEFORE SHE FIRED IT OFF, BUT...
...CHIKA PUT UP A SHIELD, SO ALL THREE ARE STILL OKAY!
RIGHT...
UNDER-STOOD.
I SHOULD HAVE PREDICTED THAT THEY'D MARK CHIKA.
WAS MY ASSESS-MENT TOO NAIVE?
SHIORI.
GIVE ME A DETAILED MAP OF THE AREA.
OKAY!

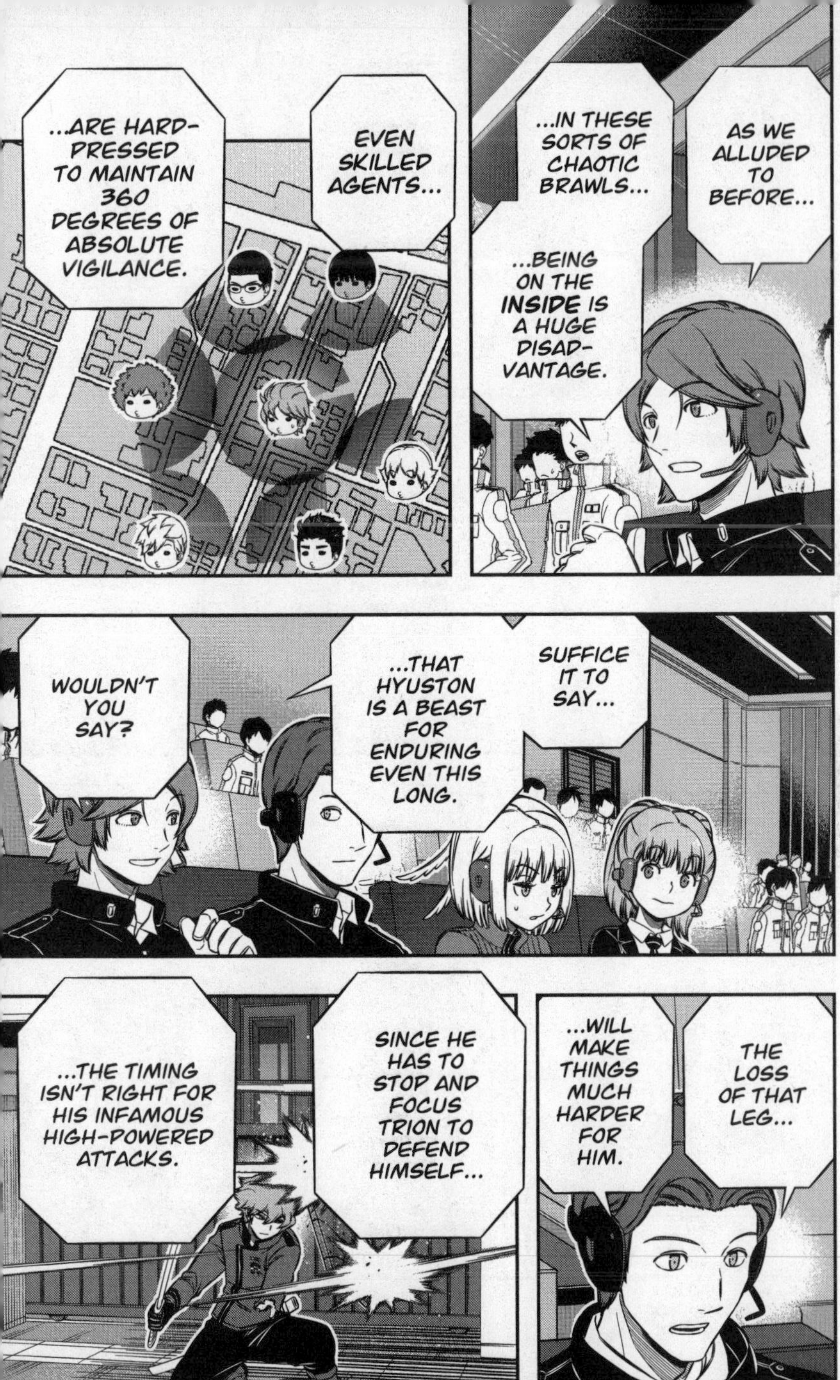
AS WE ALLUDED TO BEFORE...
...IN THESE SORTS OF CHAOTIC BRAWLS...
...BEING ON THE INSIDE IS A HUGE DISADVANTAGE.
EVEN SKILLED AGENTS...
...ARE HARD-PRESSED TO MAINTAIN 360 DEGREES OF ABSOLUTE VIGILANCE.
SUFFICE IT TO SAY...
...THAT HYUSTON IS A BEAST FOR ENDURING EVEN THIS LONG.
WOULDN'T YOU SAY?
THE LOSS OF THAT LEG...
...WILL MAKE THINGS MUCH HARDER FOR HIM.
SINCE HE HAS TO STOP AND FOCUS TRION TO DEFEND HIMSELF...
...THE TIMING ISN'T RIGHT FOR HIS INFAMOUS HIGH-POWERED ATTACKS.

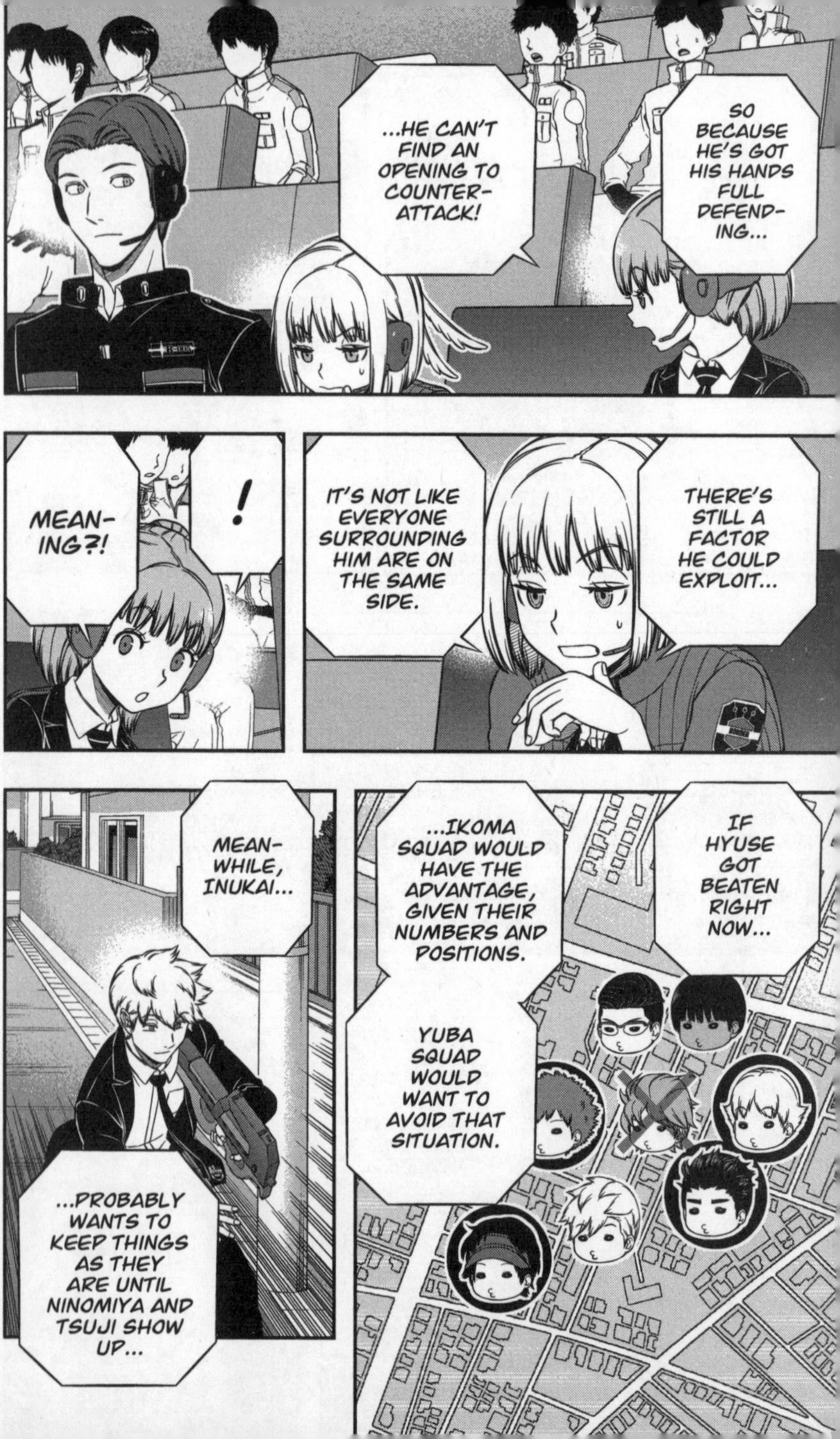
SO BECAUSE HE'S GOT HIS HANDS FULL DEFENDING...
...HE CAN'T FIND AN OPENING TO COUNTER-ATTACK!
THERE'S STILL A FACTOR HE COULD EXPLOIT...
IT'S NOT LIKE EVERYONE SURROUNDING HIM ARE ON THE SAME SIDE.
!
MEANING?!
IF HYUSE GOT BEATEN RIGHT NOW...
...IKOMA SQUAD WOULD HAVE THE ADVANTAGE, GIVEN THEIR NUMBERS AND POSITIONS.
YUBA SQUAD WOULD WANT TO AVOID THAT SITUATION.
MEANWHILE, INUKAI...
...PROBABLY WANTS TO KEEP THINGS AS THEY ARE UNTIL NINOMIYA AND TSUJI SHOW UP...

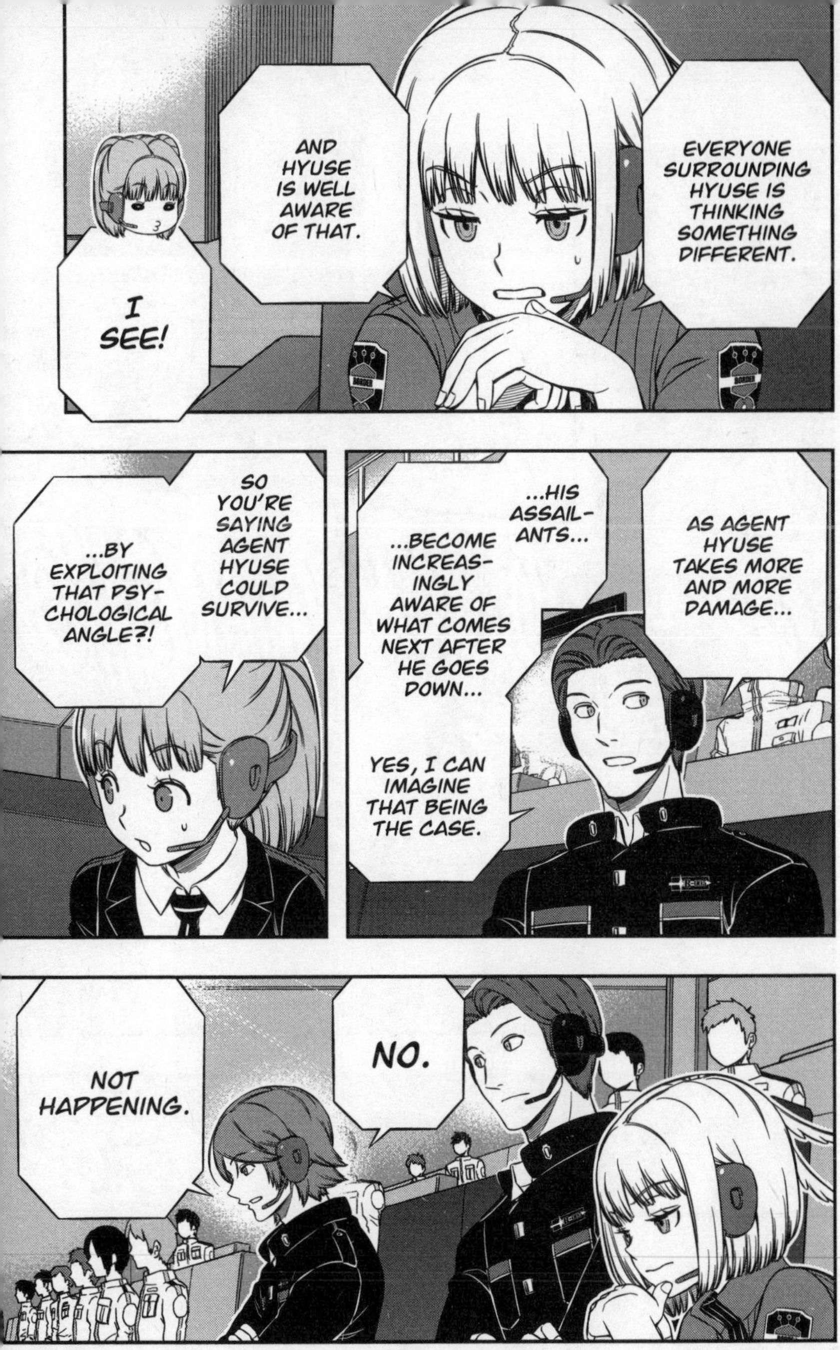
EVERYONE SURROUNDING HYUSE IS THINKING SOMETHING DIFFERENT.
AND HYUSE IS WELL AWARE OF THAT.
I SEE!
AS AGENT HYUSE TAKES MORE AND MORE DAMAGE...
...HIS ASSAIL-ANTS...
...BECOME INCREAS-INGLY AWARE OF WHAT COMES NEXT AFTER HE GOES DOWN...
YES, I CAN IMAGINE THAT BEING THE CASE.
SO YOU'RE SAYING AGENT HYUSE COULD SURVIVE...
...BY EXPLOITING THAT PSY-CHOLOGICAL ANGLE?!
NO.
NOT HAPPENING.

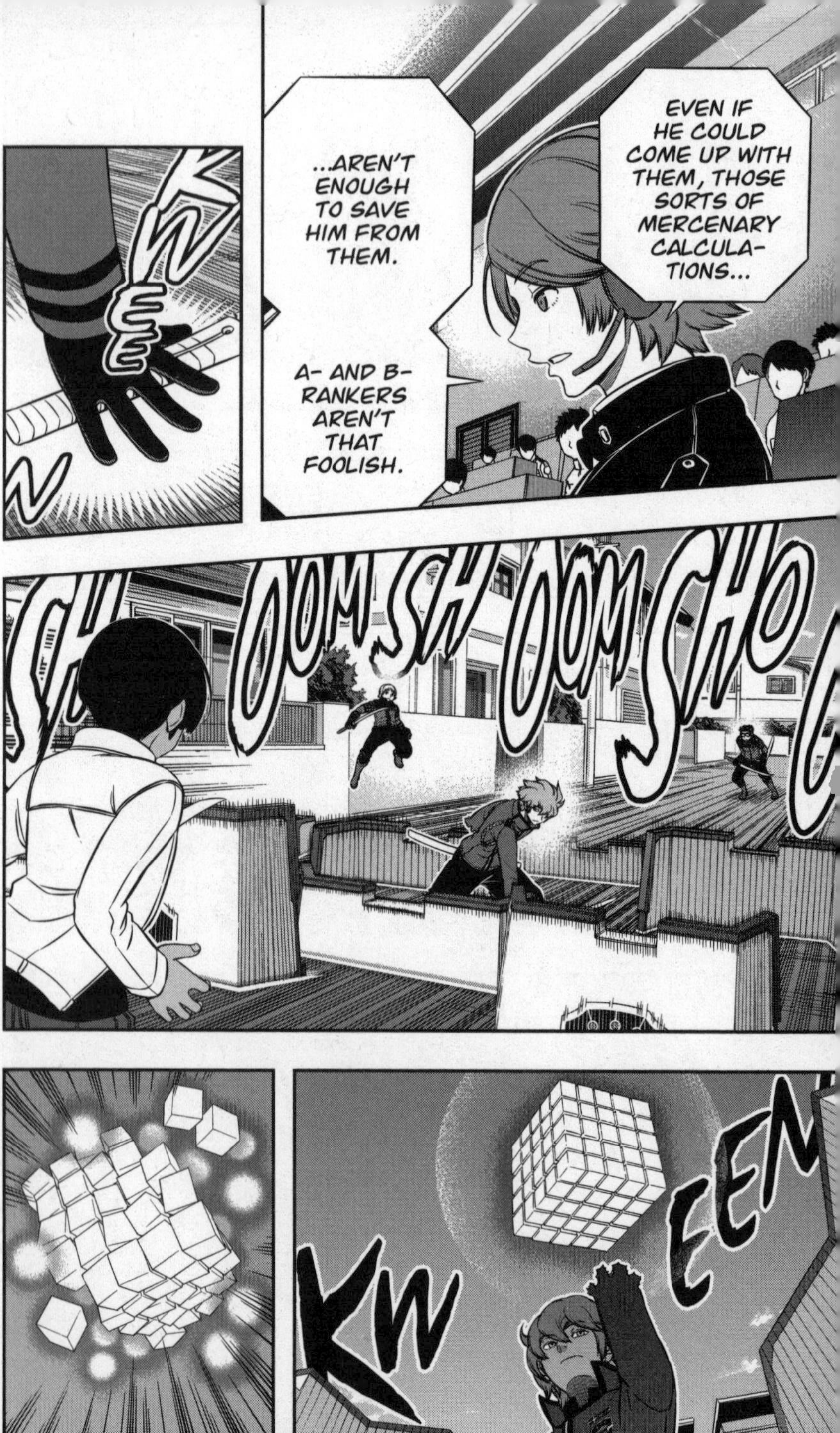
EVEN IF HE COULD COME UP WITH THEM, THOSE SORTS OF MERCENARY CALCULATIONS...
...AREN'T ENOUGH TO SAVE HIM FROM THEM.
A- AND B-RANKERS AREN'T THAT FOOLISH.

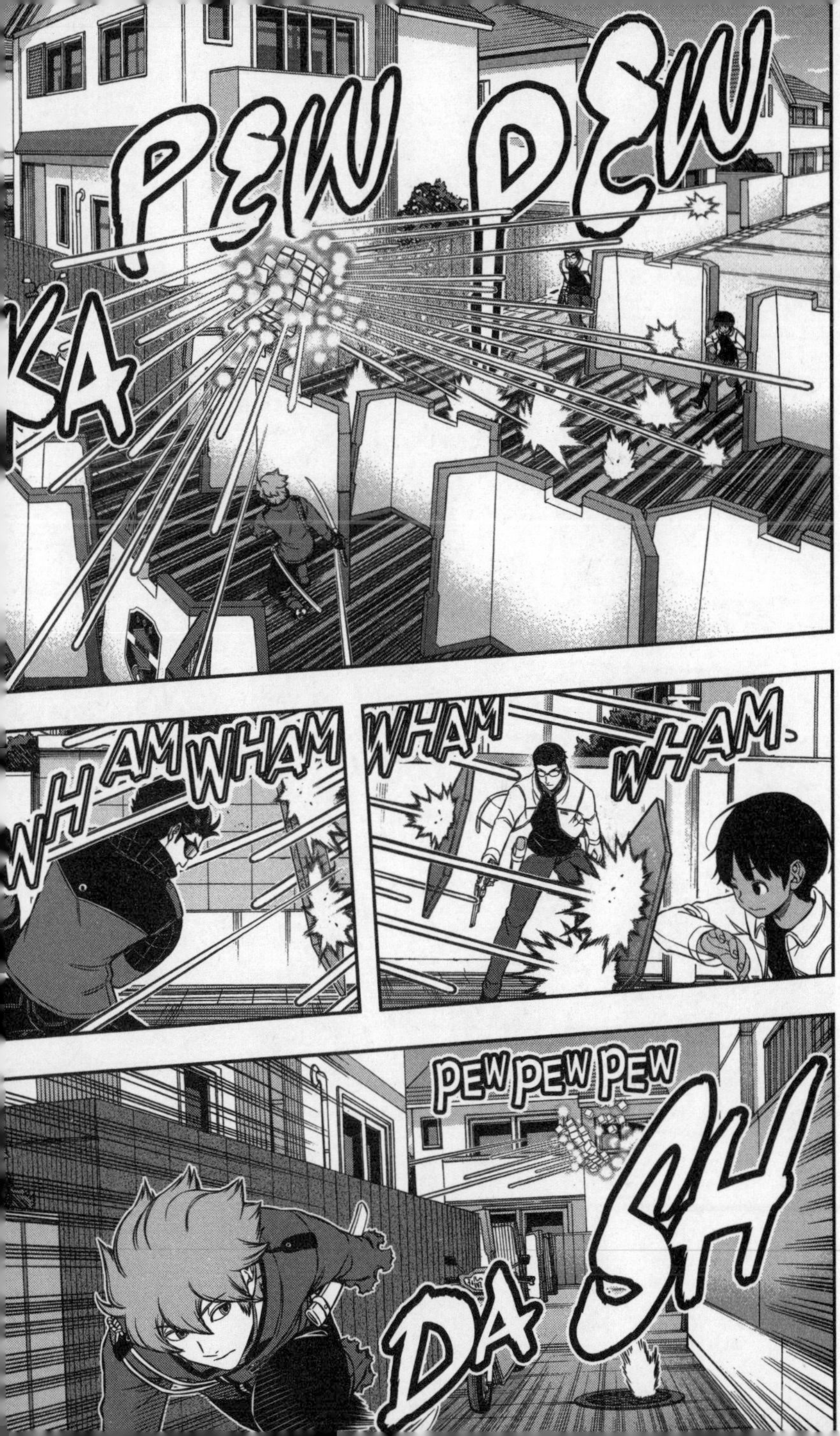

PEW PEW
KA
WHAM
WHAM
WHAM
WH AM
PEW PEW PEW
DASH

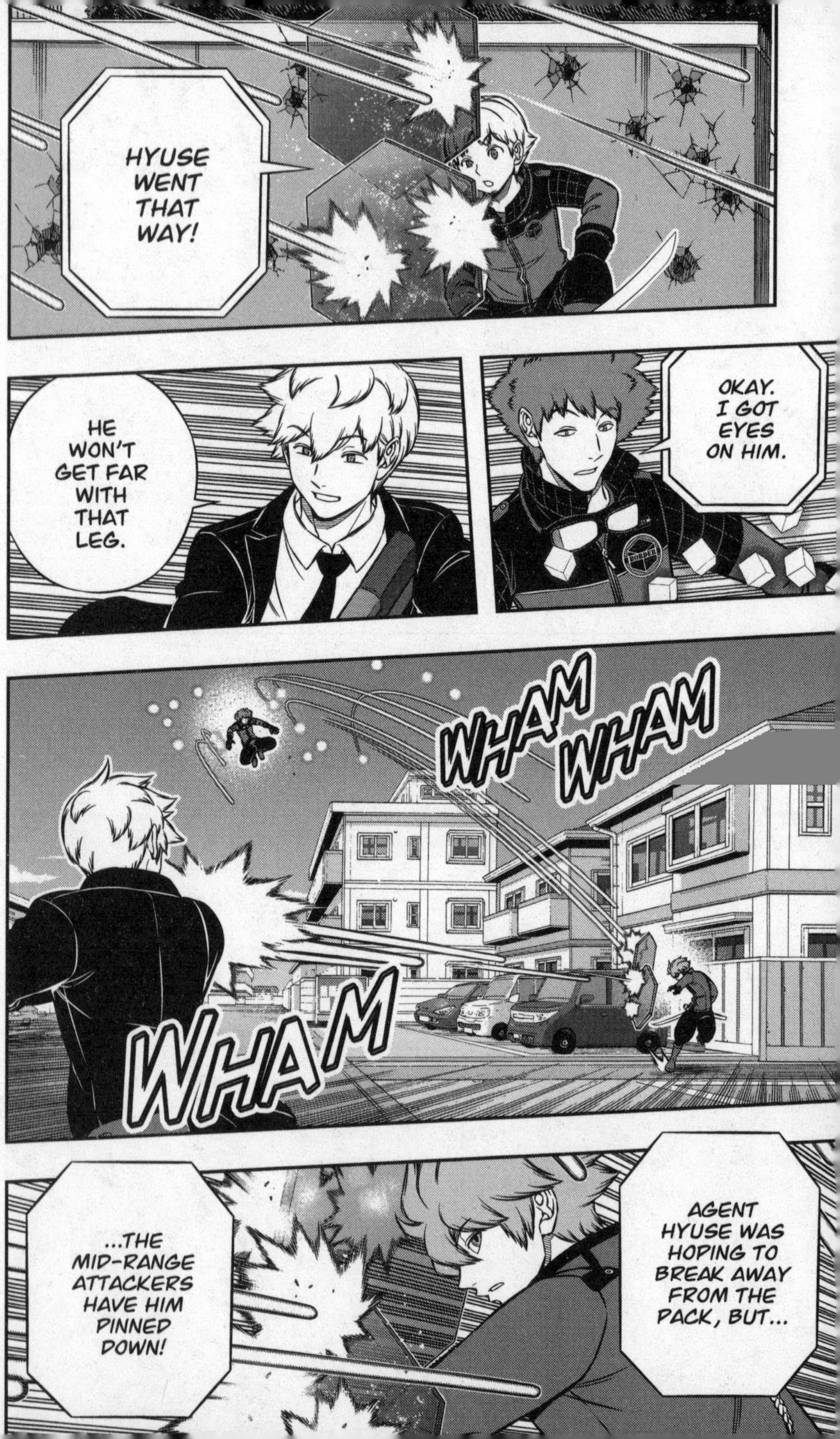
HYUSE WENT THAT WAY!
OKAY. I GOT EYES ON HIM.
HE WON'T GET FAR WITH THAT LEG.
WHAM
WHAM
WHAM
AGENT HYUSE WAS HOPING TO BREAK AWAY FROM THE PACK, BUT...
...THE MID-RANGE ATTACKERS HAVE HIM PINNED DOWN!

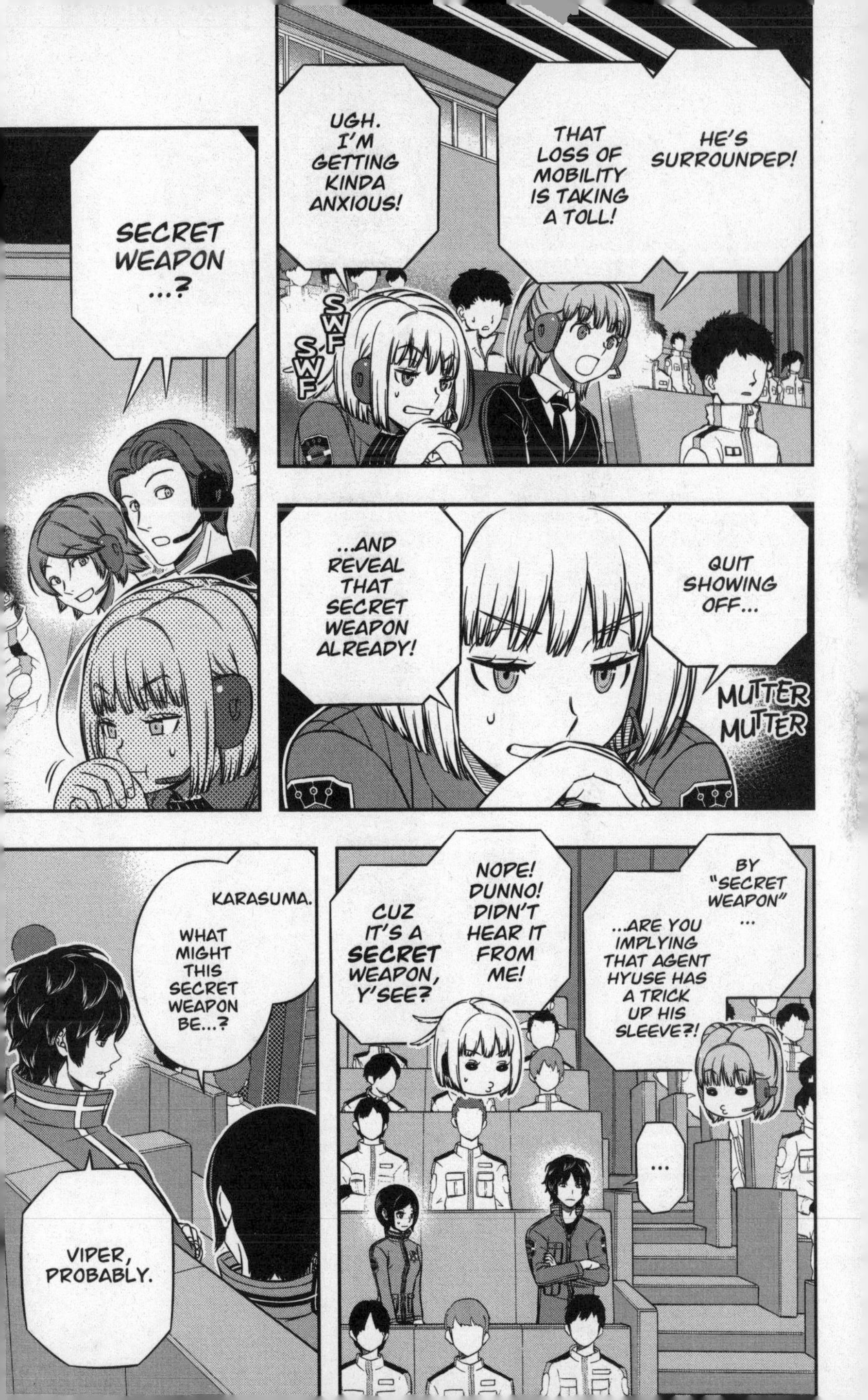
HE'S SURROUNDED!
THAT LOSS OF MOBILITY IS TAKING A TOLL!
UGH. I'M GETTING KINDA ANXIOUS!
SWF SWF
QUIT SHOWING OFF...
MUTTER MUTTER
...AND REVEAL THAT SECRET WEAPON ALREADY!
SECRET WEAPON ...?
BY "SECRET WEAPON" ...
...ARE YOU IMPLYING THAT AGENT HYUSE HAS A TRICK UP HIS SLEEVE?!
NOPE! DUNNO! DIDN'T HEAR IT FROM ME!
CUZ IT'S A SECRET WEAPON, Y'SEE?
...
KARASUMA.
WHAT MIGHT THIS SECRET WEAPON BE...?
VIPER, PROBABLY.

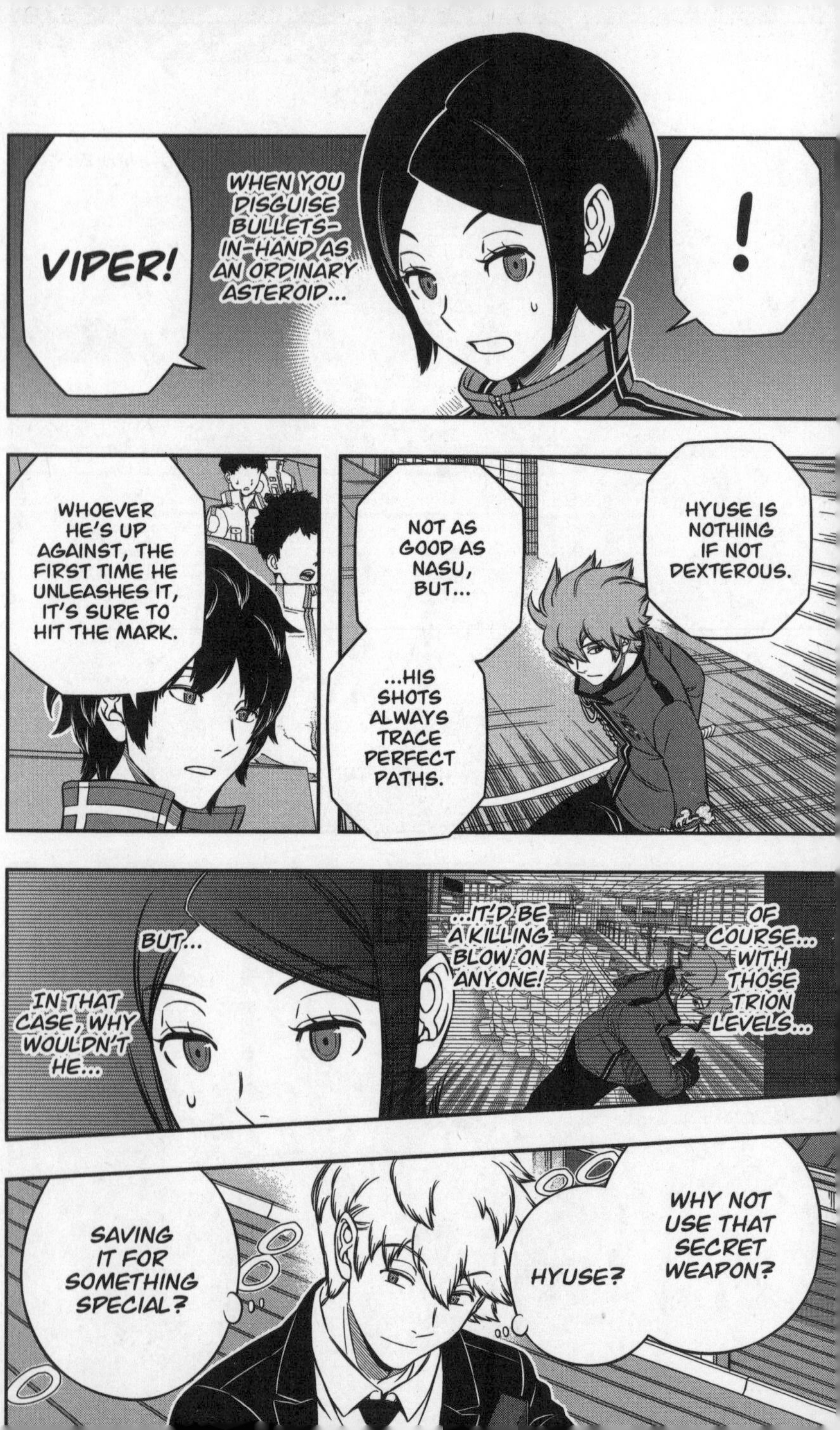
!
WHEN YOU DISGUISE BULLETS-IN-HAND AS AN ORDINARY ASTEROID...
VIPER!
HYUSE IS NOTHING IF NOT DEXTEROUS.
NOT AS GOOD AS NASU, BUT...
...HIS SHOTS ALWAYS TRACE PERFECT PATHS.
WHOEVER HE'S UP AGAINST, THE FIRST TIME HE UNLEASHES IT, IT'S SURE TO HIT THE MARK.
OF COURSE... WITH THOSE TRION LEVELS...
...IT'D BE A KILLING BLOW ON ANYONE!
BUT...
IN THAT CASE, WHY WOULDN'T HE...
WHY NOT USE THAT SECRET WEAPON?
HYUSE?
SAVING IT FOR SOMETHING SPECIAL?

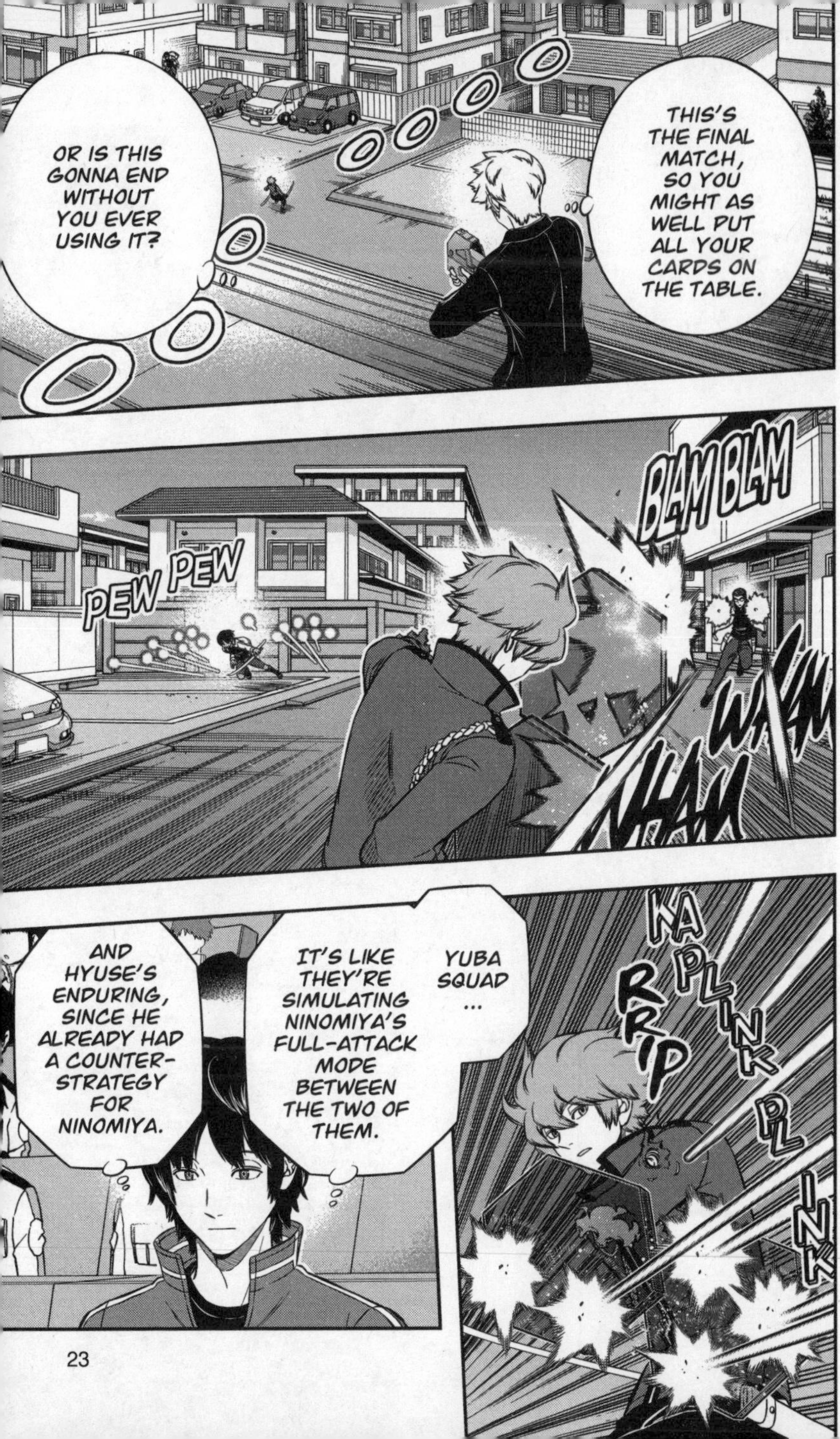
THIS'S THE FINAL MATCH, SO YOU MIGHT AS WELL PUT ALL YOUR CARDS ON THE TABLE.
OR IS THIS GONNA END WITHOUT YOU EVER USING IT?
BLAM BLAM
WHAM WHAM
PEW PEW
KA PLINK
RRIP
PLINK
YUBA SQUAD ...
IT'S LIKE THEY'RE SIMULATING NINOMIYA'S FULL-ATTACK MODE BETWEEN THE TWO OF THEM.
AND HYUSE'S ENDURING, SINCE HE ALREADY HAD A COUNTER-STRATEGY FOR NINOMIYA.

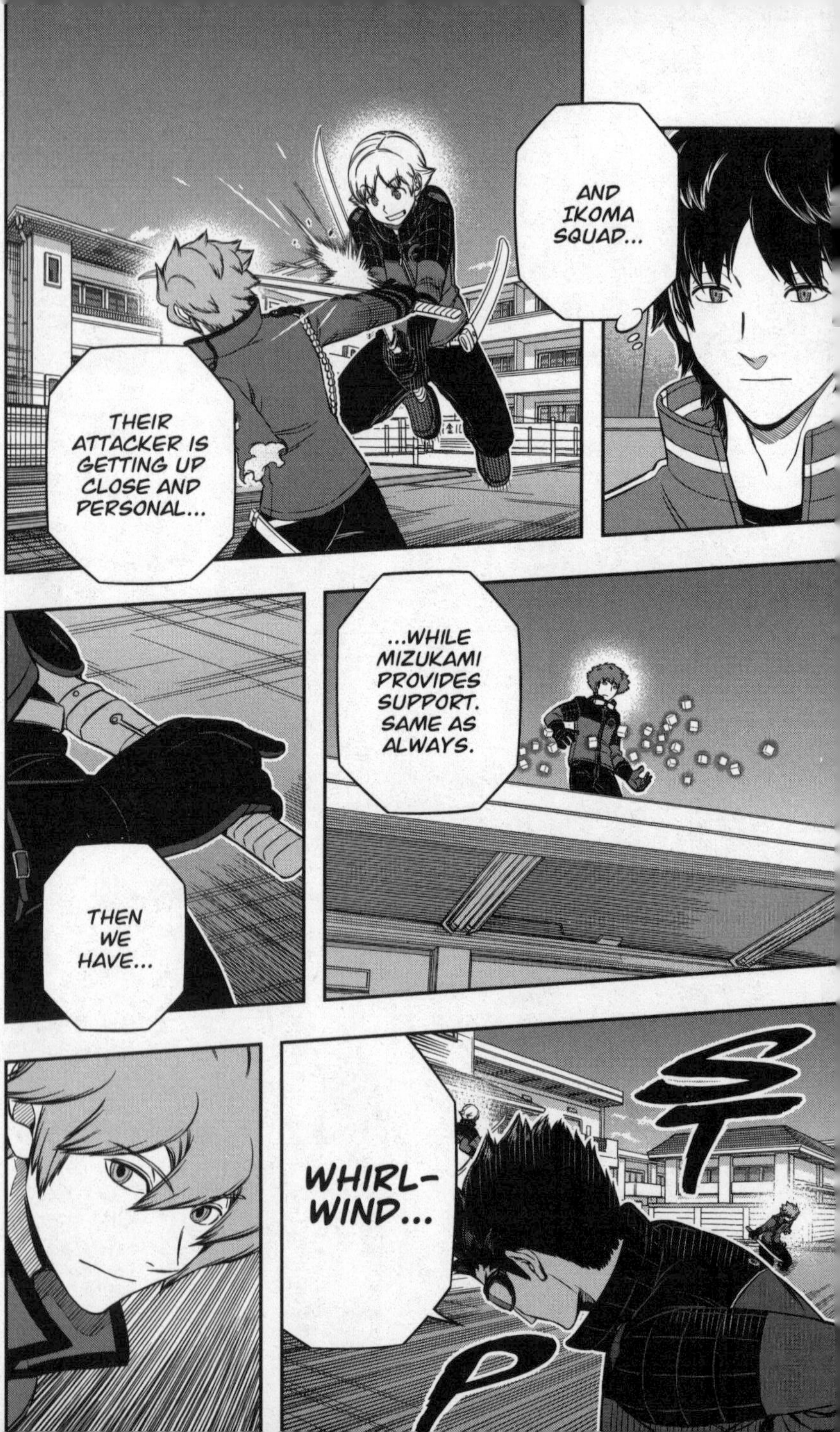
AND IKOMA SQUAD...
THEIR ATTACKER IS GETTING UP CLOSE AND PERSONAL...
...WHILE MIZUKAMI PROVIDES SUPPORT. SAME AS ALWAYS.
THEN WE HAVE...
WHIRL-WIND...

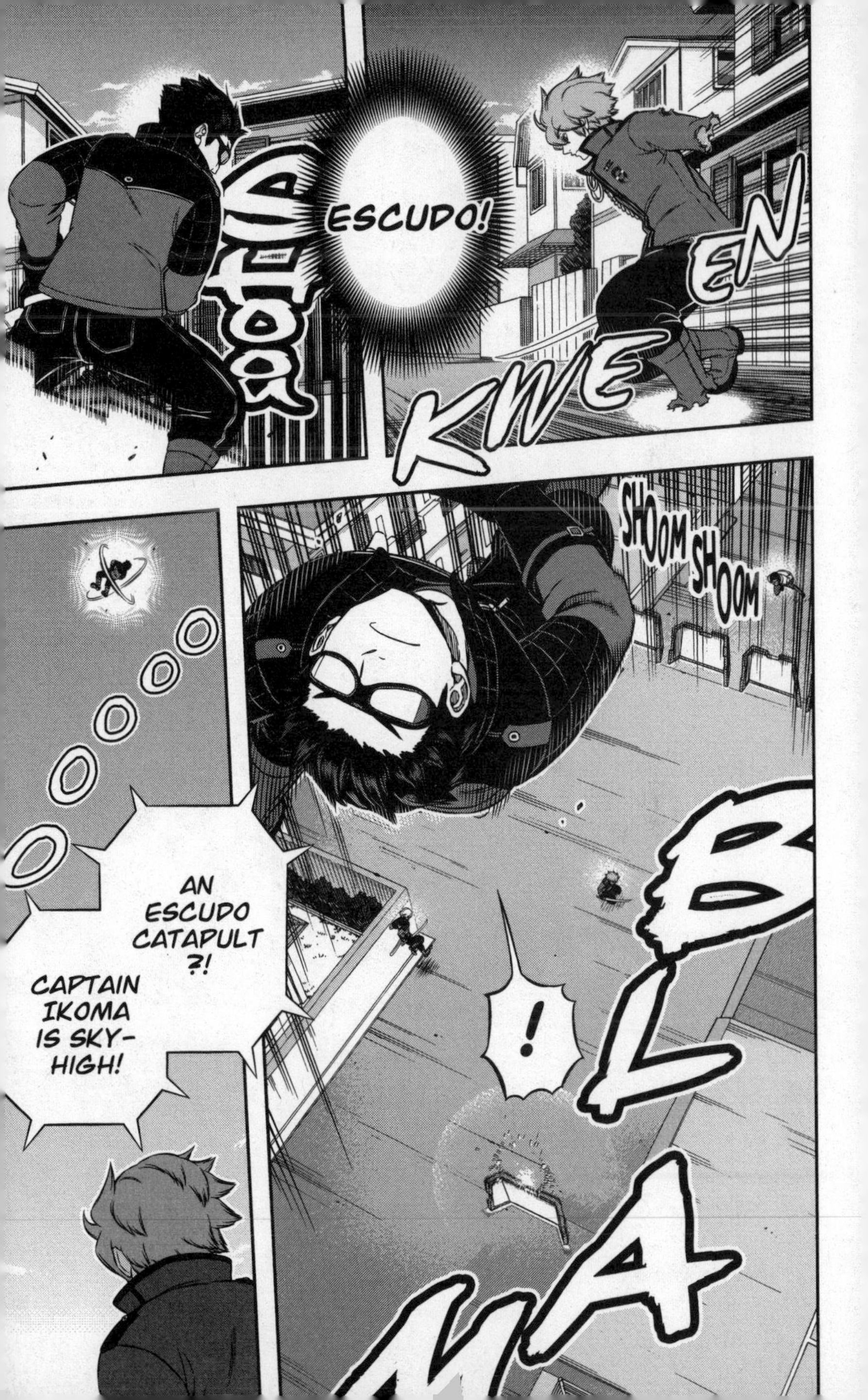
KWE EN
ESCUDO!
SHOOM SHOOM
!
AN ESCUDO CATAPULT ?!
CAPTAIN IKOMA IS SKY-HIGH!

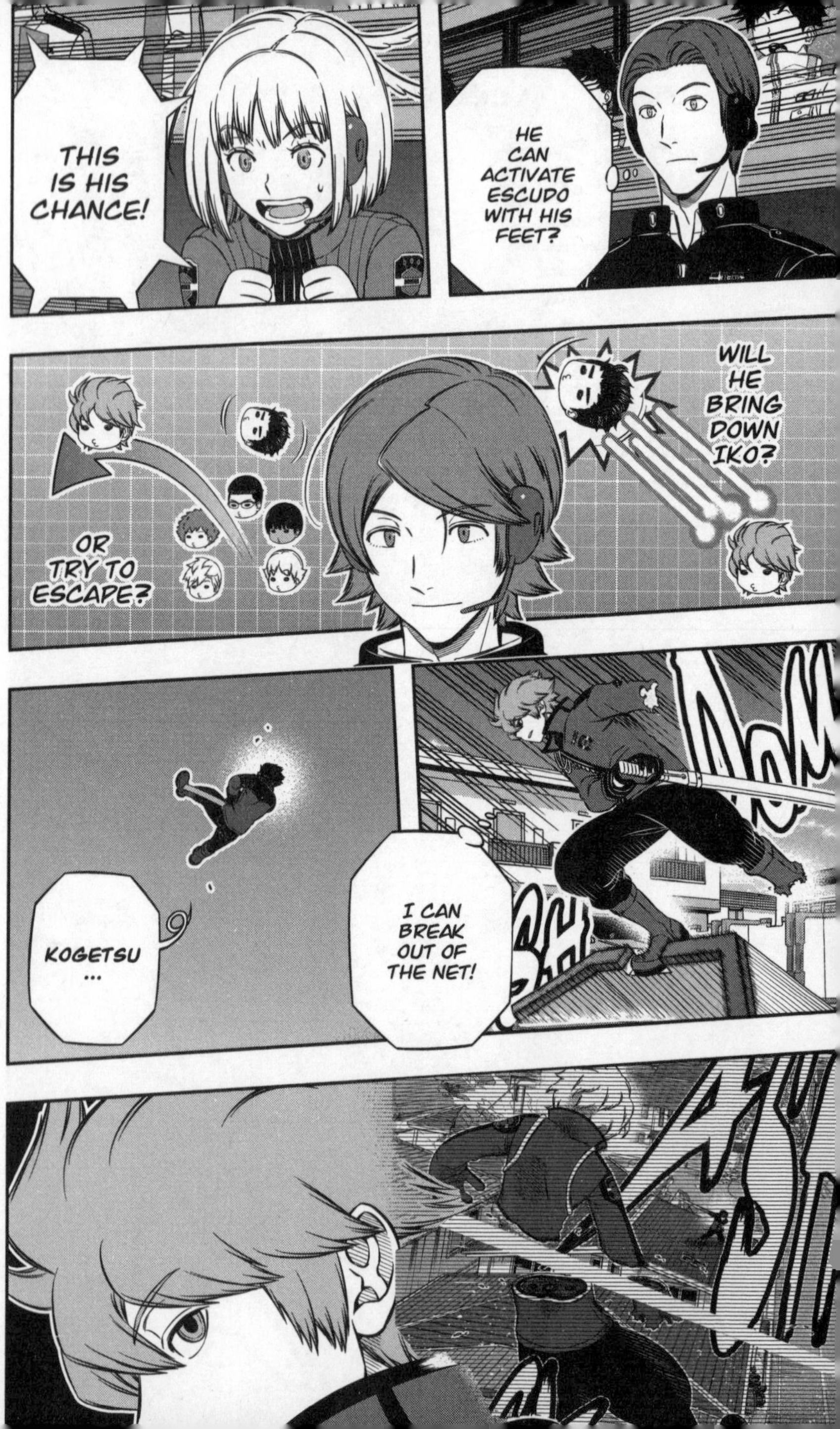
HE CAN ACTIVATE ESCUDO WITH HIS FEET?
THIS IS HIS CHANCE!
WILL HE BRING DOWN IKO?
OR TRY TO ESCAPE?
I CAN BREAK OUT OF THE NET!
KOGETSU ...

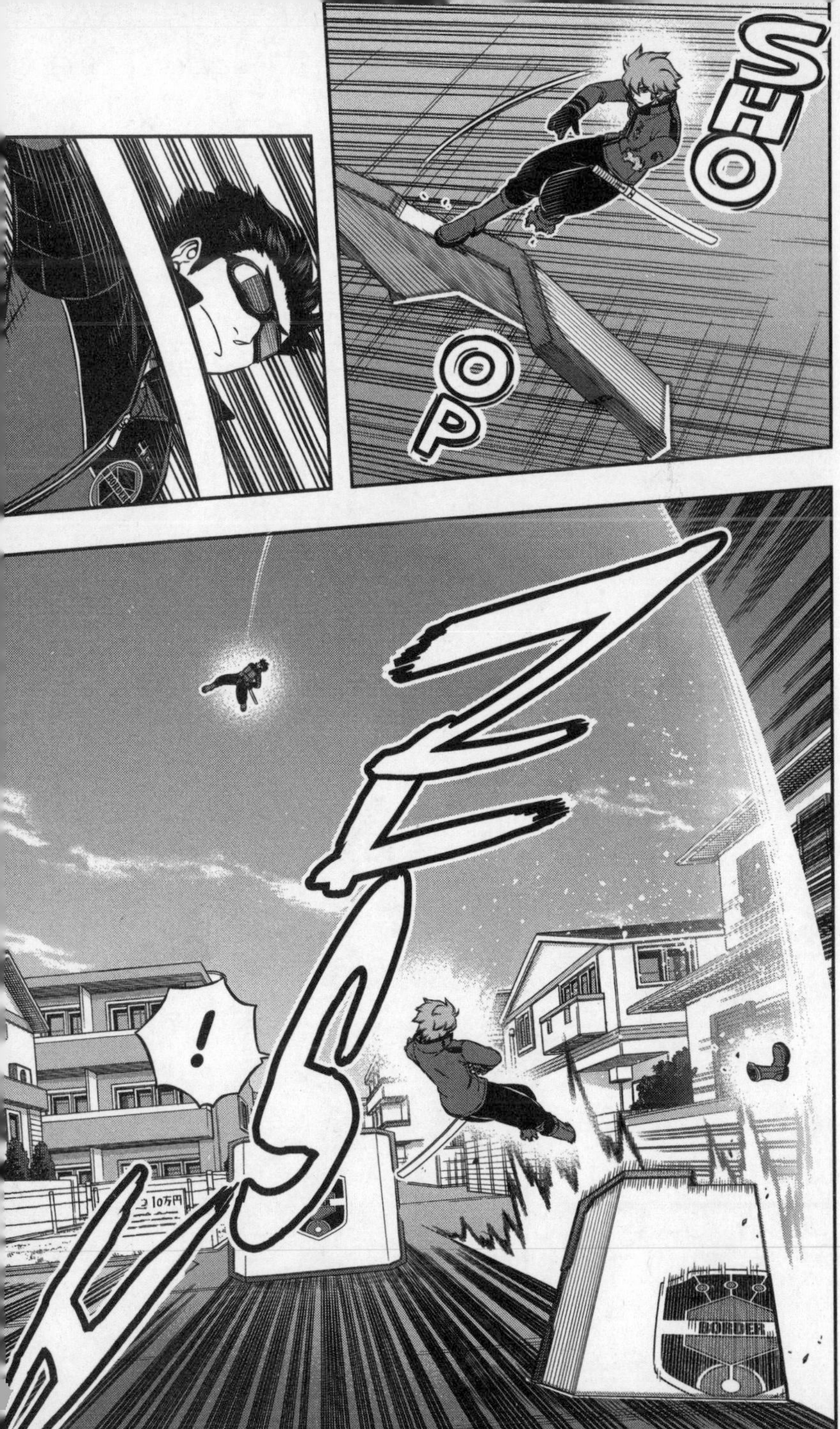
SHOOP
!
BORDER

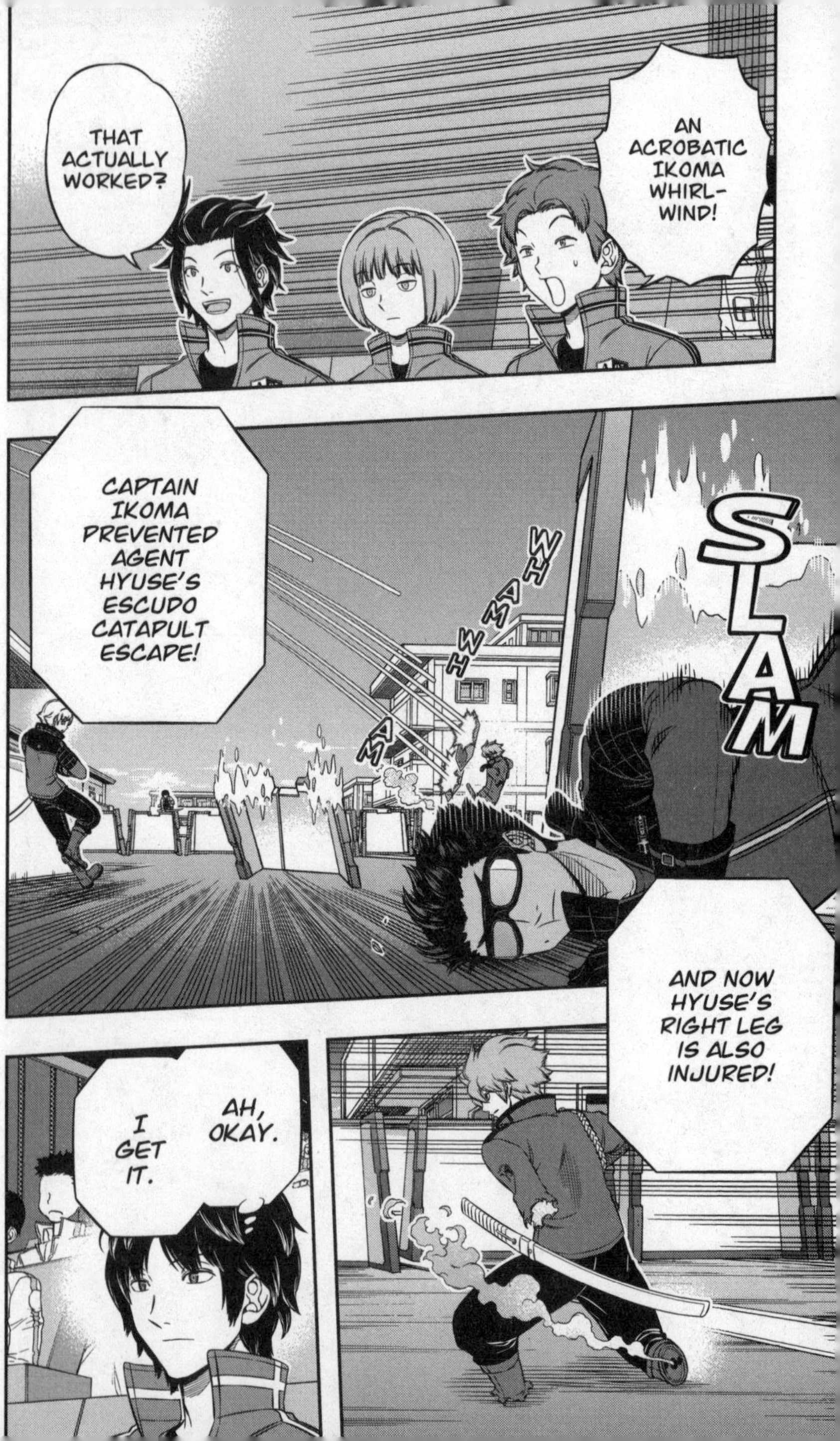
AN ACROBATIC IKOMA WHIRL-WIND!
THAT ACTUALLY WORKED?
SLAM
WHAM WHAM
CAPTAIN IKOMA PREVENTED AGENT HYUSE'S ESCUDO CATAPULT ESCAPE!
AND NOW HYUSE'S RIGHT LEG IS ALSO INJURED!
AH, OKAY.
I GET IT.

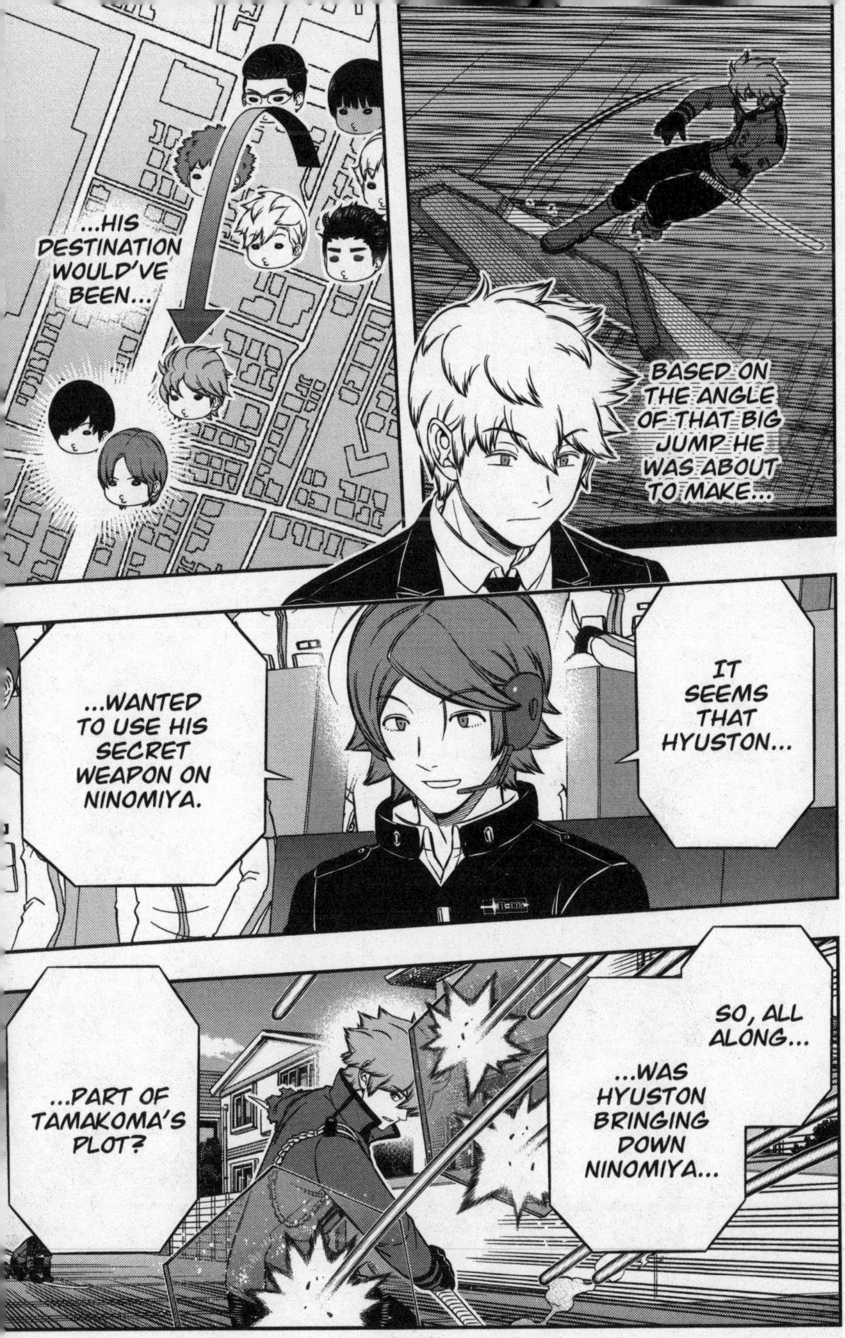
BASED ON THE ANGLE OF THAT BIG JUMP HE WAS ABOUT TO MAKE...
...HIS DESTINATION WOULD'VE BEEN...
IT SEEMS THAT HYUSTON...
...WANTED TO USE HIS SECRET WEAPON ON NINOMIYA.
SO, ALL ALONG...
...WAS HYUSTON BRINGING DOWN NINOMIYA...
...PART OF TAMAKOMA'S PLOT?

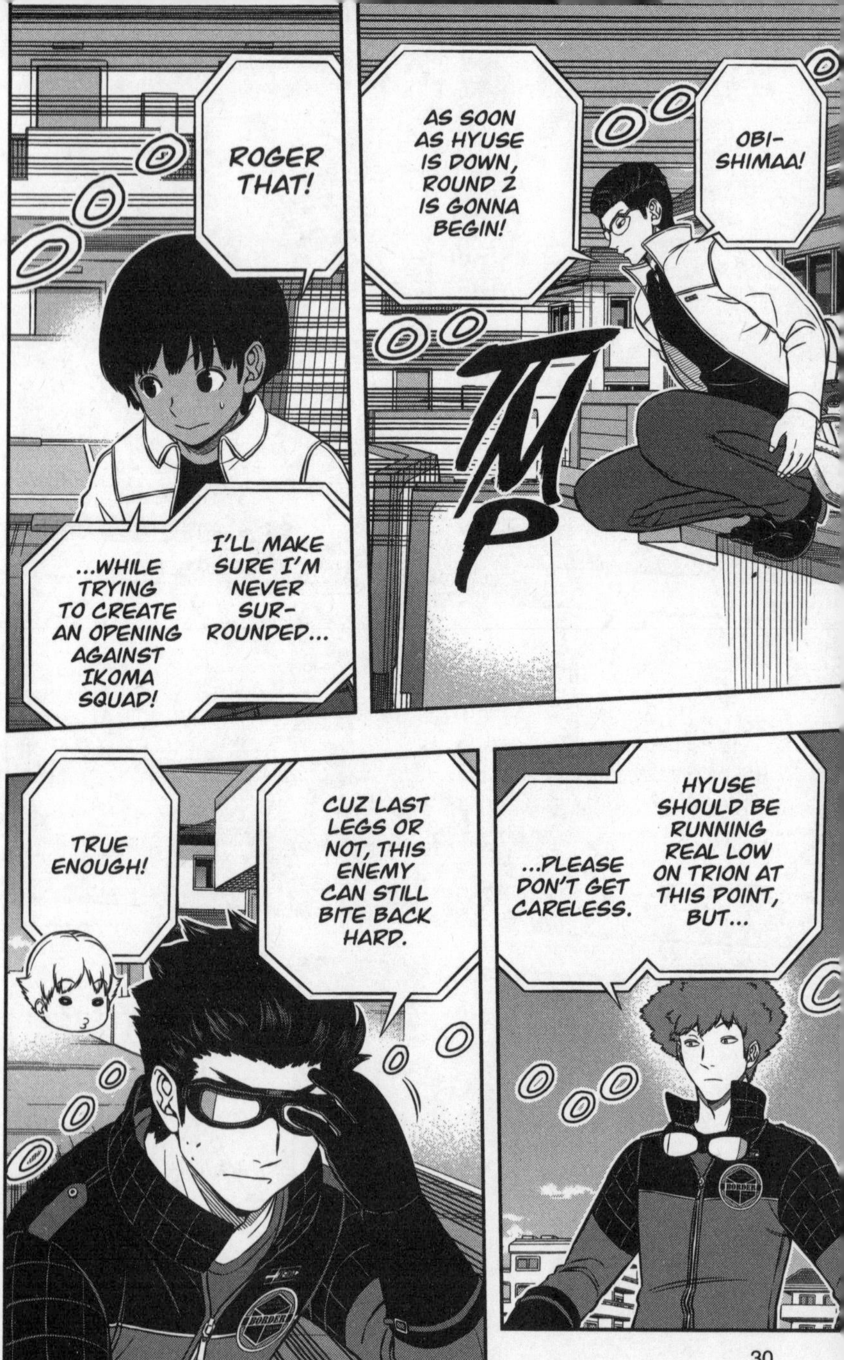
OBI-SHIMAA!
AS SOON AS HYUSE IS DOWN, ROUND 2 IS GONNA BEGIN!
TMP
ROGER THAT!
I'LL MAKE SURE I'M NEVER SUR-ROUNDED...
...WHILE TRYING TO CREATE AN OPENING AGAINST IKOMA SQUAD!
HYUSE SHOULD BE RUNNING REAL LOW ON TRION AT THIS POINT, BUT...
...PLEASE DON'T GET CARELESS.
CUZ LAST LEGS OR NOT, THIS ENEMY CAN STILL BITE BACK HARD.
TRUE ENOUGH!

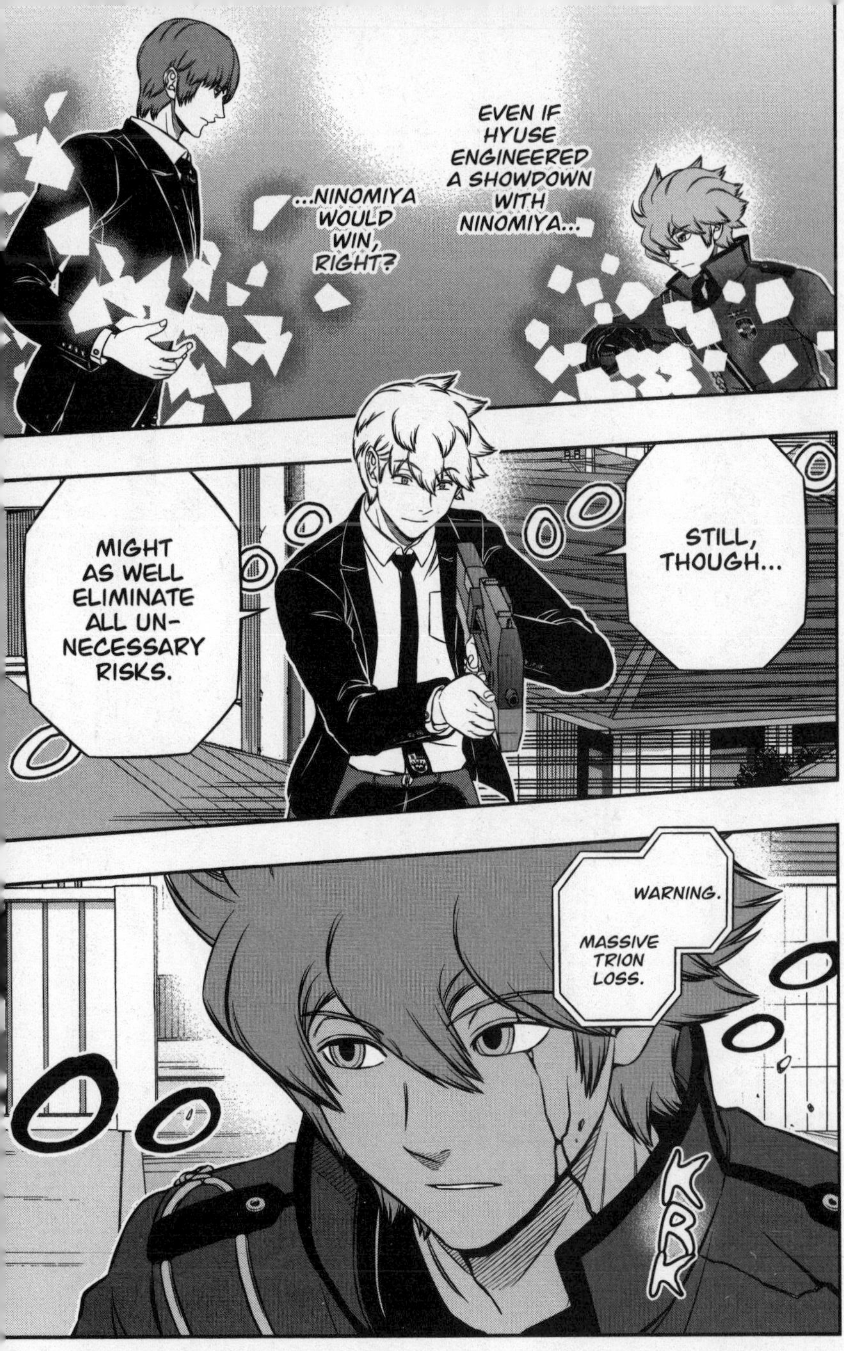
EVEN IF HYUSE ENGINEERED A SHOWDOWN WITH NINOMIYA...
...NINOMIYA WOULD WIN, RIGHT?
STILL, THOUGH...
MIGHT AS WELL ELIMINATE ALL UN-NECESSARY RISKS.
WARNING.
MASSIVE TRION LOSS.

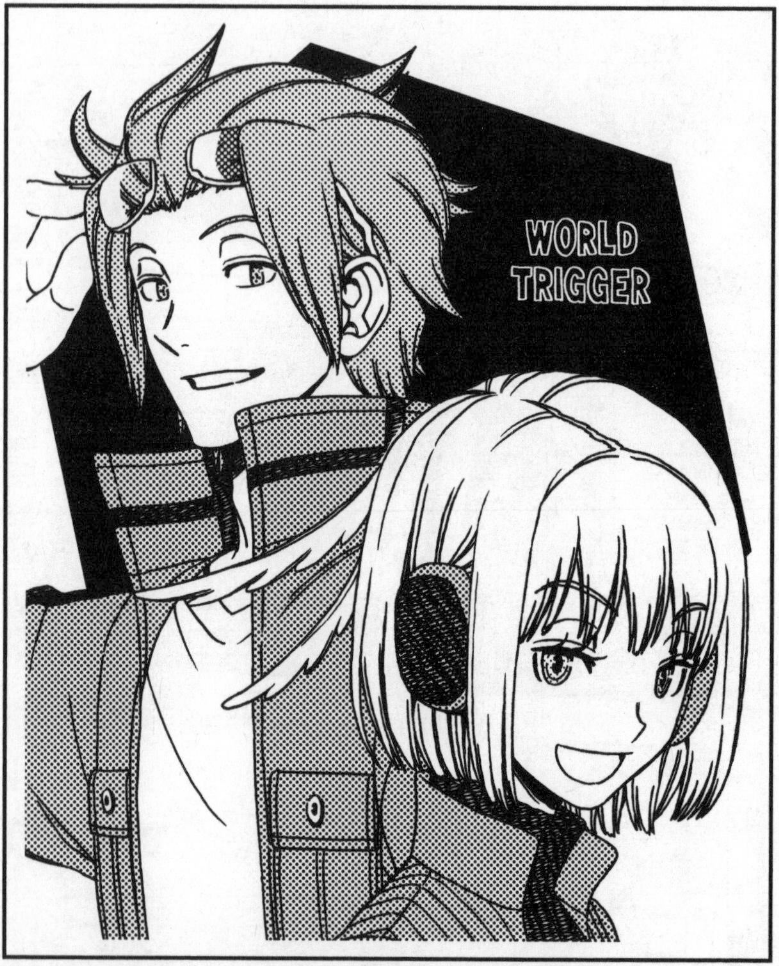
WORLD
TRIGGER

■ **Autograph Board celebrating *Jump SQ*s 12th Anniversary [December 2019 Issue] [Originally in color]**

I drew this as a gift for readers in celebration of *SQ*'s 12th anniversary. It was displayed at Jump Festa and even got turned into a key chain. Past years always had Osamu and Yuma, but I thought it was time for a change of pace, so I went with Jin and Konami. There's something nice and fresh about that, right? I wonder who'll show up next time!

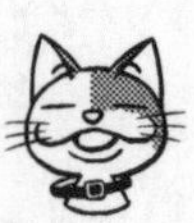

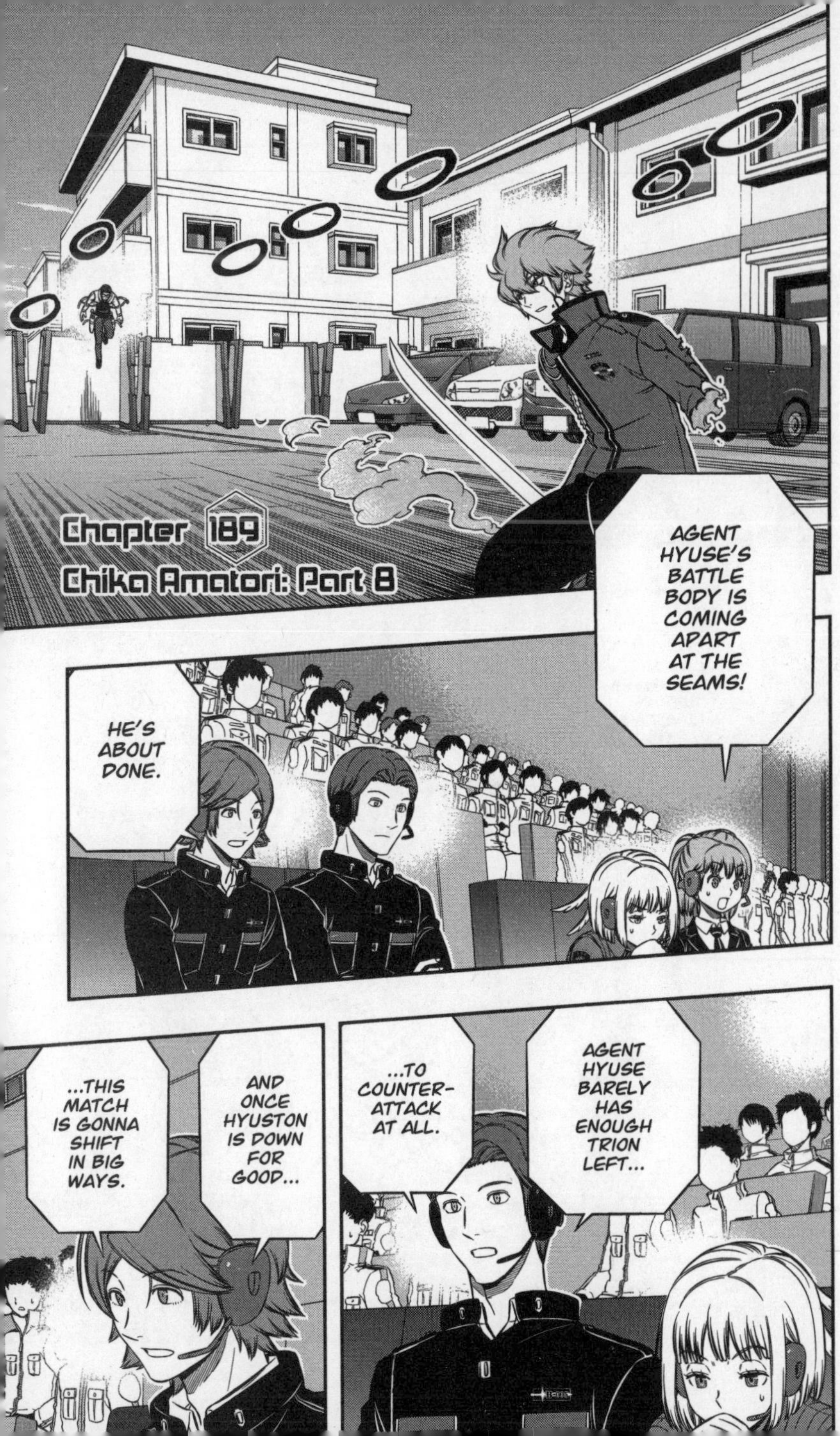
Chapter 189
Chika Amatori: Part 8
AGENT HYUSE'S BATTLE BODY IS COMING APART AT THE SEAMS!
HE'S ABOUT DONE.
AGENT HYUSE BARELY HAS ENOUGH TRION LEFT...
...TO COUNTER-ATTACK AT ALL.
AND ONCE HYUSTON IS DOWN FOR GOOD...
...THIS MATCH IS GONNA SHIFT IN BIG WAYS.

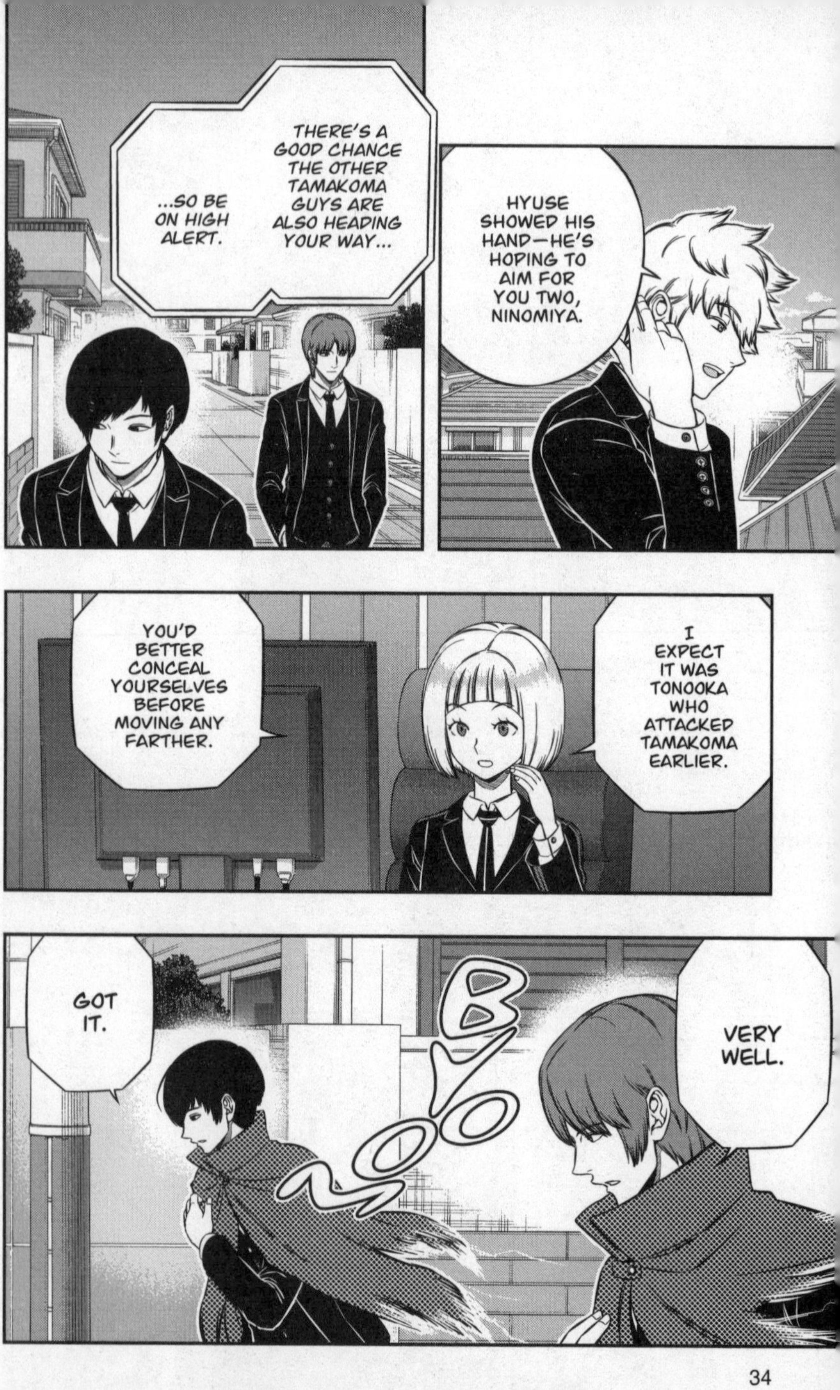
HYUSE SHOWED HIS HAND—HE'S HOPING TO AIM FOR YOU TWO, NINOMIYA.
THERE'S A GOOD CHANCE THE OTHER TAMAKOMA GUYS ARE ALSO HEADING YOUR WAY...
...SO BE ON HIGH ALERT.
I EXPECT IT WAS TONOOKA WHO ATTACKED TAMAKOMA EARLIER.
YOU'D BETTER CONCEAL YOURSELVES BEFORE MOVING ANY FARTHER.
VERY WELL.
GOT IT.

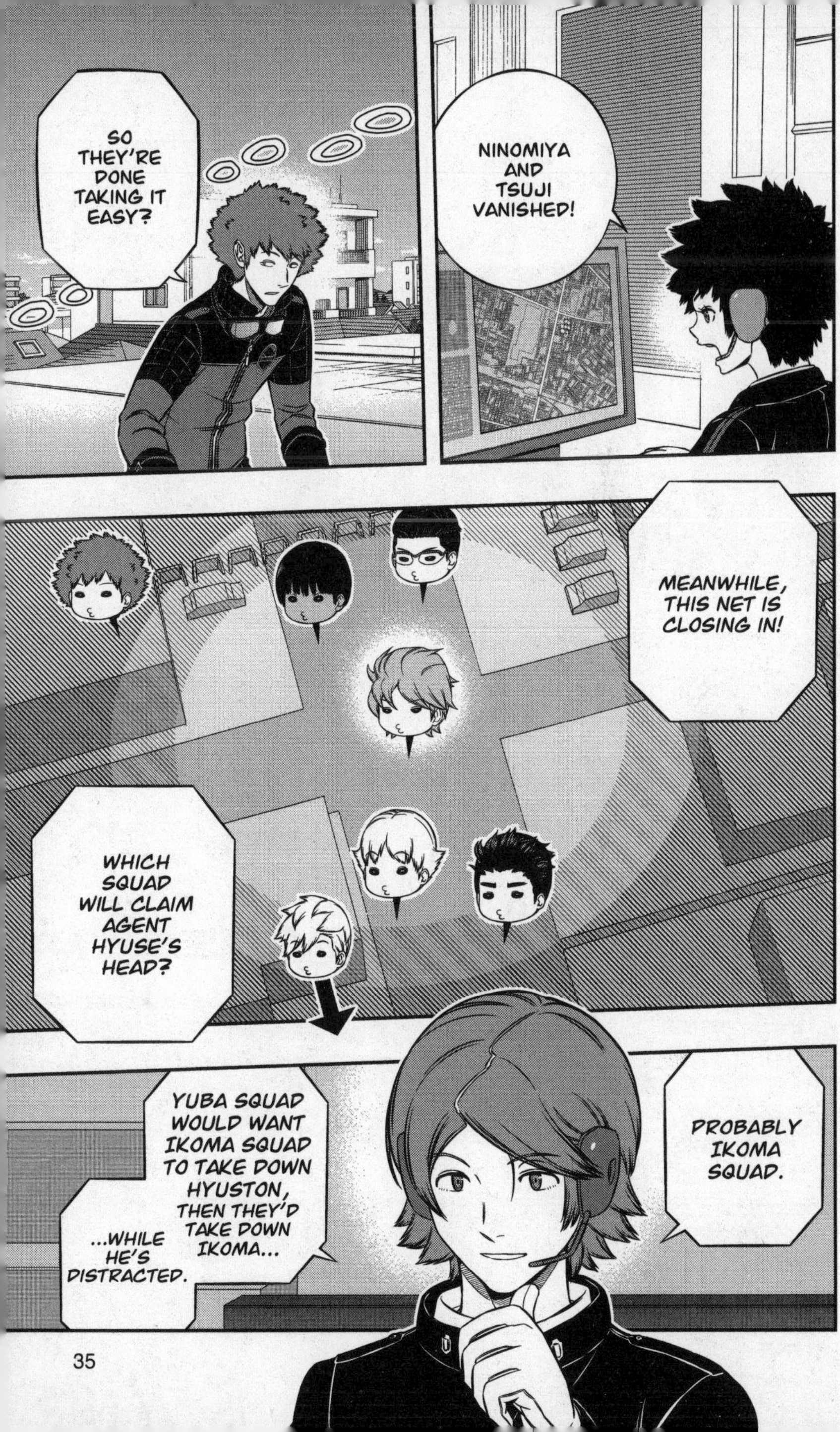
NINOMIYA AND TSUJI VANISHED!
SO THEY'RE DONE TAKING IT EASY?
MEANWHILE, THIS NET IS CLOSING IN!
WHICH SQUAD WILL CLAIM AGENT HYUSE'S HEAD?
PROBABLY IKOMA SQUAD.
YUBA SQUAD WOULD WANT IKOMA SQUAD TO TAKE DOWN HYUSTON, THEN THEY'D TAKE DOWN IKOMA...
...WHILE HE'S DISTRACTED.

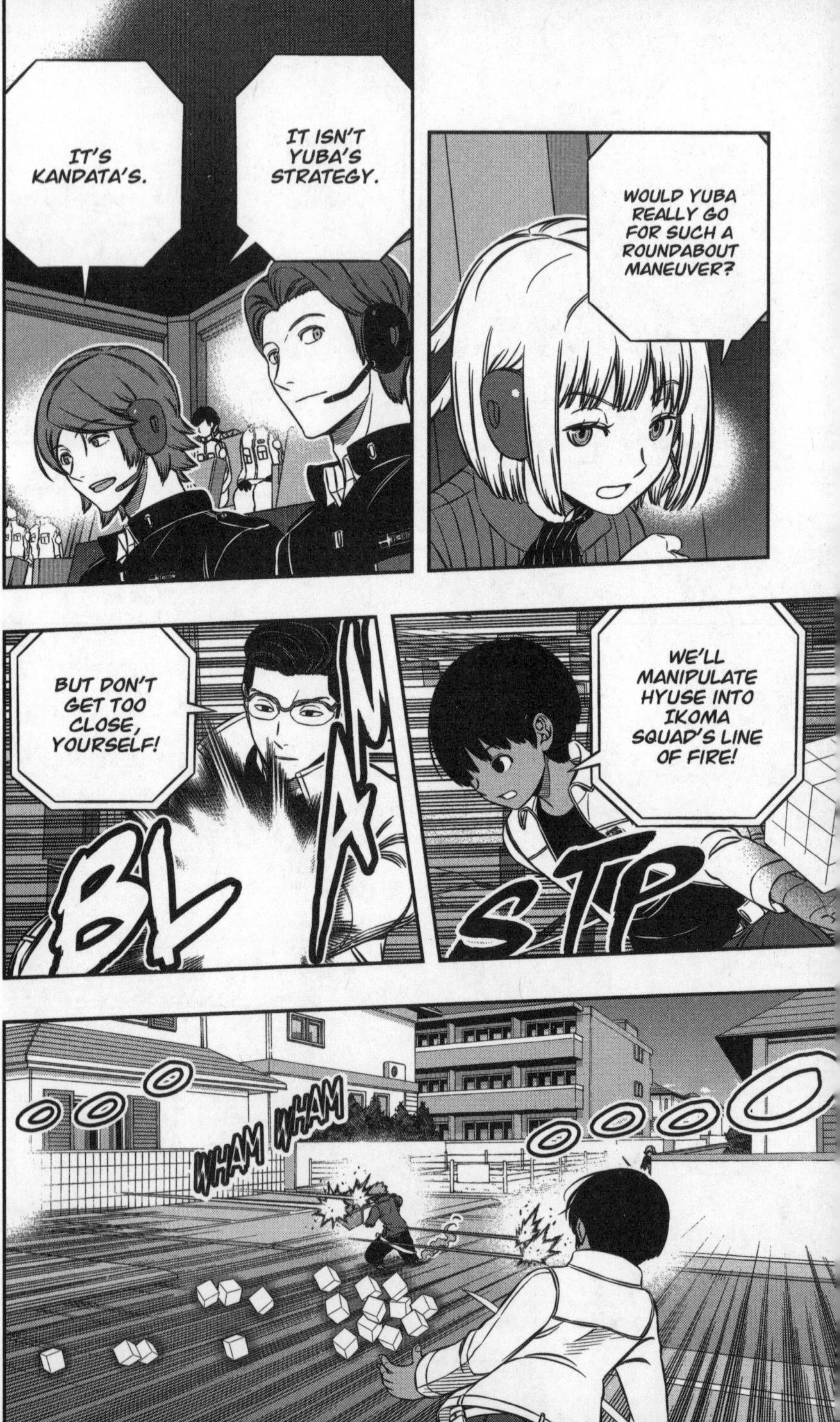
WOULD YUBA REALLY GO FOR SUCH A ROUNDABOUT MANEUVER?
IT ISN'T YUBA'S STRATEGY.
IT'S KANDATA'S.
WE'LL MANIPULATE HYUSE INTO IKOMA SQUAD'S LINE OF FIRE!
BUT DON'T GET TOO CLOSE, YOURSELF!
WHAM WHAM

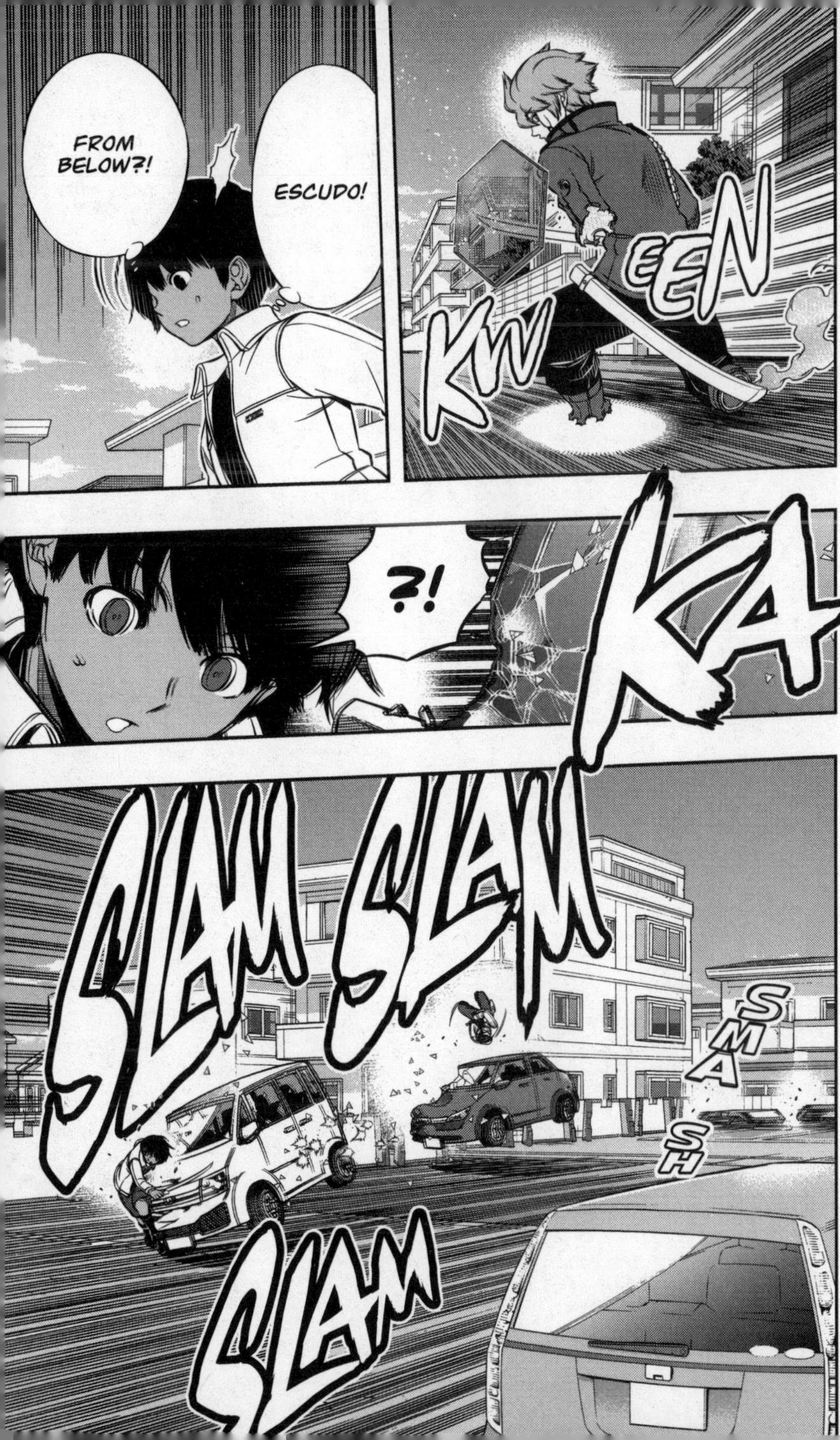
KWEEN
ESCUDO!
FROM BELOW?!
KA
?!
SLAM SLAM
SMASH
SLAM

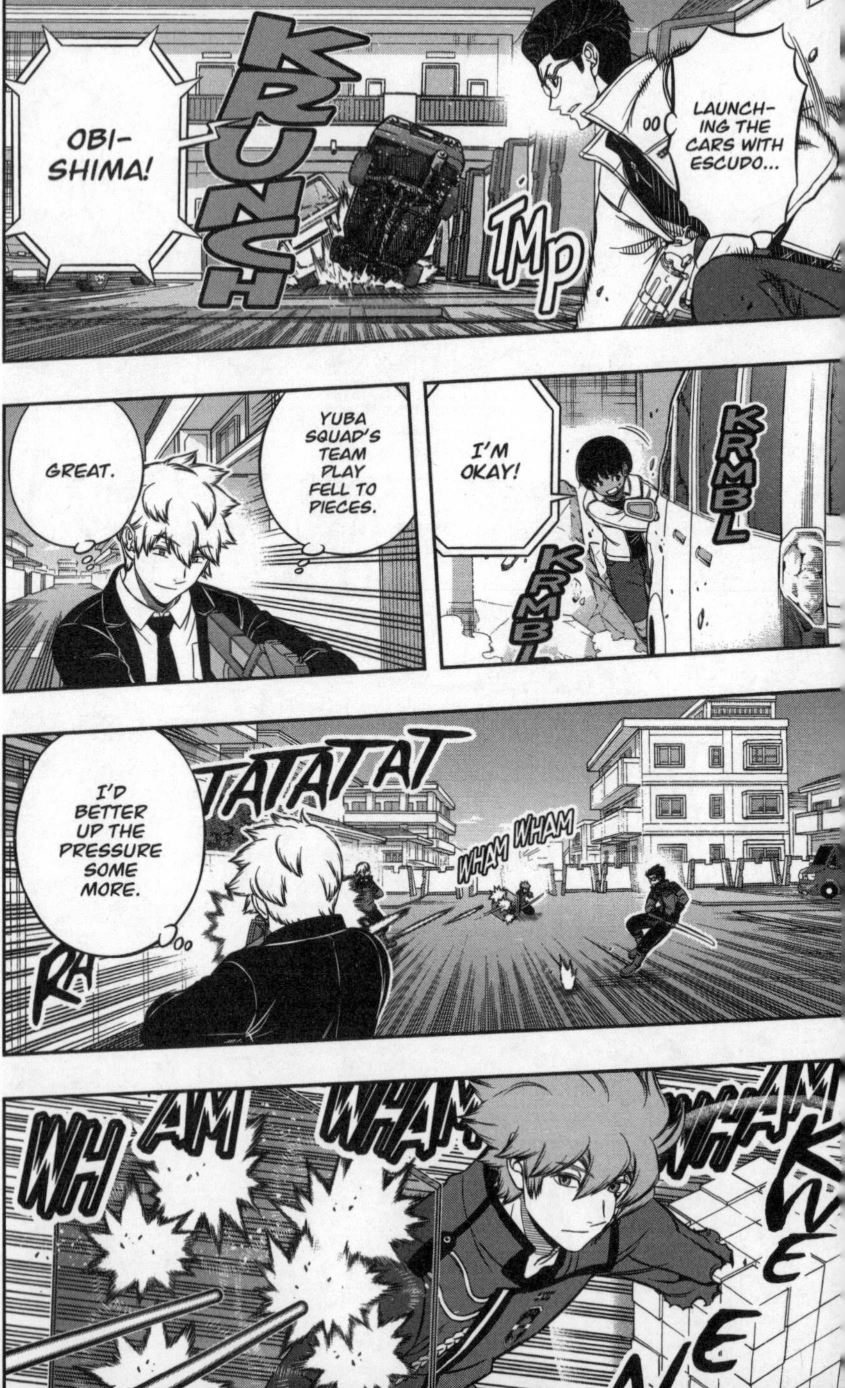
LAUNCHING THE CARS WITH ESCUDO...
KRUNCH
OBI-SHIMA!
TMP
KRMBL
I'M OKAY!
KRMBL
YUBA SQUAD'S TEAM PLAY FELL TO PIECES.
GREAT.
TATATAT
WHAM WHAM
I'D BETTER UP THE PRESSURE SOME MORE.
KA
KWEE
WHAM
WHAM
WHAM

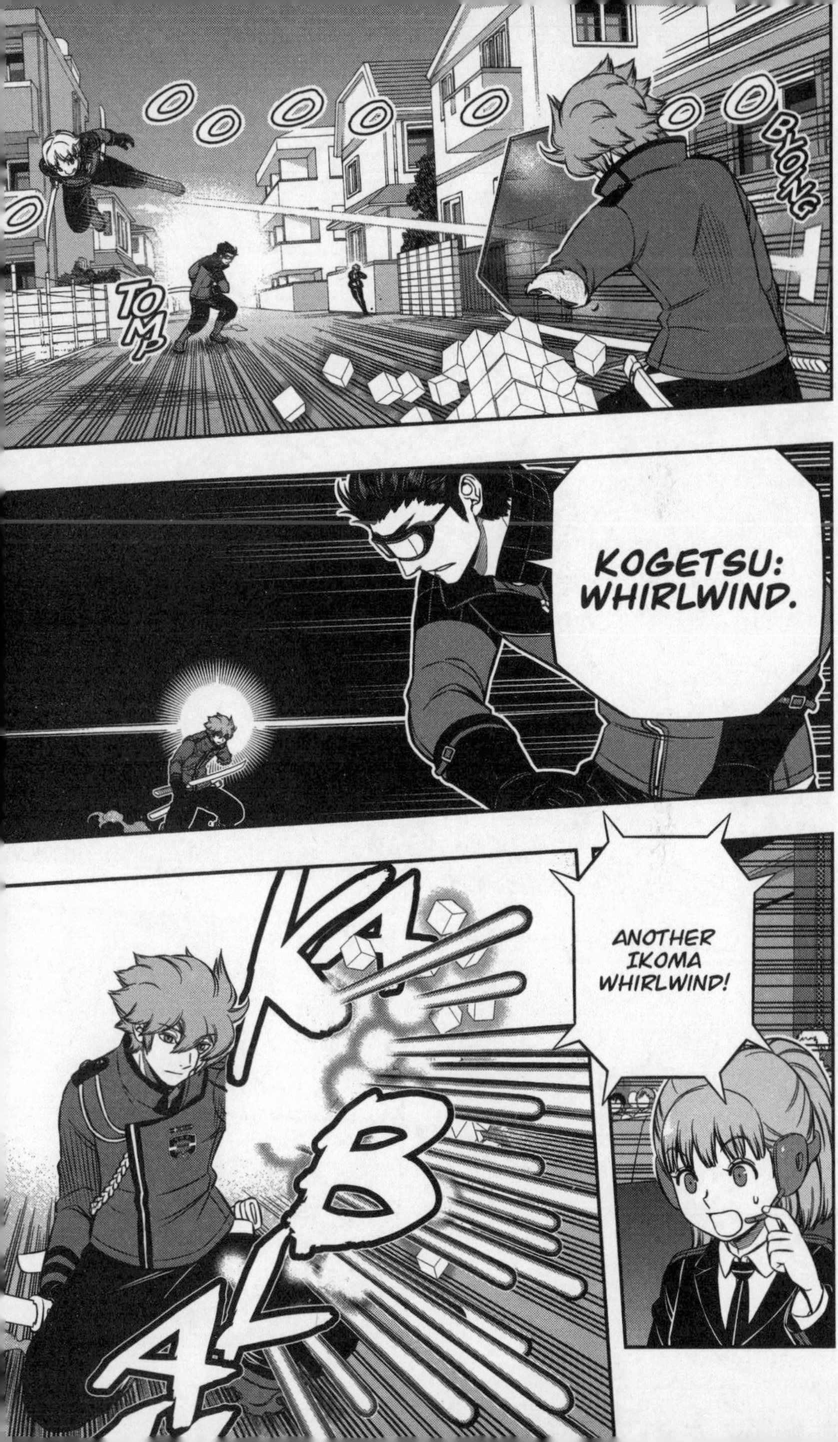
BYONG
TOMP
KOGETSU: WHIRLWIND.
ANOTHER IKOMA WHIRLWIND!
KA
BAM

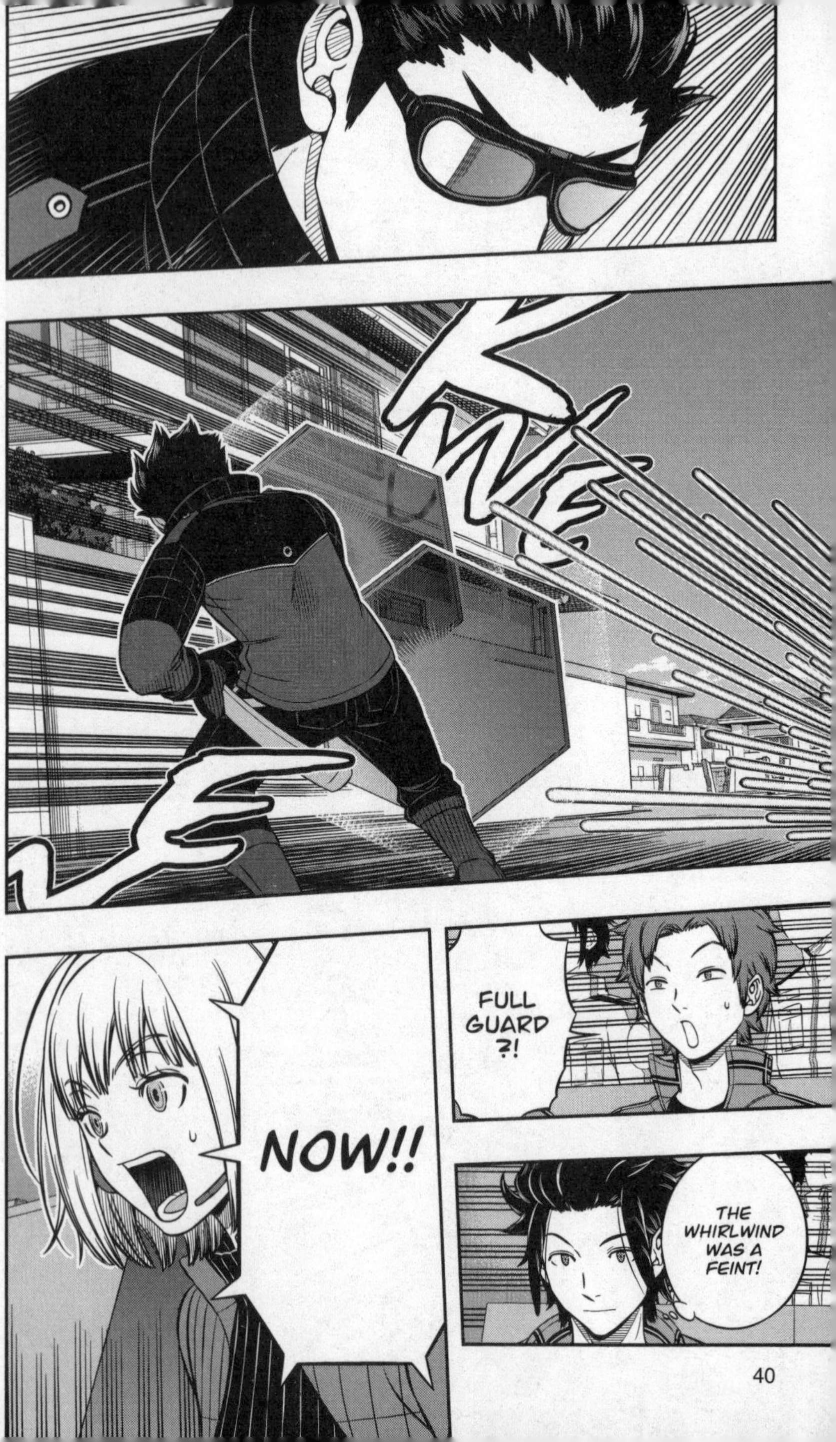
FULL GUARD ?!
THE WHIRLWIND WAS A FEINT!
NOW!!

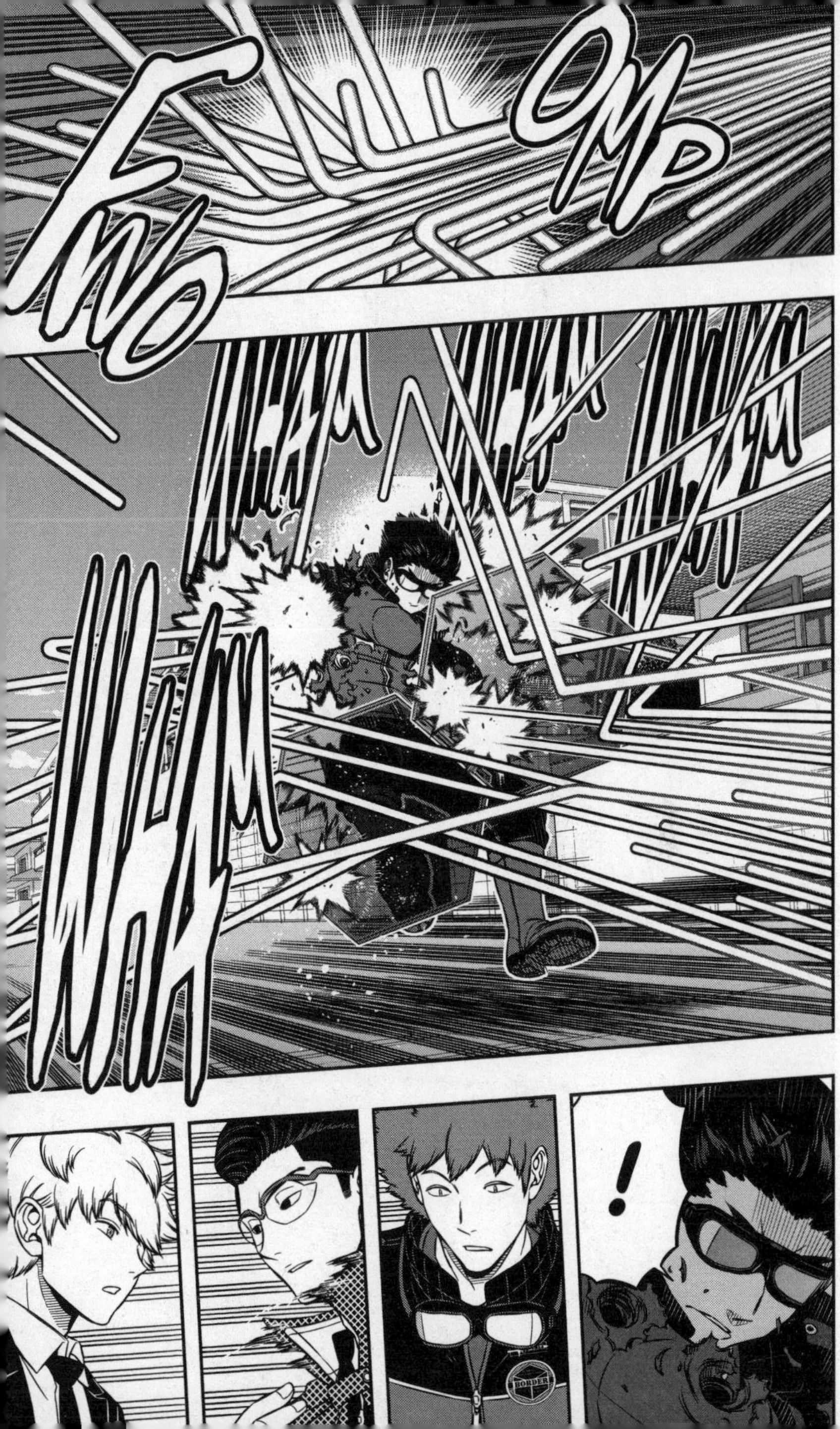
FWOOMP
WHAM
WHAM
BORDER
!

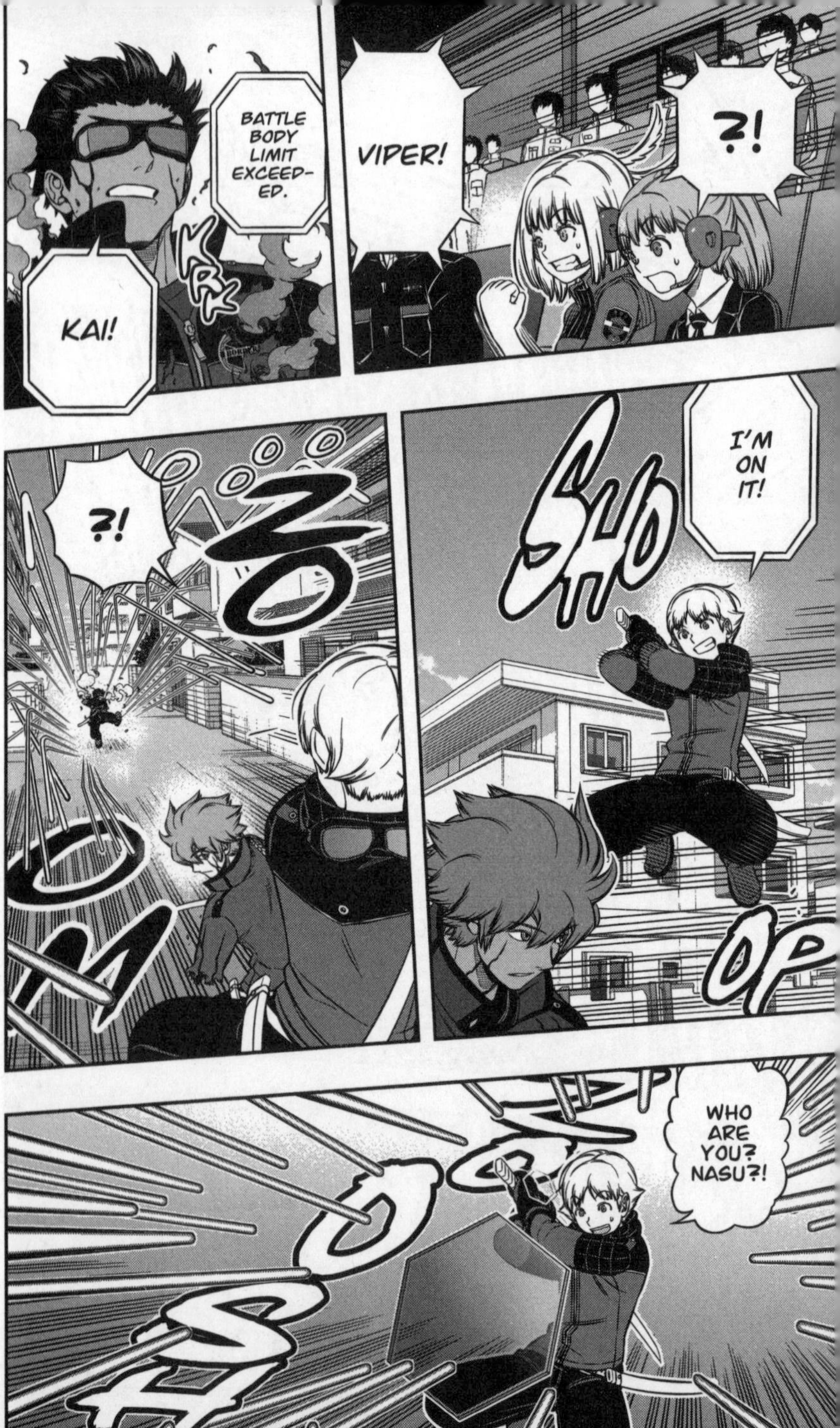
?!
VIPER!
BATTLE BODY LIMIT EXCEED-ED.
KRK
KAI!
I'M ON IT!
SHO
OP
?!
ZO
WHO ARE YOU? NASU?!

WEEN
K

PLINK PLINK
!
PLINK
PKAKKA

TOOK
LONG
ENOUGH.

BUT
YOU'RE
DONE.

43

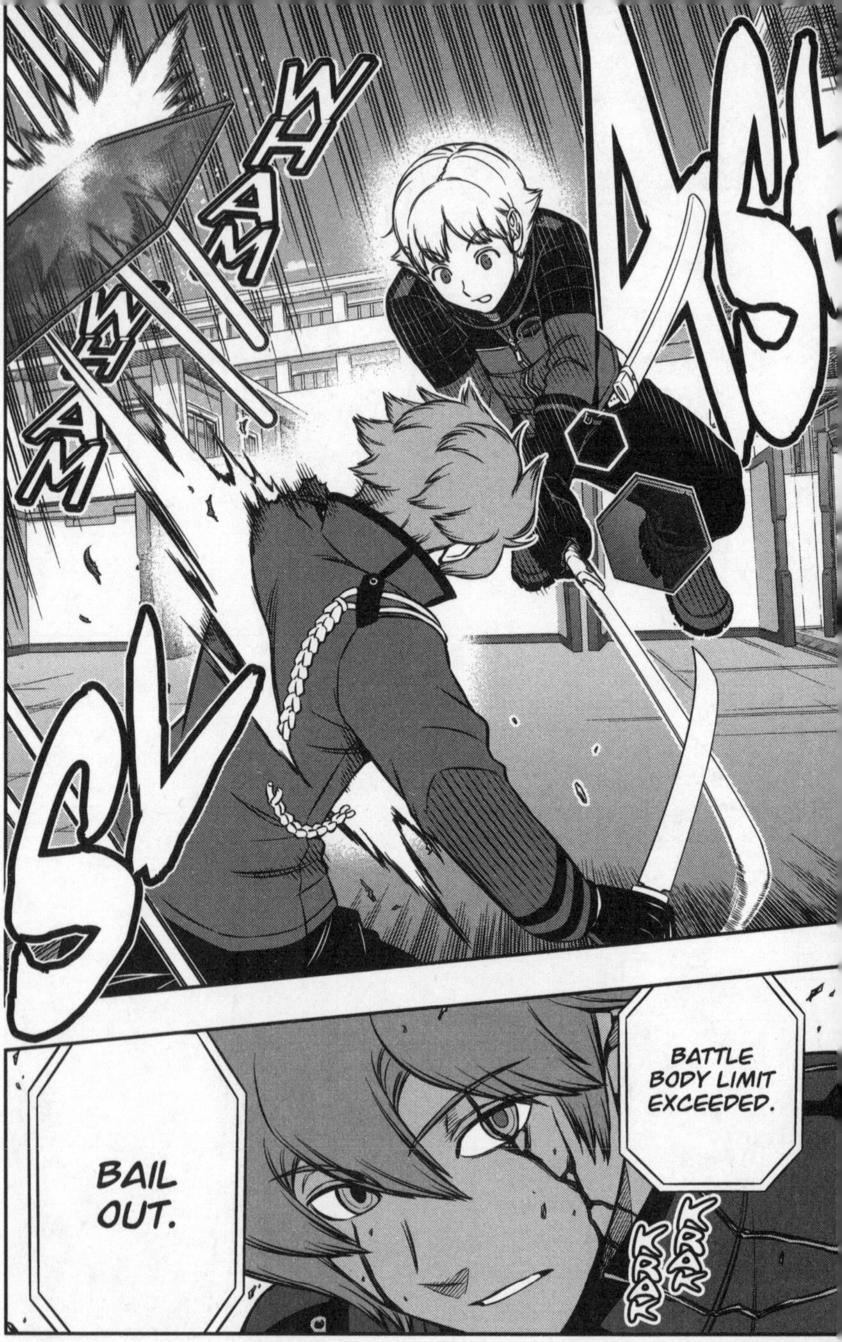
WHAM
WHAM
BATTLE BODY LIMIT EXCEEDED.
KRAK KRAK
BAIL OUT.

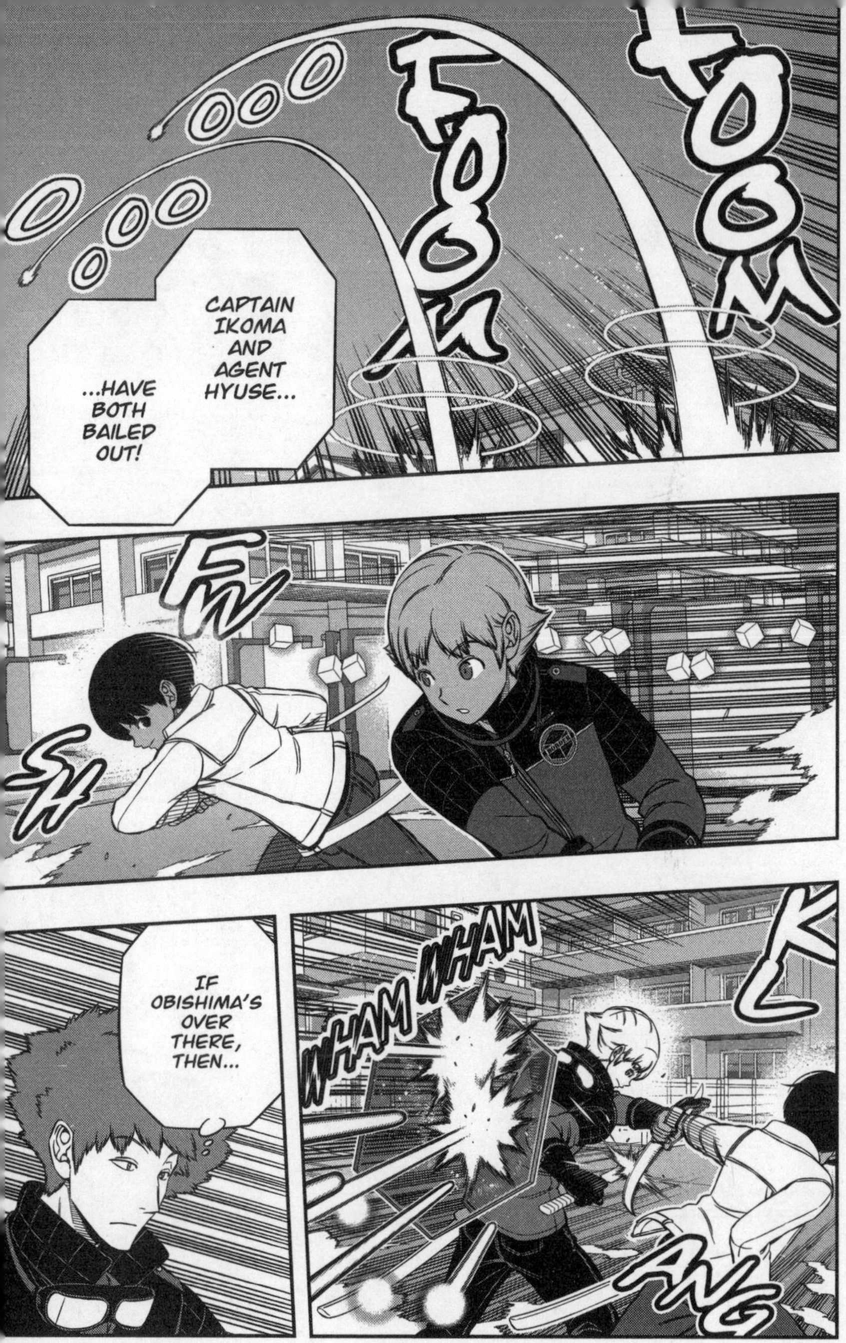
FOOOM
FOOOM
CAPTAIN IKOMA AND AGENT HYUSE...
...HAVE BOTH BAILED OUT!
FW
SH
KL
ANG
WHAM WHAM
IF OBISHIMA'S OVER THERE, THEN...

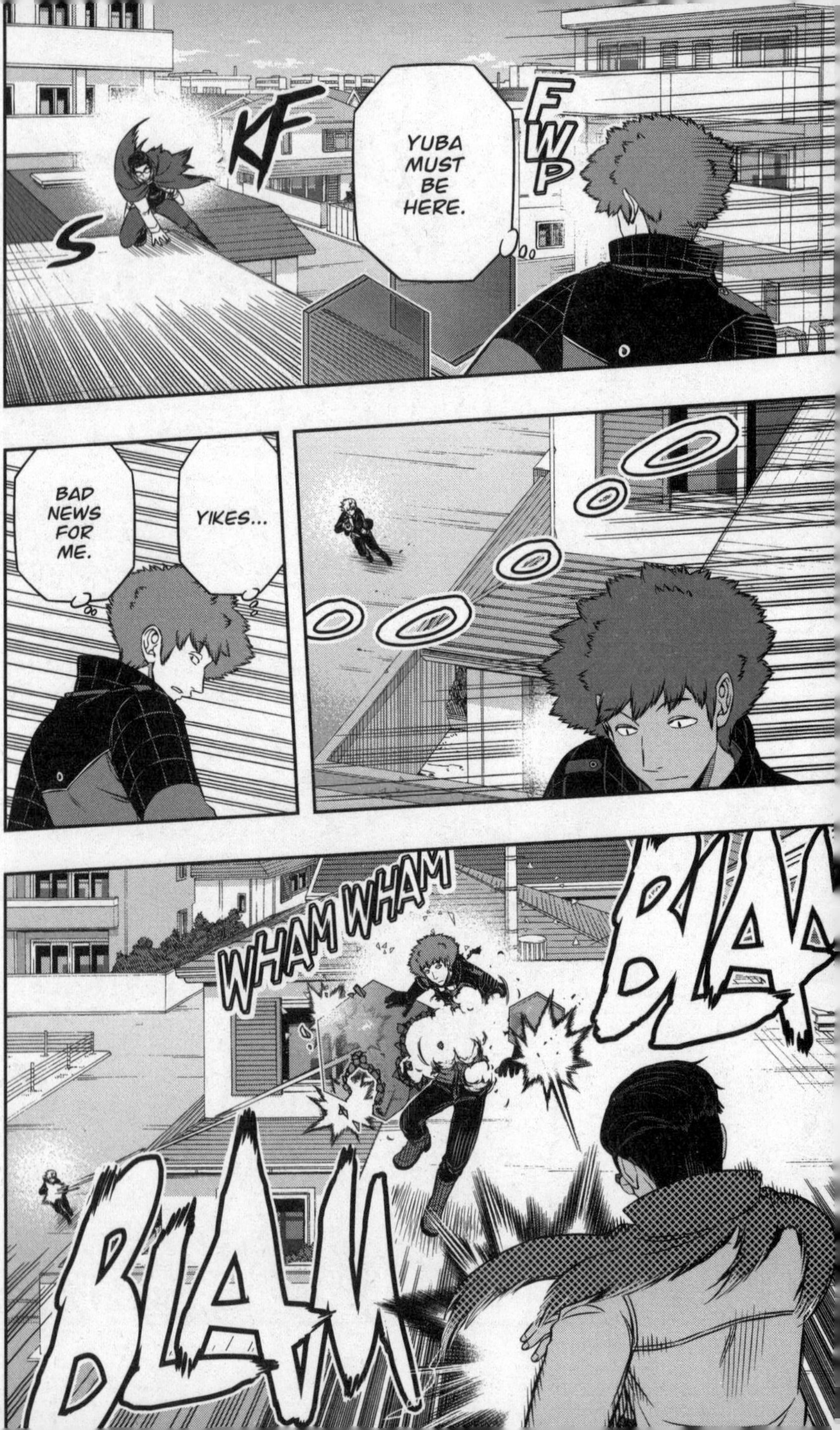
FWP
YUBA MUST BE HERE.
KF
S
YIKES...
BAD NEWS FOR ME.
BLAM
WHAM WHAM
BLAM

CAPTAIN YUBA'S QUICK TRIGGER FINGER ENSURED THAT THAT POINT WENT TO HIM!

THAT'S A POINT FOR YUBA SQUAD!

FO OM

CAUGHT BETWEEN CAPTAIN YUBA AND AGENT INUKAI...

...AGENT MIZUKAMI HAS ALSO BAILED OUT!

007 YUBA SQUAD

TOTAL : 1 pt

	1 pt
	0 pt

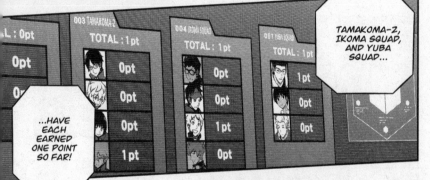

TAMAKOMA-2, IKOMA SQUAD, AND YUBA SQUAD...

...HAVE EACH EARNED ONE POINT SO FAR!

...L : 0 pt	003 TAMAKOMA-2 TOTAL : 1 pt	004 IKOMA SQUAD TOTAL : 1 pt	007 YUBA SQUAD TOTAL : 1 pt
0 pt	0 pt	0 pt	1 pt
0	0 pt	0 pt	0 pt
	0 pt	1 pt	0 pt
	1 pt	0 pt	0 pt

RIGHT.

I WAS NERVOUS HE'D GO DOWN WITHOUT GETTING A CHANCE TO USE IT.

SO AGENT HYUSE'S SECRET WEAPON...

...TURNED OUT TO BE VIPER!

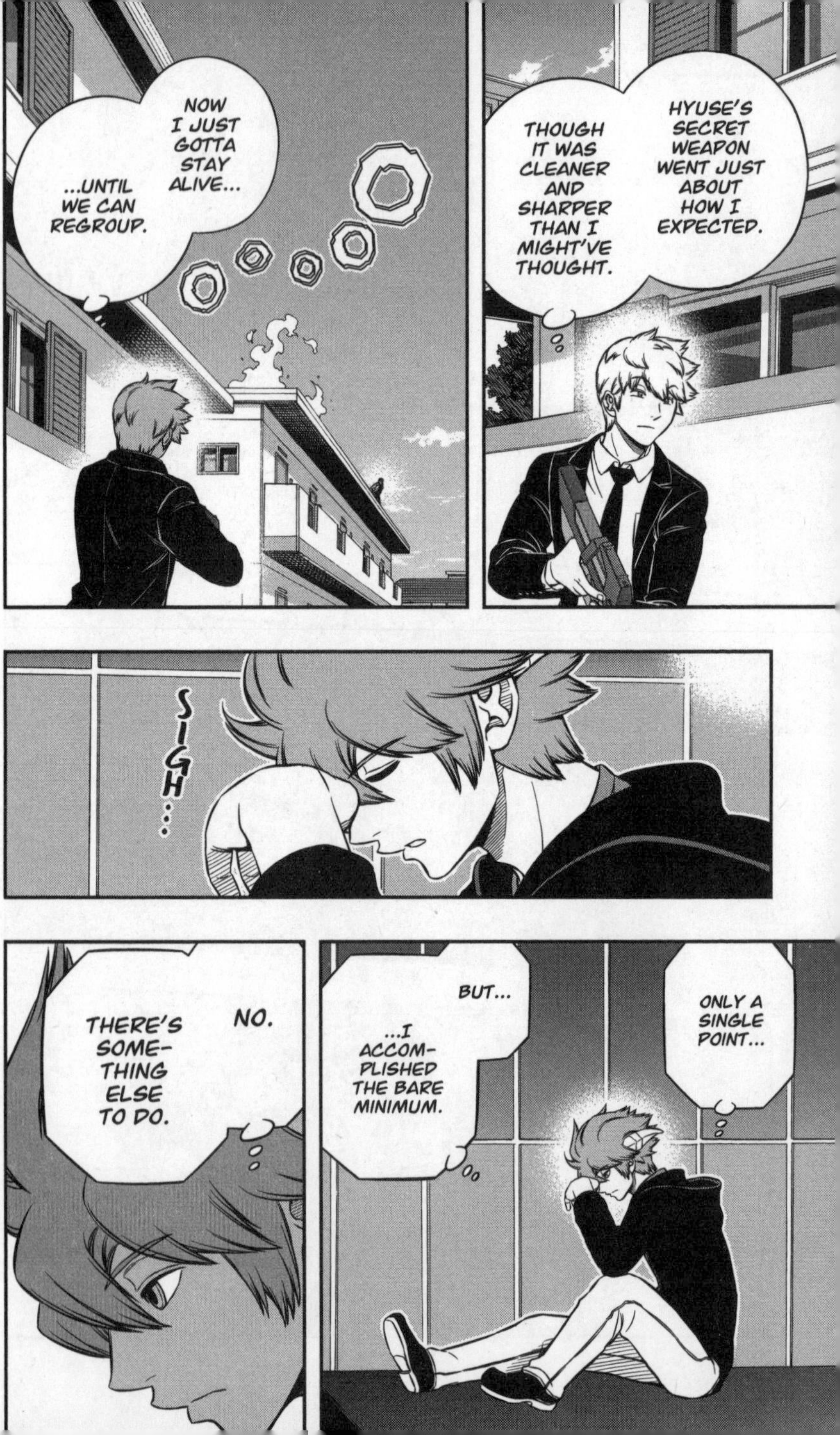
HYUSE'S SECRET WEAPON WENT JUST ABOUT HOW I EXPECTED.
THOUGH IT WAS CLEANER AND SHARPER THAN I MIGHT'VE THOUGHT.
NOW I JUST GOTTA STAY ALIVE...
...UNTIL WE CAN REGROUP.
SIGH...
ONLY A SINGLE POINT...
BUT...
...I ACCOM-PLISHED THE BARE MINIMUM.
NO.
THERE'S SOME-THING ELSE TO DO.

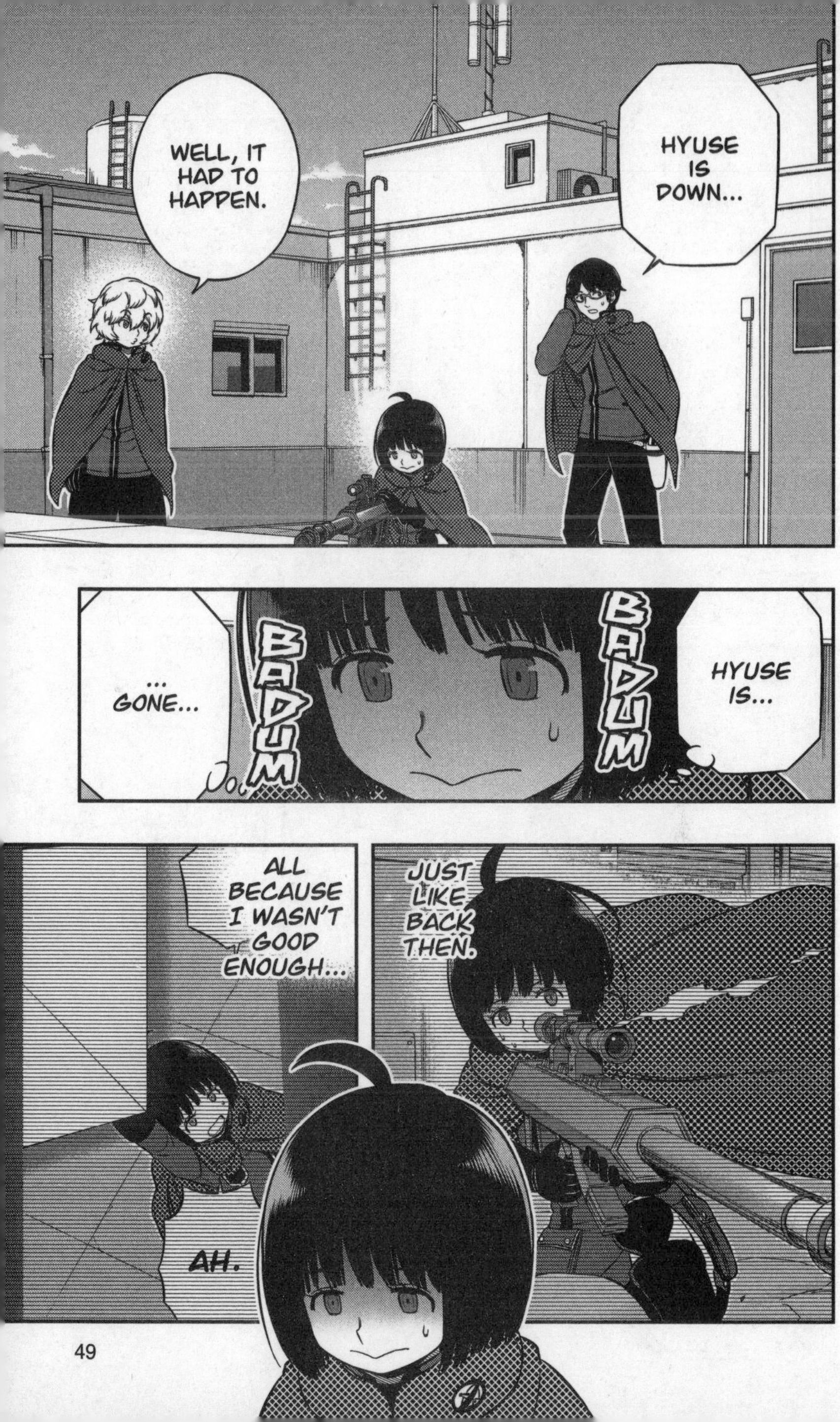
HYUSE IS DOWN...
WELL, IT HAD TO HAPPEN.
HYUSE IS...
BADUM
BADUM
... GONE...
JUST LIKE BACK THEN.
ALL BECAUSE I WASN'T GOOD ENOUGH...
AH.

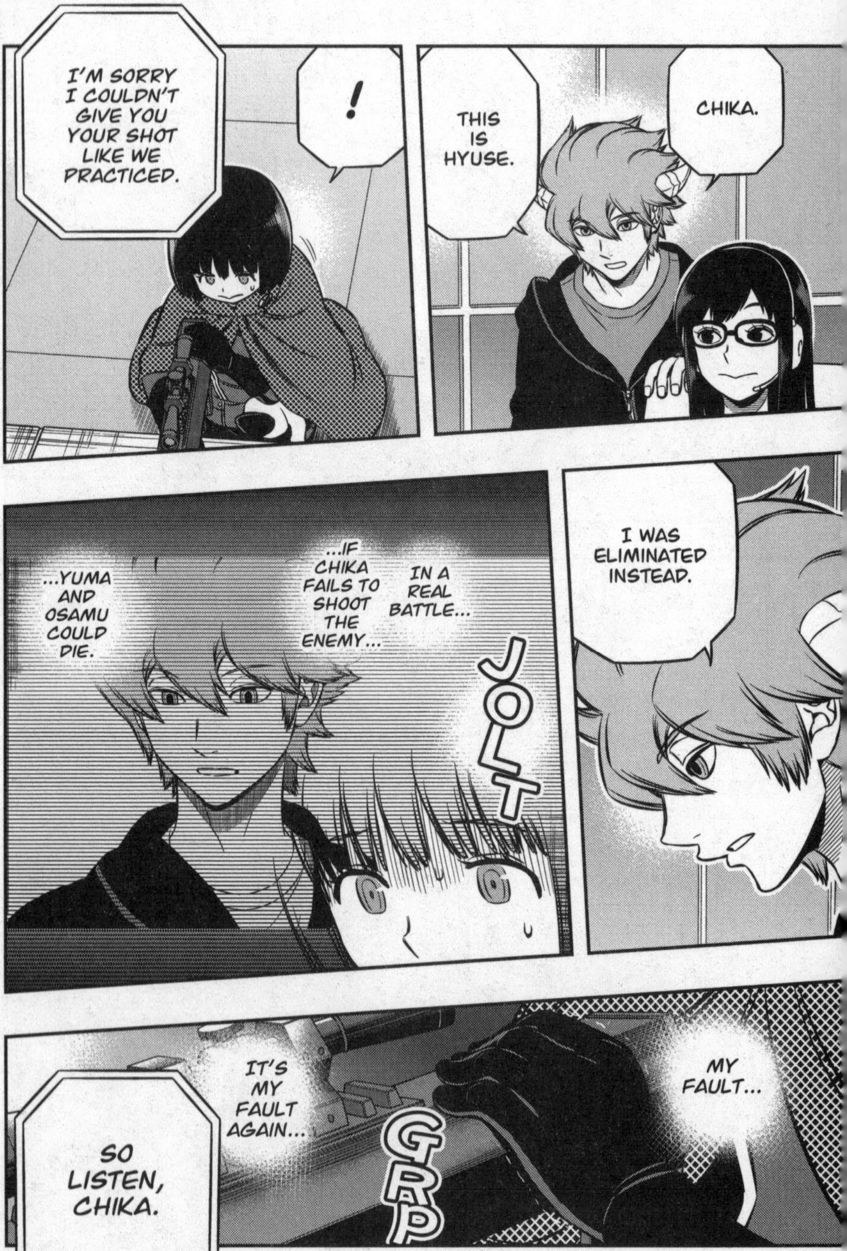
CHIKA.
THIS IS HYUSE.
I'M SORRY I COULDN'T GIVE YOU YOUR SHOT LIKE WE PRACTICED.
!
I WAS ELIMINATED INSTEAD.
JOLT
IN A REAL BATTLE...
...IF CHIKA FAILS TO SHOOT THE ENEMY...
...YUMA AND OSAMU COULD DIE.
MY FAULT...
GRP
IT'S MY FAULT AGAIN...
SO LISTEN, CHIKA.

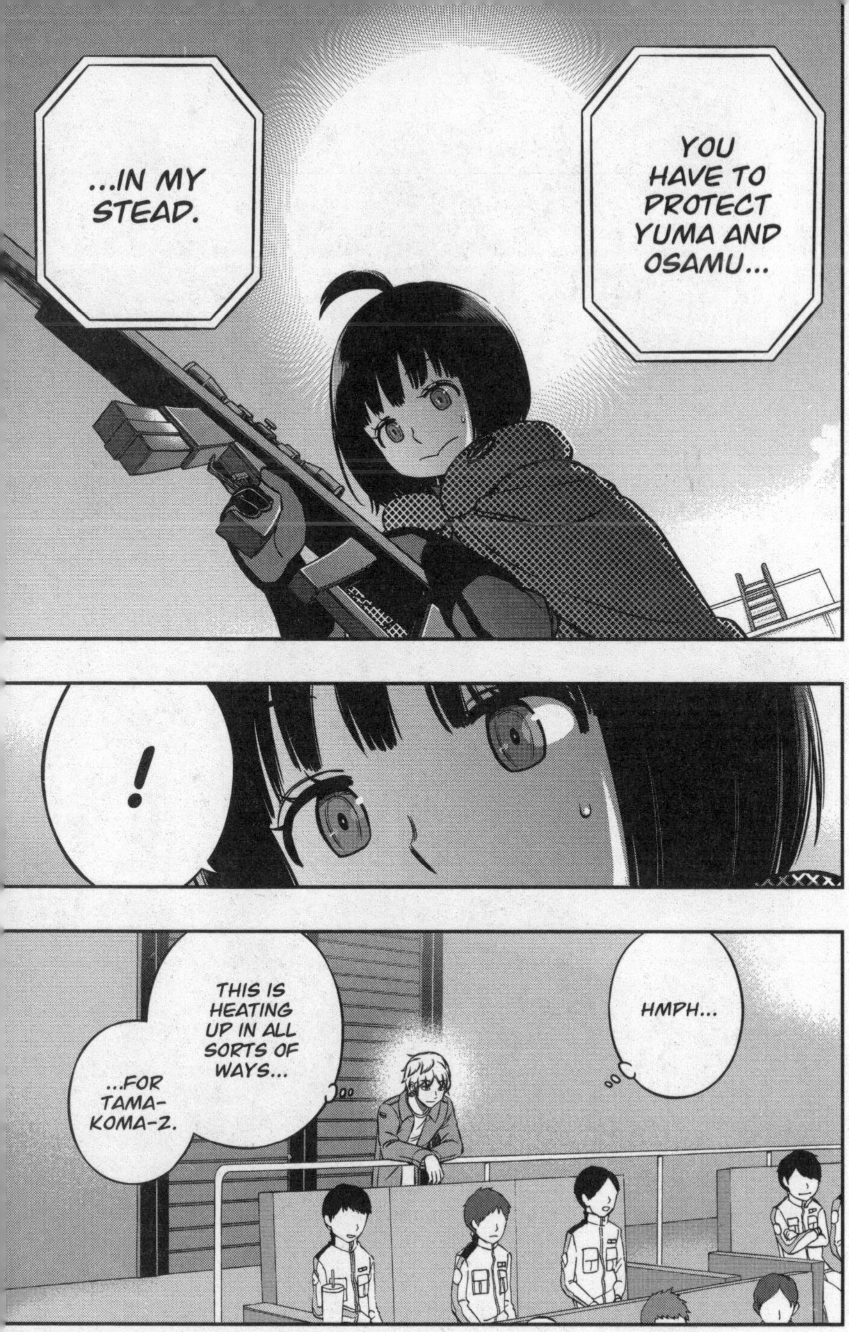
YOU HAVE TO PROTECT YUMA AND OSAMU...
...IN MY STEAD.
!
HMPH...
THIS IS HEATING UP IN ALL SORTS OF WAYS...
...FOR TAMA-KOMA-2.

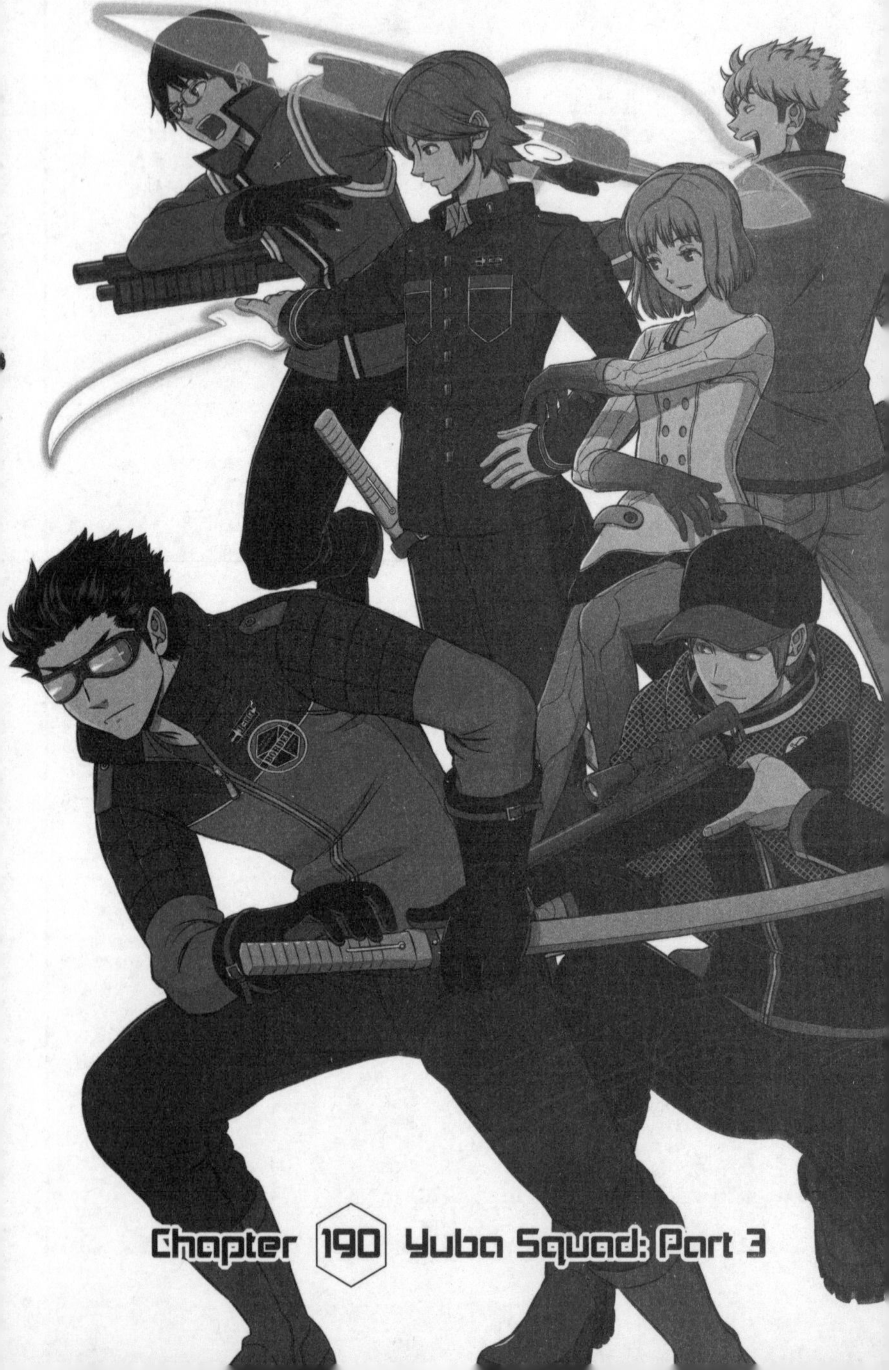

Chapter 190 Yuba Squad: Part 3

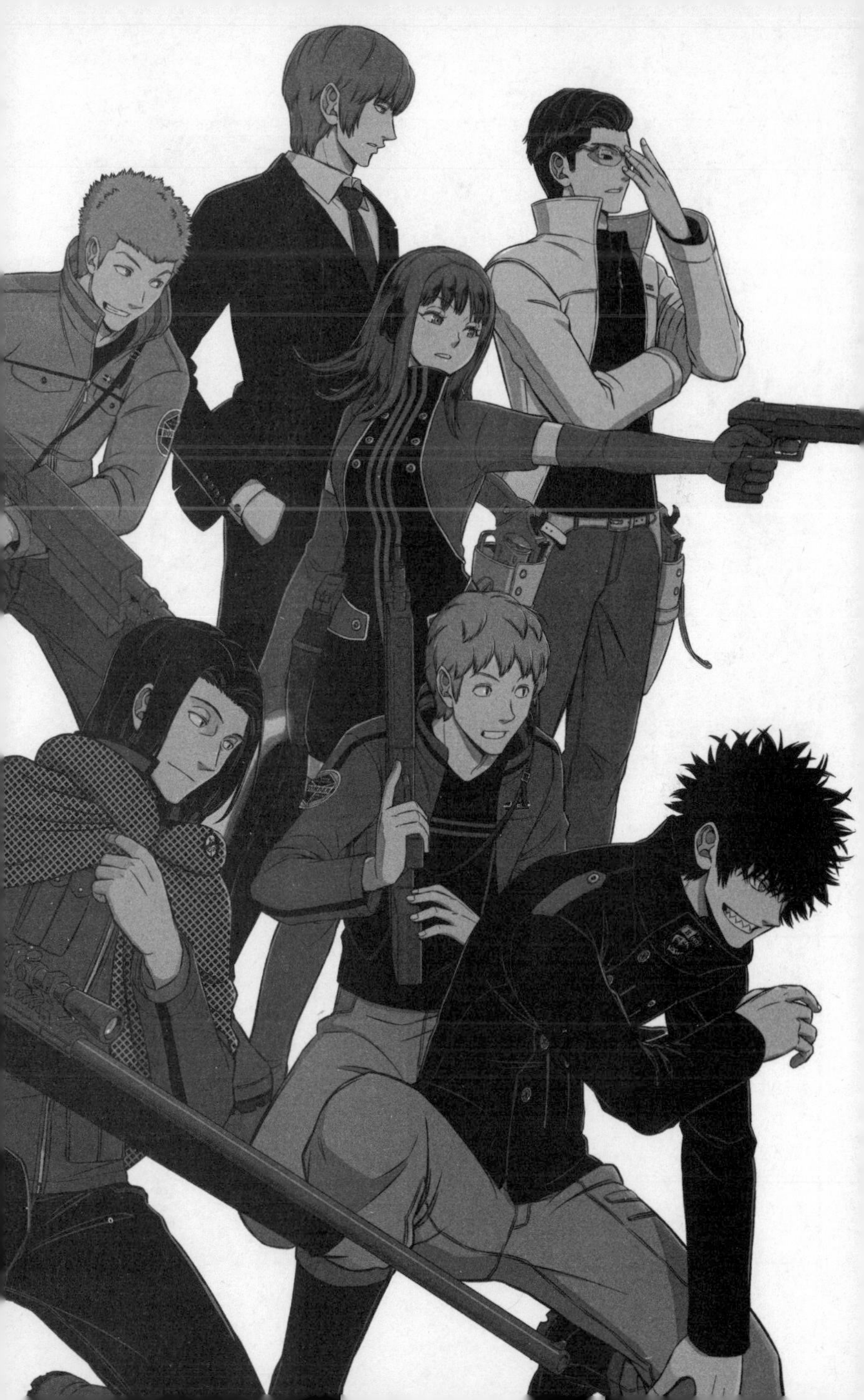

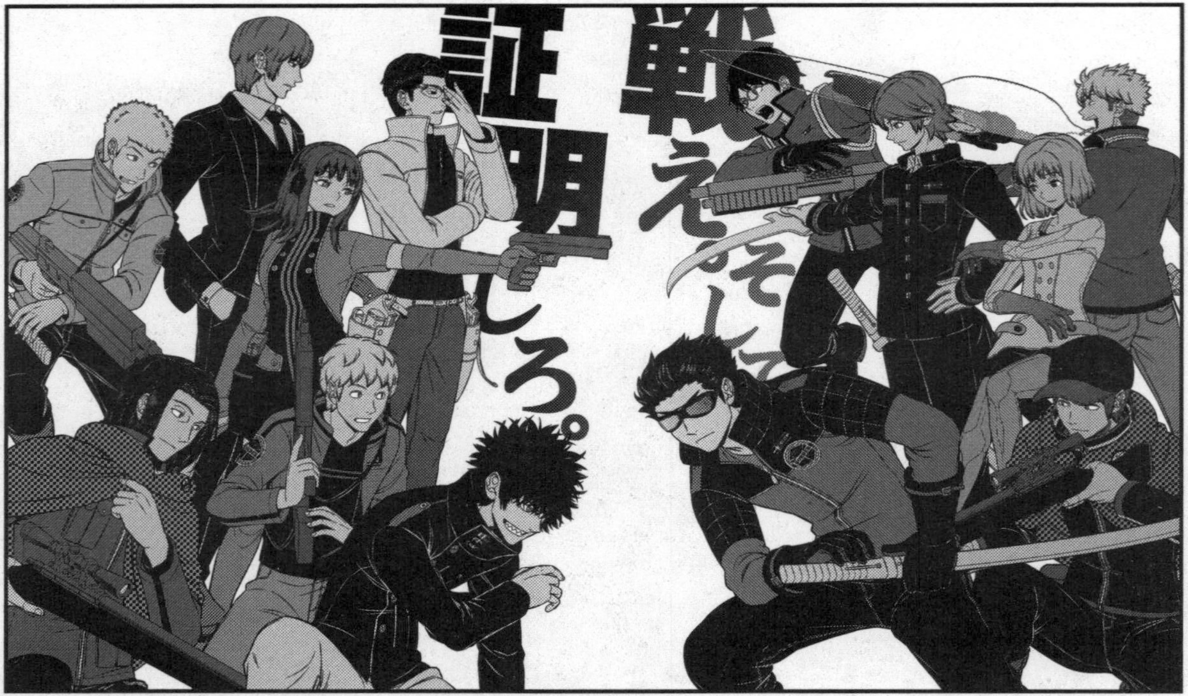
戦え。そして
証明しろ。

■ Color Title Page from *Jump SQ*, February 2020 Issue

The B-Rank captains in a group shot. This was a spread I wanted to draw before the B-Rank Wars arc ended, so I'm glad it got to happen. The big background text says, "Fight. Prove yourselves," and was originally copy provided by my second editor, Saito, for the book wrapper on volume 13. But it was perfectly suited for the B-Rank Wars, so I got to use it again. So cool.

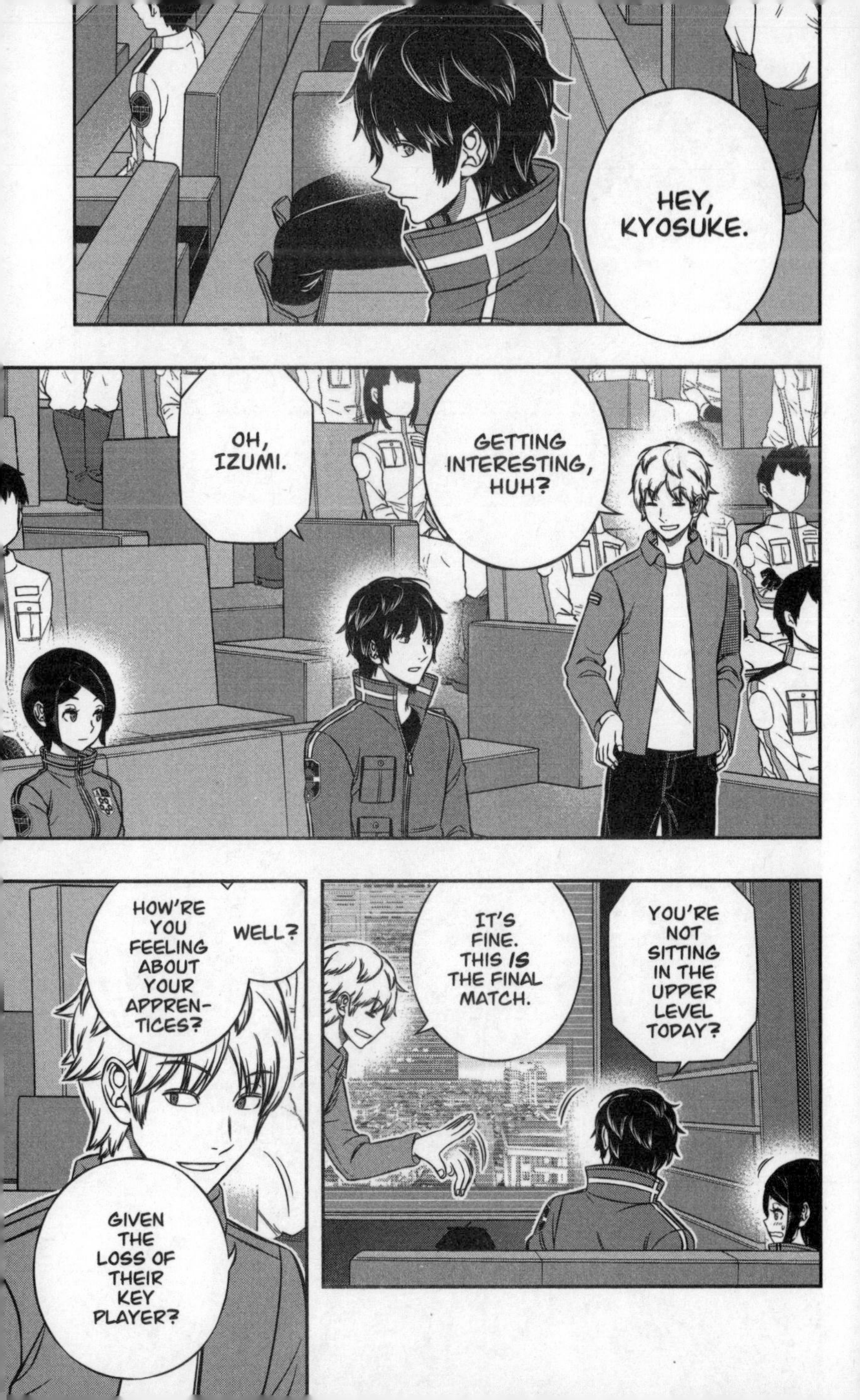
HEY, KYOSUKE.
GETTING INTERESTING, HUH?
OH, IZUMI.
YOU'RE NOT SITTING IN THE UPPER LEVEL TODAY?
IT'S FINE. THIS *IS* THE FINAL MATCH.
WELL?
HOW'RE YOU FEELING ABOUT YOUR APPREN-TICES?
GIVEN THE LOSS OF THEIR KEY PLAYER?

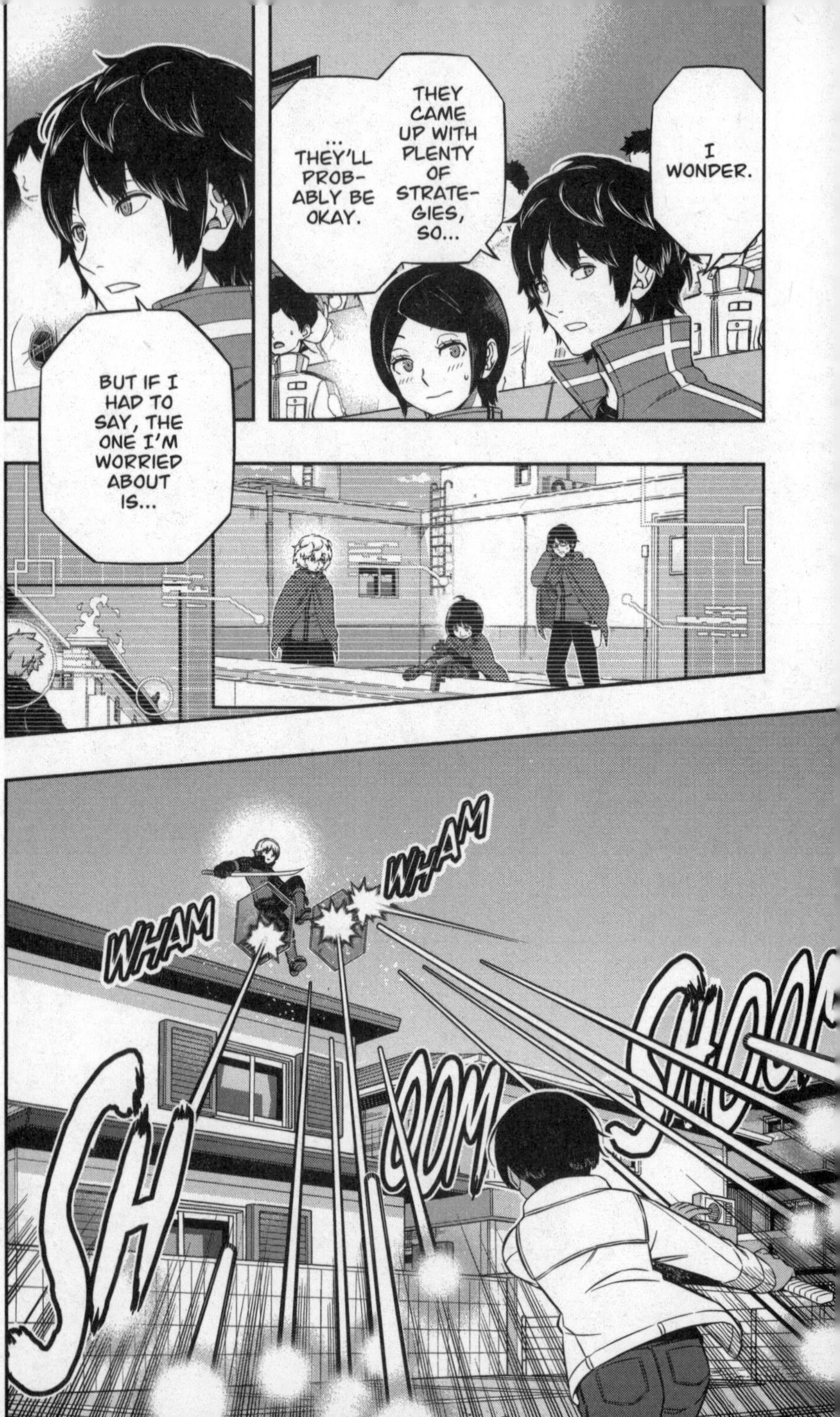
I WONDER.
THEY CAME UP WITH PLENTY OF STRATE-GIES, SO...
...THEY'LL PROB-ABLY BE OKAY.
BUT IF I HAD TO SAY, THE ONE I'M WORRIED ABOUT IS...
WHAM
WHAM
OOM
SH

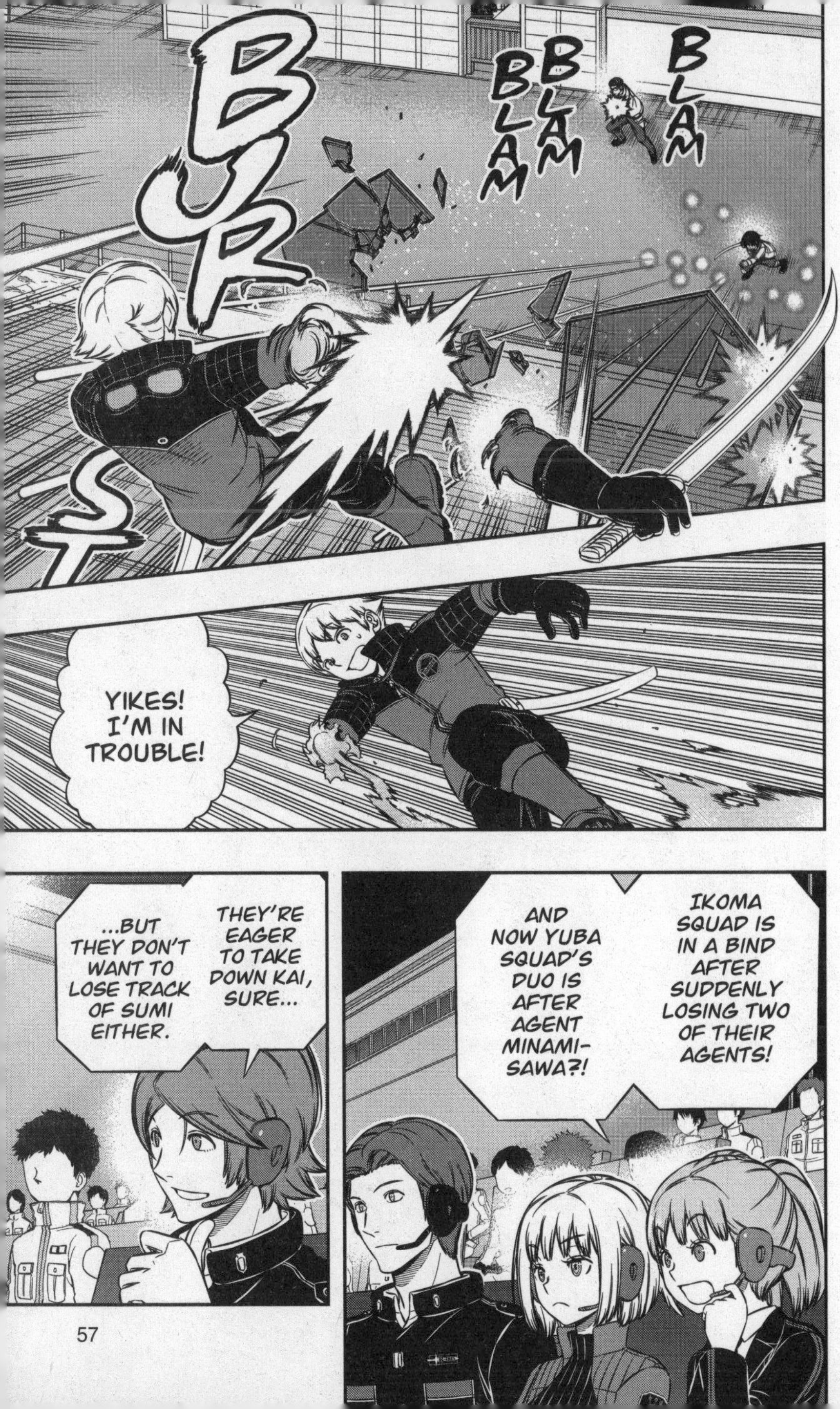
BLAM
BLAM
BLAM
BURST
YIKES! I'M IN TROUBLE!
IKOMA SQUAD IS IN A BIND AFTER SUDDENLY LOSING TWO OF THEIR AGENTS!
AND NOW YUBA SQUAD'S DUO IS AFTER AGENT MINAMI-SAWA?!
THEY'RE EAGER TO TAKE DOWN KAI, SURE...
...BUT THEY DON'T WANT TO LOSE TRACK OF SUMI EITHER.

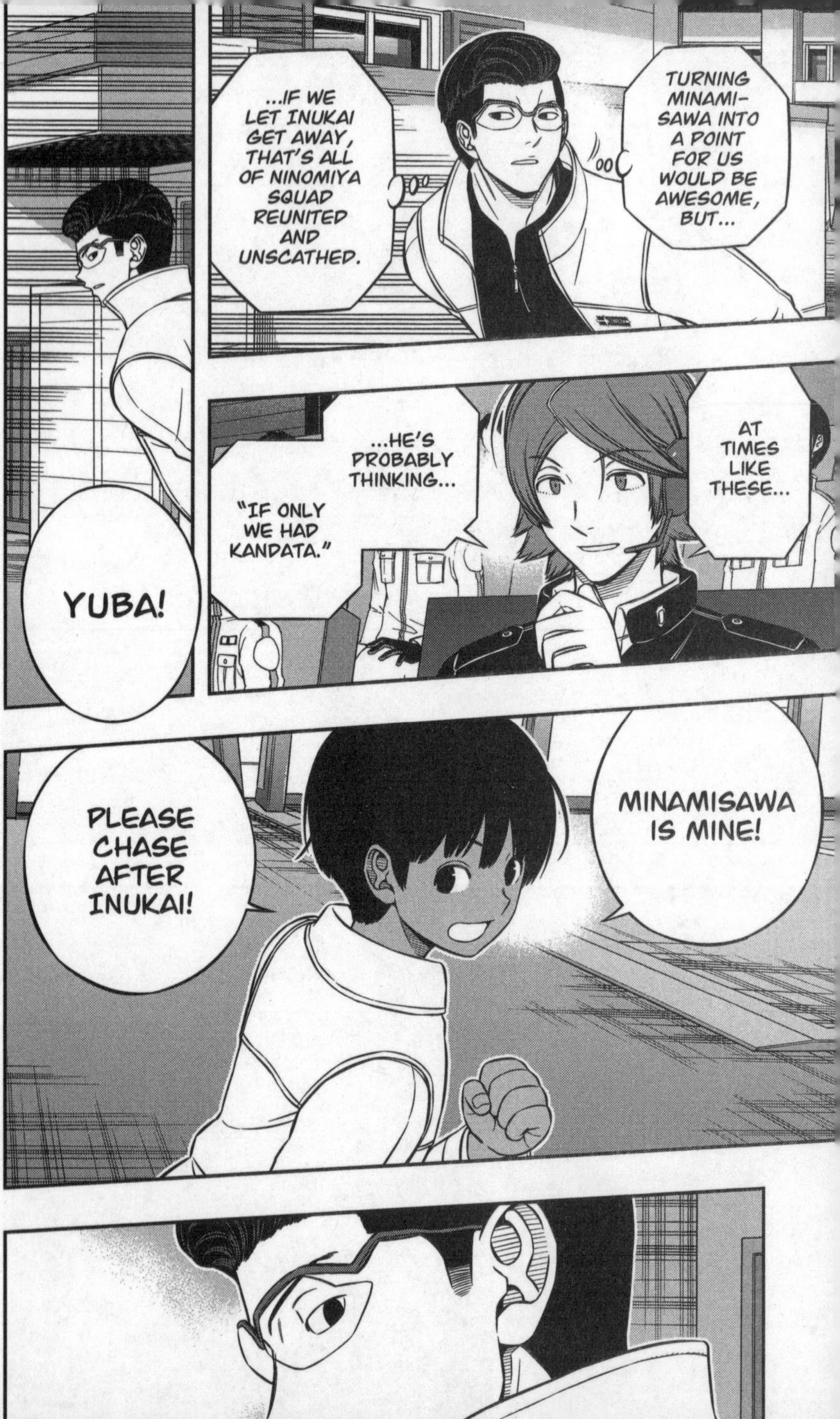
TURNING MINAMI-SAWA INTO A POINT FOR US WOULD BE AWESOME, BUT...
...IF WE LET INUKAI GET AWAY, THAT'S ALL OF NINOMIYA SQUAD REUNITED AND UNSCATHED.
AT TIMES LIKE THESE...
...HE'S PROBABLY THINKING...
“IF ONLY WE HAD KANDATA.”
YUBA!
MINAMISAWA IS MINE!
PLEASE CHASE AFTER INUKAI!

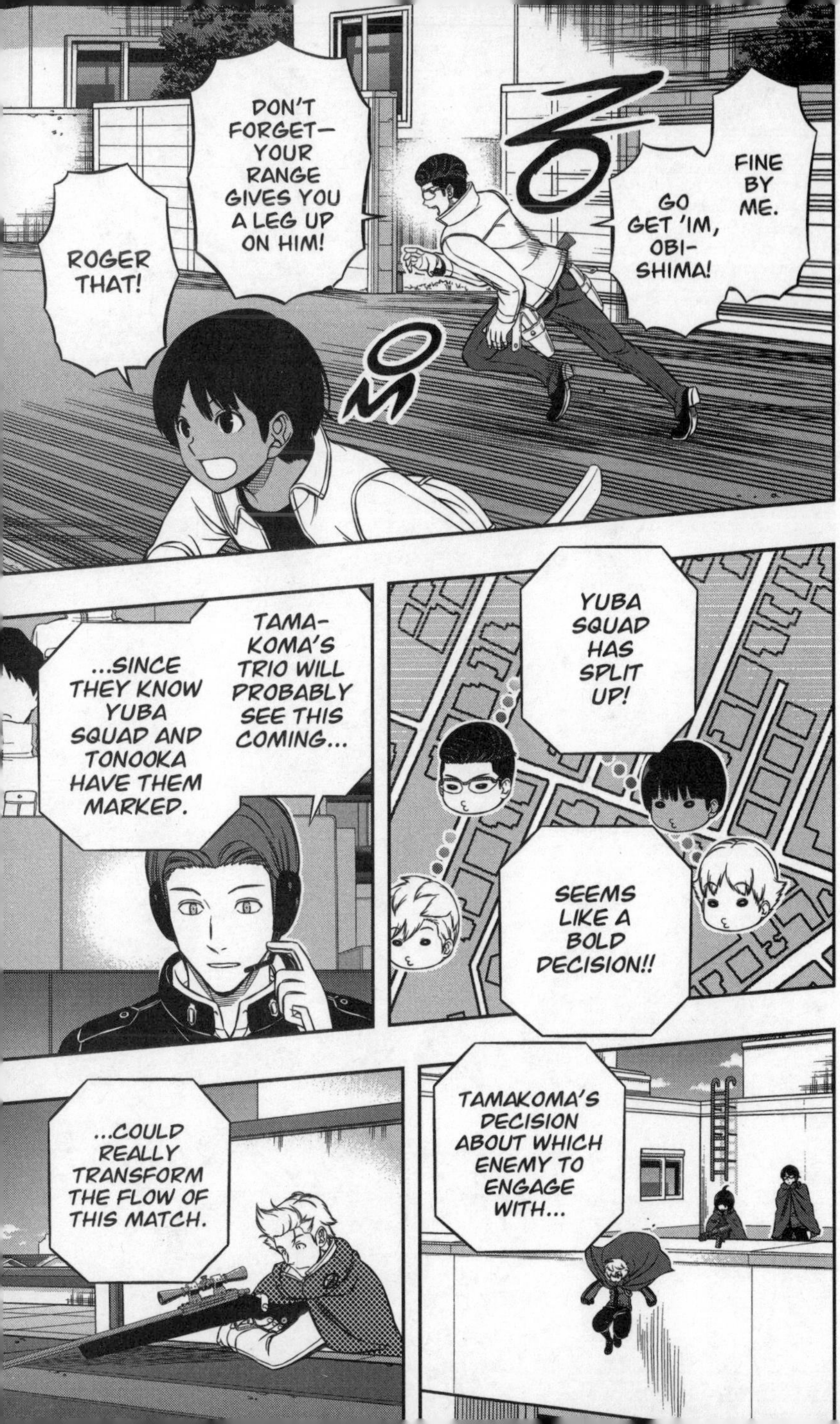
FINE BY ME.
GO GET 'IM, OBI-SHIMA!
ZOOM
DON'T FORGET— YOUR RANGE GIVES YOU A LEG UP ON HIM!
ROGER THAT!
YUBA SQUAD HAS SPLIT UP!
SEEMS LIKE A BOLD DECISION!!
TAMA-KOMA'S TRIO WILL PROBABLY SEE THIS COMING...
...SINCE THEY KNOW YUBA SQUAD AND TONOOKA HAVE THEM MARKED.
TAMAKOMA'S DECISION ABOUT WHICH ENEMY TO ENGAGE WITH...
...COULD REALLY TRANSFORM THE FLOW OF THIS MATCH.

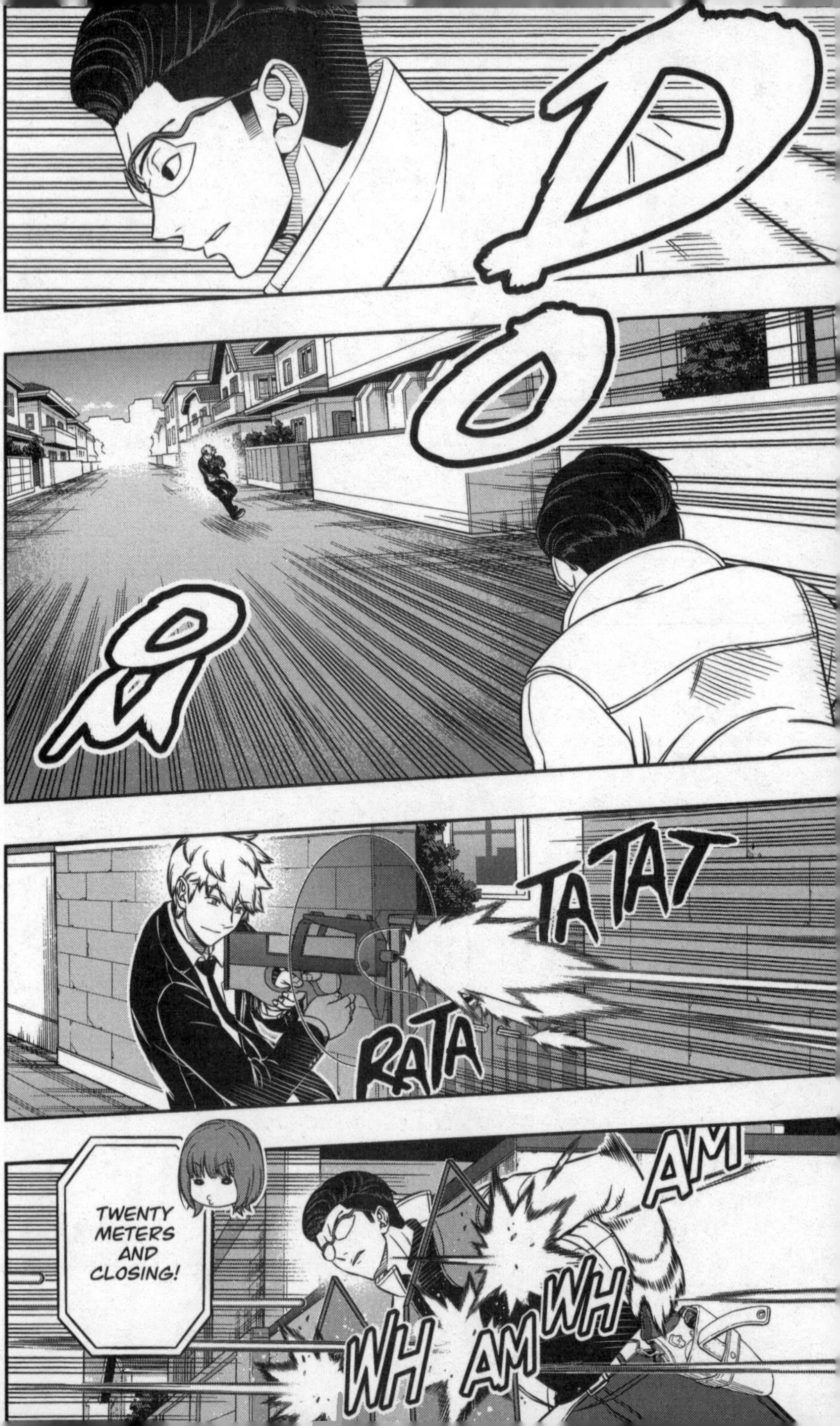
RATA
TA TAT
TWENTY METERS AND CLOSING!
WH AM
WH AM

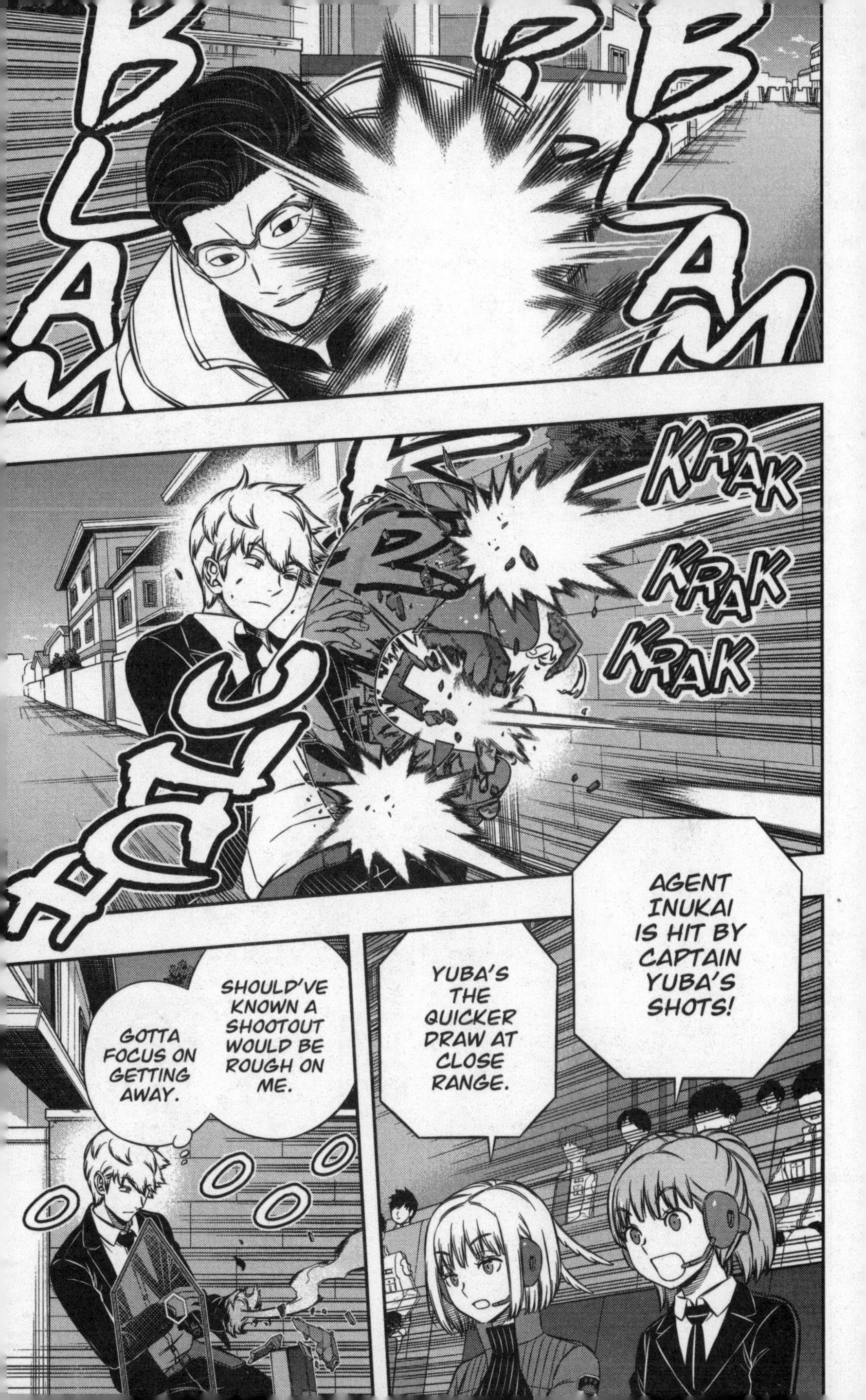
BLAM
BLAM
KRAK
KRAK
KRAK
AGENT INUKAI IS HIT BY CAPTAIN YUBA'S SHOTS!
YUBA'S THE QUICKER DRAW AT CLOSE RANGE.
SHOULD'VE KNOWN A SHOOTOUT WOULD BE ROUGH ON ME.
GOTTA FOCUS ON GETTING AWAY.

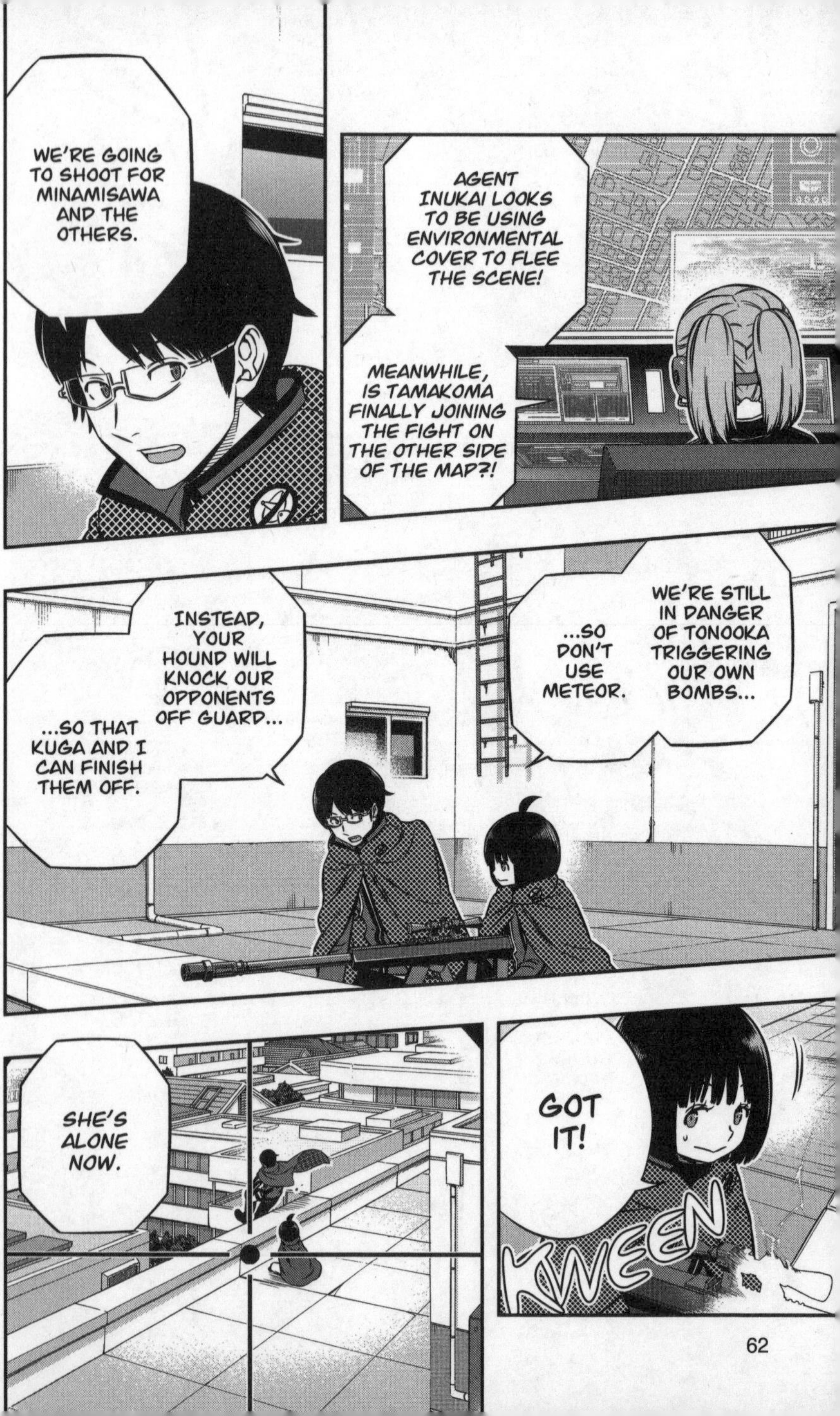
AGENT INUKAI LOOKS TO BE USING ENVIRONMENTAL COVER TO FLEE THE SCENE!
MEANWHILE, IS TAMAKOMA FINALLY JOINING THE FIGHT ON THE OTHER SIDE OF THE MAP?!
WE'RE GOING TO SHOOT FOR MINAMISAWA AND THE OTHERS.
WE'RE STILL IN DANGER OF TONOOKA TRIGGERING OUR OWN BOMBS...
...SO DON'T USE METEOR.
INSTEAD, YOUR HOUND WILL KNOCK OUR OPPONENTS OFF GUARD...
...SO THAT KUGA AND I CAN FINISH THEM OFF.
GOT IT!
KWEEN
SHE'S ALONE NOW.

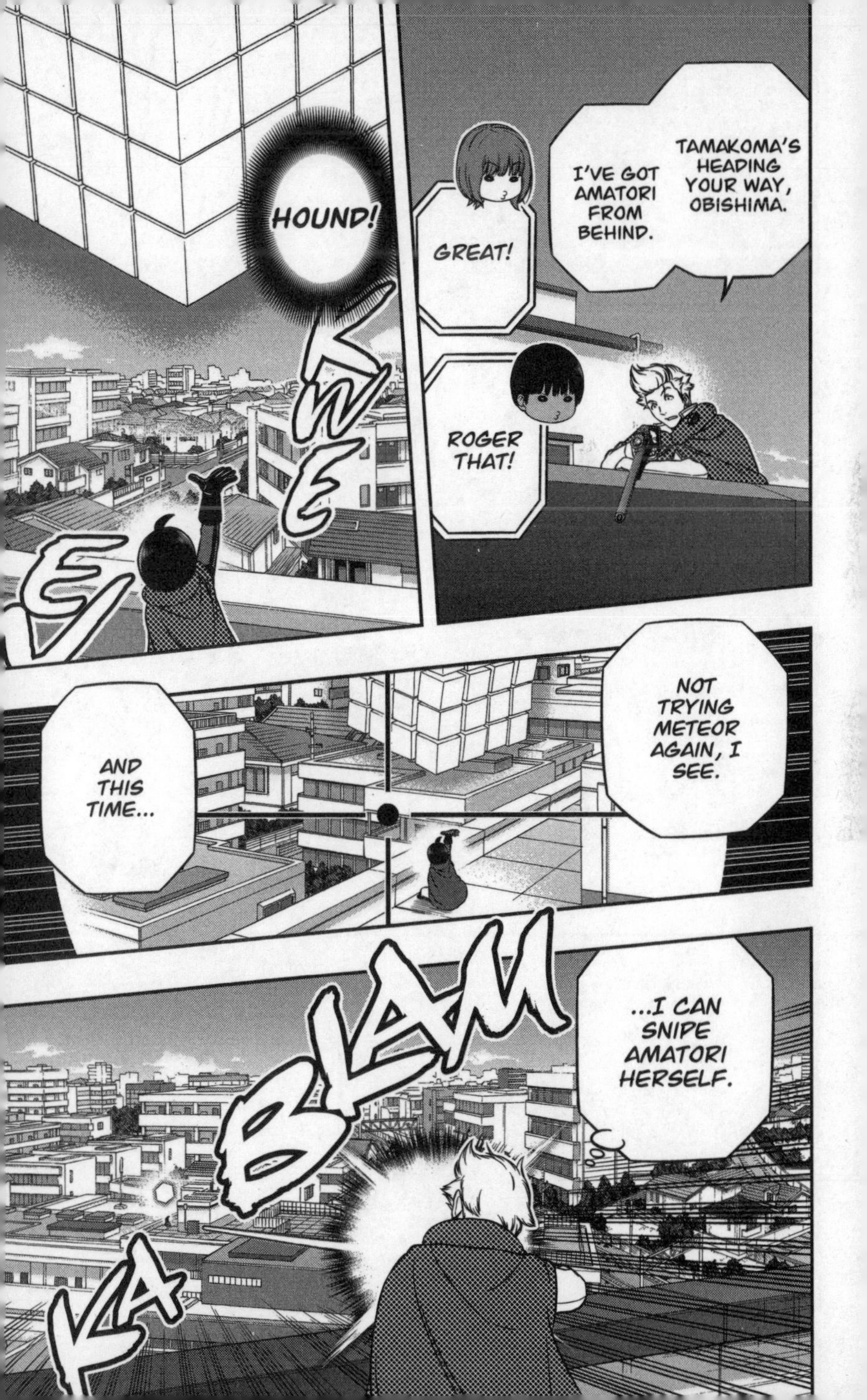
TAMAKOMA'S HEADING YOUR WAY, OBISHIMA.
I'VE GOT AMATORI FROM BEHIND.
GREAT!
ROGER THAT!
HOUND!
NOT TRYING METEOR AGAIN, I SEE.
AND THIS TIME...
...I CAN SNIPE AMATORI HERSELF.
KA
BLAM

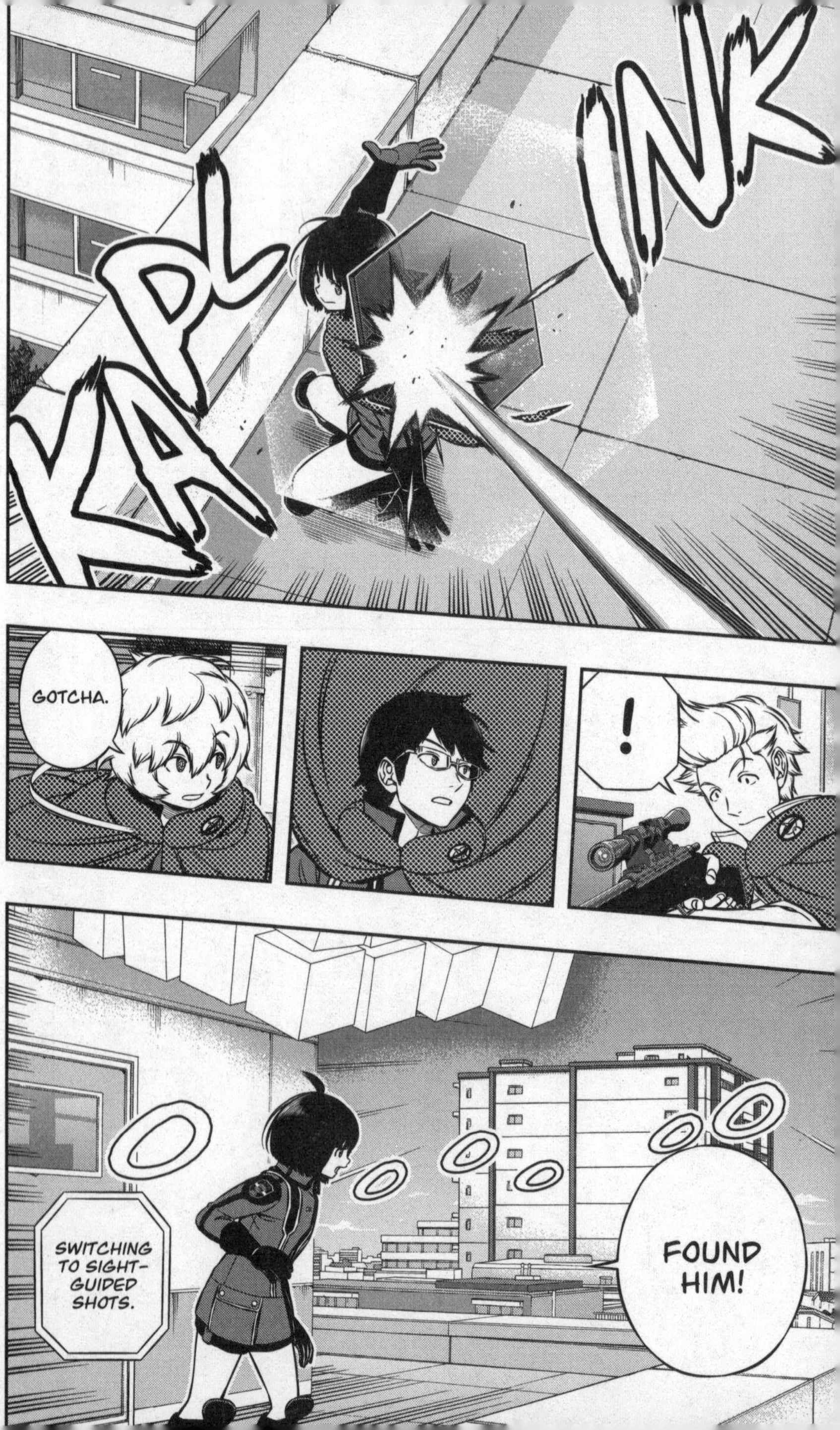
KAPLINK
!
GOTCHA.
FOUND HIM!
SWITCHING TO SIGHT-GUIDED SHOTS.

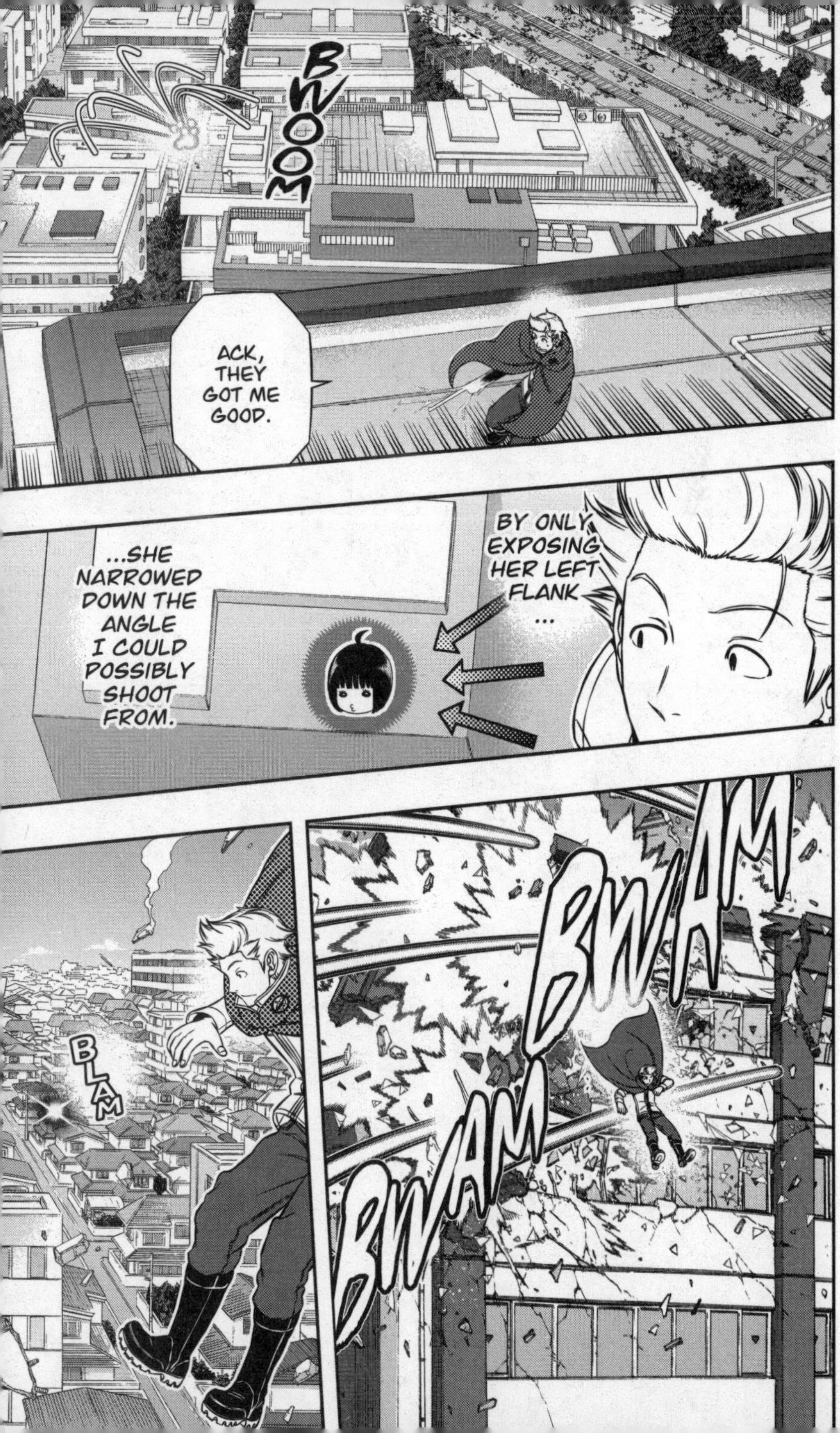
BWOOM
ACK, THEY GOT ME GOOD.
BY ONLY EXPOSING HER LEFT FLANK ...
...SHE NARROWED DOWN THE ANGLE I COULD POSSIBLY SHOOT FROM.
BWAM
BWAM
BLAM

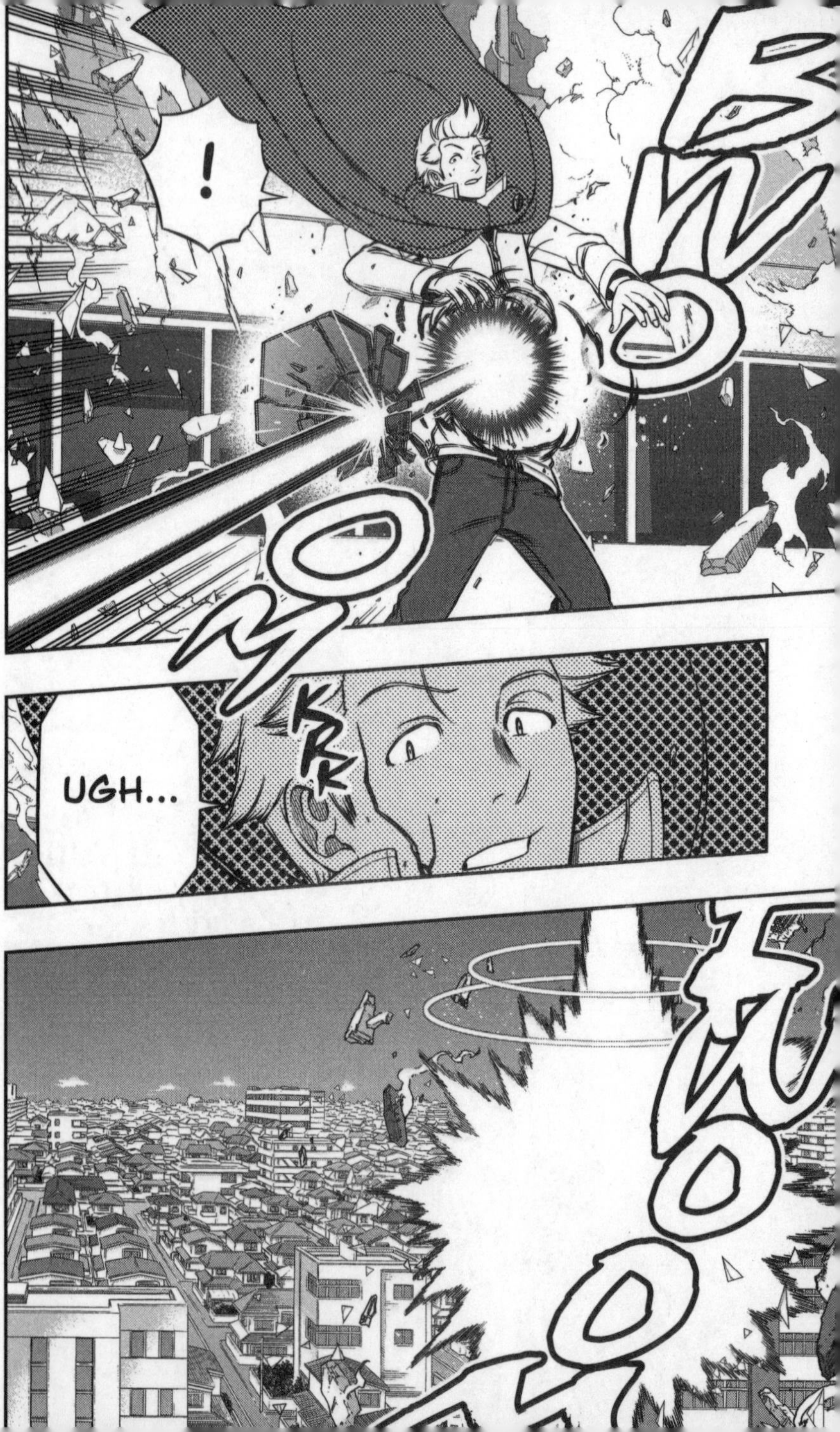
BWOOM
!
UGH...

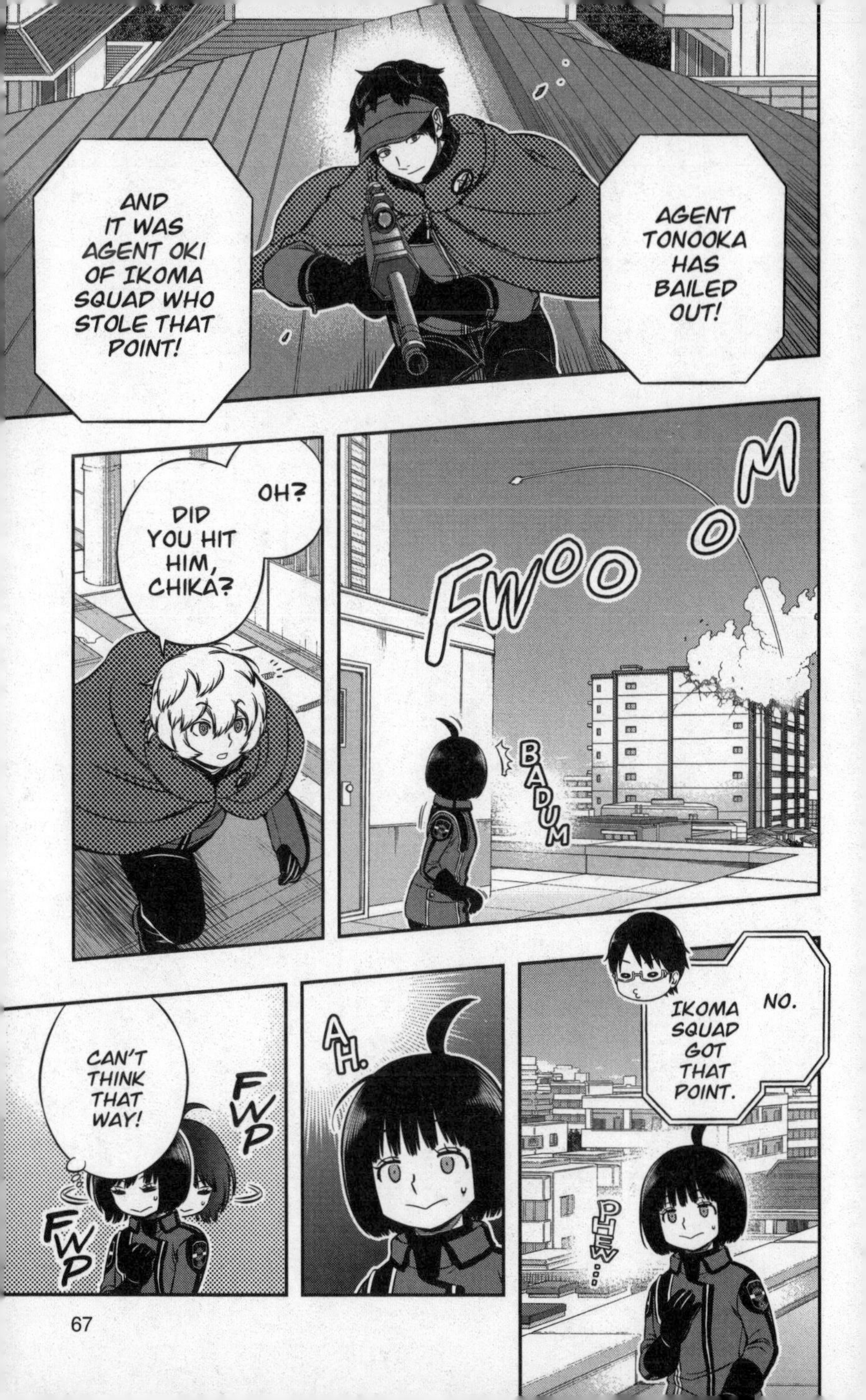
AGENT TONOOKA HAS BAILED OUT!
AND IT WAS AGENT OKI OF IKOMA SQUAD WHO STOLE THAT POINT!
FWOOOM
BADUM
OH?
DID YOU HIT HIM, CHIKA?
NO.
IKOMA SQUAD GOT THAT POINT.
PHEW...
AH.
CAN'T THINK THAT WAY!
FWP
FWP

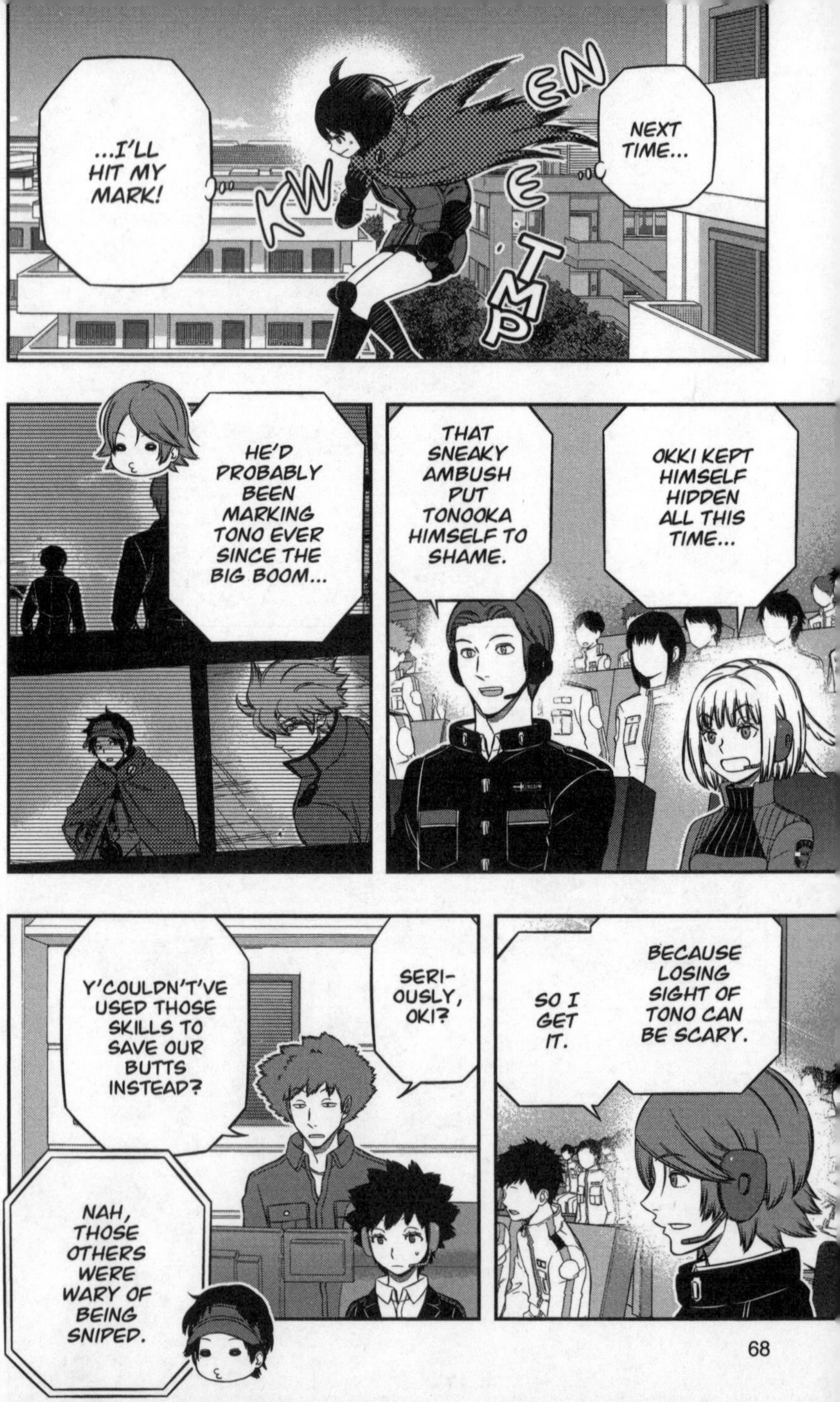
NEXT TIME...
...I'LL HIT MY MARK!
KWEEN
TMP
OKKI KEPT HIMSELF HIDDEN ALL THIS TIME...
THAT SNEAKY AMBUSH PUT TONOOKA HIMSELF TO SHAME.
HE'D PROBABLY BEEN MARKING TONO EVER SINCE THE BIG BOOM...
BECAUSE LOSING SIGHT OF TONO CAN BE SCARY.
SO I GET IT.
SERIOUSLY, OKI?
Y'COULDN'T'VE USED THOSE SKILLS TO SAVE OUR BUTTS INSTEAD?
NAH, THOSE OTHERS WERE WARY OF BEING SNIPED.

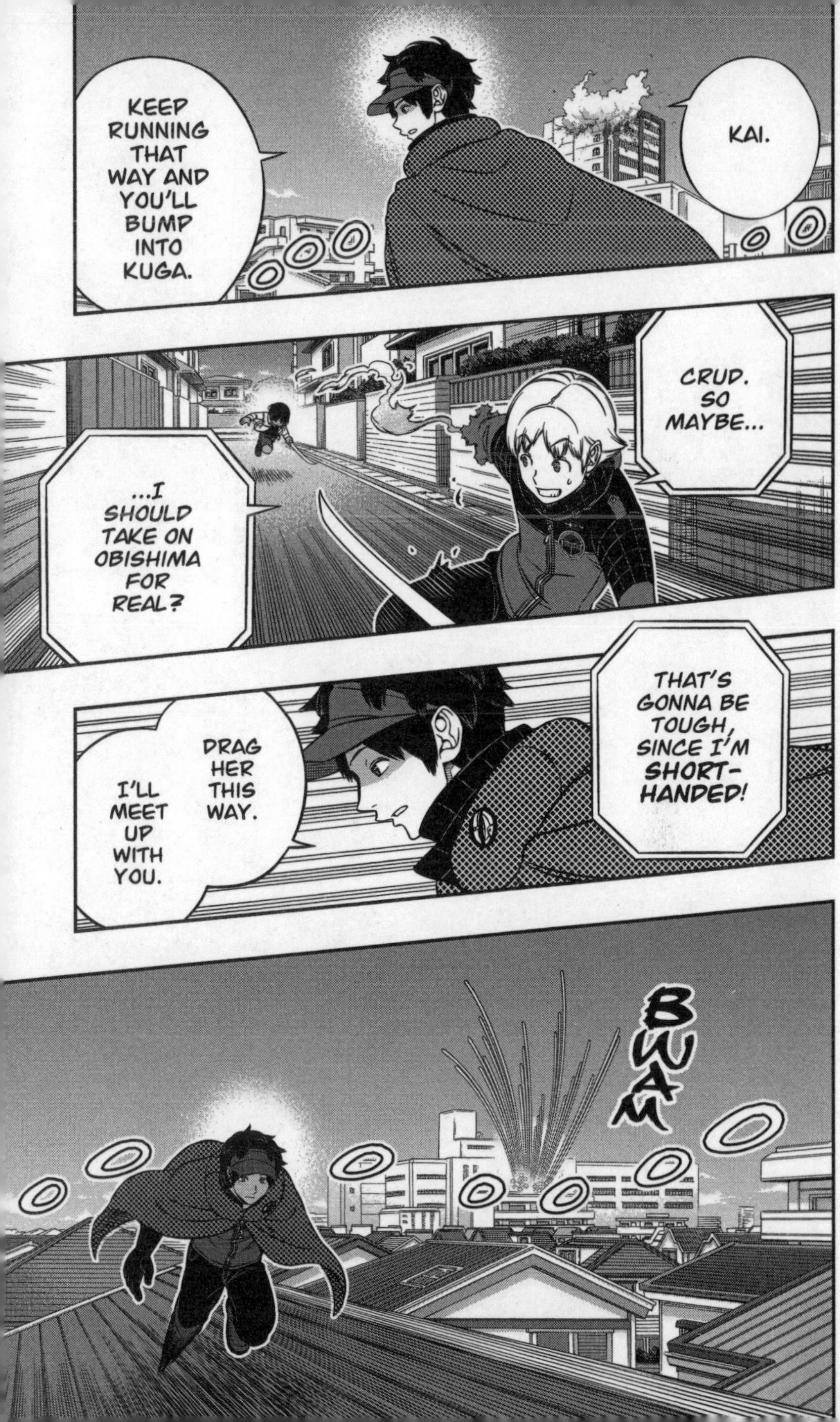
KAI.
KEEP RUNNING THAT WAY AND YOU'LL BUMP INTO KUGA.
CRUD. SO MAYBE...
...I SHOULD TAKE ON OBISHIMA FOR REAL?
THAT'S GONNA BE TOUGH, SINCE I'M **SHORT-HANDED!**
DRAG HER THIS WAY.
I'LL MEET UP WITH YOU.
BWAM

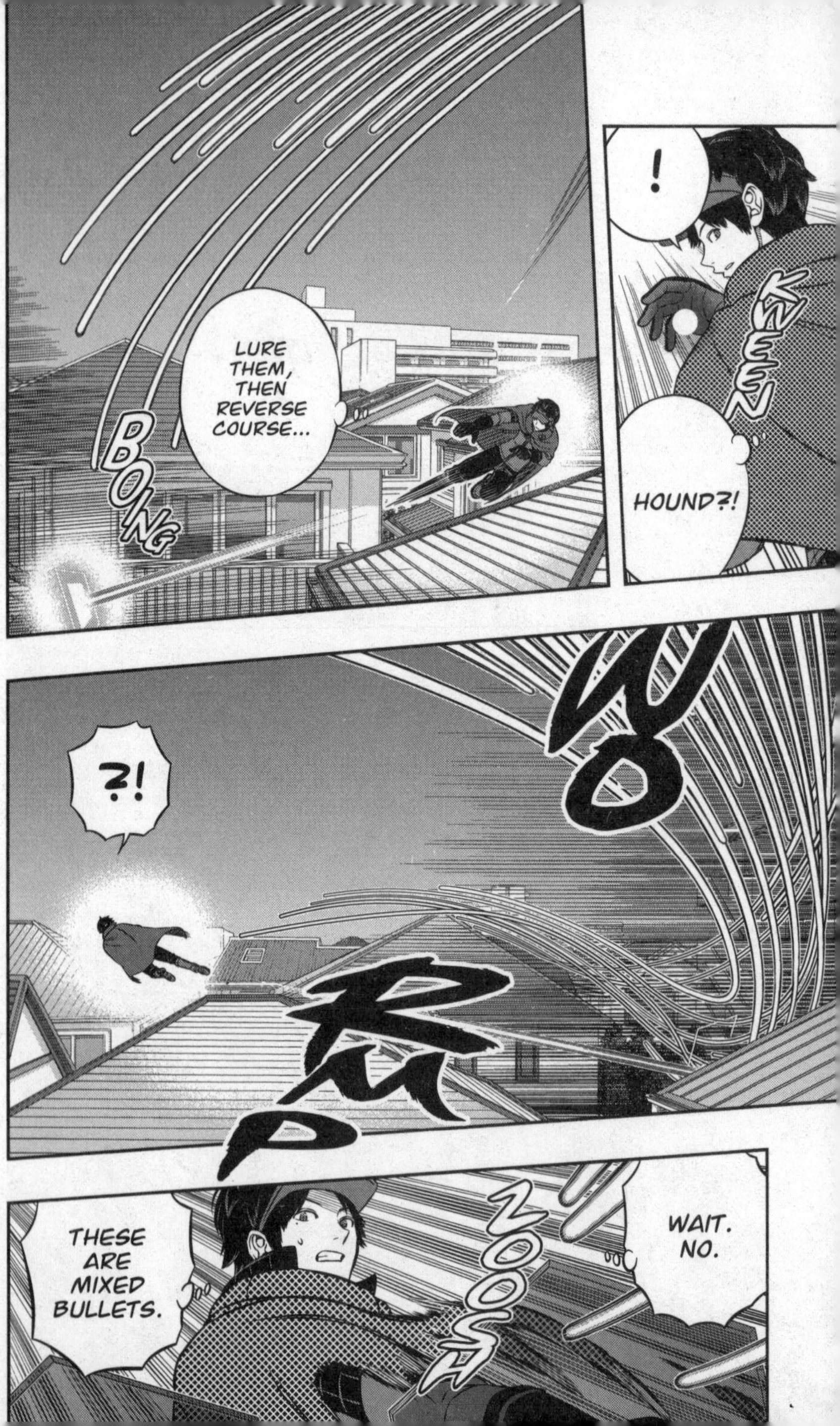
!
KWEEN
HOUND?!
LURE THEM, THEN REVERSE COURSE...
BOING
?!
WAIT. NO.
ZOOOSH
THESE ARE MIXED BULLETS.

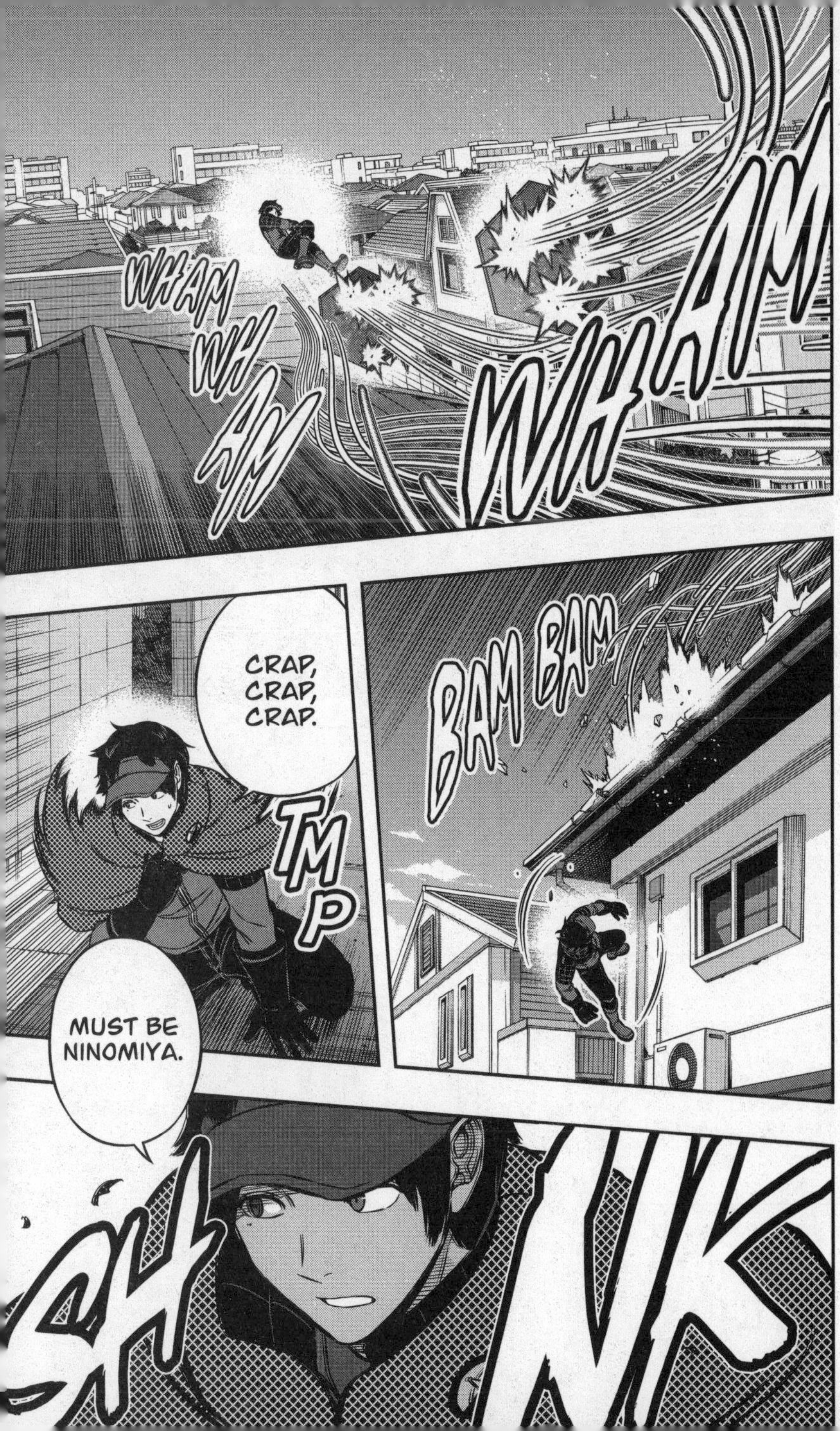
WHAM
WHAM
WHAM
BAM BAM
CRAP, CRAP, CRAP.
TMP
MUST BE NINOMIYA.

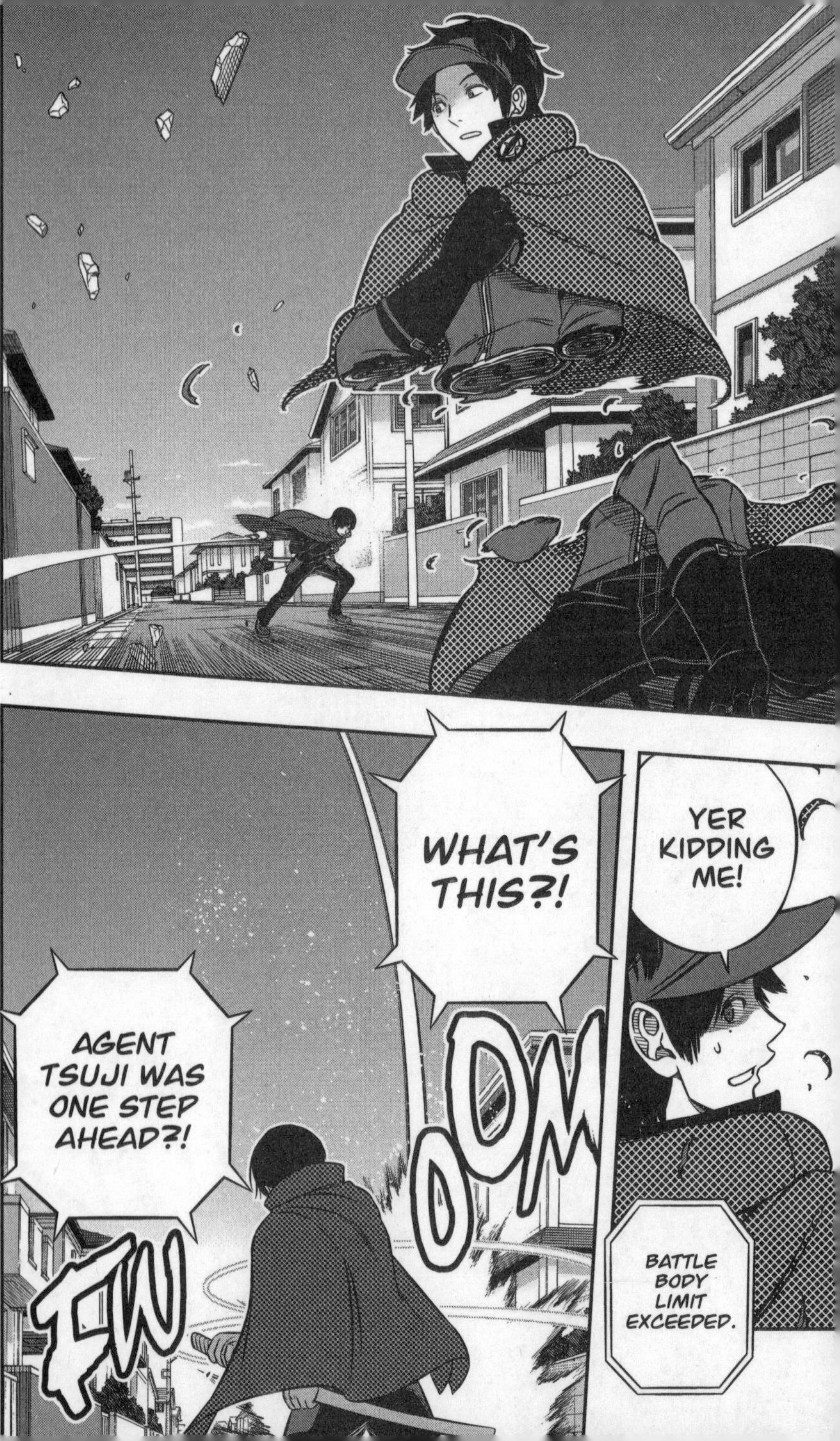
YER KIDDING ME!
WHAT'S THIS?!
DOOM
AGENT TSUJI WAS ONE STEP AHEAD?!
BATTLE BODY LIMIT EXCEEDED.
FW

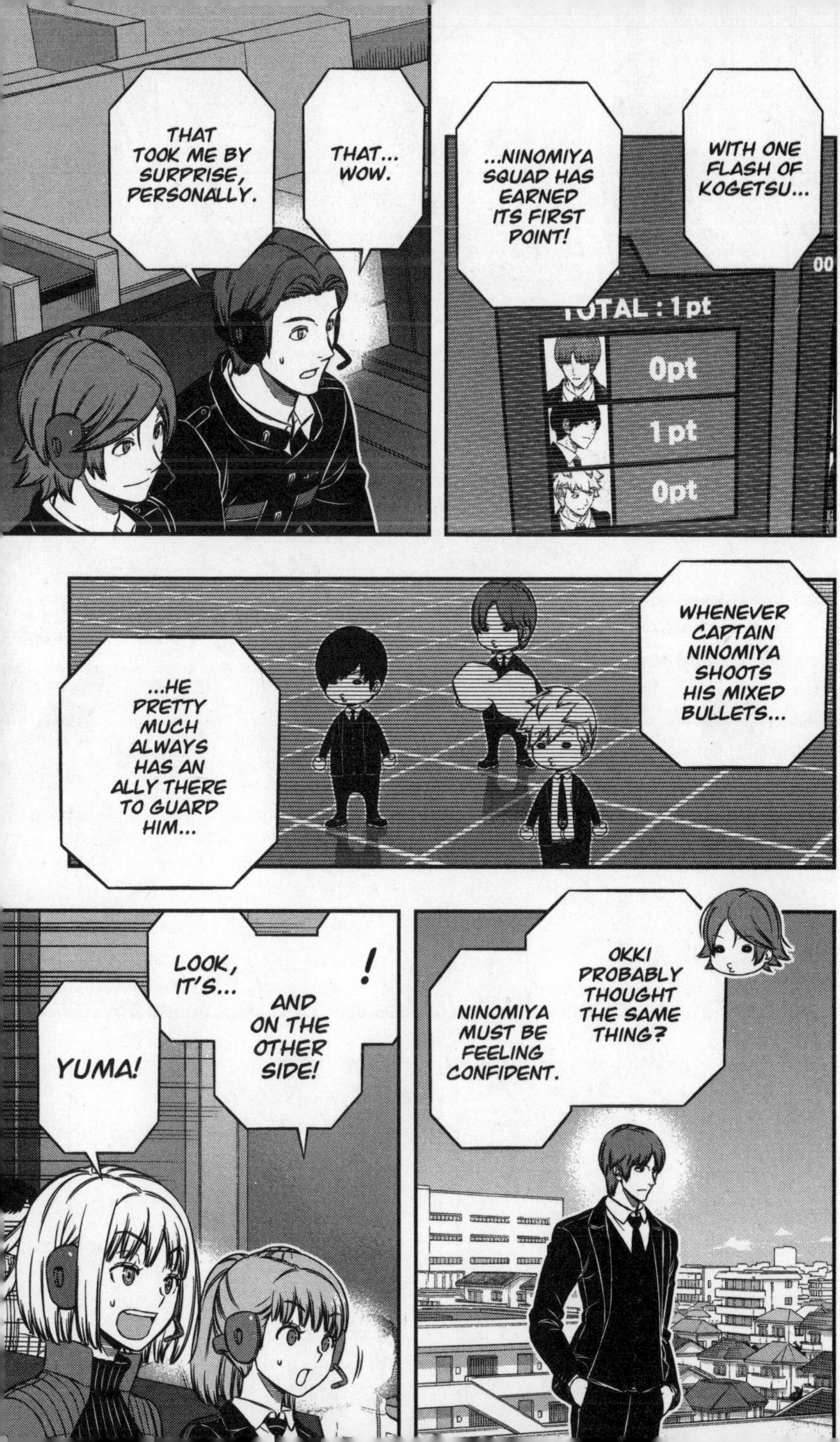
WITH ONE FLASH OF KOGETSU...
...NINOMIYA SQUAD HAS EARNED ITS FIRST POINT!
TOTAL : 1pt
0pt
1pt
0pt
THAT... WOW.
THAT TOOK ME BY SURPRISE, PERSONALLY.
WHENEVER CAPTAIN NINOMIYA SHOOTS HIS MIXED BULLETS...
...HE PRETTY MUCH ALWAYS HAS AN ALLY THERE TO GUARD HIM...
OKKI PROBABLY THOUGHT THE SAME THING?
NINOMIYA MUST BE FEELING CONFIDENT.
!
AND ON THE OTHER SIDE!
LOOK, IT'S...
YUMA!

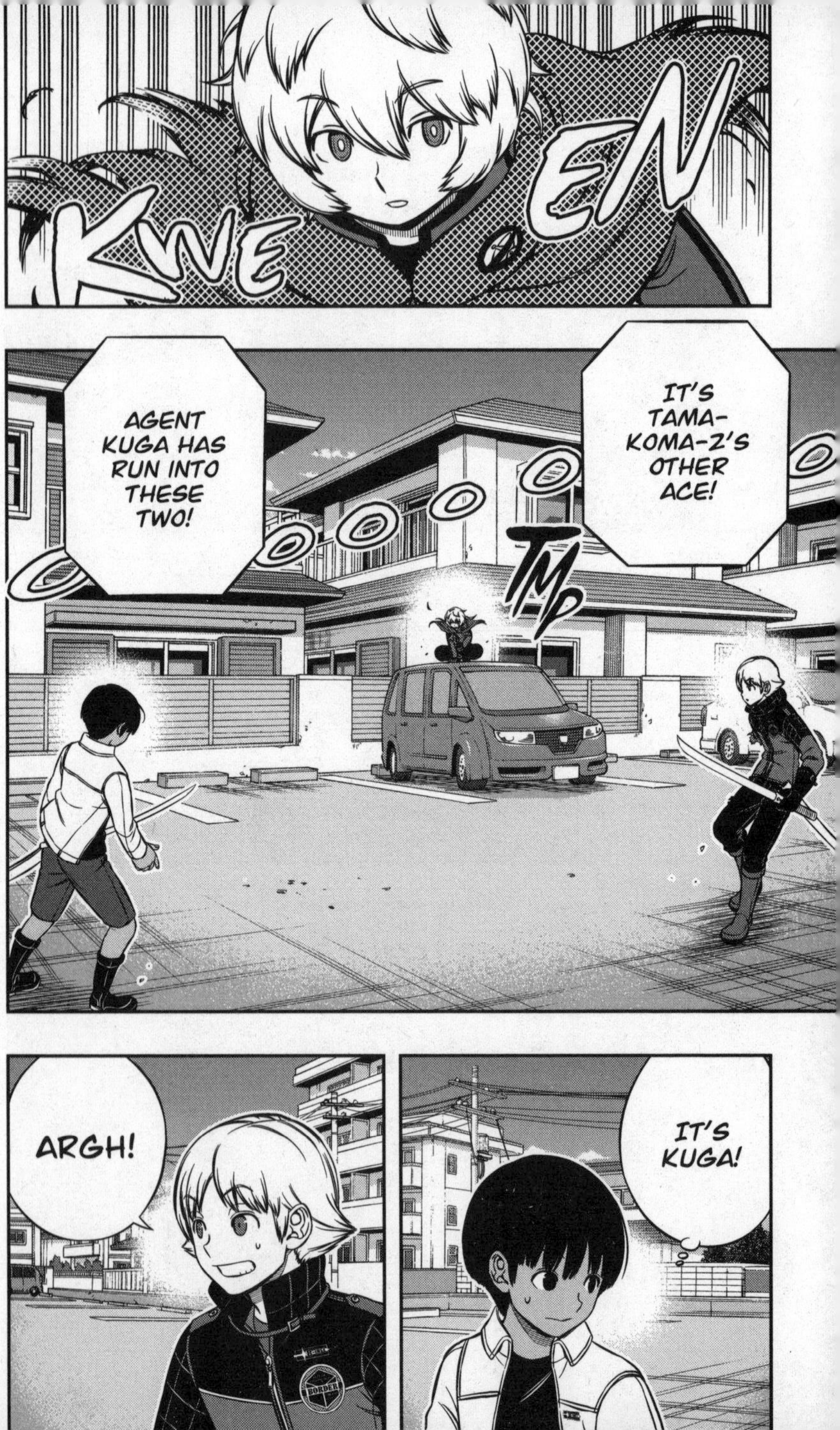
KWEEN
IT'S TAMA-KOMA-2'S OTHER ACE!
AGENT KUGA HAS RUN INTO THESE TWO!
TMP
IT'S KUGA!
ARGH!

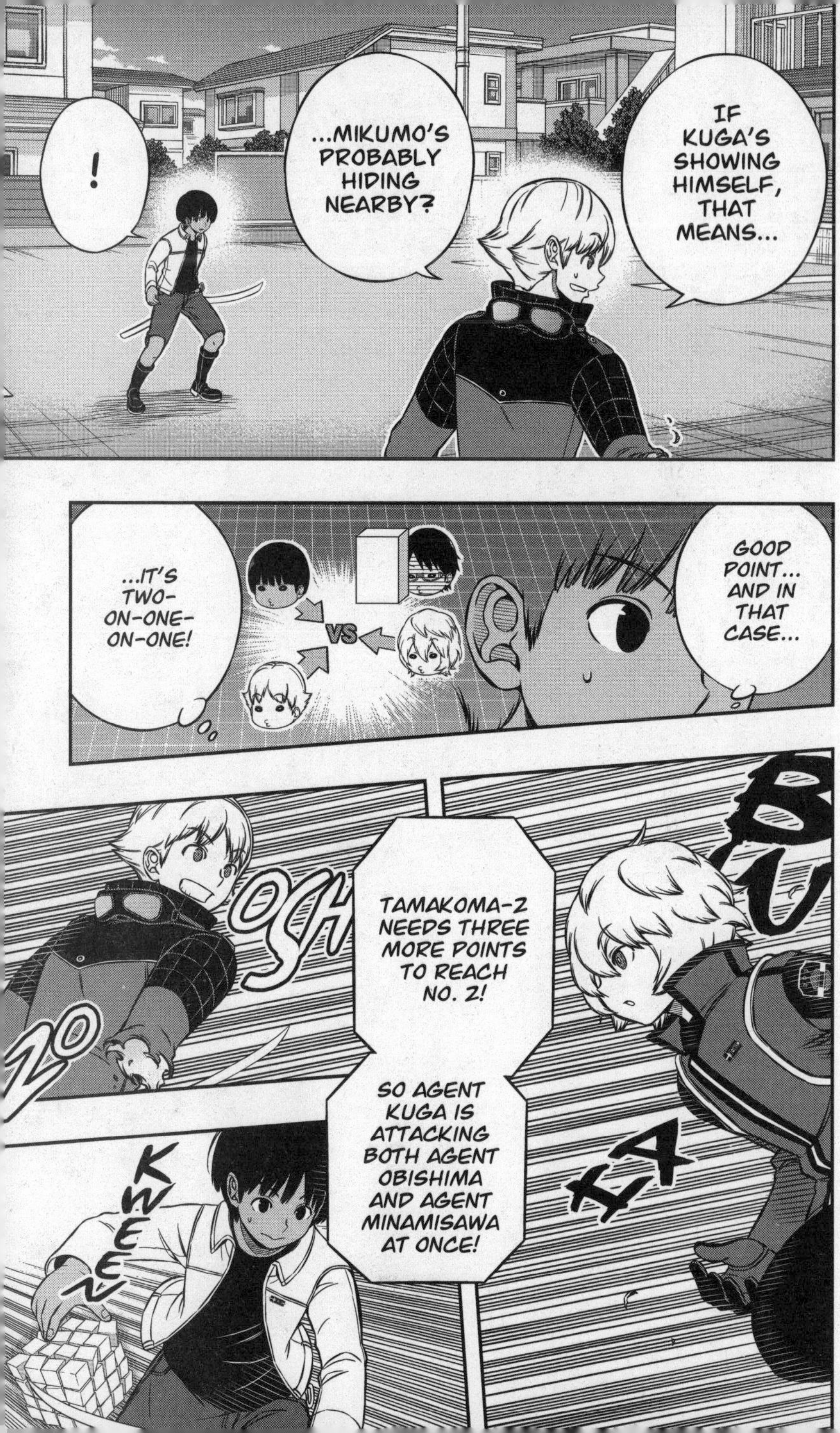
IF KUGA'S SHOWING HIMSELF, THAT MEANS...
...MIKUMO'S PROBABLY HIDING NEARBY?
!
GOOD POINT... AND IN THAT CASE...
VS
...IT'S TWO-ON-ONE-ON-ONE!
TAMAKOMA-2 NEEDS THREE MORE POINTS TO REACH NO. 2!
SO AGENT KUGA IS ATTACKING BOTH AGENT OBISHIMA AND AGENT MINAMISAWA AT ONCE!
KWEEN

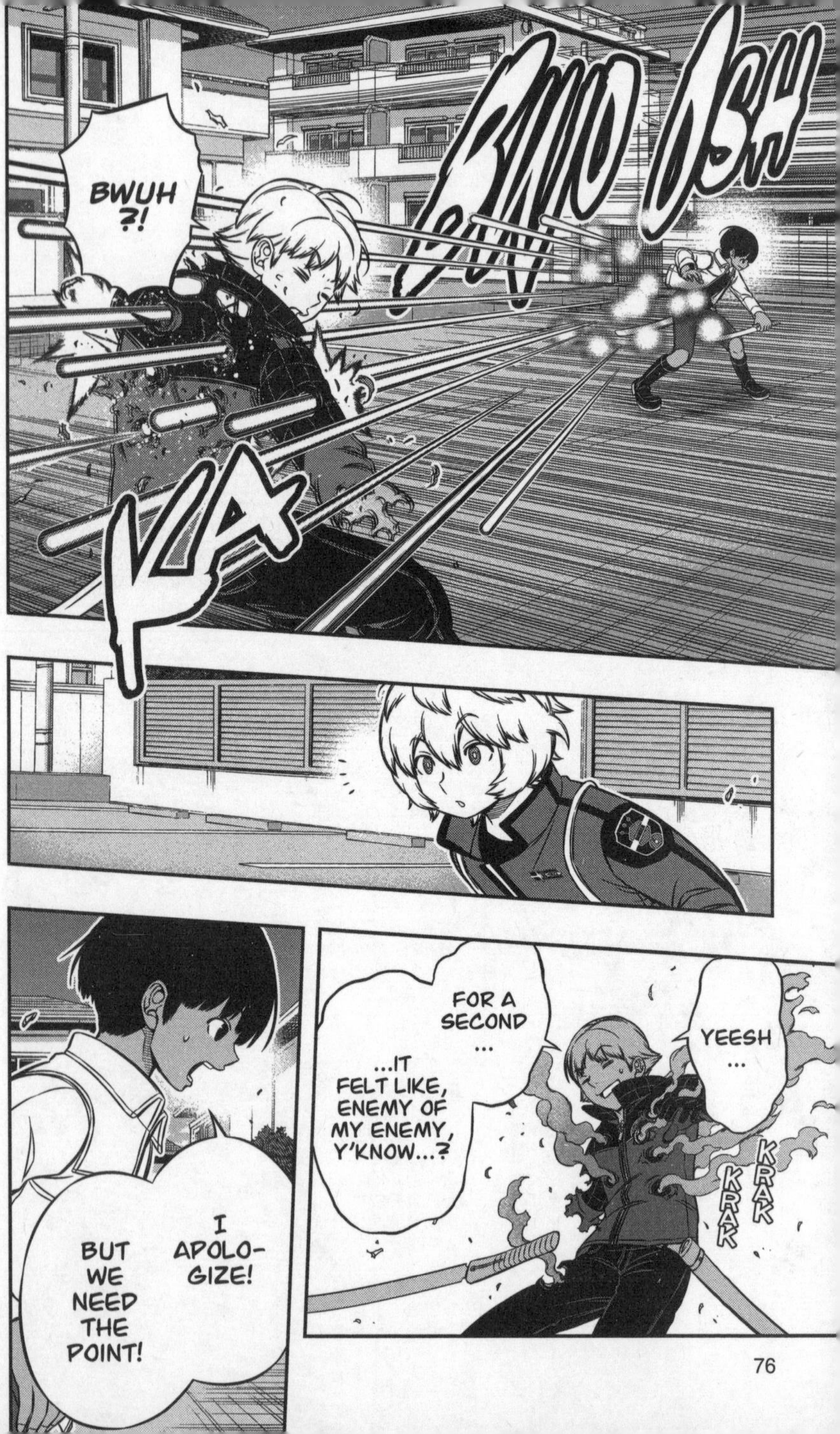
BWUH ?!
YEESH ...
FOR A SECOND ...
...IT FELT LIKE, ENEMY OF MY ENEMY, Y'KNOW...?
KRAK KRAK
I APOLO-GIZE!
BUT WE NEED THE POINT!

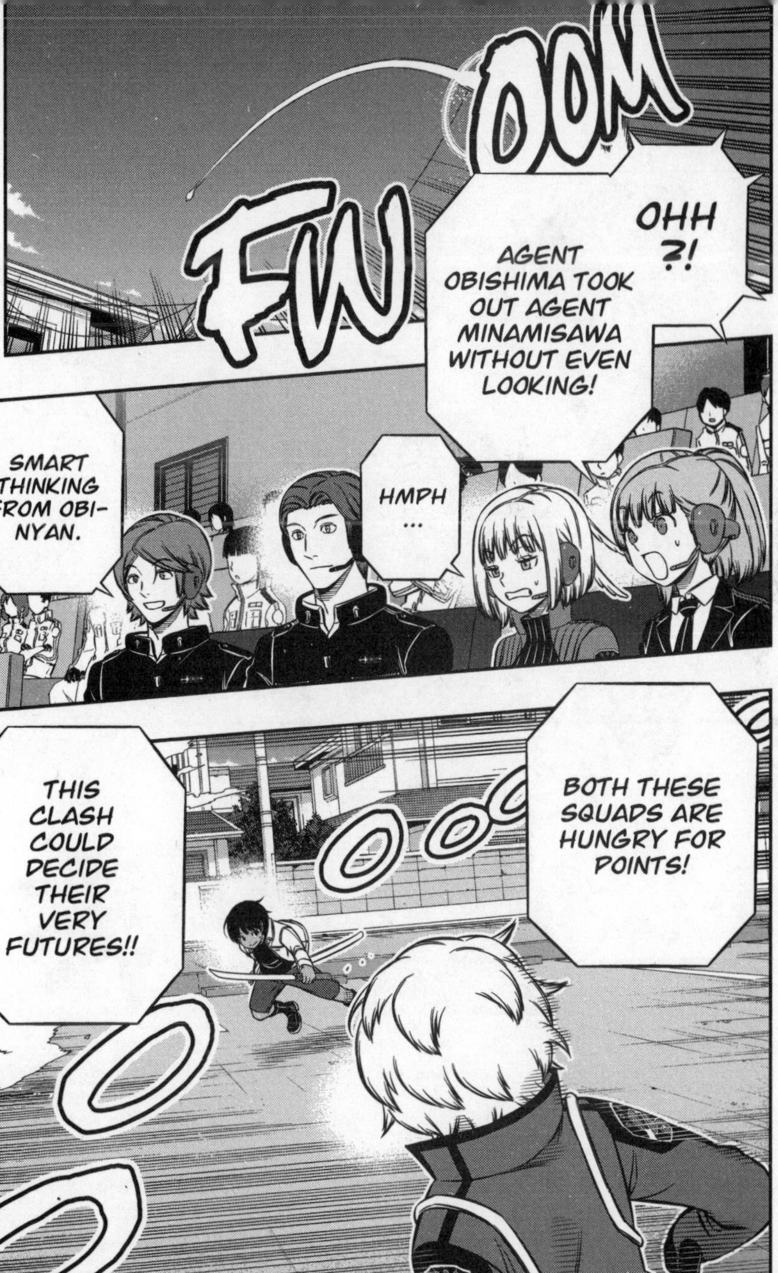
FWOOM
OHH ?!
AGENT OBISHIMA TOOK OUT AGENT MINAMISAWA WITHOUT EVEN LOOKING!
HMPH ...
SMART THINKING FROM OBI-NYAN.
BOTH THESE SQUADS ARE HUNGRY FOR POINTS!
THIS CLASH COULD DECIDE THEIR VERY FUTURES!!

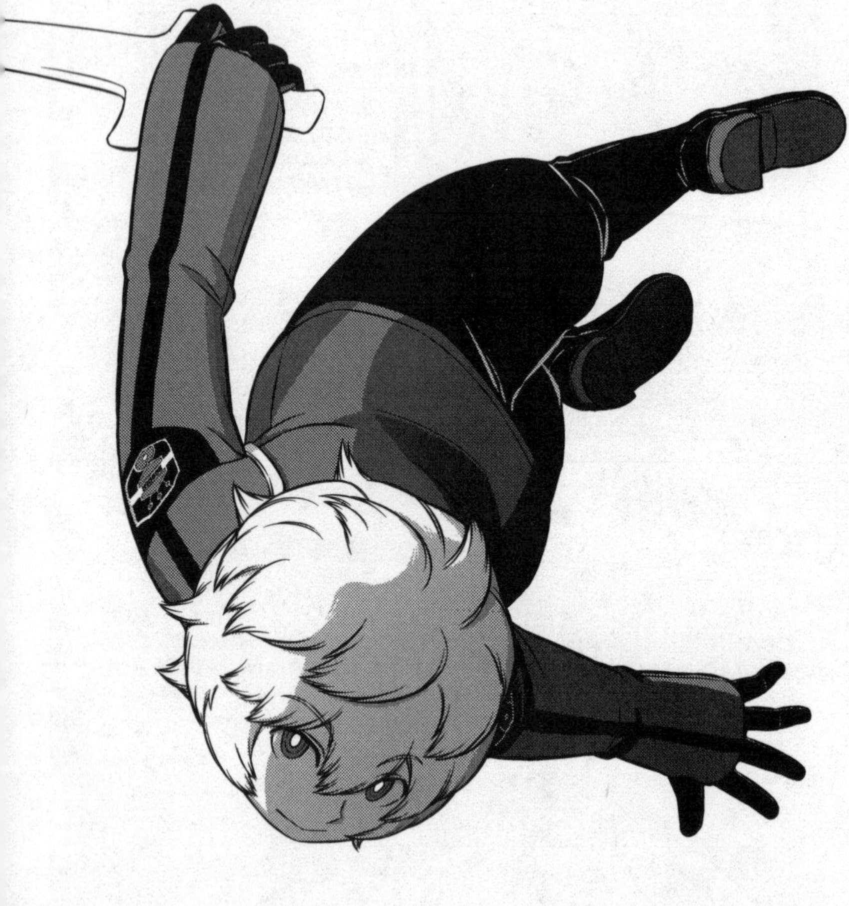

■ Cover Contribution from *Jump SQ*, January 2020 Issue (originally in color)

I drew this in accordance with the request from the *SQ* cover designer. There were two design options: either make a character falling down from above, or climbing up from below. I chose the former. When I stop to think about it, I realize that Yuma's face was probably cut off when the magazine was placed on shelves. But his face would show up well enough when the magazines were arranged in stacks at the convenience stores. Yuma has a big head-to-body ratio, so it's easy to fit his whole tiny body in a shot like this.

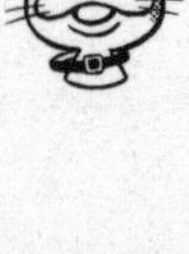

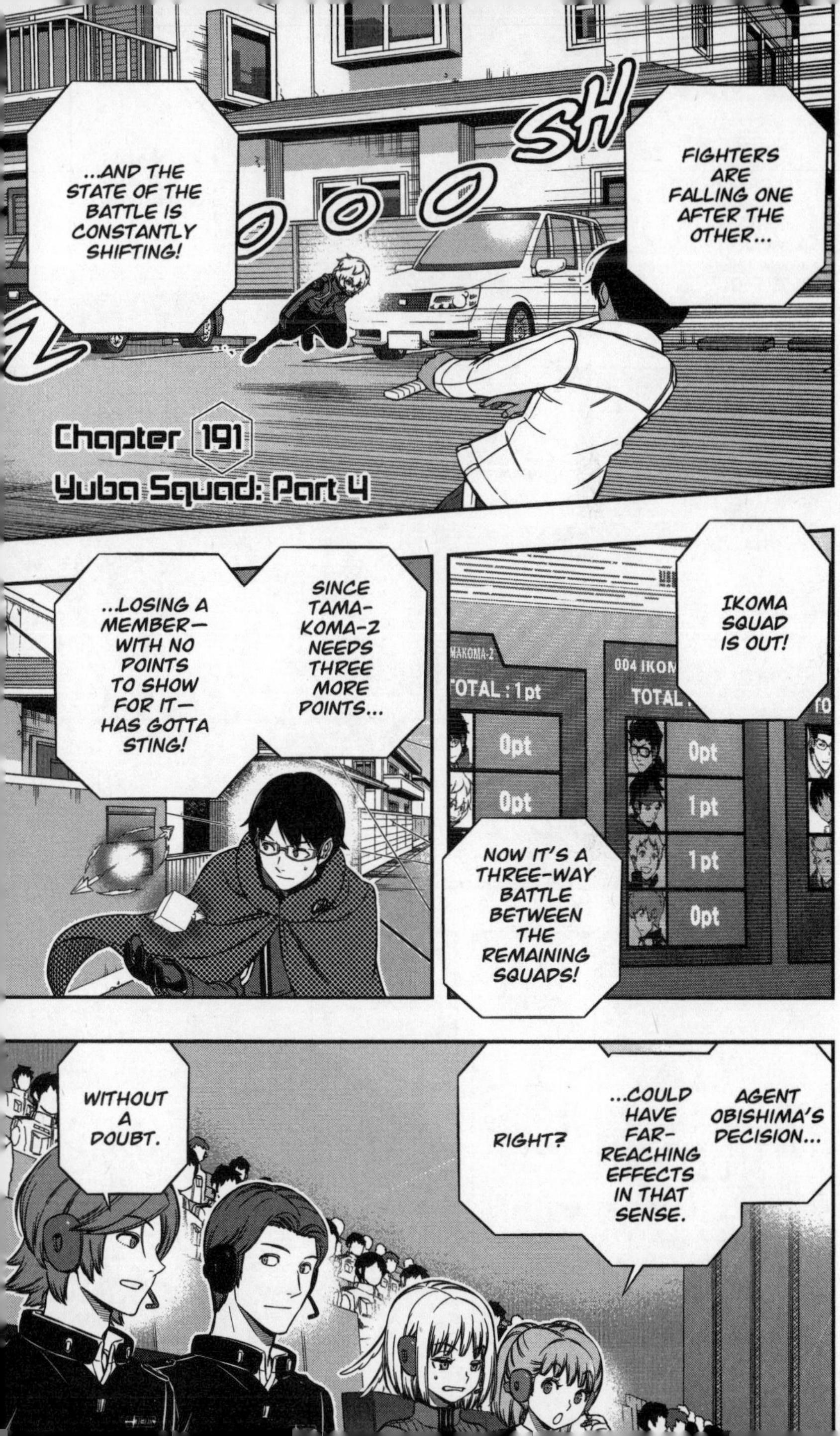
FIGHTERS ARE FALLING ONE AFTER THE OTHER...
ZOOOOSH
...AND THE STATE OF THE BATTLE IS CONSTANTLY SHIFTING!
Chapter 191
Yuba Squad: Part 4
IKOMA SQUAD IS OUT!
MAKOMA-2
TOTAL : 1pt
0pt
0pt
004 IKOM
TOTAL
0pt
1pt
1pt
0pt
NOW IT'S A THREE-WAY BATTLE BETWEEN THE REMAINING SQUADS!
SINCE TAMA-KOMA-2 NEEDS THREE MORE POINTS...
...LOSING A MEMBER—WITH NO POINTS TO SHOW FOR IT—HAS GOTTA STING!
AGENT OBISHIMA'S DECISION...
...COULD HAVE FAR-REACHING EFFECTS IN THAT SENSE.
RIGHT?
WITHOUT A DOUBT.

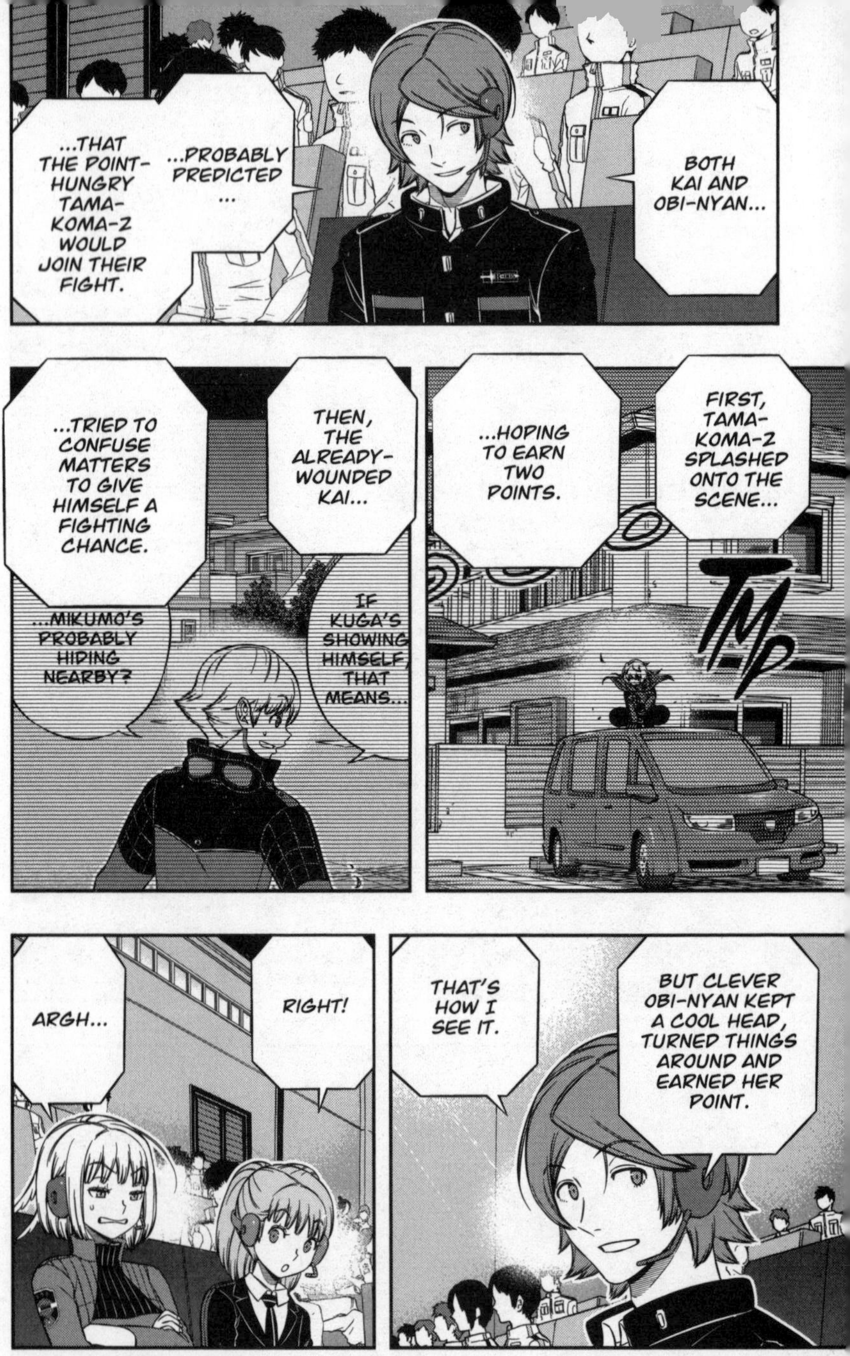
BOTH KAI AND OBI-NYAN...
...PROBABLY PREDICTED ...
...THAT THE POINT-HUNGRY TAMA-KOMA-2 WOULD JOIN THEIR FIGHT.
FIRST, TAMA-KOMA-2 SPLASHED ONTO THE SCENE...
...HOPING TO EARN TWO POINTS.
TMP
THEN, THE ALREADY-WOUNDED KAI...
...TRIED TO CONFUSE MATTERS TO GIVE HIMSELF A FIGHTING CHANCE.
IF KUGA'S SHOWING HIMSELF, THAT MEANS...
...MIKUMO'S PROBABLY HIDING NEARBY?
BUT CLEVER OBI-NYAN KEPT A COOL HEAD, TURNED THINGS AROUND AND EARNED HER POINT.
THAT'S HOW I SEE IT.
RIGHT!
ARGH...

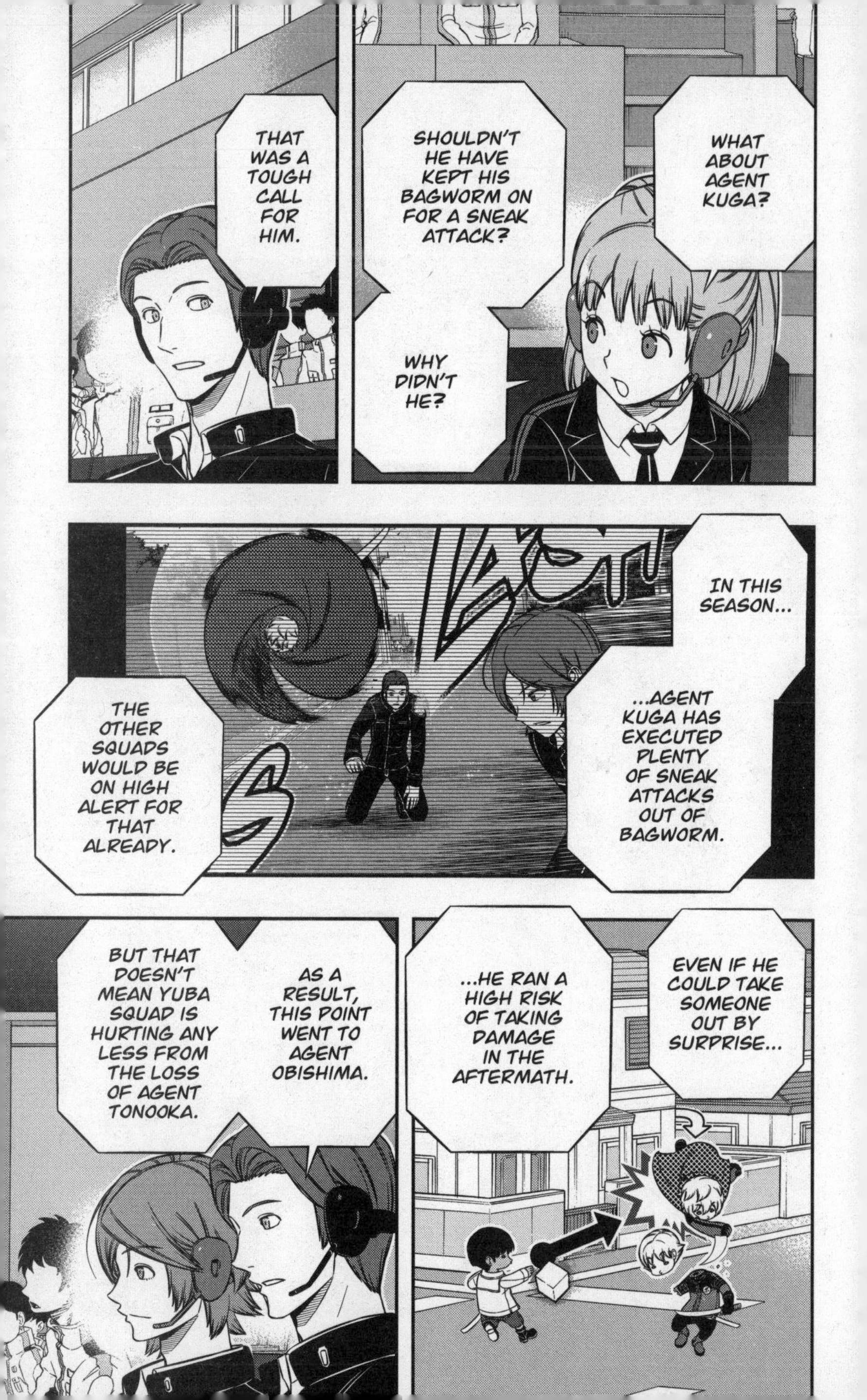
WHAT ABOUT AGENT KUGA?
SHOULDN'T HE HAVE KEPT HIS BAGWORM ON FOR A SNEAK ATTACK?
WHY DIDN'T HE?
THAT WAS A TOUGH CALL FOR HIM.
IN THIS SEASON...
...AGENT KUGA HAS EXECUTED PLENTY OF SNEAK ATTACKS OUT OF BAGWORM.
THE OTHER SQUADS WOULD BE ON HIGH ALERT FOR THAT ALREADY.
EVEN IF HE COULD TAKE SOMEONE OUT BY SURPRISE...
...HE RAN A HIGH RISK OF TAKING DAMAGE IN THE AFTERMATH.
AS A RESULT, THIS POINT WENT TO AGENT OBISHIMA.
BUT THAT DOESN'T MEAN YUBA SQUAD IS HURTING ANY LESS FROM THE LOSS OF AGENT TONOOKA.

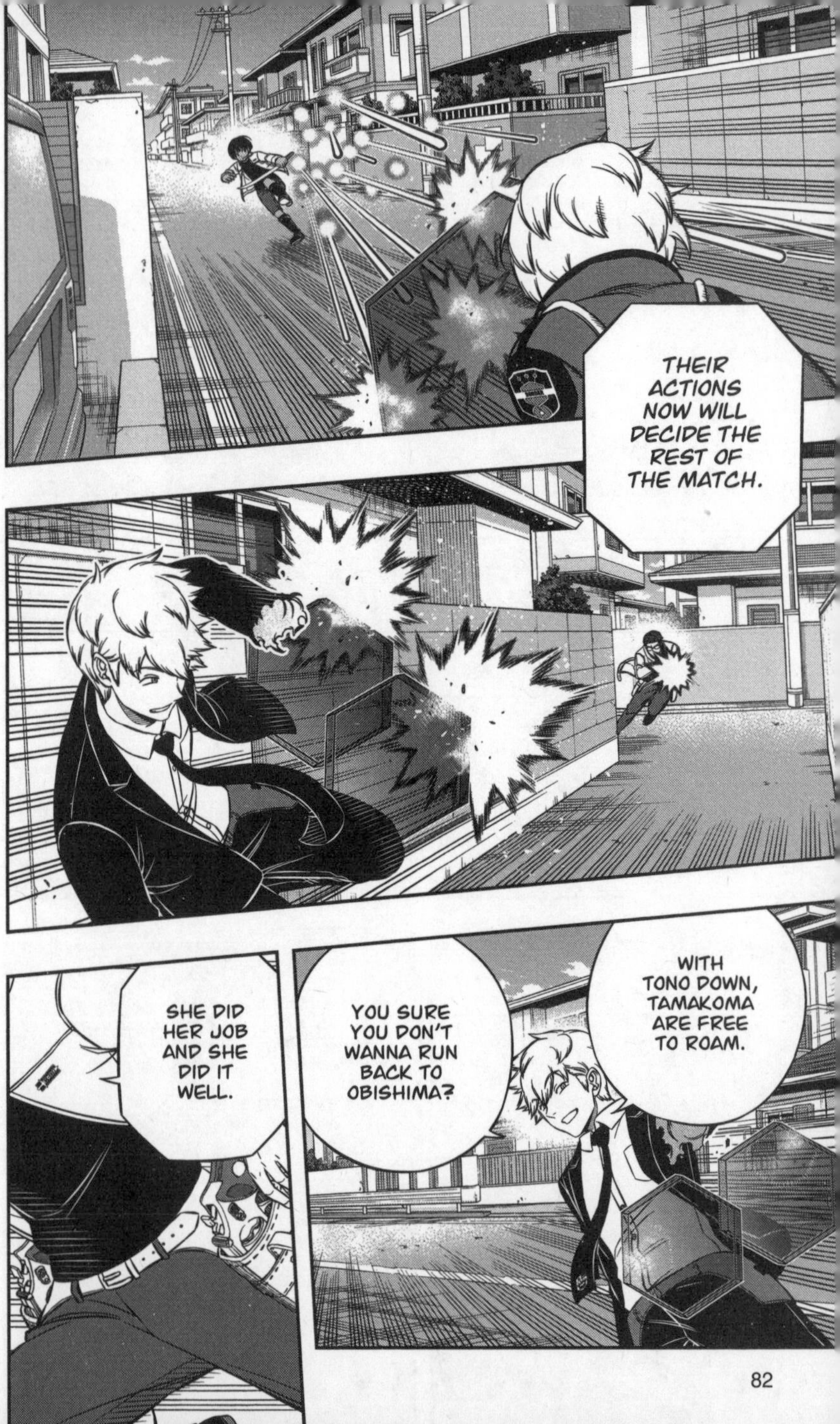
THEIR ACTIONS NOW WILL DECIDE THE REST OF THE MATCH.
WITH TONO DOWN, TAMAKOMA ARE FREE TO ROAM.
YOU SURE YOU DON'T WANNA RUN BACK TO OBISHIMA?
SHE DID HER JOB AND SHE DID IT WELL.

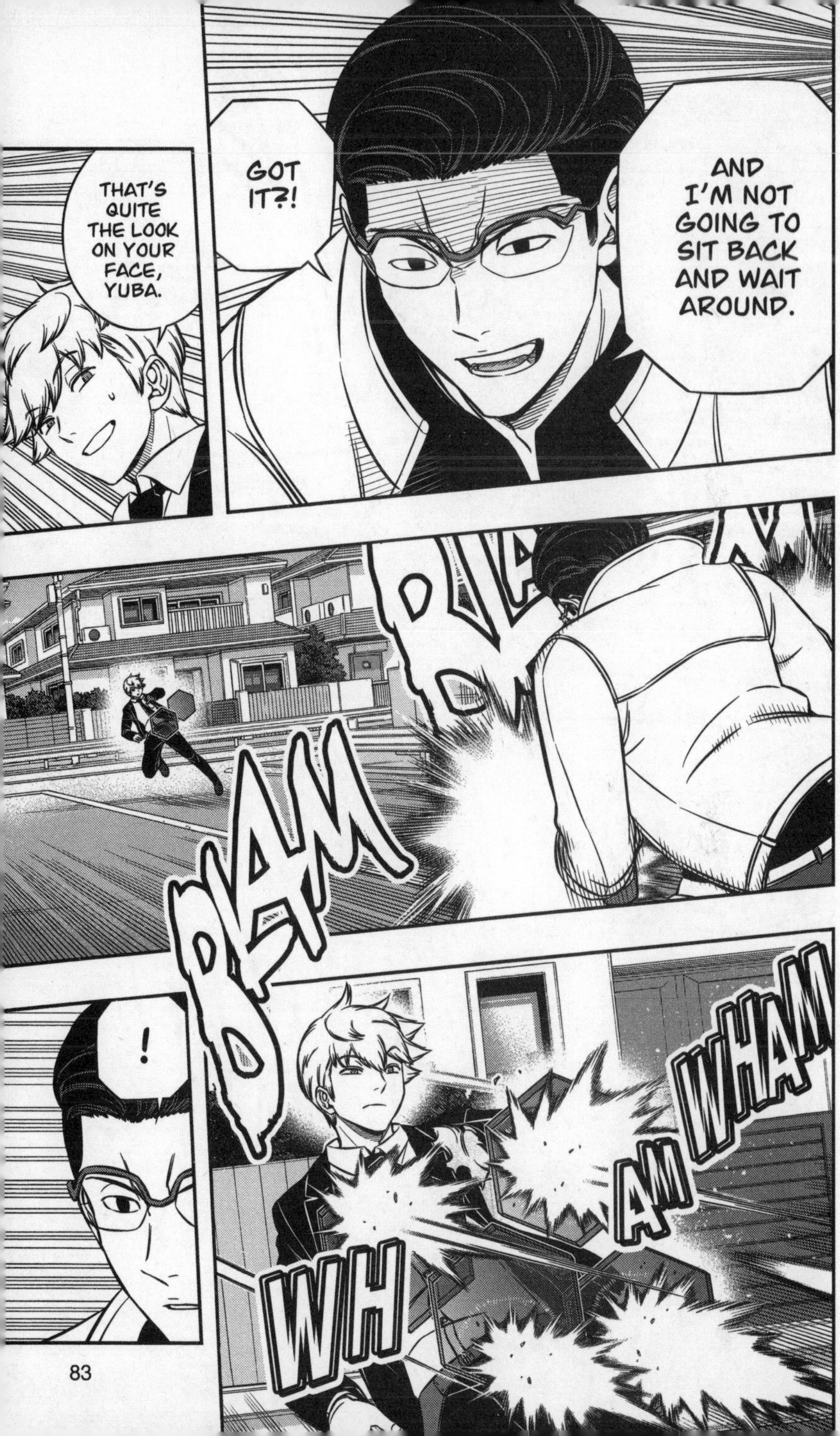
AND I'M NOT GOING TO SIT BACK AND WAIT AROUND.
GOT IT?!
THAT'S QUITE THE LOOK ON YOUR FACE, YUBA.
BLAM
BLAM
WHAM
WHAM
!

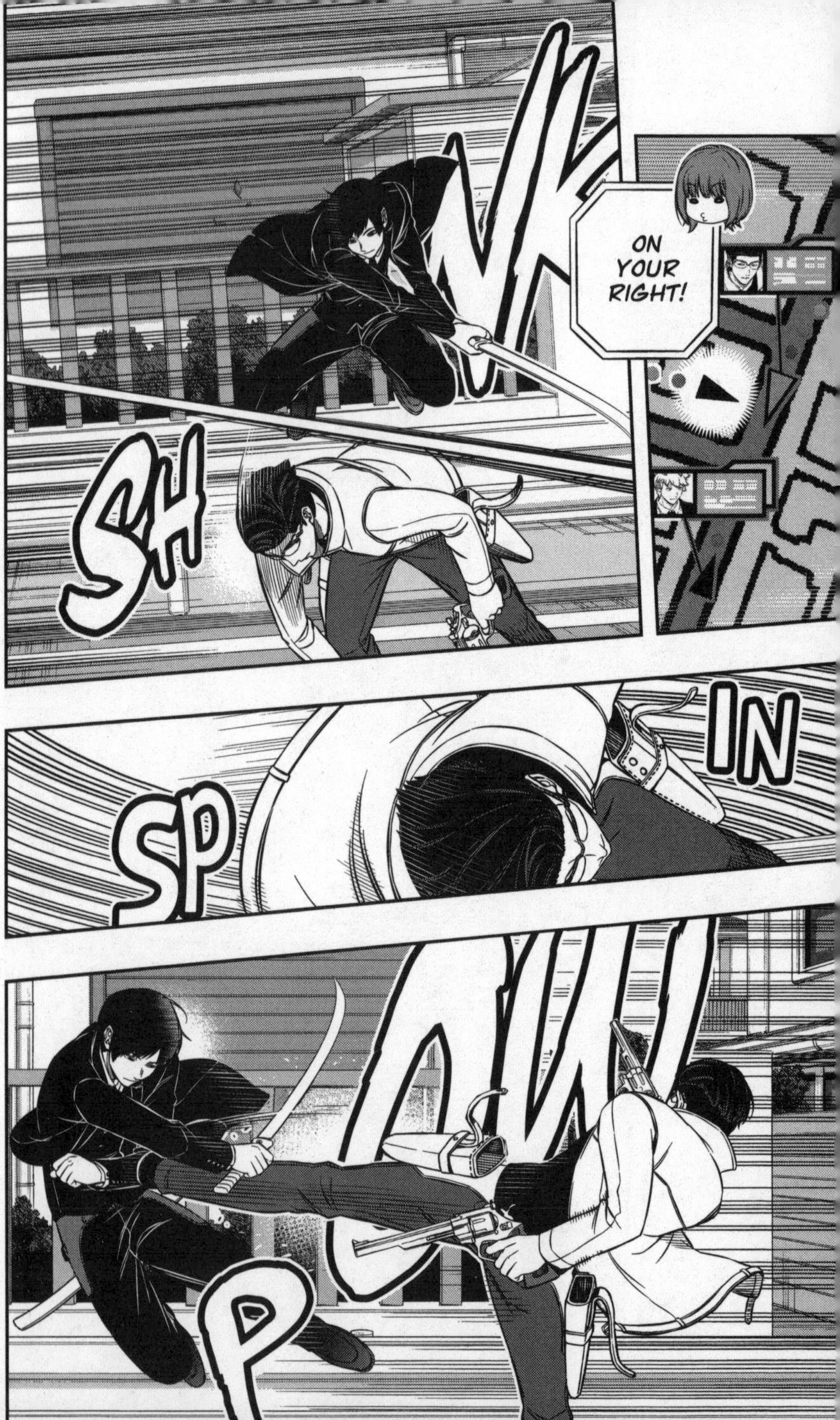
ON YOUR RIGHT!
SH
IN
SP
P

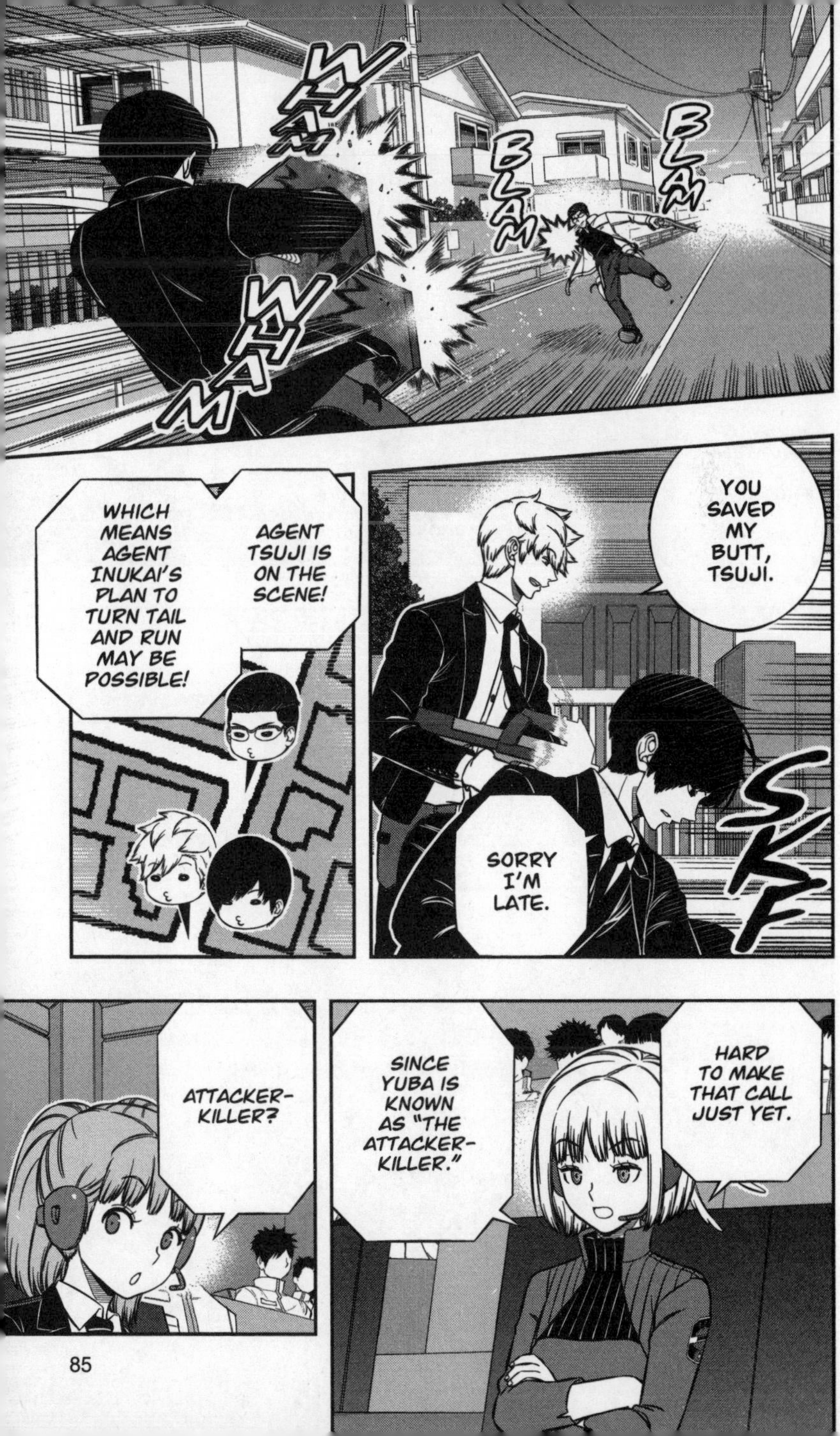
BLAM
BLAM
WHAM
WHAM
YOU SAVED MY BUTT, TSUJI.
SKF
SORRY I'M LATE.
AGENT TSUJI IS ON THE SCENE!
WHICH MEANS AGENT INUKAI'S PLAN TO TURN TAIL AND RUN MAY BE POSSIBLE!
HARD TO MAKE THAT CALL JUST YET.
SINCE YUBA IS KNOWN AS "THE ATTACKER-KILLER."
ATTACKER-KILLER?

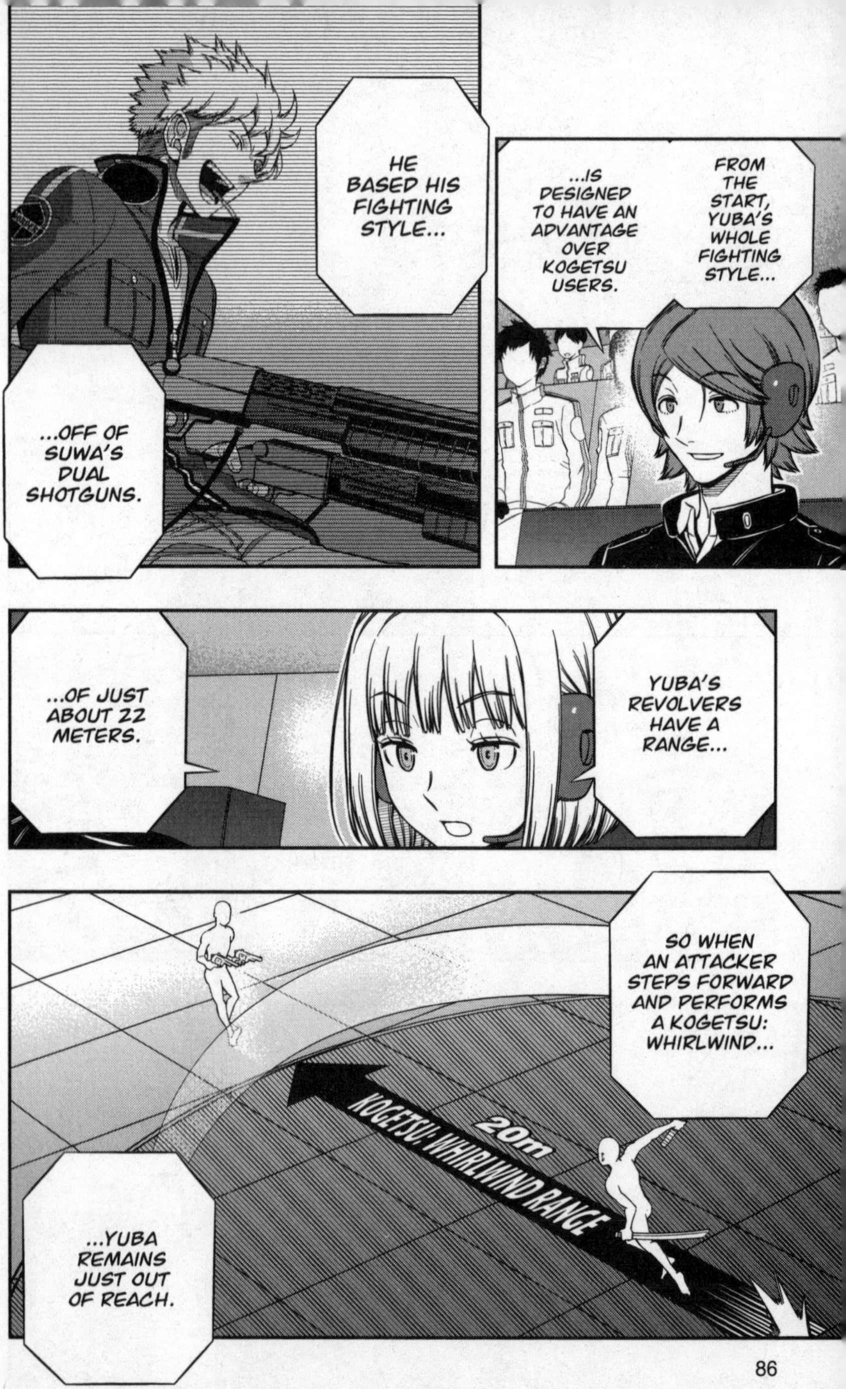
FROM THE START, YUBA'S WHOLE FIGHTING STYLE...
...IS DESIGNED TO HAVE AN ADVANTAGE OVER KOGETSU USERS.
HE BASED HIS FIGHTING STYLE...
...OFF OF SUWA'S DUAL SHOTGUNS.
YUBA'S REVOLVERS HAVE A RANGE...
...OF JUST ABOUT 22 METERS.
SO WHEN AN ATTACKER STEPS FORWARD AND PERFORMS A KOGETSU: WHIRLWIND...
20m
KOGETSU: WHIRLWIND RANGE
...YUBA REMAINS JUST OUT OF REACH.

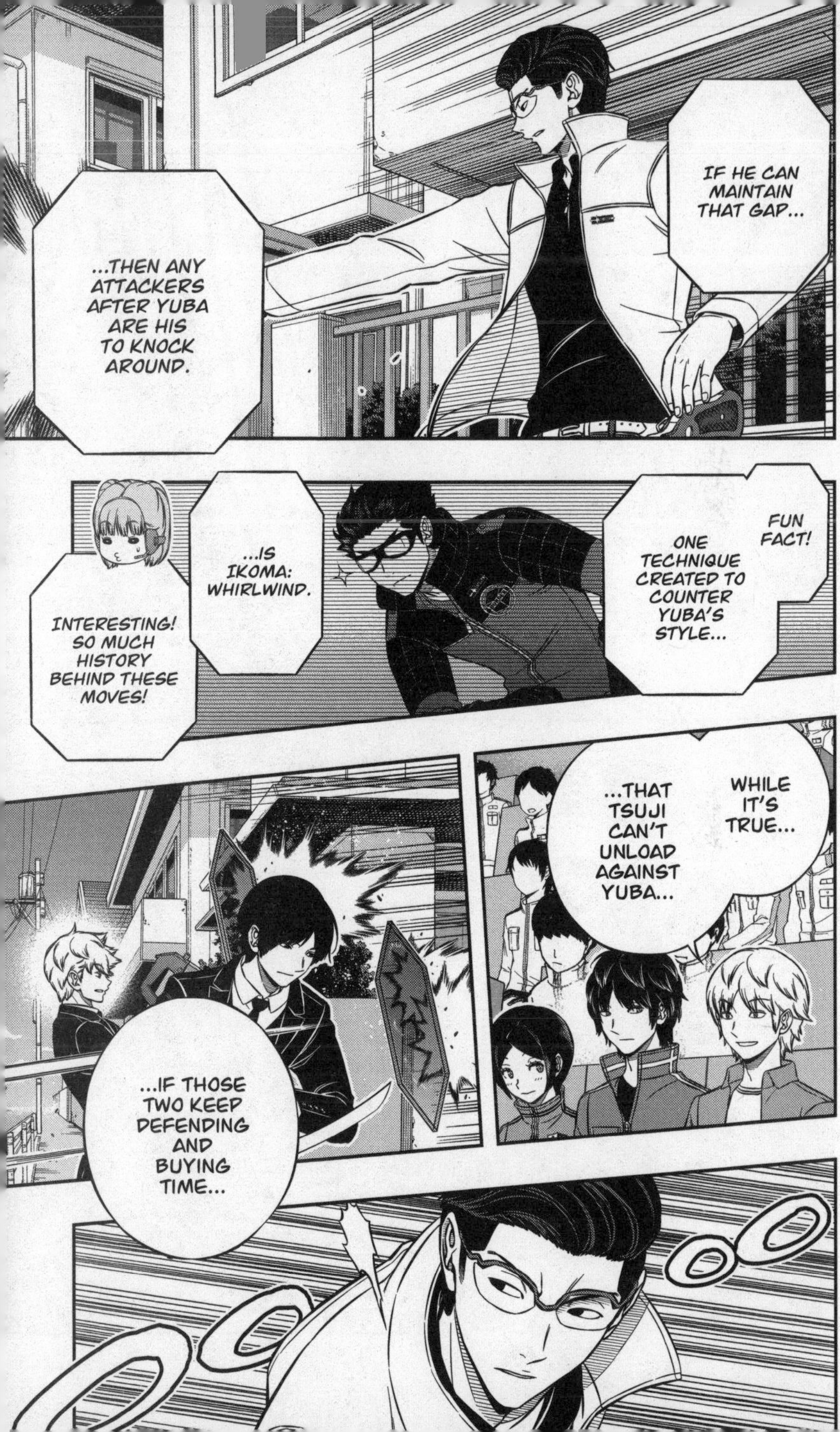
IF HE CAN MAINTAIN THAT GAP...
...THEN ANY ATTACKERS AFTER YUBA ARE HIS TO KNOCK AROUND.
FUN FACT!
ONE TECHNIQUE CREATED TO COUNTER YUBA'S STYLE...
...IS IKOMA: WHIRLWIND.
INTERESTING! SO MUCH HISTORY BEHIND THESE MOVES!
WHILE IT'S TRUE...
...THAT TSUJI CAN'T UNLOAD AGAINST YUBA...
...IF THOSE TWO KEEP DEFENDING AND BUYING TIME...

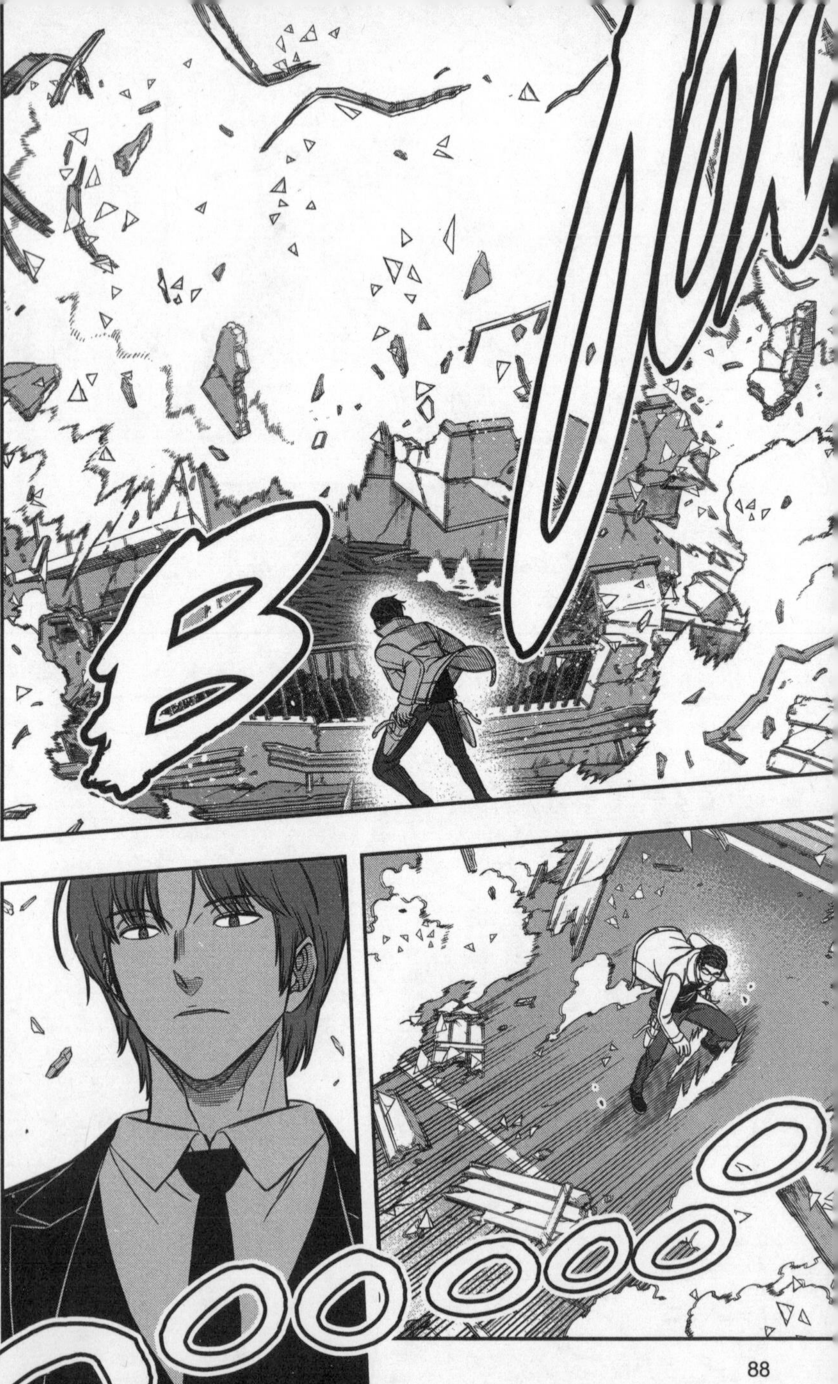
B
OOOOOOOO

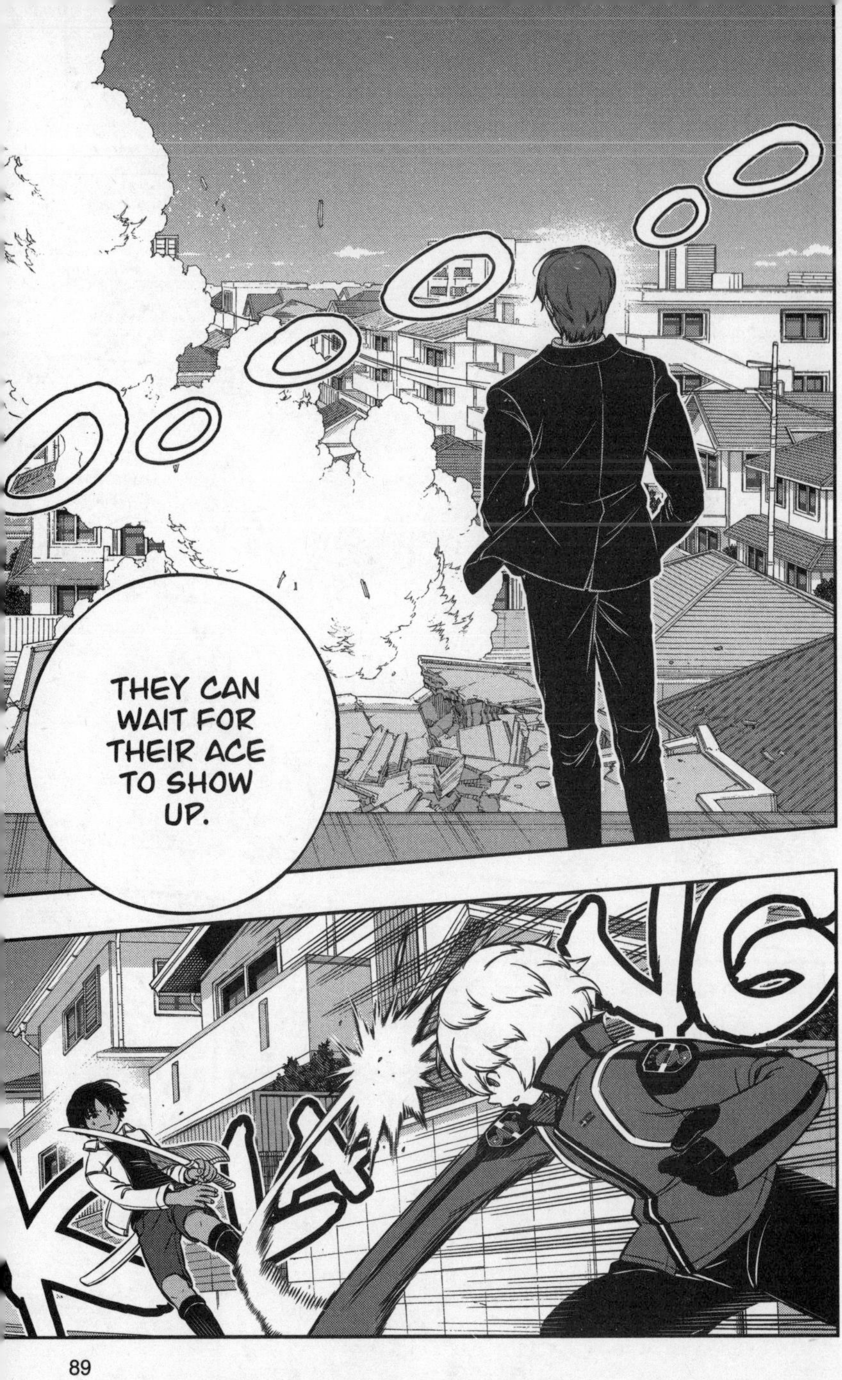
THEY CAN WAIT FOR THEIR ACE TO SHOW UP.

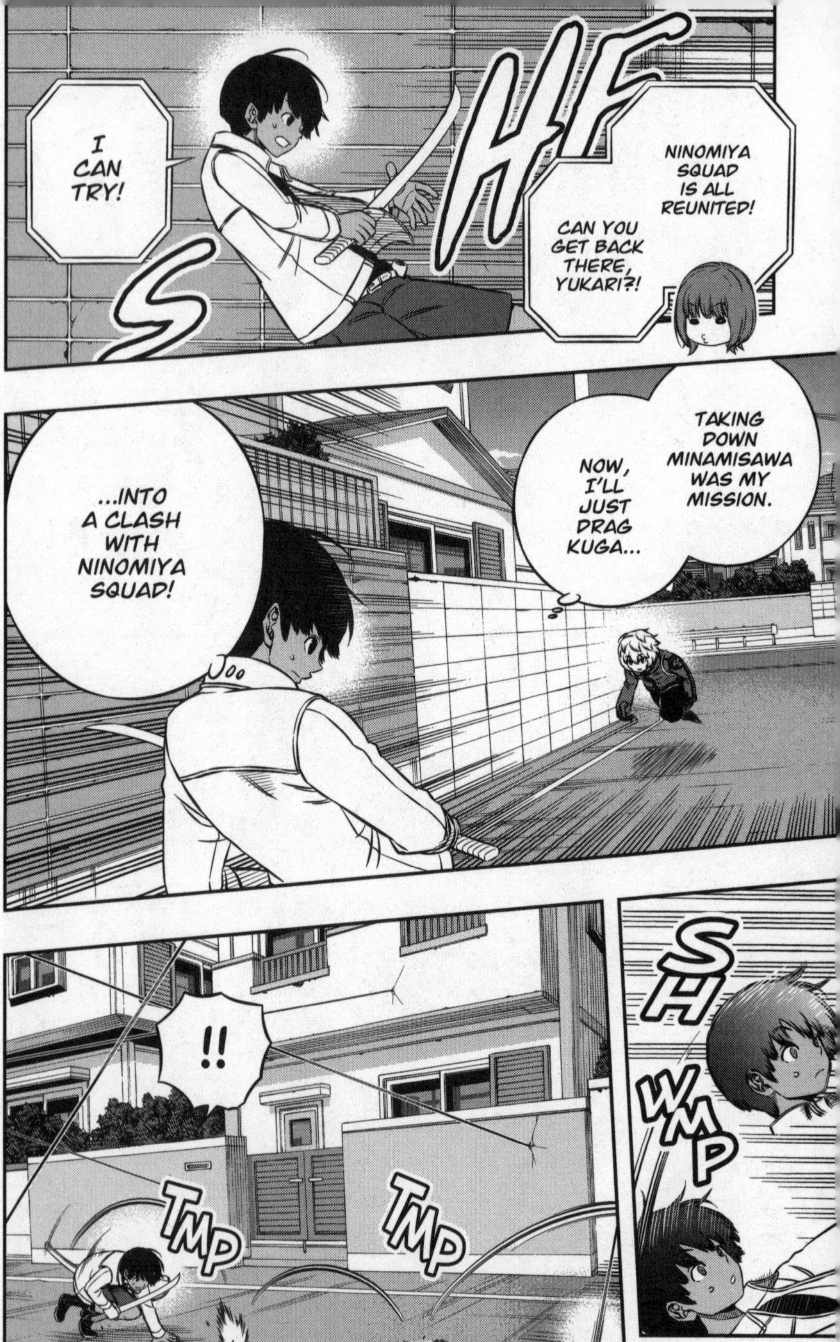
HF
NINOMIYA SQUAD IS ALL REUNITED!
CAN YOU GET BACK THERE, YUKARI?!
I CAN TRY!
S
TAKING DOWN MINAMISAWA WAS MY MISSION.
NOW, I'LL JUST DRAG KUGA...
...INTO A CLASH WITH NINOMIYA SQUAD!
SH
WMP
!!
TMP
TMP

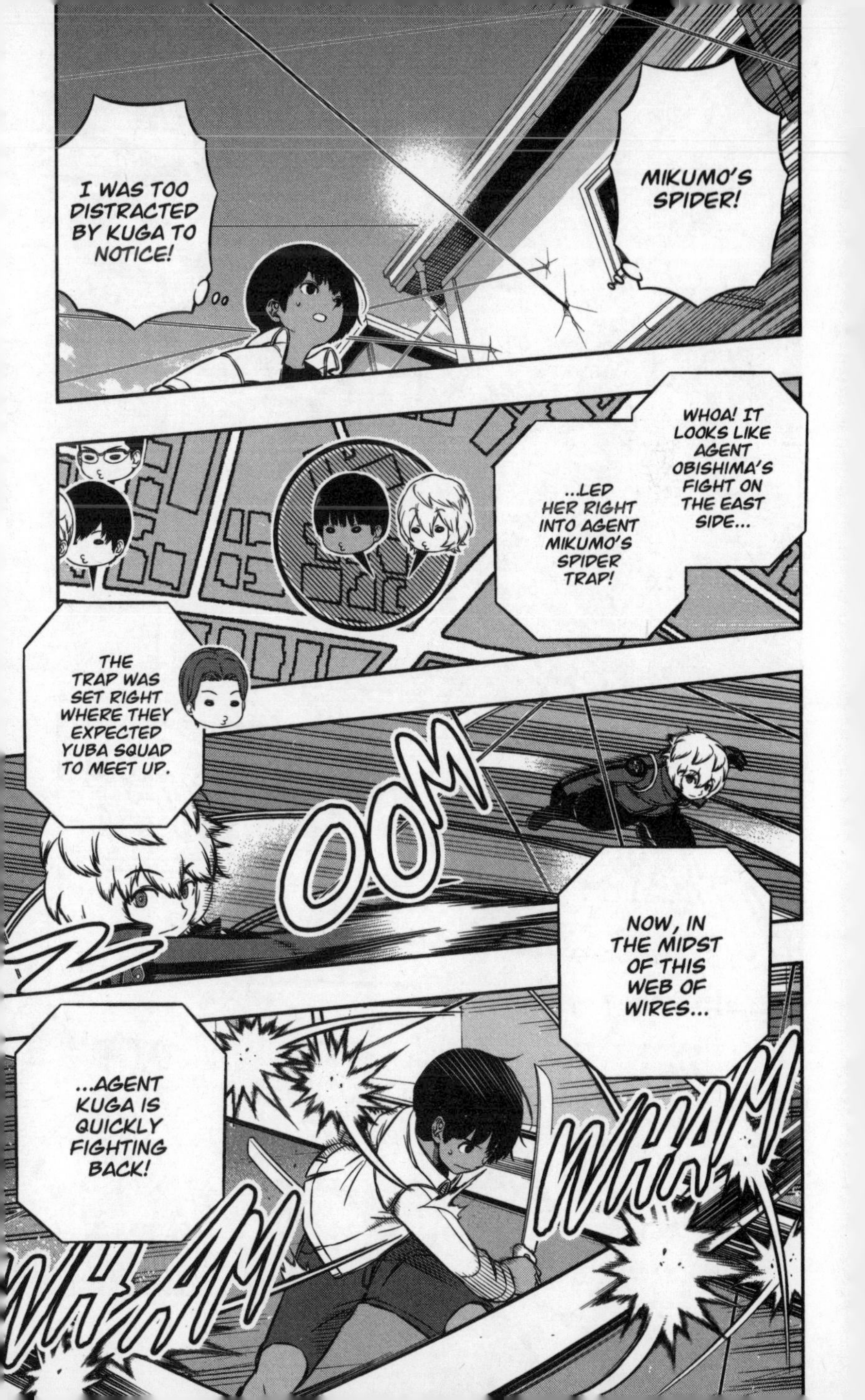
MIKUMO'S SPIDER!
I WAS TOO DISTRACTED BY KUGA TO NOTICE!
WHOA! IT LOOKS LIKE AGENT OBISHIMA'S FIGHT ON THE EAST SIDE...
...LED HER RIGHT INTO AGENT MIKUMO'S SPIDER TRAP!
THE TRAP WAS SET RIGHT WHERE THEY EXPECTED YUBA SQUAD TO MEET UP.
ZOOM
NOW, IN THE MIDST OF THIS WEB OF WIRES...
...AGENT KUGA IS QUICKLY FIGHTING BACK!
WHAM
WHAM

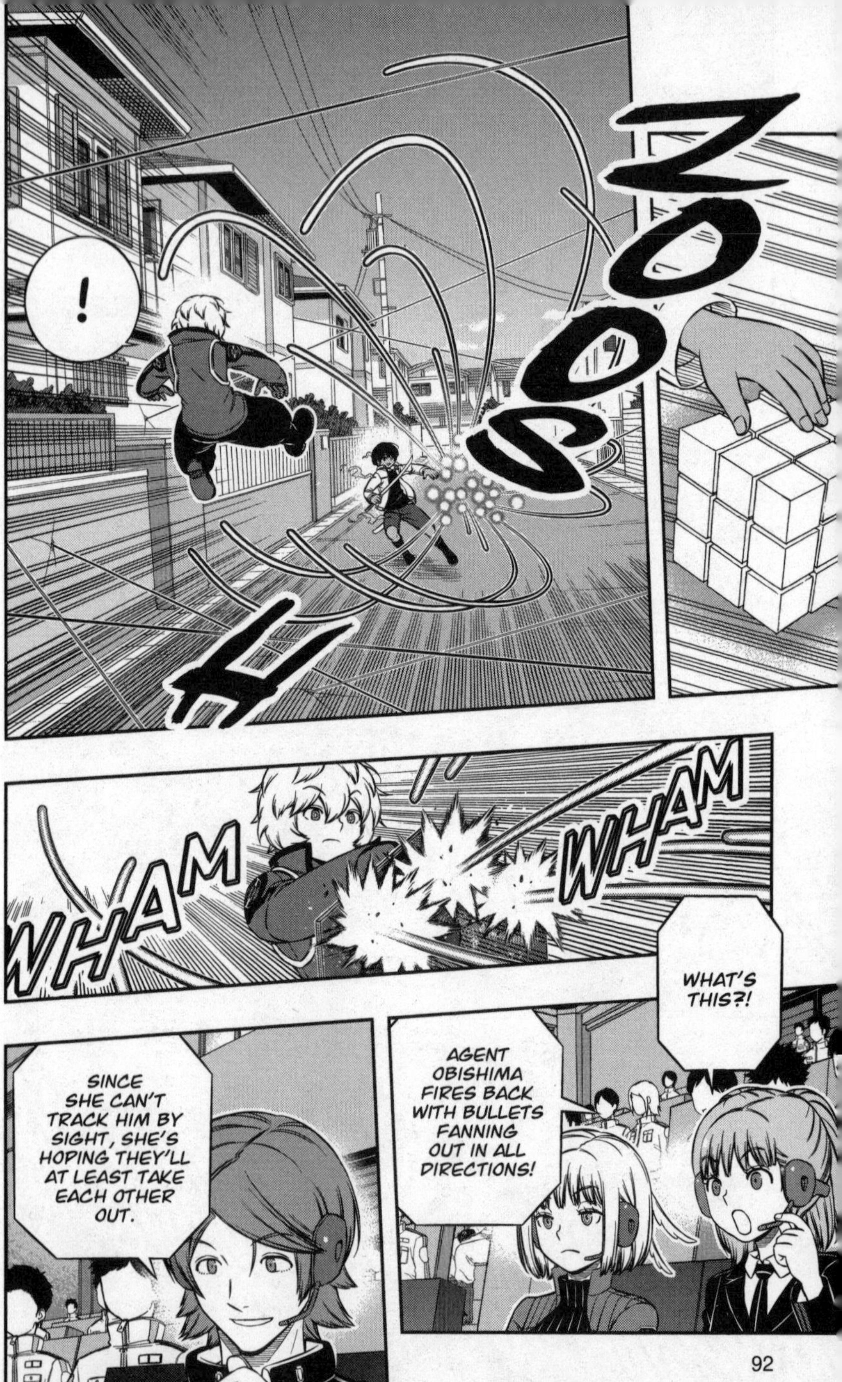
ZOOSH
!
WHAM WHAM
WHAT'S THIS?!
AGENT OBISHIMA FIRES BACK WITH BULLETS FANNING OUT IN ALL DIRECTIONS!
SINCE SHE CAN'T TRACK HIM BY SIGHT, SHE'S HOPING THEY'LL AT LEAST TAKE EACH OTHER OUT.

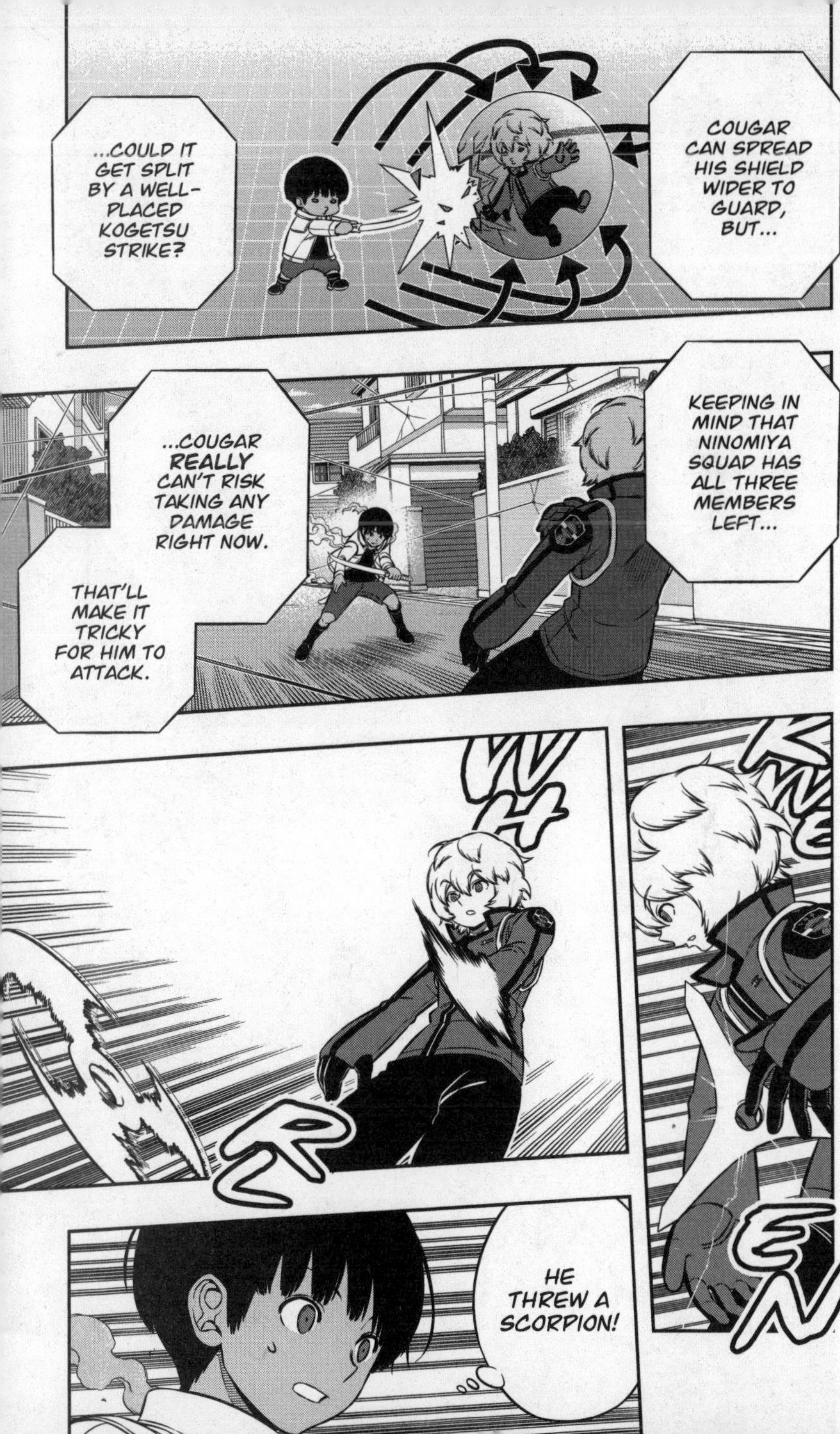
COUGAR CAN SPREAD HIS SHIELD WIDER TO GUARD, BUT...
...COULD IT GET SPLIT BY A WELL-PLACED KOGETSU STRIKE?
KEEPING IN MIND THAT NINOMIYA SQUAD HAS ALL THREE MEMBERS LEFT...
...COUGAR REALLY CAN'T RISK TAKING ANY DAMAGE RIGHT NOW.
THAT'LL MAKE IT TRICKY FOR HIM TO ATTACK.
HE THREW A SCORPION!

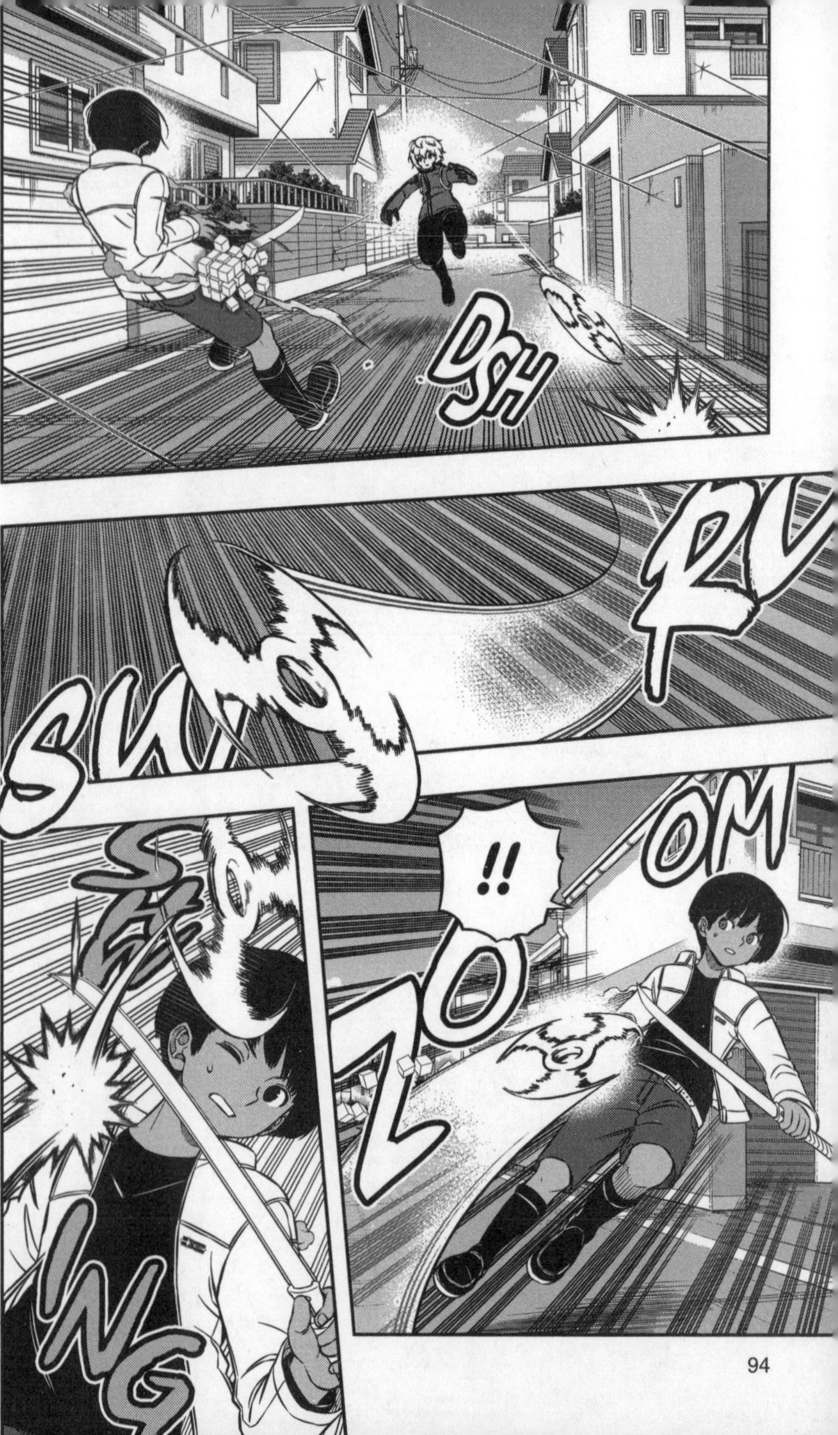
DSH
SHVRV
!!
ZOOM
SWING

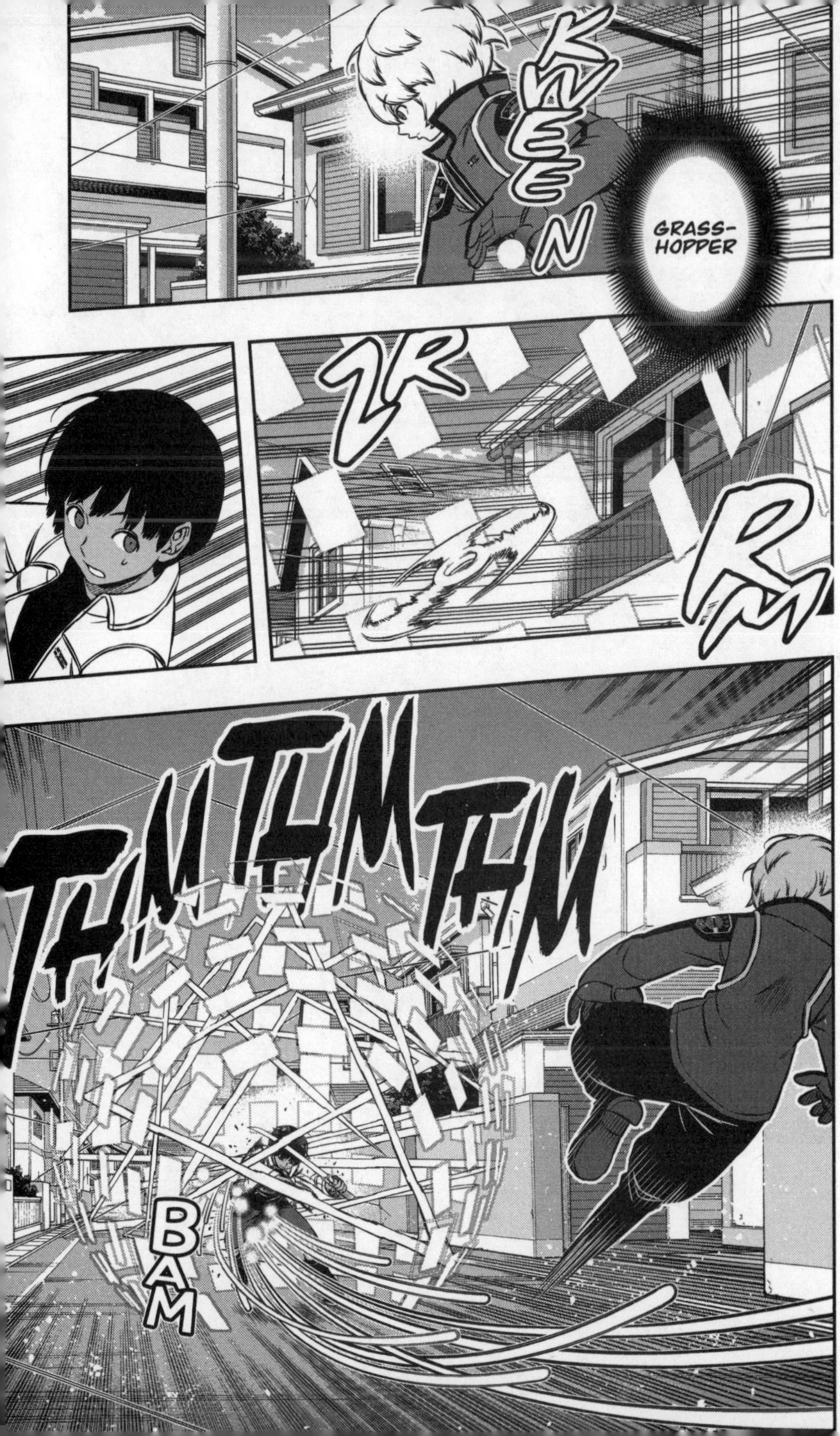
KWEEN
GRASS-HOPPER
ZR
RM
THM THM THM THM
BAM

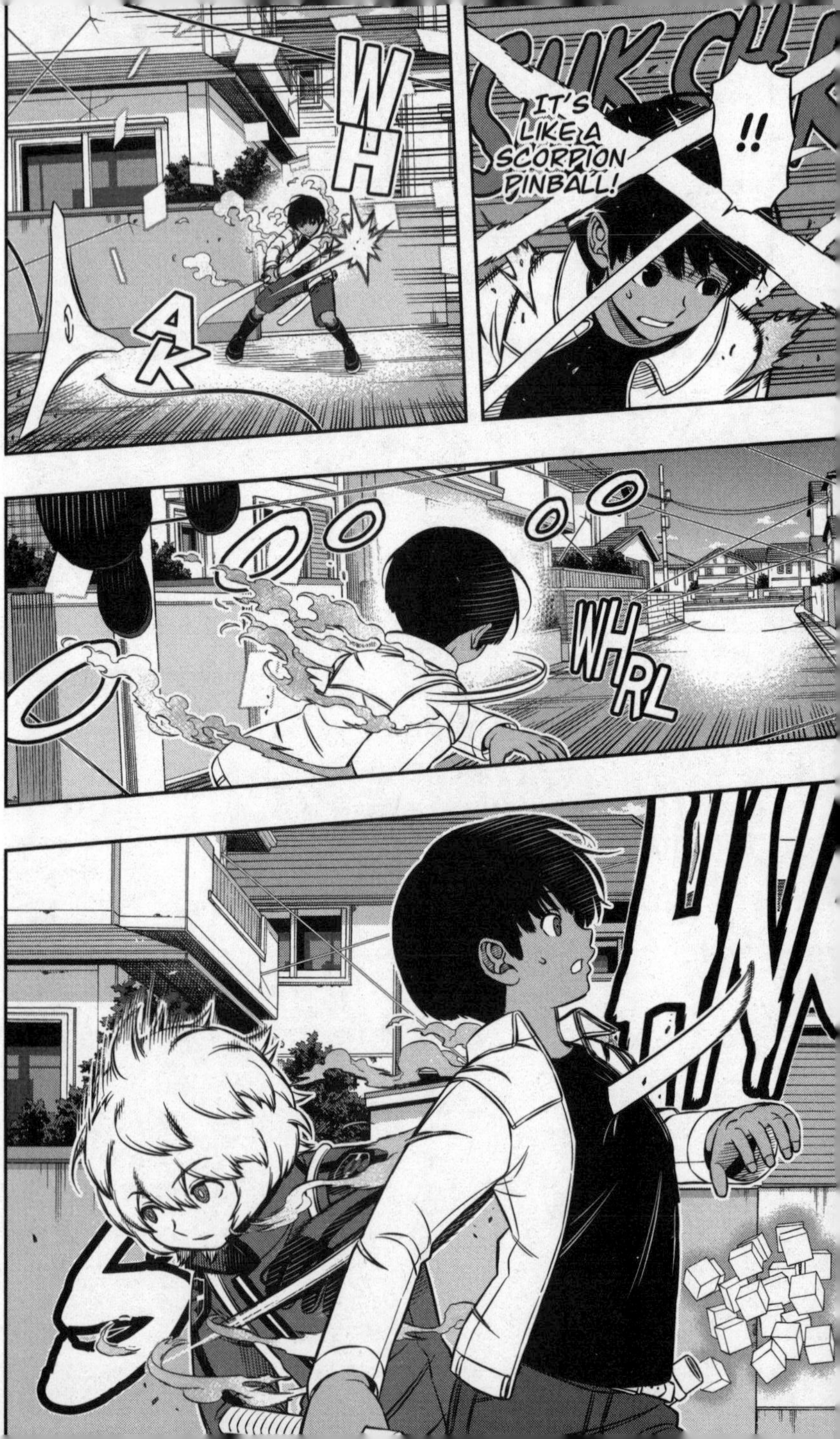
IT'S LIKE A SCORPION PINBALL!
!!
WH
AK
WHRL

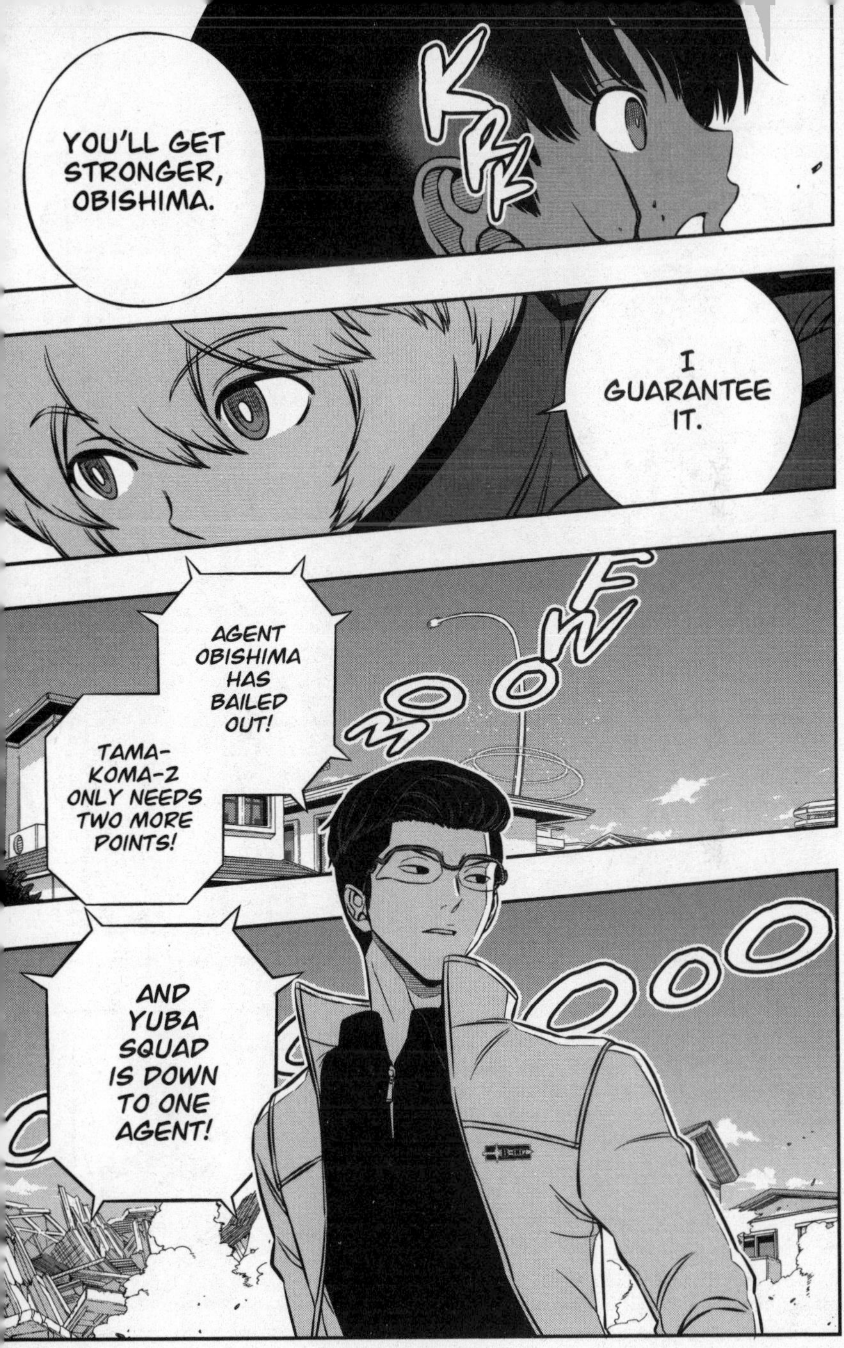
KRK
YOU'LL GET STRONGER, OBISHIMA.
I GUARANTEE IT.
FWOOM
AGENT OBISHIMA HAS BAILED OUT!
TAMA-KOMA-2 ONLY NEEDS TWO MORE POINTS!
AND YUBA SQUAD IS DOWN TO ONE AGENT!

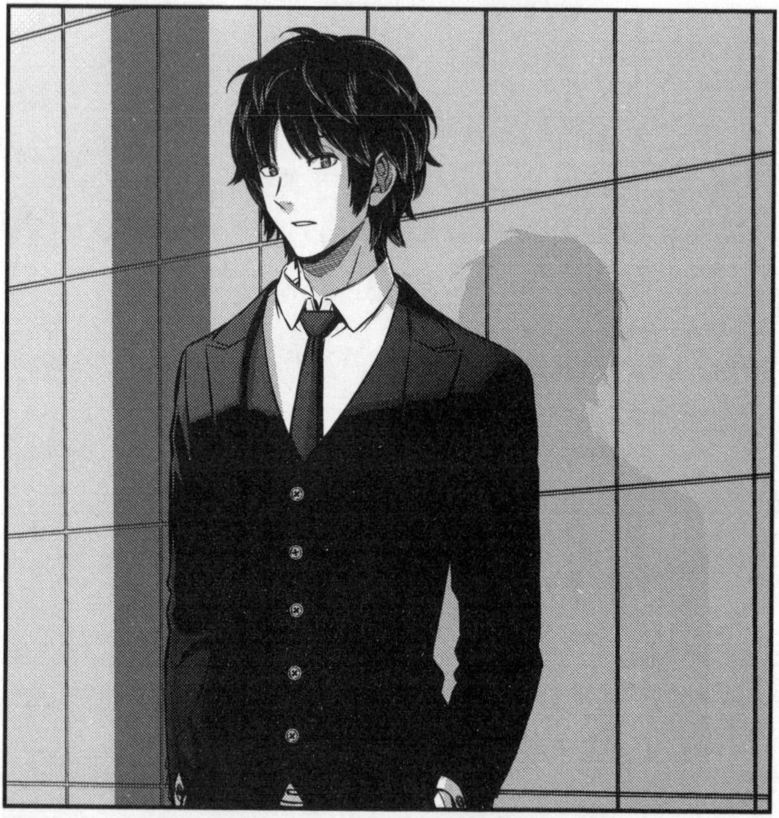

■ Ninomaru glamor shot for *Jump SQ*, January 2020 Issue (originally in color)

This basically came about because of a prank by my editor and manager, but it turned into a fun joke, so I have no regrets about it. This raw, unedited photo was brought into HQ by dubious means, and then Yotaro declared, "I'll give this to whomsoever provides me with the tastiest snack." This triggered a bidding war among a certain group of girls, but it all ended in a draw when Yotaro wound up with a stuffed tummy. Later, he distributed high-res scans of the image to everyone who participated. Nobody knows where the original photo is now...

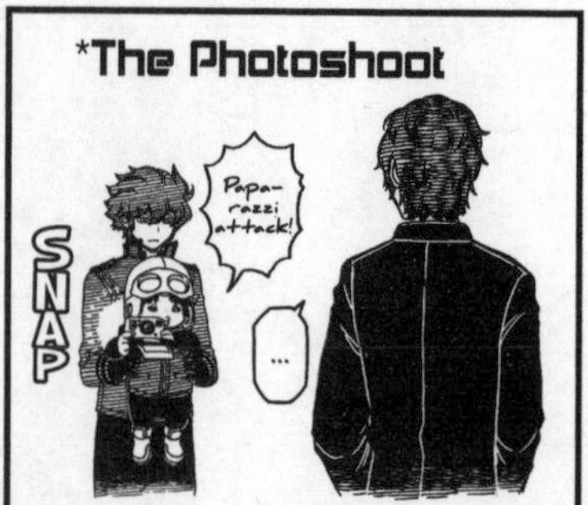
*The Photoshoot
...
Papa-razzi attack!
SNAP

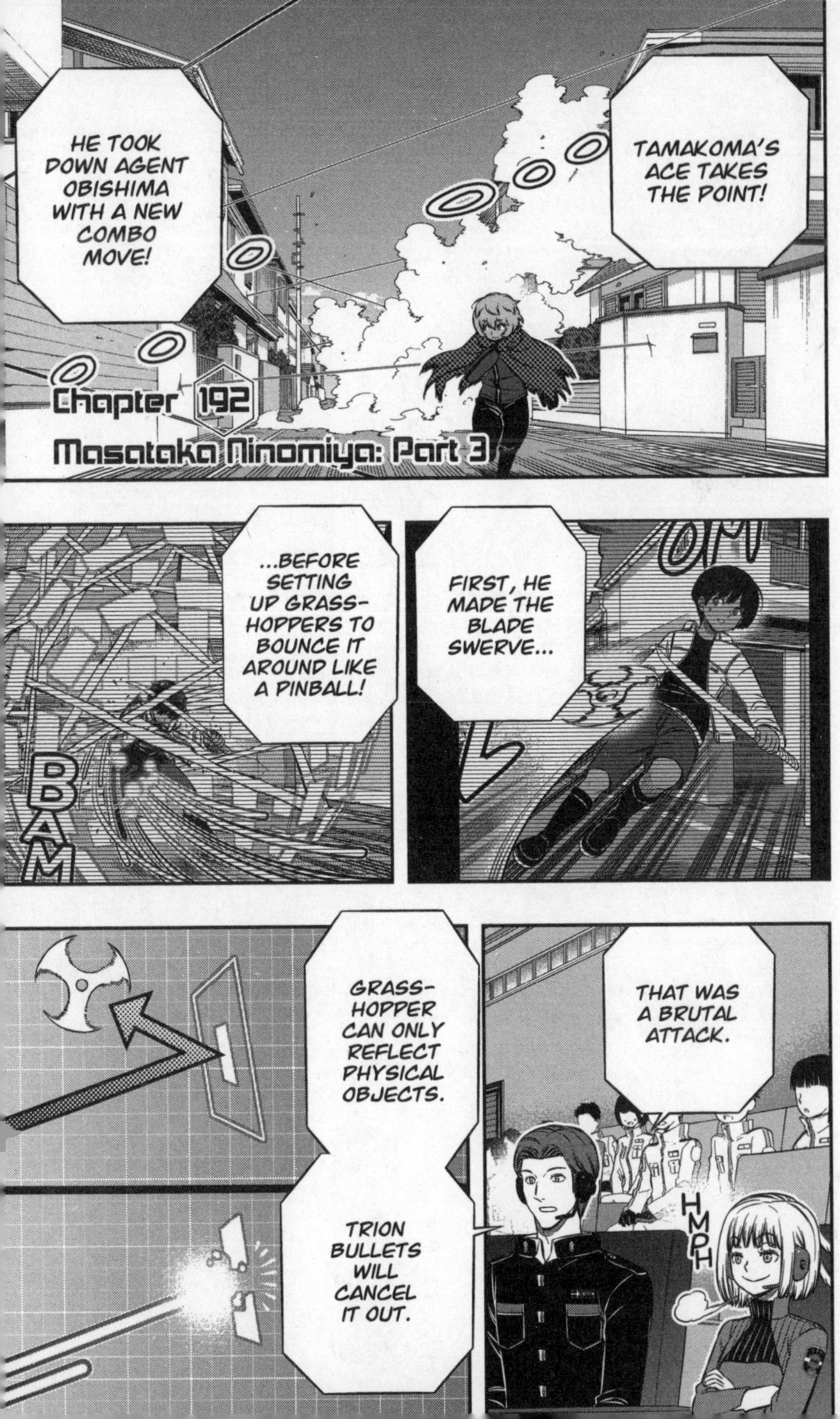
TAMAKOMA'S ACE TAKES THE POINT!
HE TOOK DOWN AGENT OBISHIMA WITH A NEW COMBO MOVE!
Chapter 192
Masataka Ninomiya: Part 3
FIRST, HE MADE THE BLADE SWERVE...
...BEFORE SETTING UP GRASS-HOPPERS TO BOUNCE IT AROUND LIKE A PINBALL!
BAM
THAT WAS A BRUTAL ATTACK.
HMPH
GRASS-HOPPER CAN ONLY REFLECT PHYSICAL OBJECTS.
TRION BULLETS WILL CANCEL IT OUT.

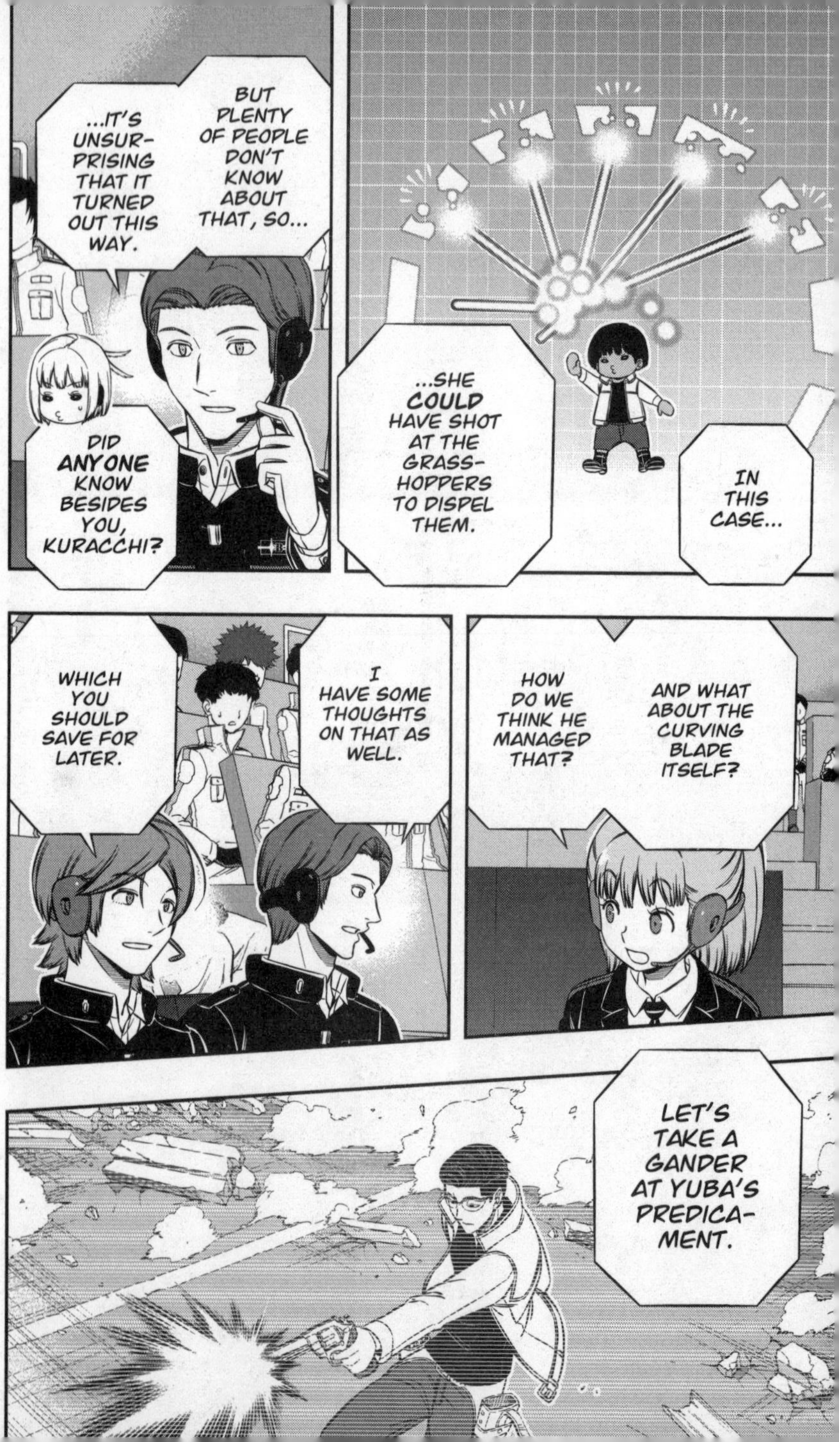

...SHE COULD HAVE SHOT AT THE GRASS-HOPPERS TO DISPEL THEM.
IN THIS CASE...
BUT PLENTY OF PEOPLE DON'T KNOW ABOUT THAT, SO...
...IT'S UNSUR-PRISING THAT IT TURNED OUT THIS WAY.
DID ANYONE KNOW BESIDES YOU, KURACCHI?
AND WHAT ABOUT THE CURVING BLADE ITSELF?
HOW DO WE THINK HE MANAGED THAT?
I HAVE SOME THOUGHTS ON THAT AS WELL.
WHICH YOU SHOULD SAVE FOR LATER.
LET'S TAKE A GANDER AT YUBA'S PREDICA-MENT.

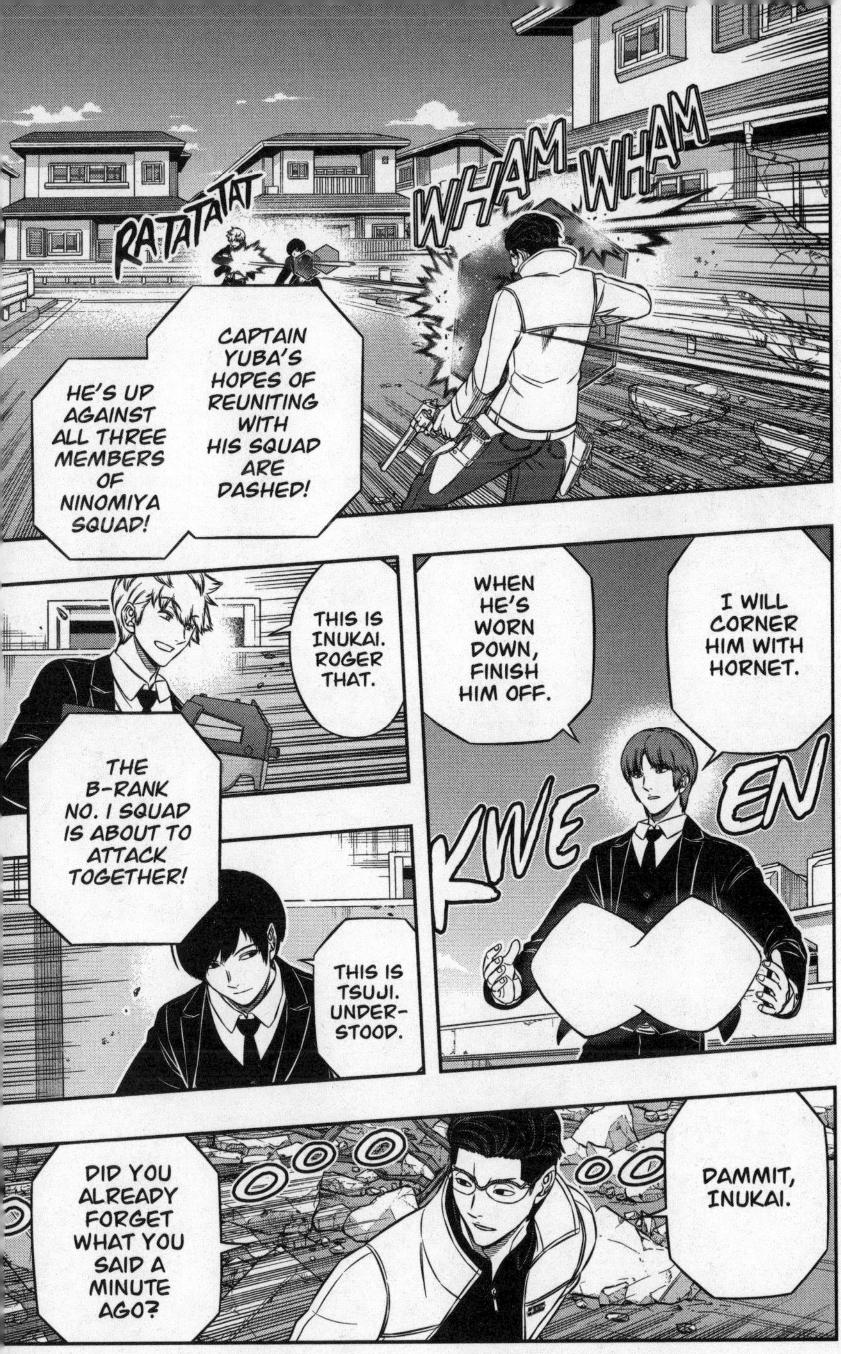
WHAM WHAM
RATATATAT
CAPTAIN YUBA'S HOPES OF REUNITING WITH HIS SQUAD ARE DASHED!
HE'S UP AGAINST ALL THREE MEMBERS OF NINOMIYA SQUAD!
I WILL CORNER HIM WITH HORNET.
WHEN HE'S WORN DOWN, FINISH HIM OFF.
KWE EN
THIS IS INUKAI. ROGER THAT.
THE B-RANK NO. 1 SQUAD IS ABOUT TO ATTACK TOGETHER!
THIS IS TSUJI. UNDER-STOOD.
DAMMIT, INUKAI.
DID YOU ALREADY FORGET WHAT YOU SAID A MINUTE AGO?

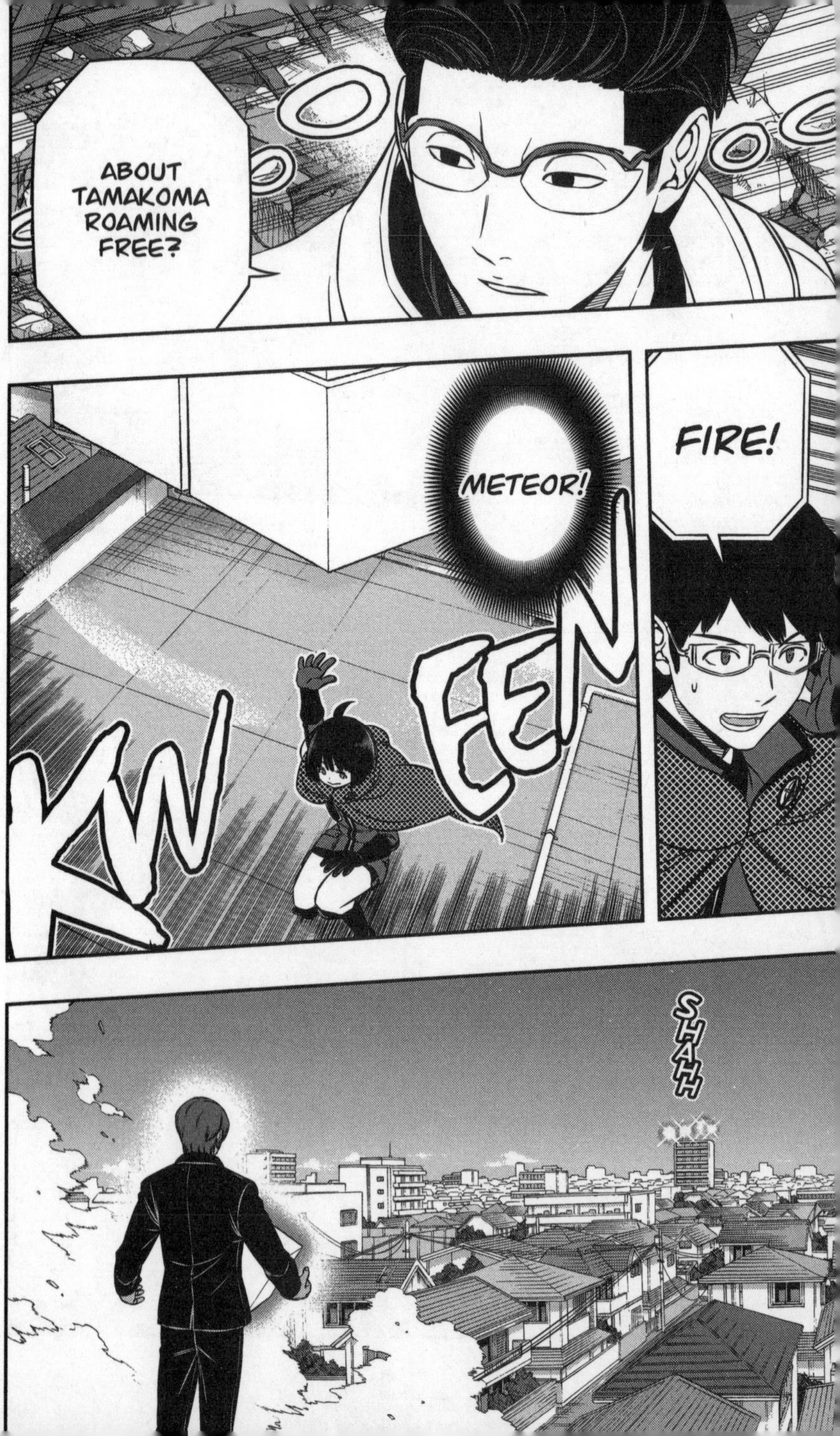
ABOUT TAMAKOMA ROAMING FREE?
FIRE!
METEOR!
KWEEN
SHAHH

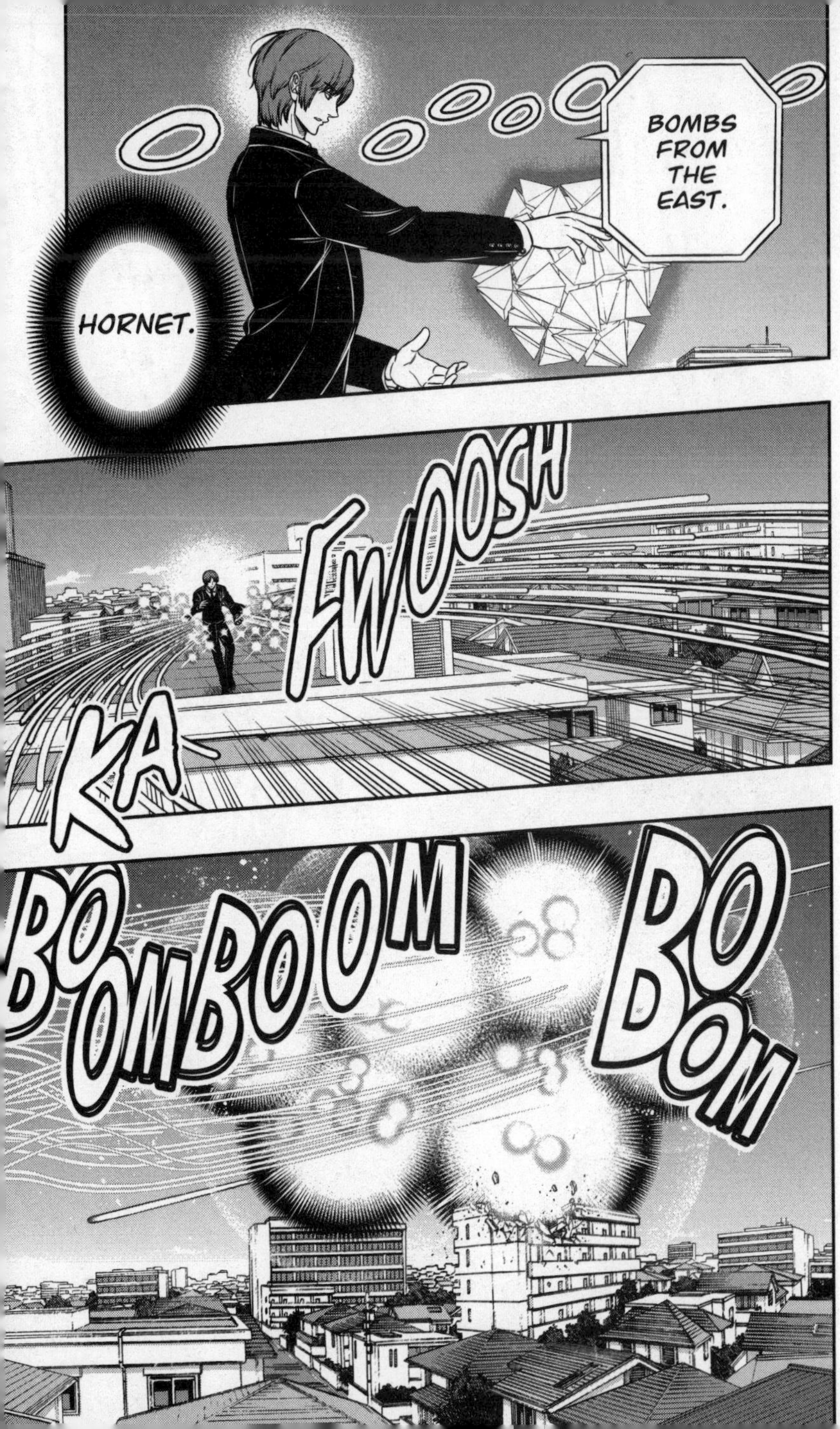
BOMBS FROM THE EAST.
HORNET.
KA-FWOOSH
BOOMBOOM
BOOM

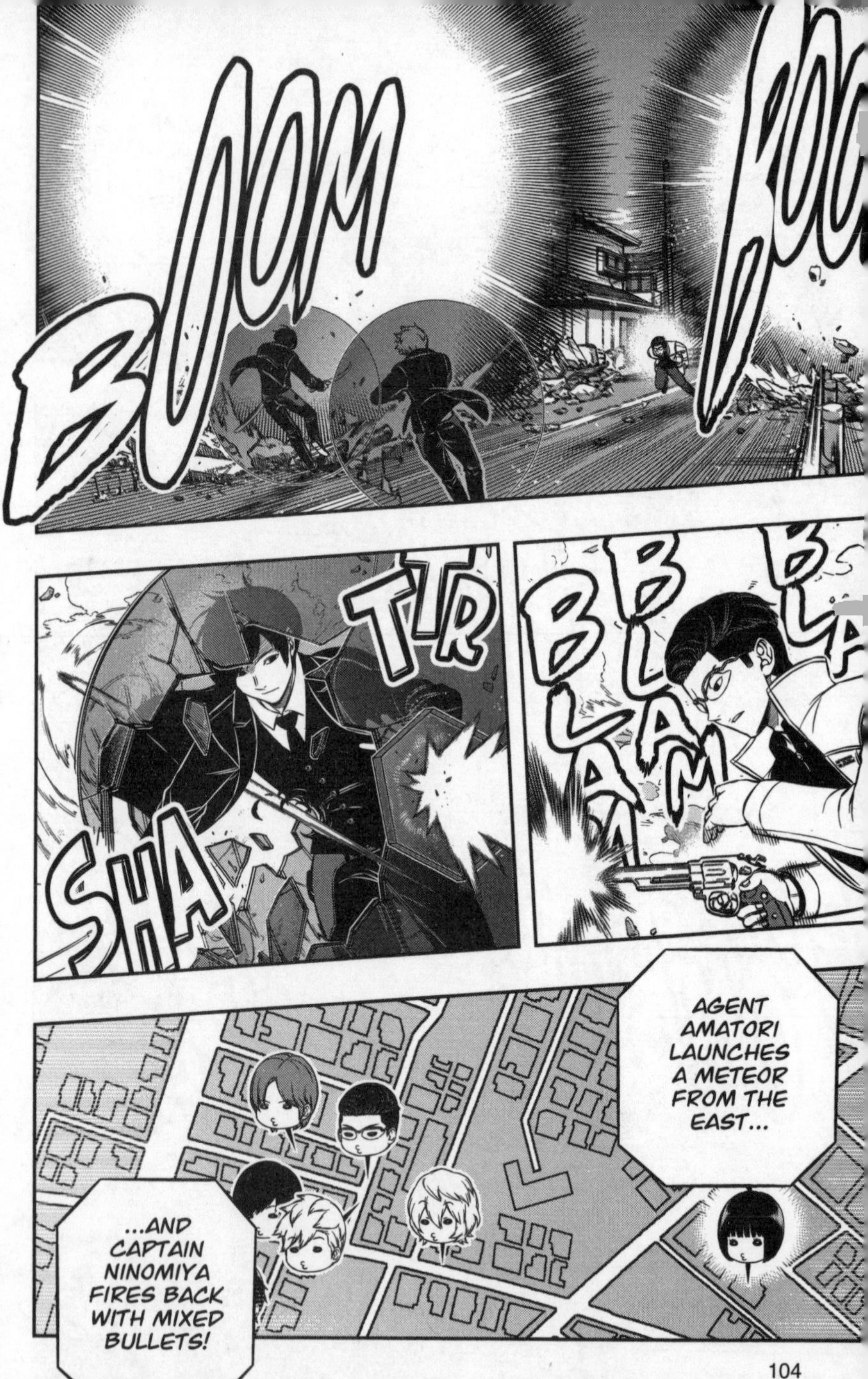
BOOM
BLAM
BLAM
TTR
SHA
AGENT AMATORI LAUNCHES A METEOR FROM THE EAST...
...AND CAPTAIN NINOMIYA FIRES BACK WITH MIXED BULLETS!

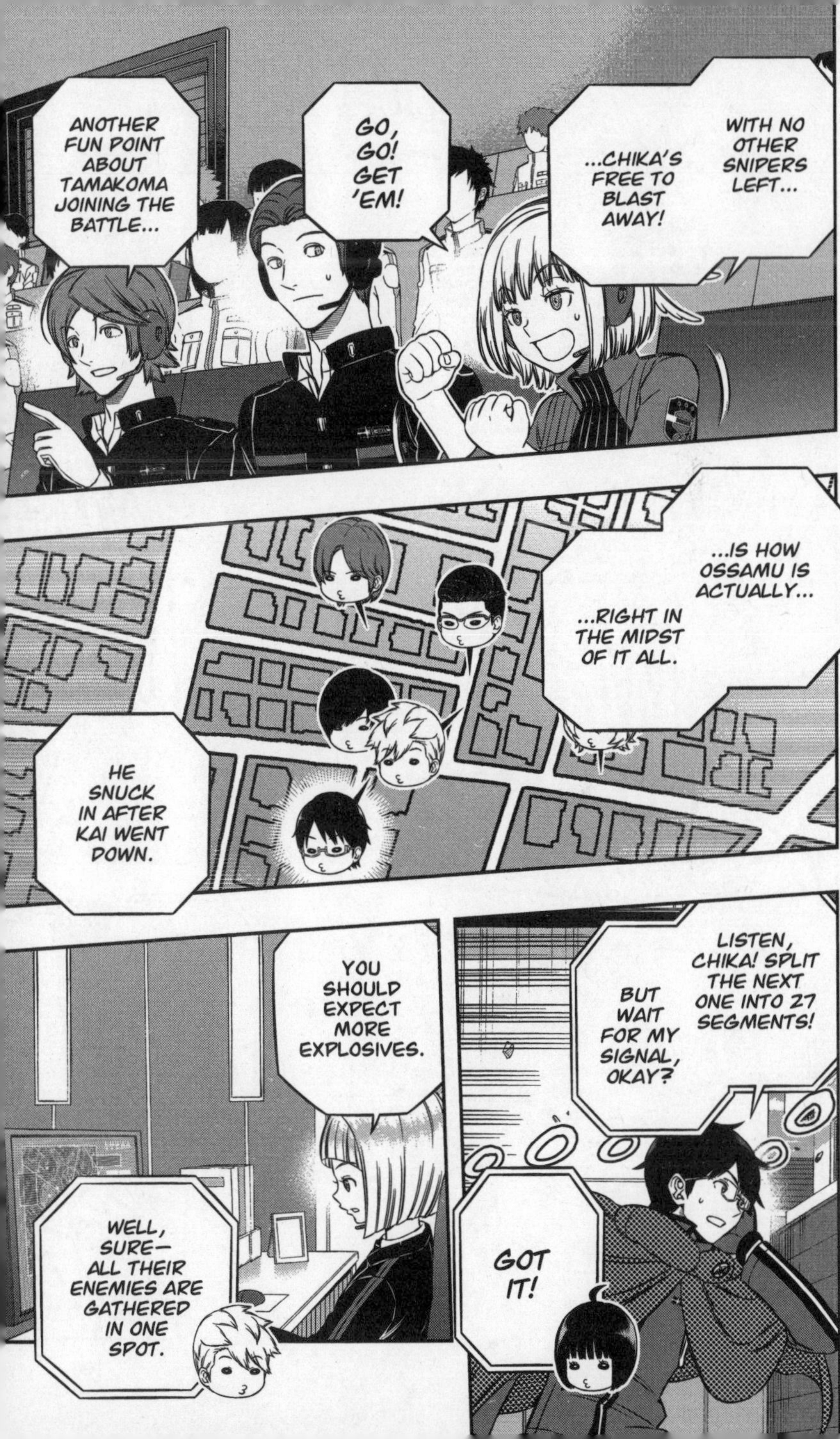
WITH NO OTHER SNIPERS LEFT...
...CHIKA'S FREE TO BLAST AWAY!
GO, GO! GET 'EM!
ANOTHER FUN POINT ABOUT TAMAKOMA JOINING THE BATTLE...
...IS HOW OSSAMU IS ACTUALLY...
...RIGHT IN THE MIDST OF IT ALL.
HE SNUCK IN AFTER KAI WENT DOWN.
LISTEN, CHIKA! SPLIT THE NEXT ONE INTO 27 SEGMENTS!
BUT WAIT FOR MY SIGNAL, OKAY?
GOT IT!
YOU SHOULD EXPECT MORE EXPLOSIVES.
WELL, SURE— ALL THEIR ENEMIES ARE GATHERED IN ONE SPOT.

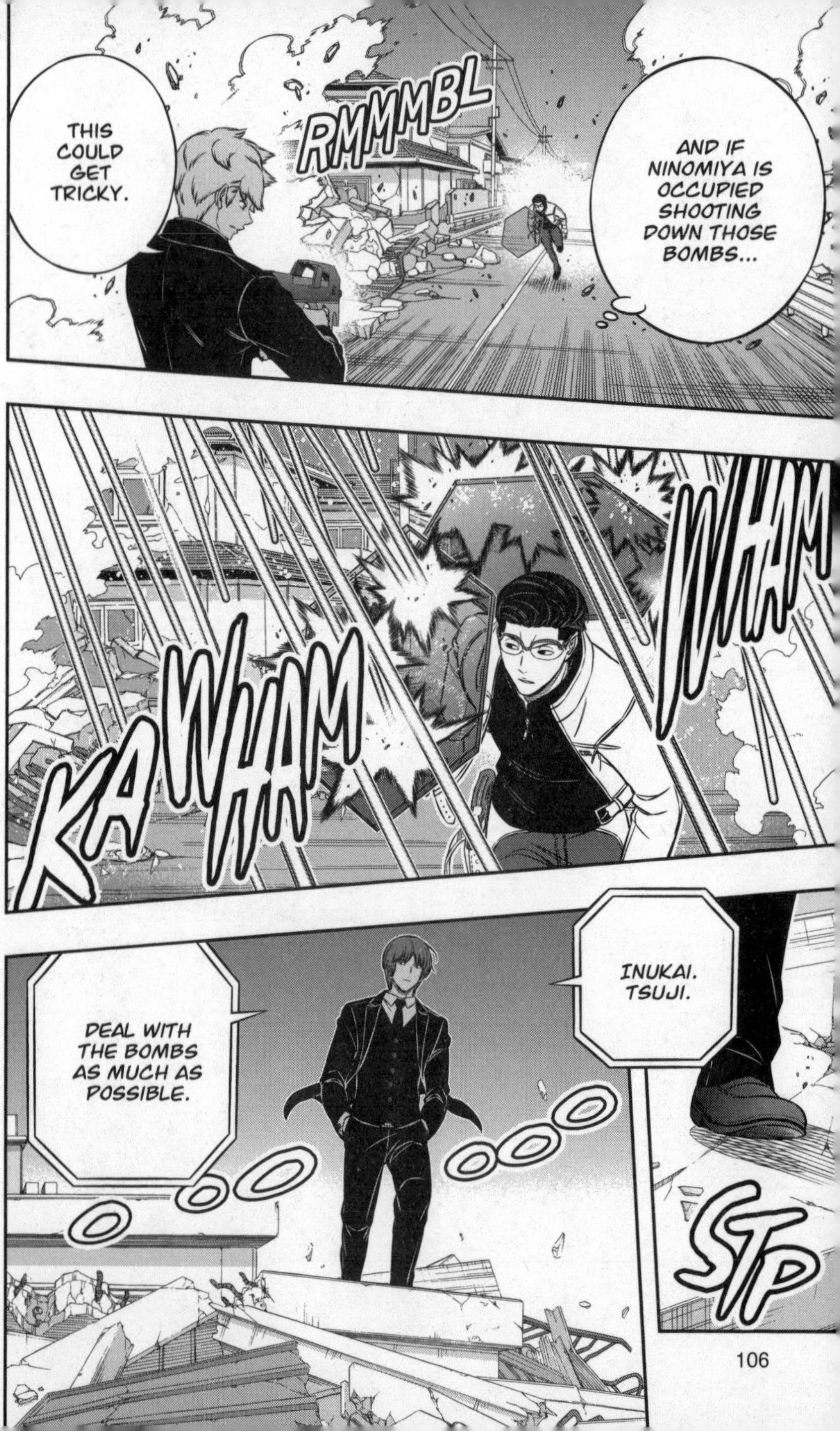
AND IF NINOMIYA IS OCCUPIED SHOOTING DOWN THOSE BOMBS...
RMMMBL
THIS COULD GET TRICKY.
WHAM
KAWHAM
STP
INUKAI. TSUJI.
DEAL WITH THE BOMBS AS MUCH AS POSSIBLE.
OOOOOOOO

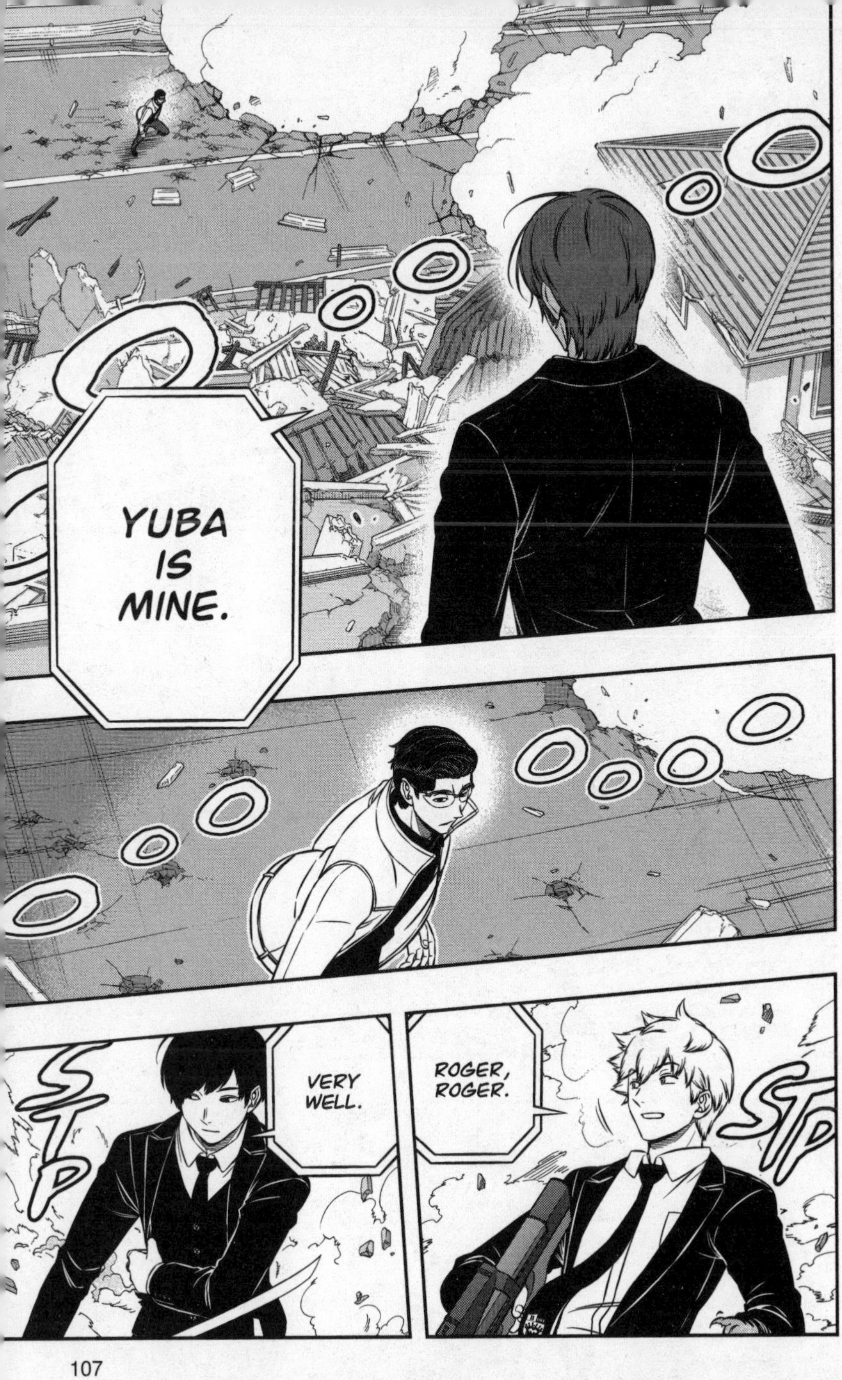
YUBA IS MINE.
ROGER, ROGER.
STP
VERY WELL.
STP

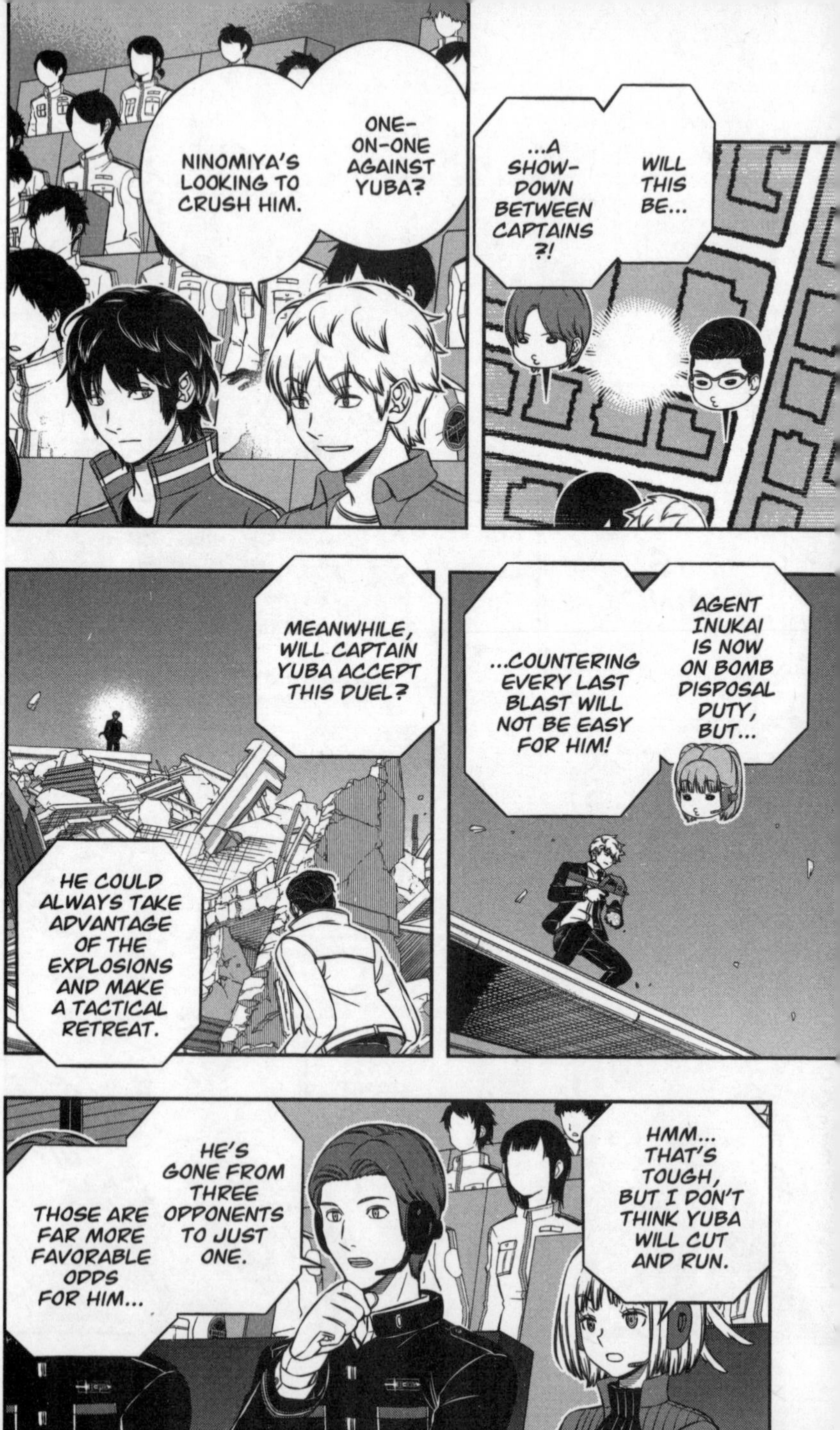
WILL THIS BE...
...A SHOWDOWN BETWEEN CAPTAINS?!
ONE-ON-ONE AGAINST YUBA?
NINOMIYA'S LOOKING TO CRUSH HIM.
AGENT INUKAI IS NOW ON BOMB DISPOSAL DUTY, BUT...
...COUNTERING EVERY LAST BLAST WILL NOT BE EASY FOR HIM!
MEANWHILE, WILL CAPTAIN YUBA ACCEPT THIS DUEL?
HE COULD ALWAYS TAKE ADVANTAGE OF THE EXPLOSIONS AND MAKE A TACTICAL RETREAT.
HMM... THAT'S TOUGH, BUT I DON'T THINK YUBA WILL CUT AND RUN.
HE'S GONE FROM THREE OPPONENTS TO JUST ONE.
THOSE ARE FAR MORE FAVORABLE ODDS FOR HIM...

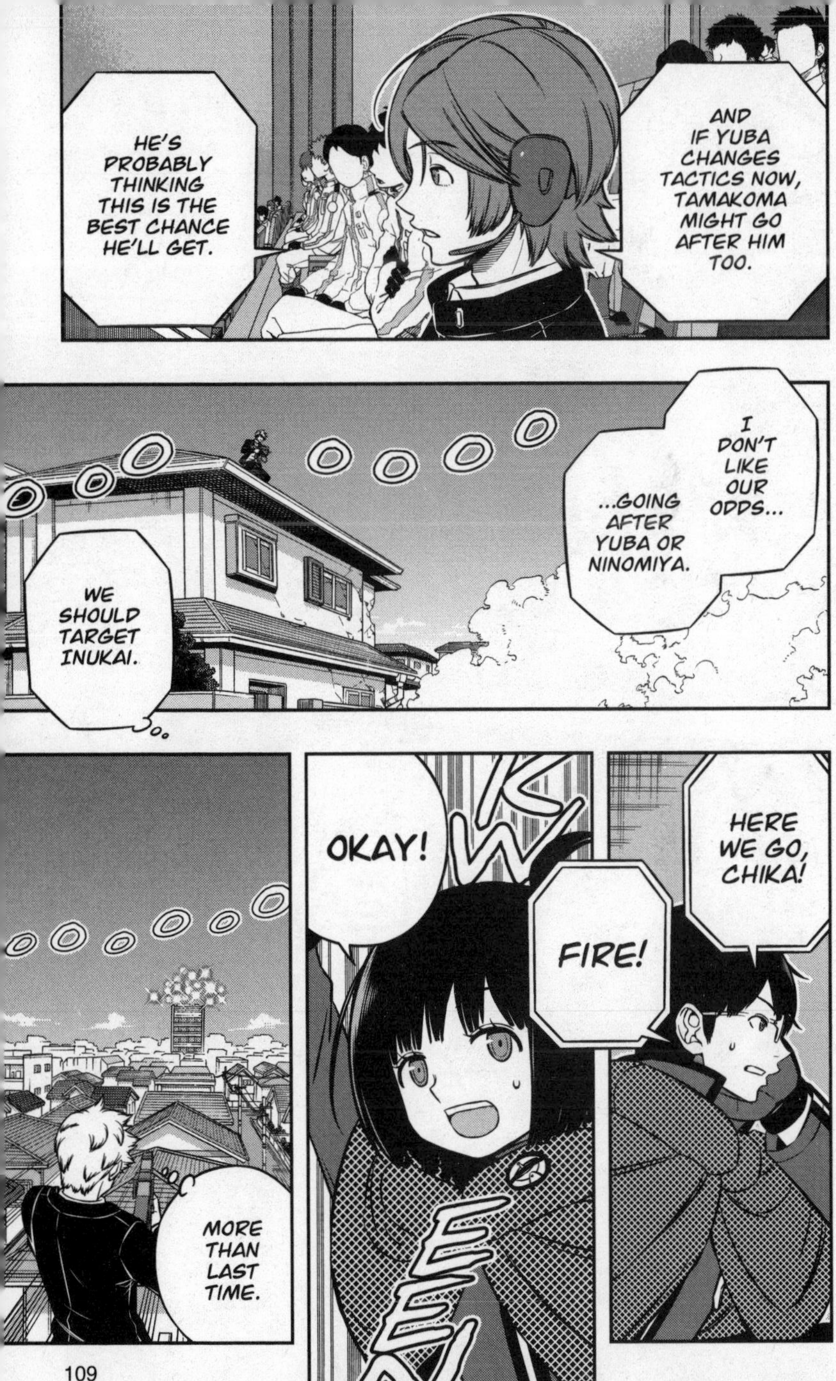
AND IF YUBA CHANGES TACTICS NOW, TAMAKOMA MIGHT GO AFTER HIM TOO.
HE'S PROBABLY THINKING THIS IS THE BEST CHANCE HE'LL GET.
I DON'T LIKE OUR ODDS...
...GOING AFTER YUBA OR NINOMIYA.
WE SHOULD TARGET INUKAI.
HERE WE GO, CHIKA!
FIRE!
OKAY!
KWEEEN
MORE THAN LAST TIME.

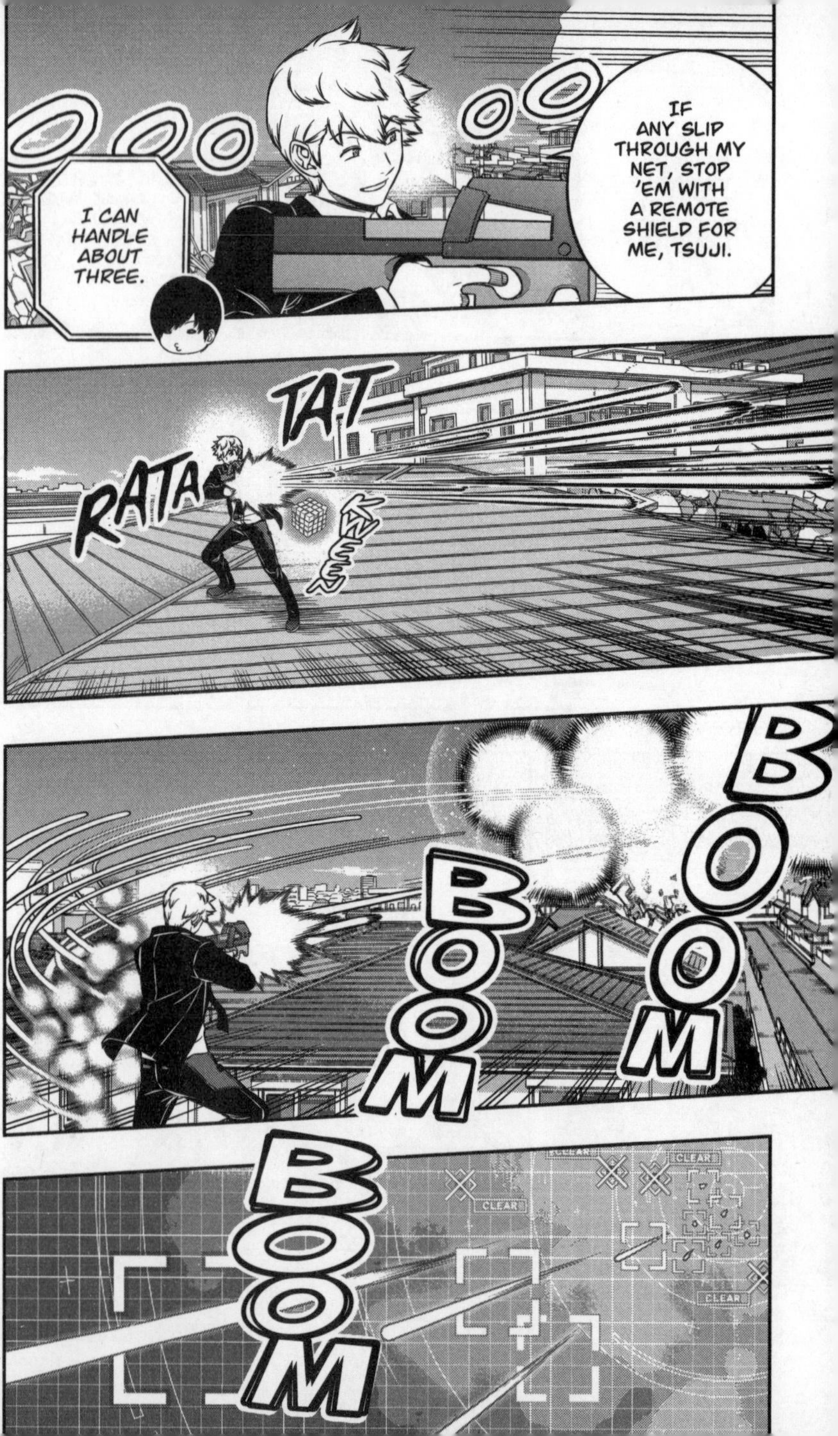
IF ANY SLIP THROUGH MY NET, STOP 'EM WITH A REMOTE SHIELD FOR ME, TSUJI.
I CAN HANDLE ABOUT THREE.
TAT
RATA
KWEEP
BOOM
BOOM
BOOM
CLEAR
CLEAR
CLEAR
CLEAR

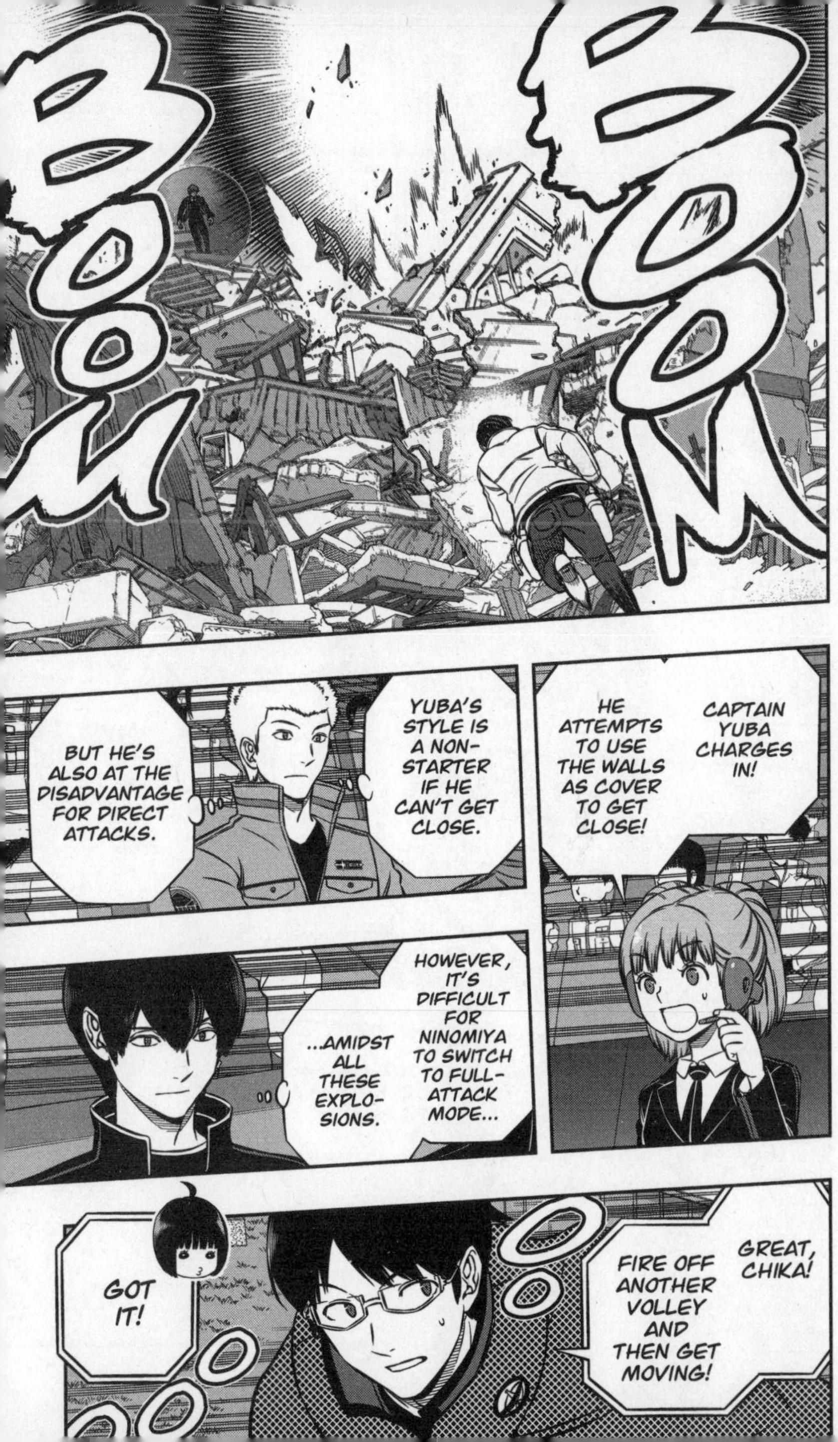
BOOM
BOOM
CAPTAIN YUBA CHARGES IN!
HE ATTEMPTS TO USE THE WALLS AS COVER TO GET CLOSE!
YUBA'S STYLE IS A NON-STARTER IF HE CAN'T GET CLOSE.
BUT HE'S ALSO AT THE DISADVANTAGE FOR DIRECT ATTACKS.
HOWEVER, IT'S DIFFICULT FOR NINOMIYA TO SWITCH TO FULL-ATTACK MODE...
...AMIDST ALL THESE EXPLOSIONS.
GREAT, CHIKA!
FIRE OFF ANOTHER VOLLEY AND THEN GET MOVING!
GOT IT!

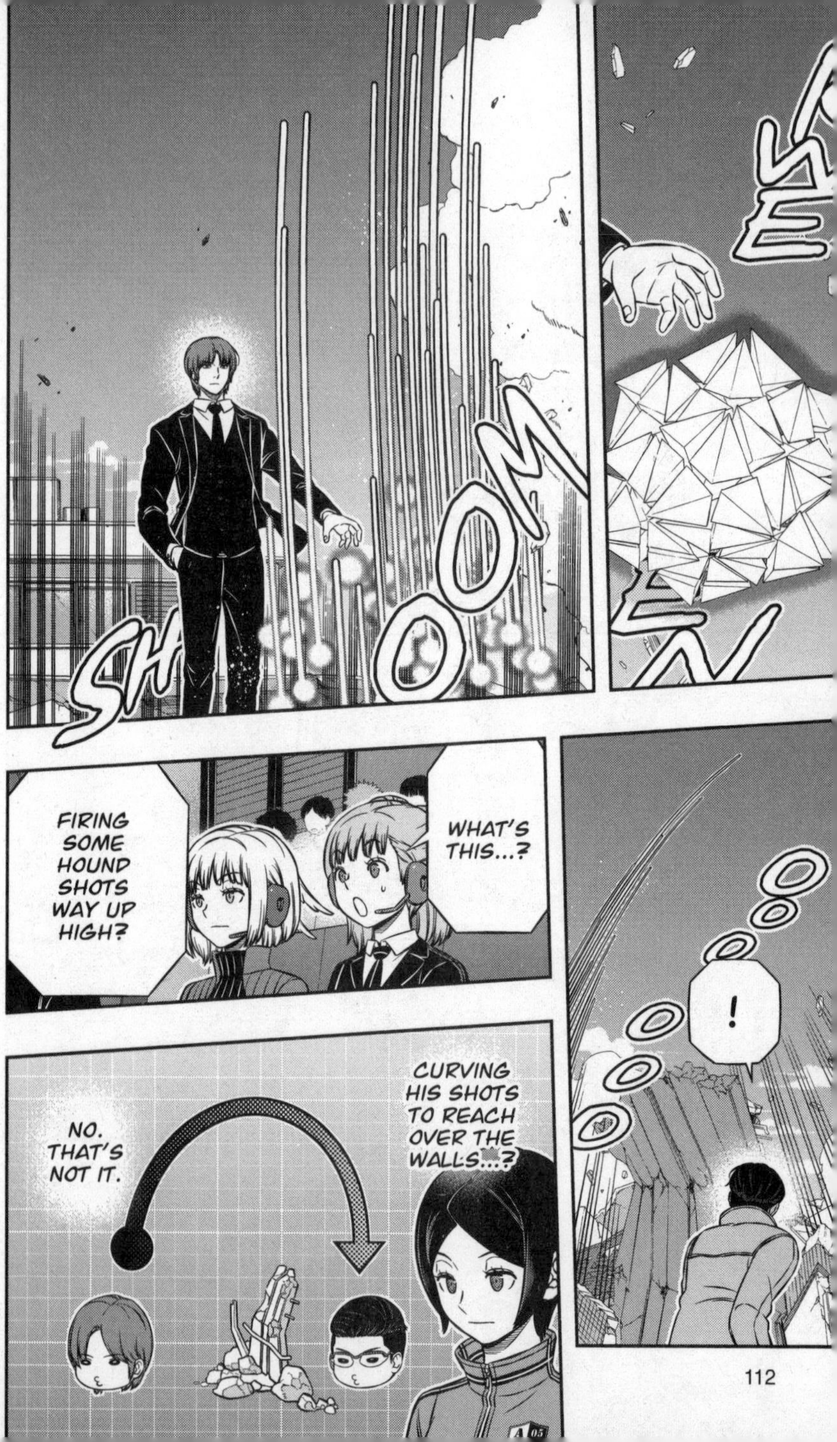
SHOOM
!
WHAT'S THIS...?
FIRING SOME HOUND SHOTS WAY UP HIGH?
CURVING HIS SHOTS TO REACH OVER THE WALLS...?
NO. THAT'S NOT IT.

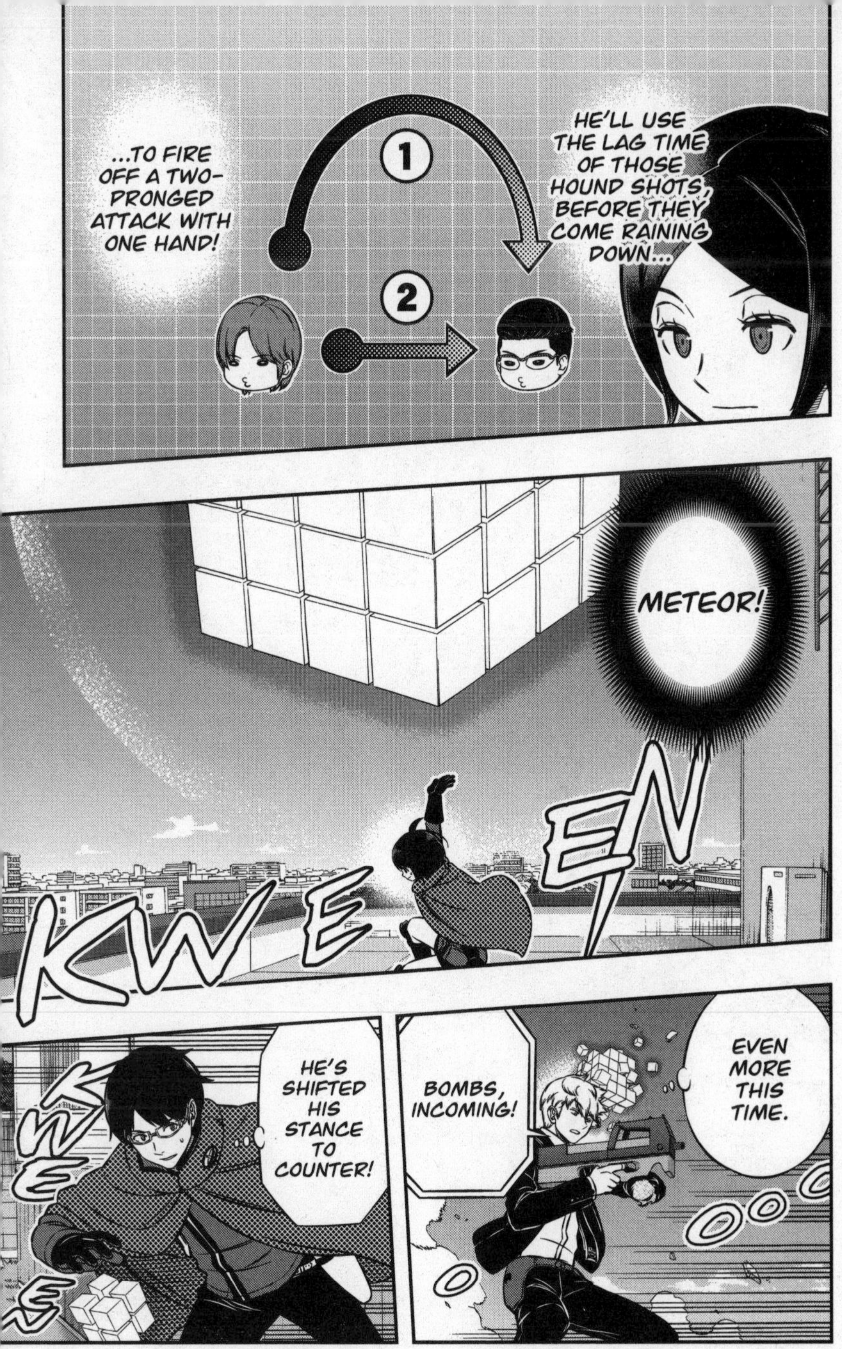
HE'LL USE THE LAG TIME OF THOSE HOUND SHOTS, BEFORE THEY COME RAINING DOWN...
...TO FIRE OFF A TWO-PRONGED ATTACK WITH ONE HAND!
1
2
METEOR!
KWEEN
EVEN MORE THIS TIME.
BOMBS, INCOMING!
HE'S SHIFTED HIS STANCE TO COUNTER!
KWEEN

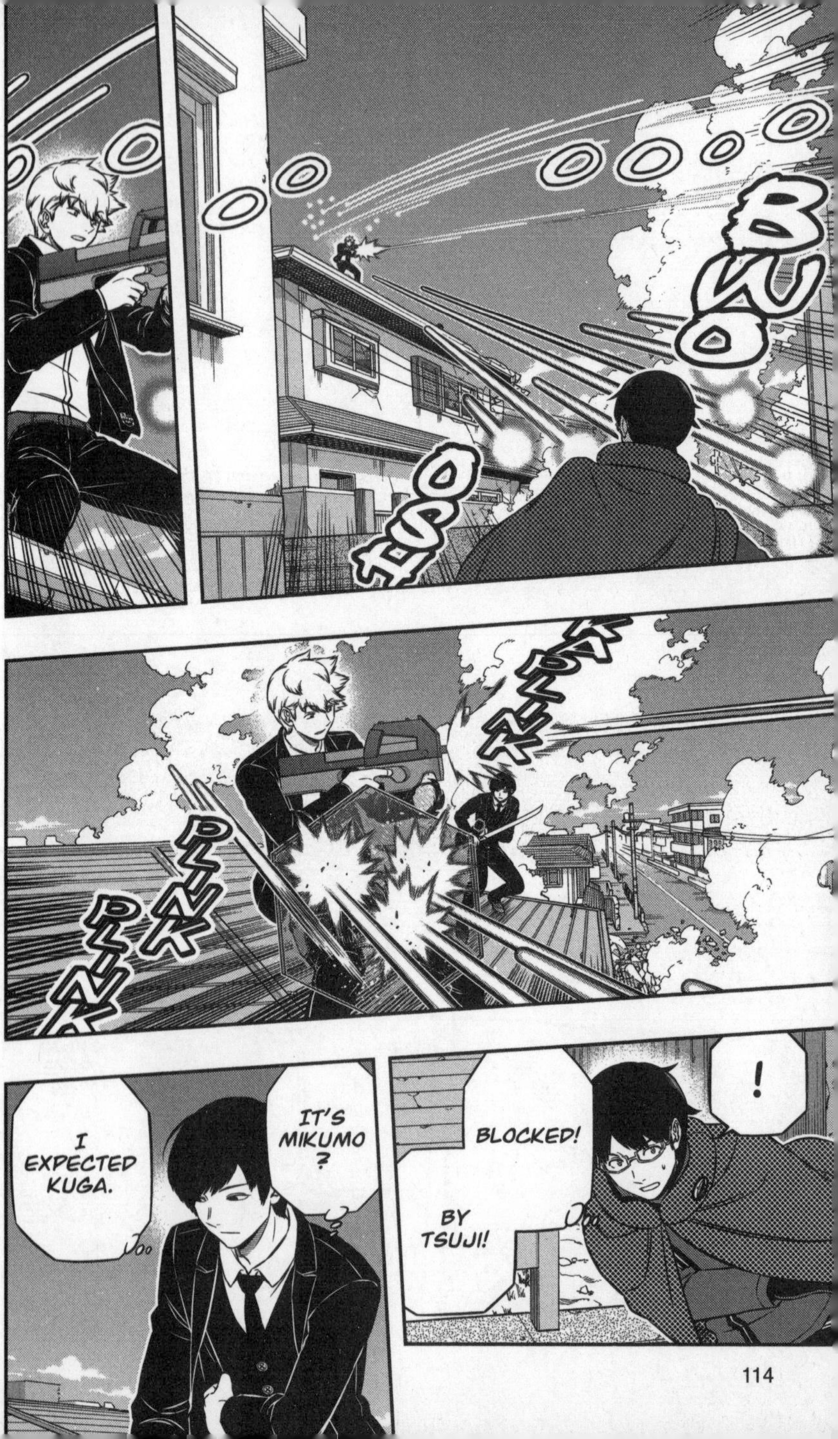
BUOOOOOOOOOO
PLINK
PLINK
PLINK
!
BLOCKED!
BY TSUJI!
IT'S MIKUMO?
I EXPECTED KUGA.

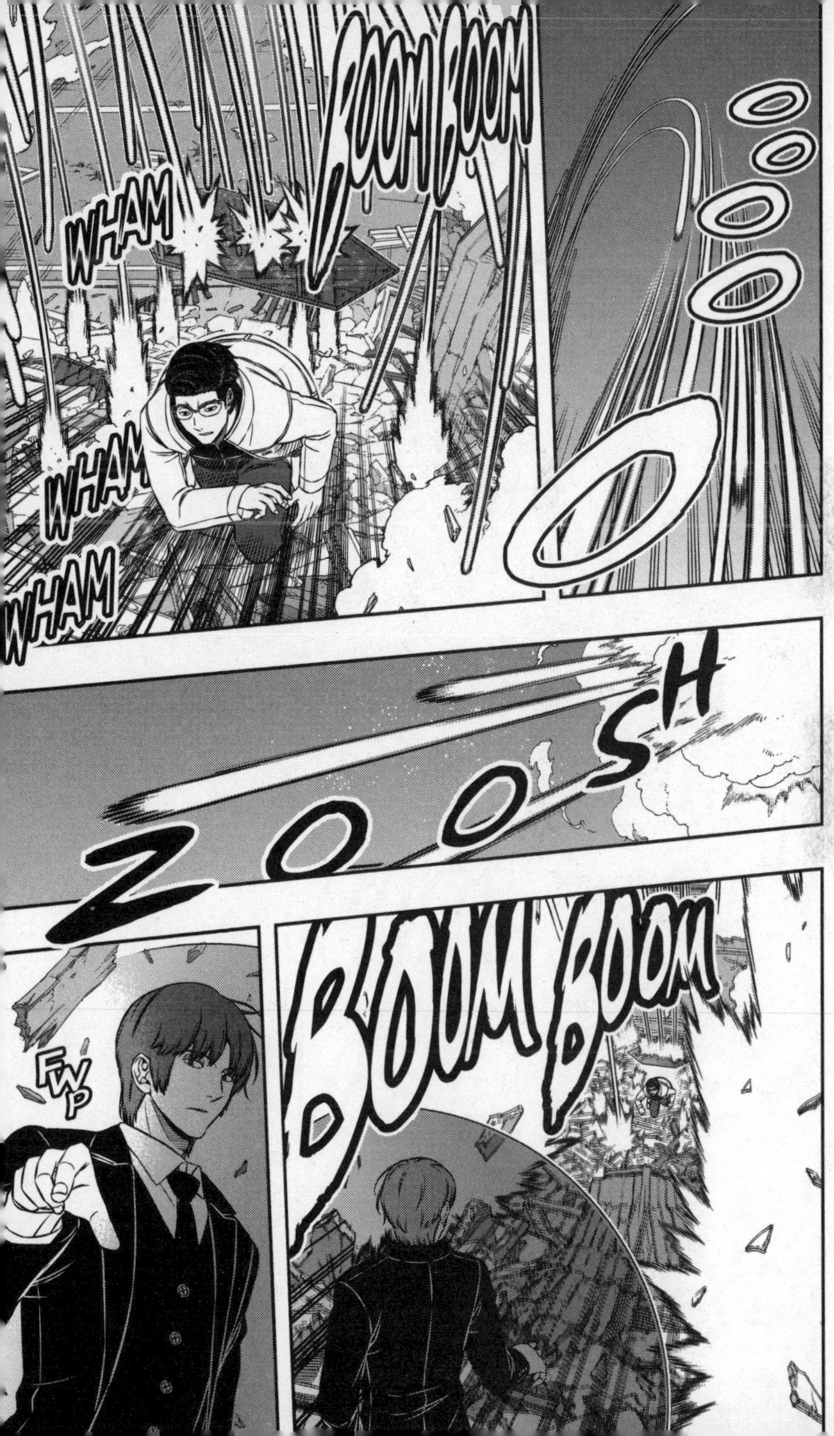
BOOM BOOM
WHAM
WHAM
WHAM
ZOOOOSH
BOOM BOOM
FWP

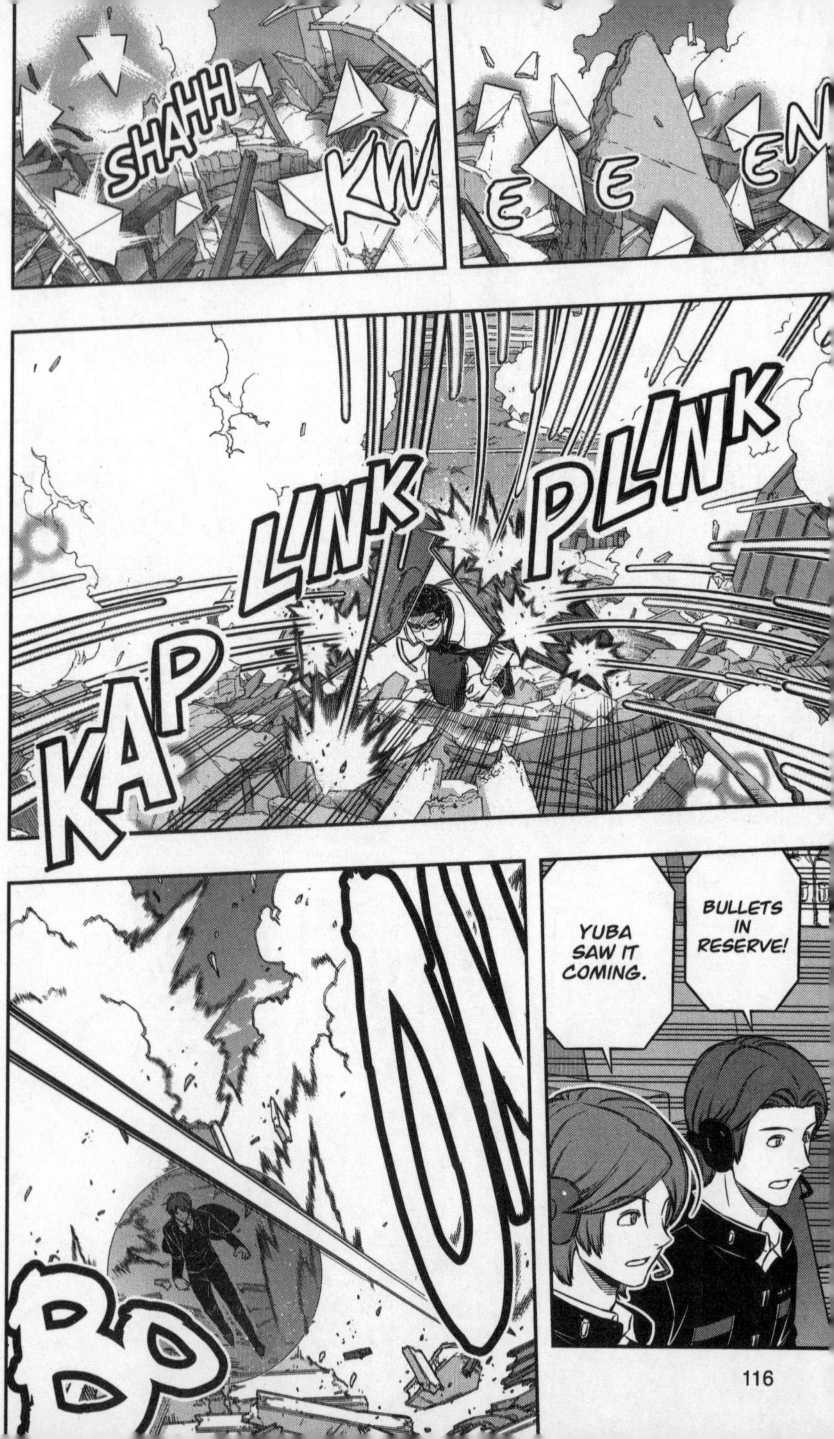

SHAHH
KW
E E EN
KAP LINK PLINK
BULLETS IN RESERVE!
YUBA SAW IT COMING.
BO

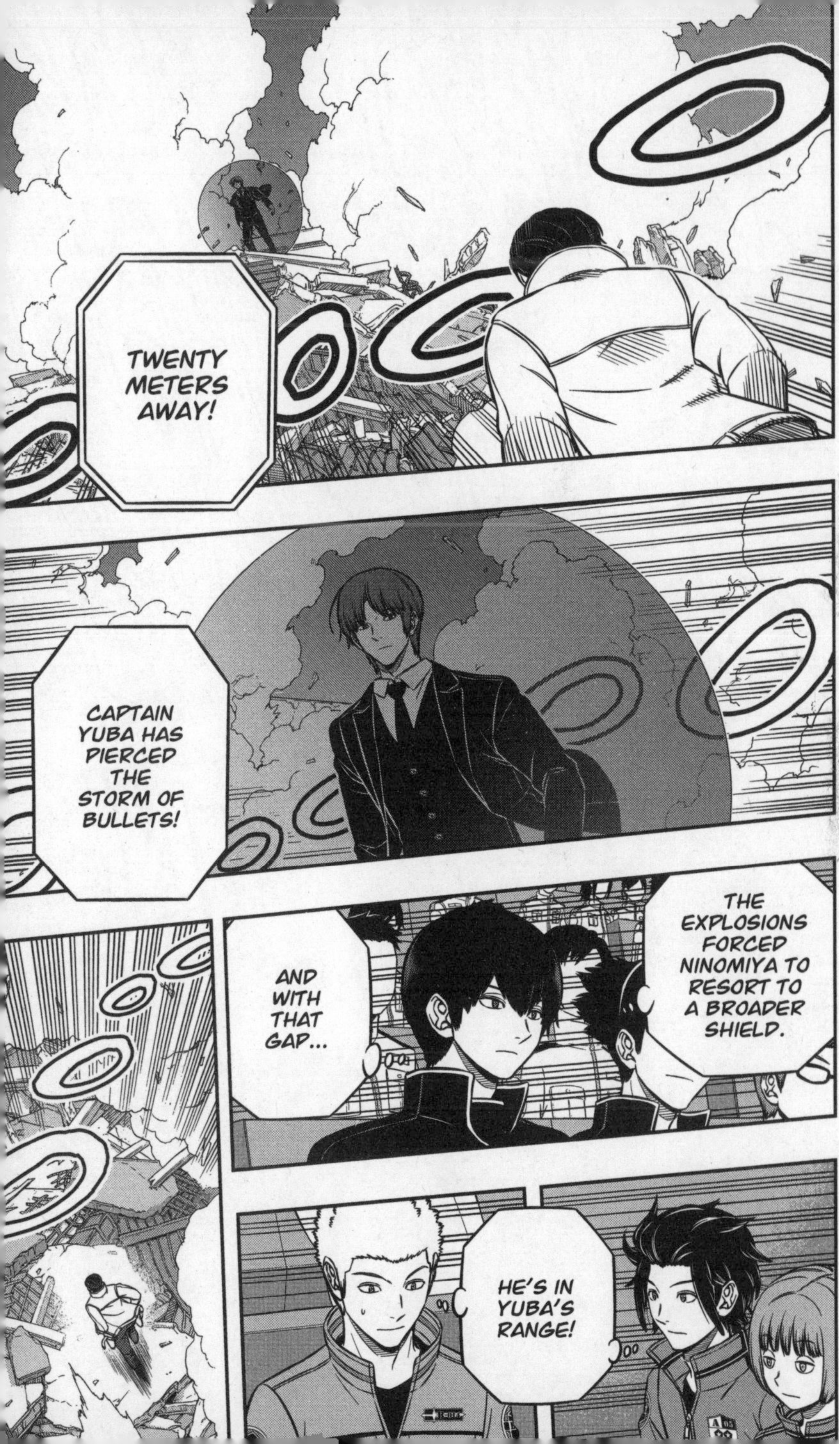
TWENTY METERS AWAY!
CAPTAIN YUBA HAS PIERCED THE STORM OF BULLETS!
THE EXPLOSIONS FORCED NINOMIYA TO RESORT TO A BROADER SHIELD.
AND WITH THAT GAP...
HE'S IN YUBA'S RANGE!

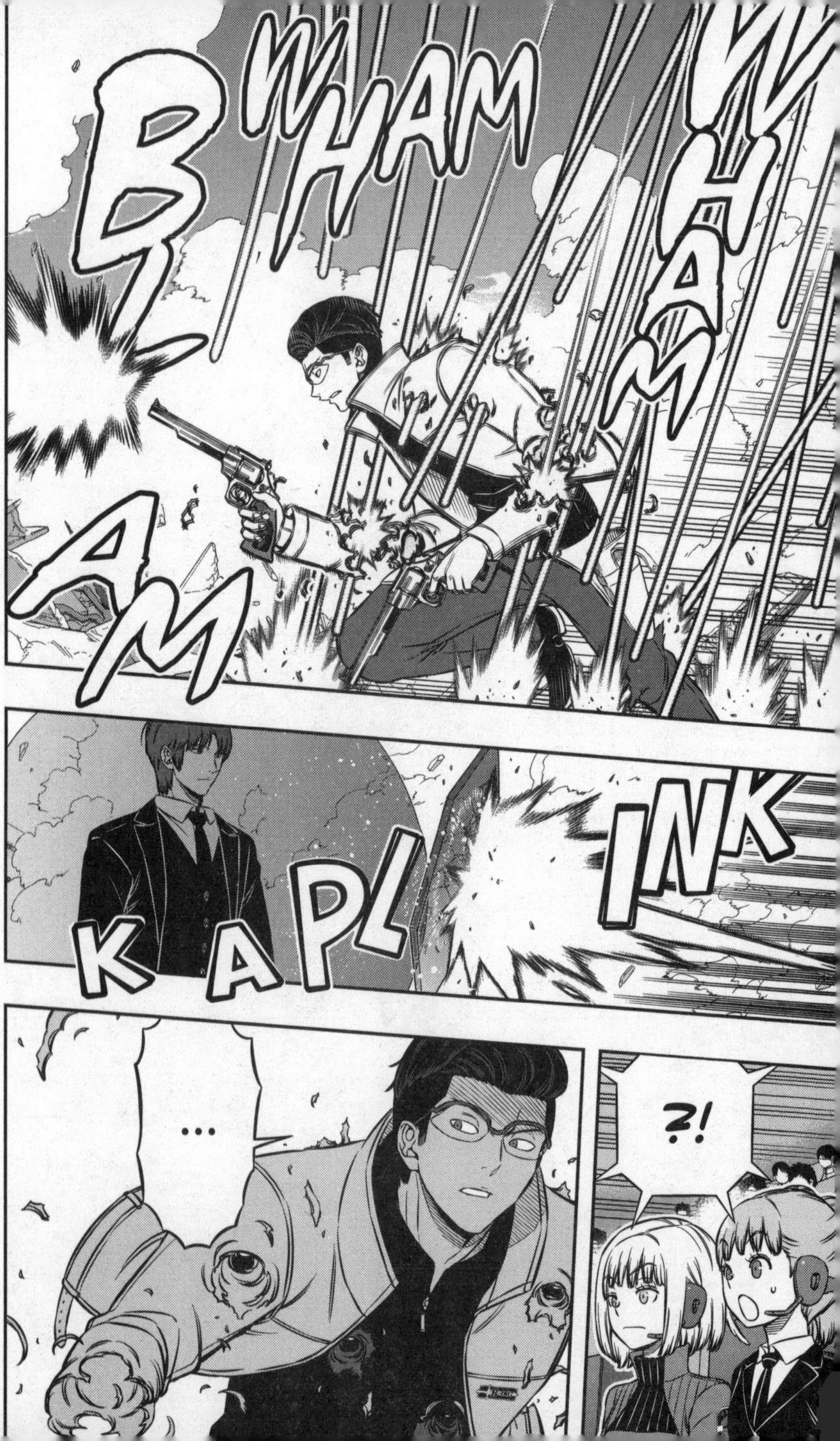
WHAM
BWHAM
AM
KAPLINK
?!
...

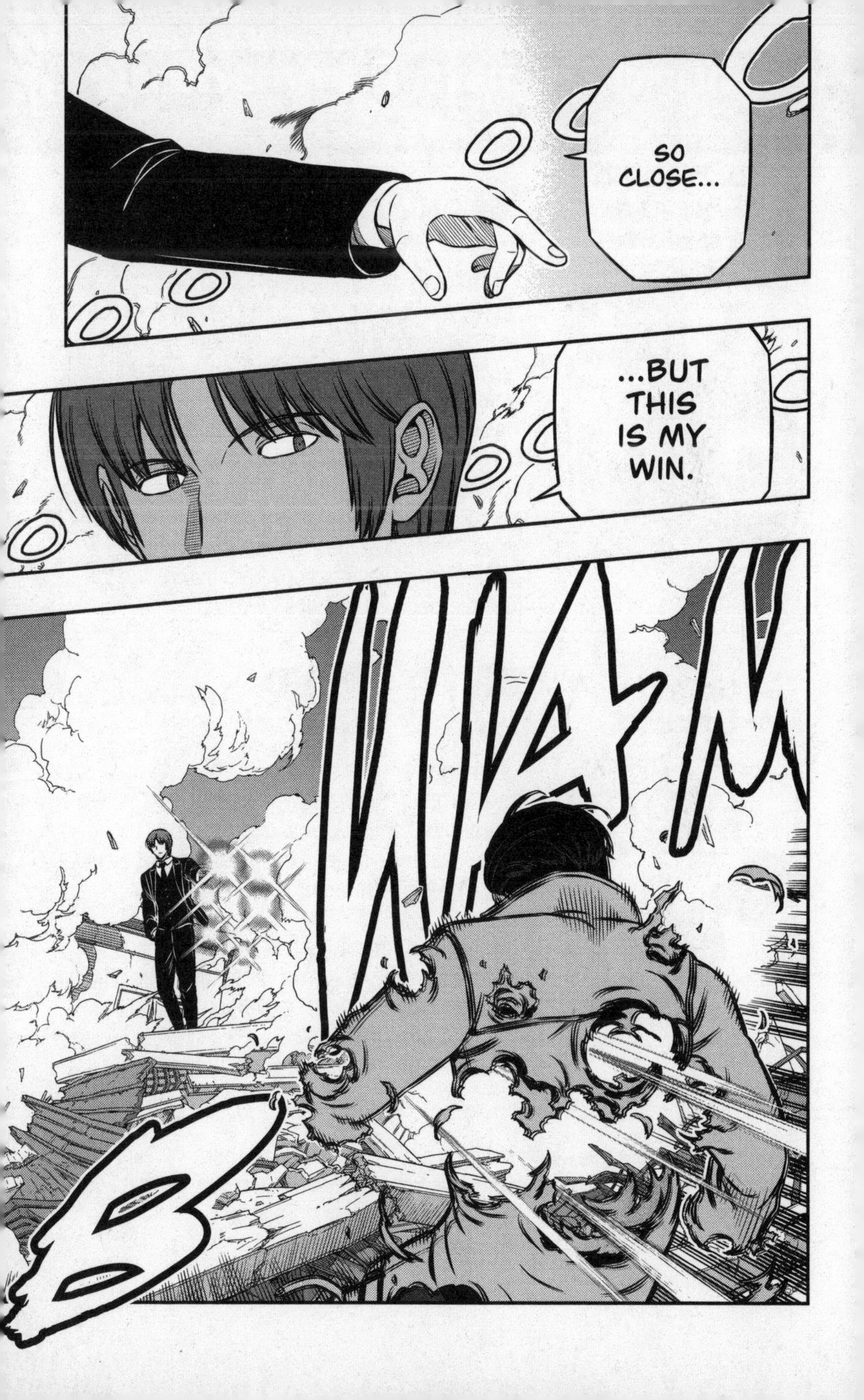
SO CLOSE...
...BUT THIS IS MY WIN.
WHAM

Squad Emblem Commentary: Part 2

Tachikawa Squad's Emblem

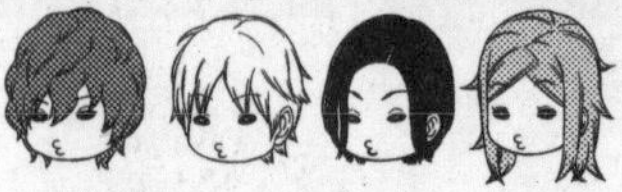

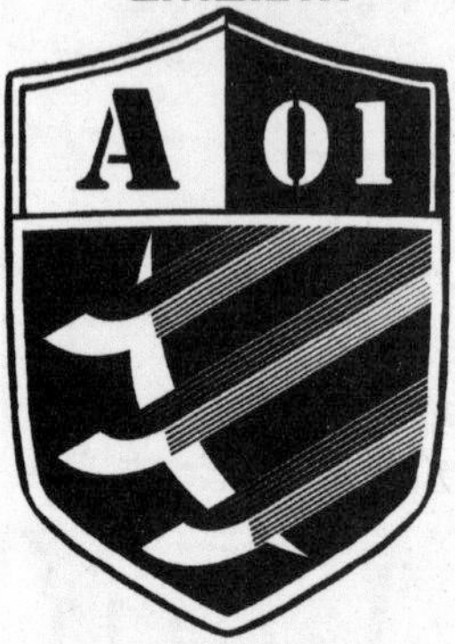
A 01

Commentary:
Clearly, you've got three katana representing the three fighters of Tachikawa Squad, plus the crescent moon in the background representing Kunichika.
However, it was designed with the original three members in mind, so Yuiga isn't technically represented.
That's why Yuiga came off so pathetic during the explanation of the emblem in volume 13.
I probably wrote this somewhere before, but the member before Yuiga was Torimaru.

Kazama Squad's Emblem

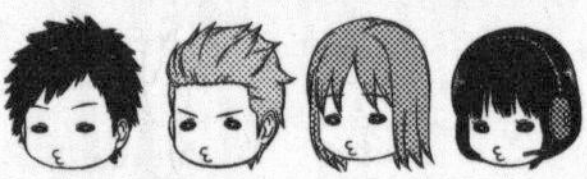

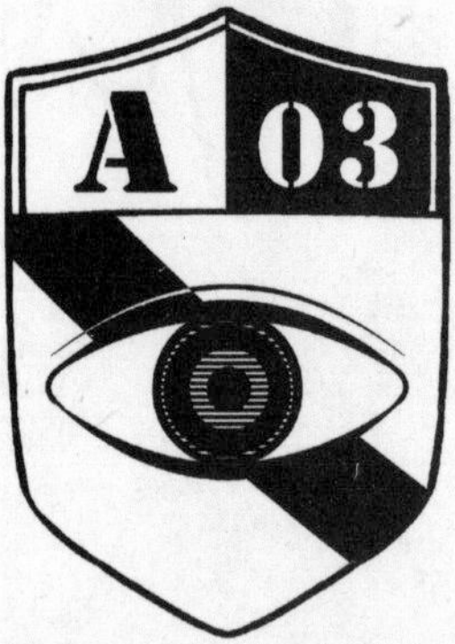
A 03

Commentary:
Stealth squad means "invisible to the eye," so we have another self-explanatory design.
It's not Kazama's style to be excessive, but what happens when those stealth tactics fall out of fashion?
It's true that Kikuchihara has particularly good hearing, but an emblem consisting of just a big ear would be pretty bizarre, so everyone's glad they went with an eye instead.
Simple is best.

I don't remember this being used for any particular event, but when the manager in charge of these bonus pages sent me a commentary page, I got to work. There are some mundane spoilers here, but nothing major, so don't worry about it.

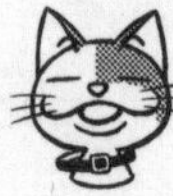

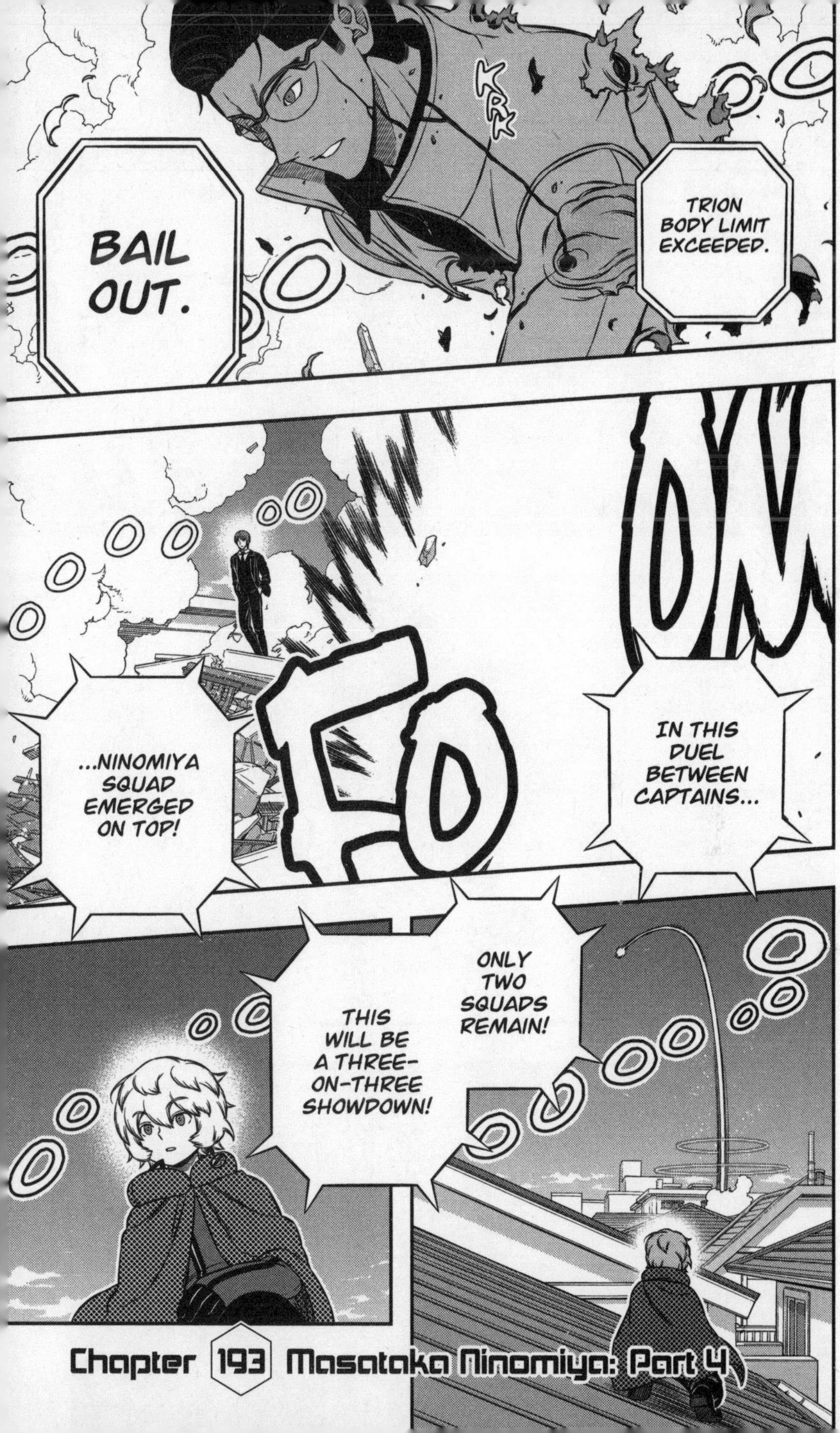
KRK
TRION BODY LIMIT EXCEEDED.
BAIL OUT.
IN THIS DUEL BETWEEN CAPTAINS...
...NINOMIYA SQUAD EMERGED ON TOP!
ONLY TWO SQUADS REMAIN!
THIS WILL BE A THREE-ON-THREE SHOWDOWN!

Chapter 193 Masataka Ninomiya: Part 4

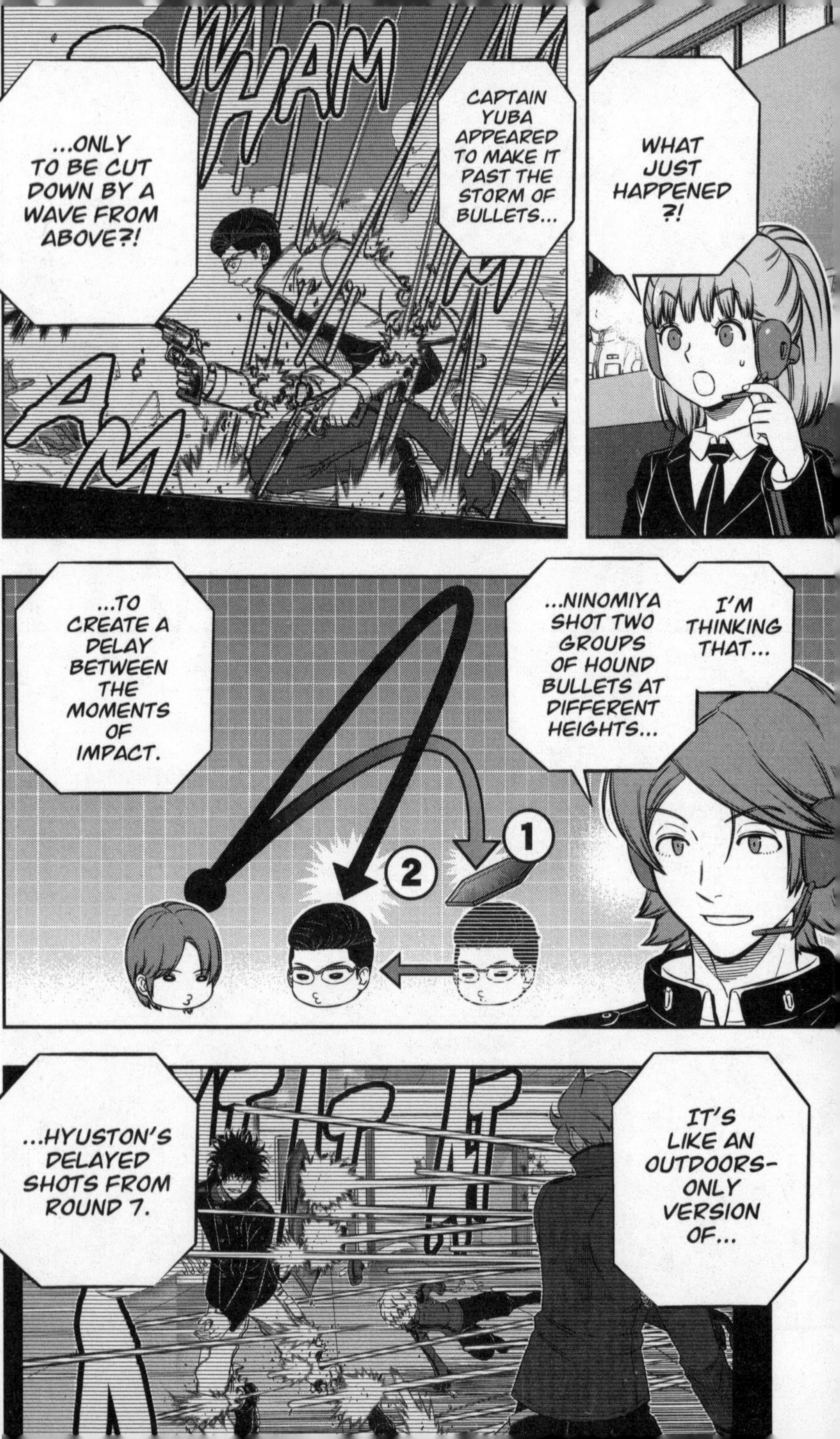
WHAT JUST HAPPENED?!
CAPTAIN YUBA APPEARED TO MAKE IT PAST THE STORM OF BULLETS...
WHAM
...ONLY TO BE CUT DOWN BY A WAVE FROM ABOVE?!
I'M THINKING THAT...
...NINOMIYA SHOT TWO GROUPS OF HOUND BULLETS AT DIFFERENT HEIGHTS...
...TO CREATE A DELAY BETWEEN THE MOMENTS OF IMPACT.
1
2
IT'S LIKE AN OUTDOORS-ONLY VERSION OF...
...HYUSTON'S DELAYED SHOTS FROM ROUND 7.

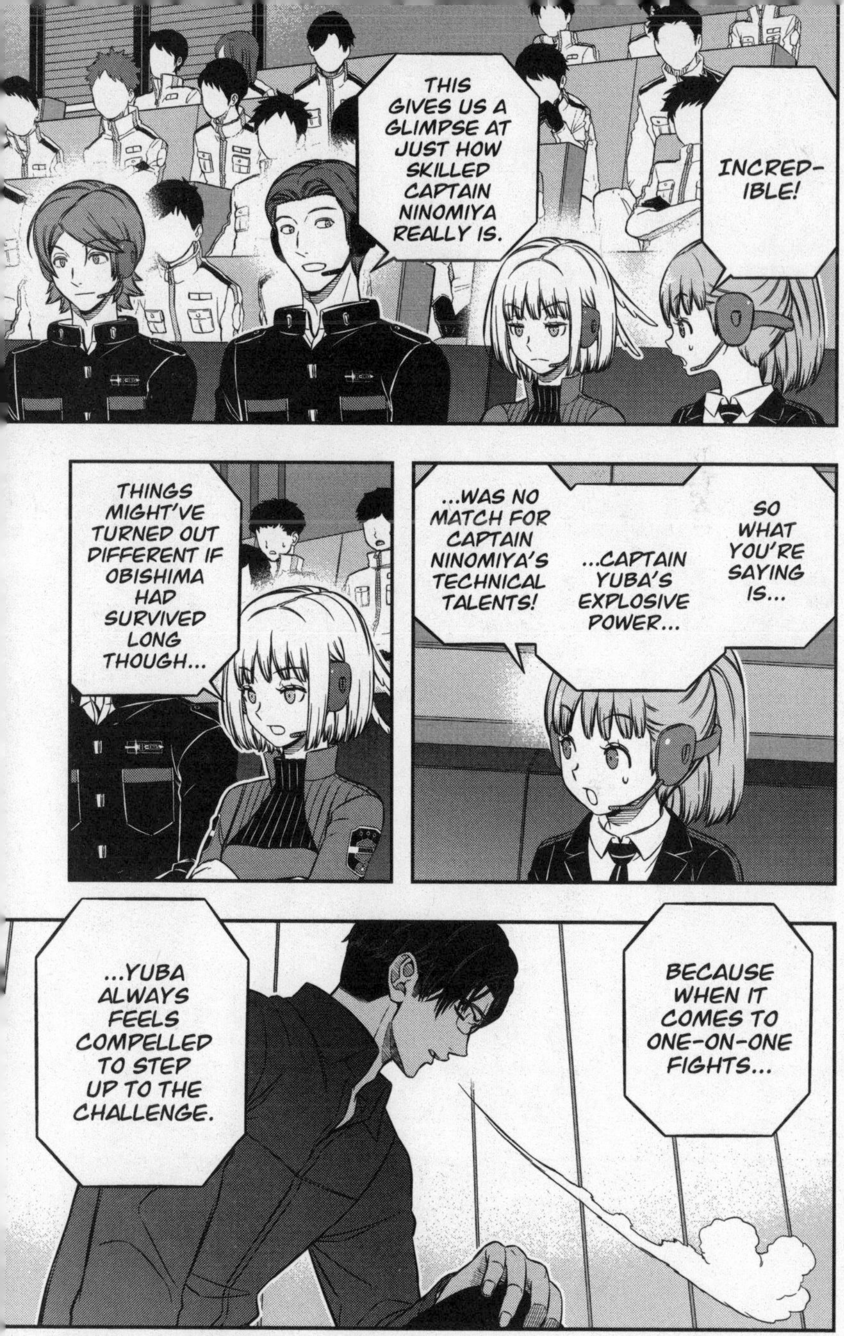
INCRED-IBLE!
THIS GIVES US A GLIMPSE AT JUST HOW SKILLED CAPTAIN NINOMIYA REALLY IS.
SO WHAT YOU'RE SAYING IS...
...CAPTAIN YUBA'S EXPLOSIVE POWER...
...WAS NO MATCH FOR CAPTAIN NINOMIYA'S TECHNICAL TALENTS!
THINGS MIGHT'VE TURNED OUT DIFFERENT IF OBISHIMA HAD SURVIVED LONG THOUGH...
BECAUSE WHEN IT COMES TO ONE-ON-ONE FIGHTS...
...YUBA ALWAYS FEELS COMPELLED TO STEP UP TO THE CHALLENGE.

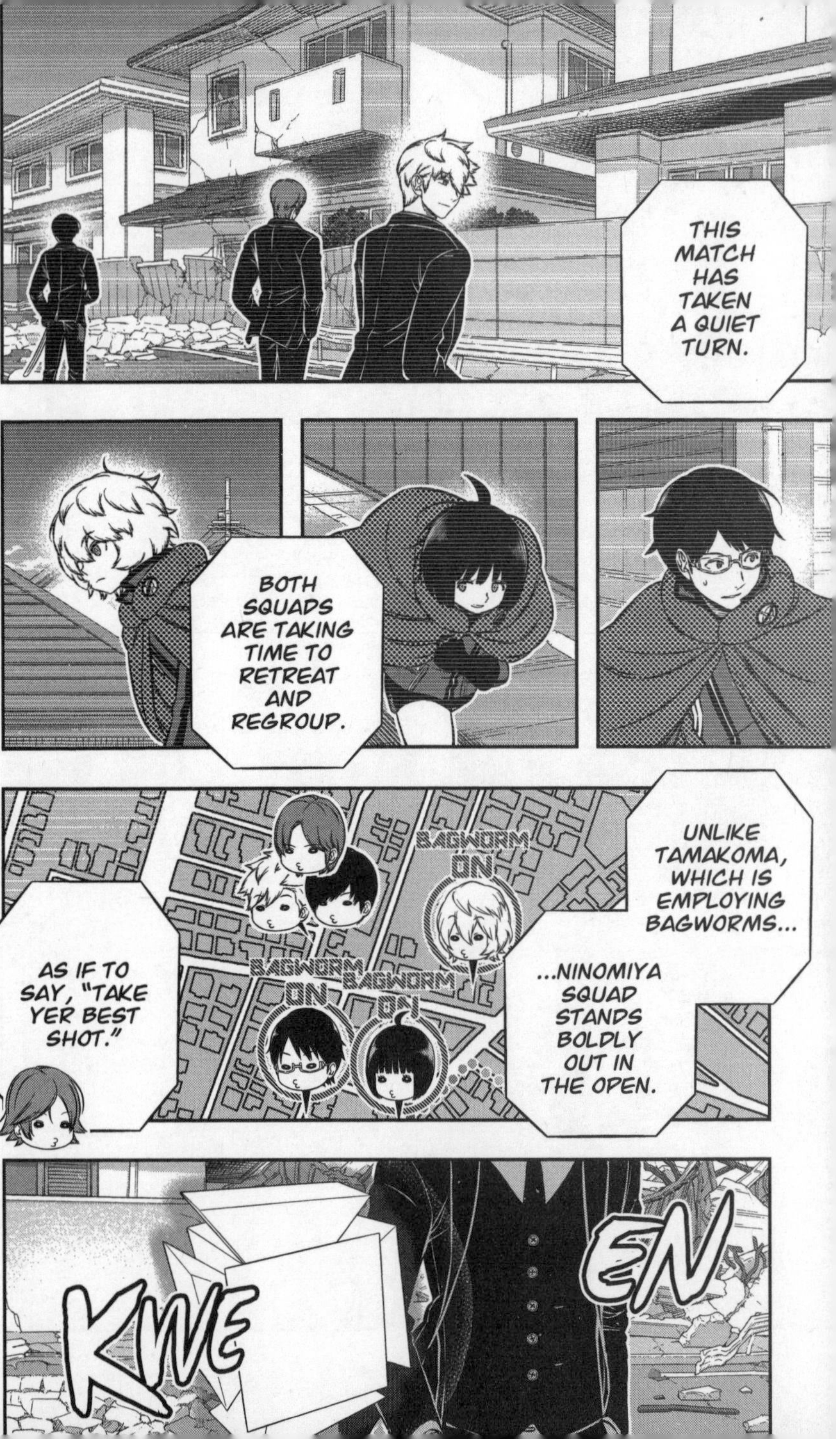
THIS MATCH HAS TAKEN A QUIET TURN.
BOTH SQUADS ARE TAKING TIME TO RETREAT AND REGROUP.
UNLIKE TAMAKOMA, WHICH IS EMPLOYING BAGWORMS...
BAGWORM ON
BAGWORM ON
BAGWORM ON
...NINOMIYA SQUAD STANDS BOLDLY OUT IN THE OPEN.
AS IF TO SAY, "TAKE YER BEST SHOT."
EN
KWE

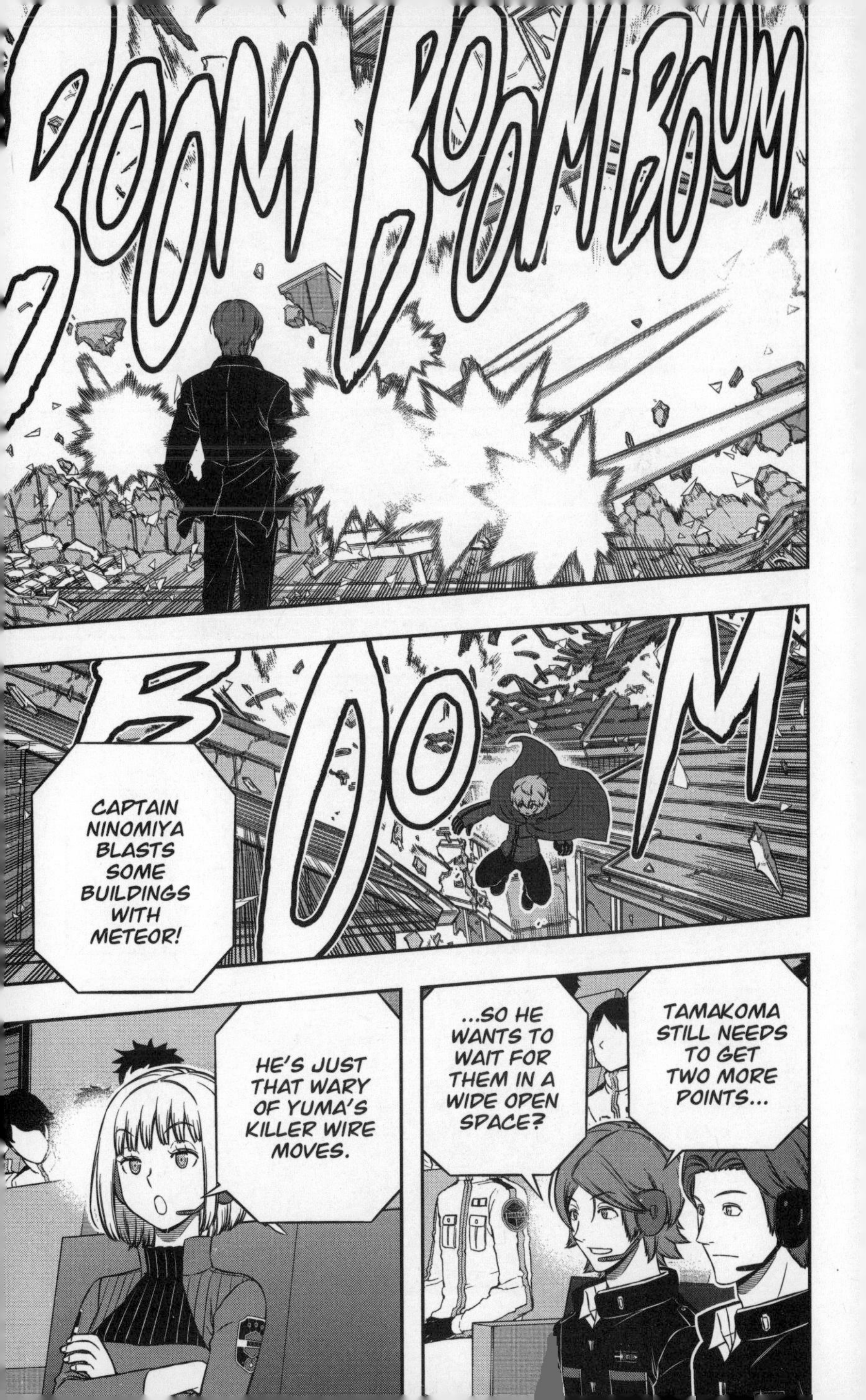
BOOM BOOM BOOM
BOOM
CAPTAIN NINOMIYA BLASTS SOME BUILDINGS WITH METEOR!
TAMAKOMA STILL NEEDS TO GET TWO MORE POINTS...
...SO HE WANTS TO WAIT FOR THEM IN A WIDE OPEN SPACE?
HE'S JUST THAT WARY OF YUMA'S KILLER WIRE MOVES.

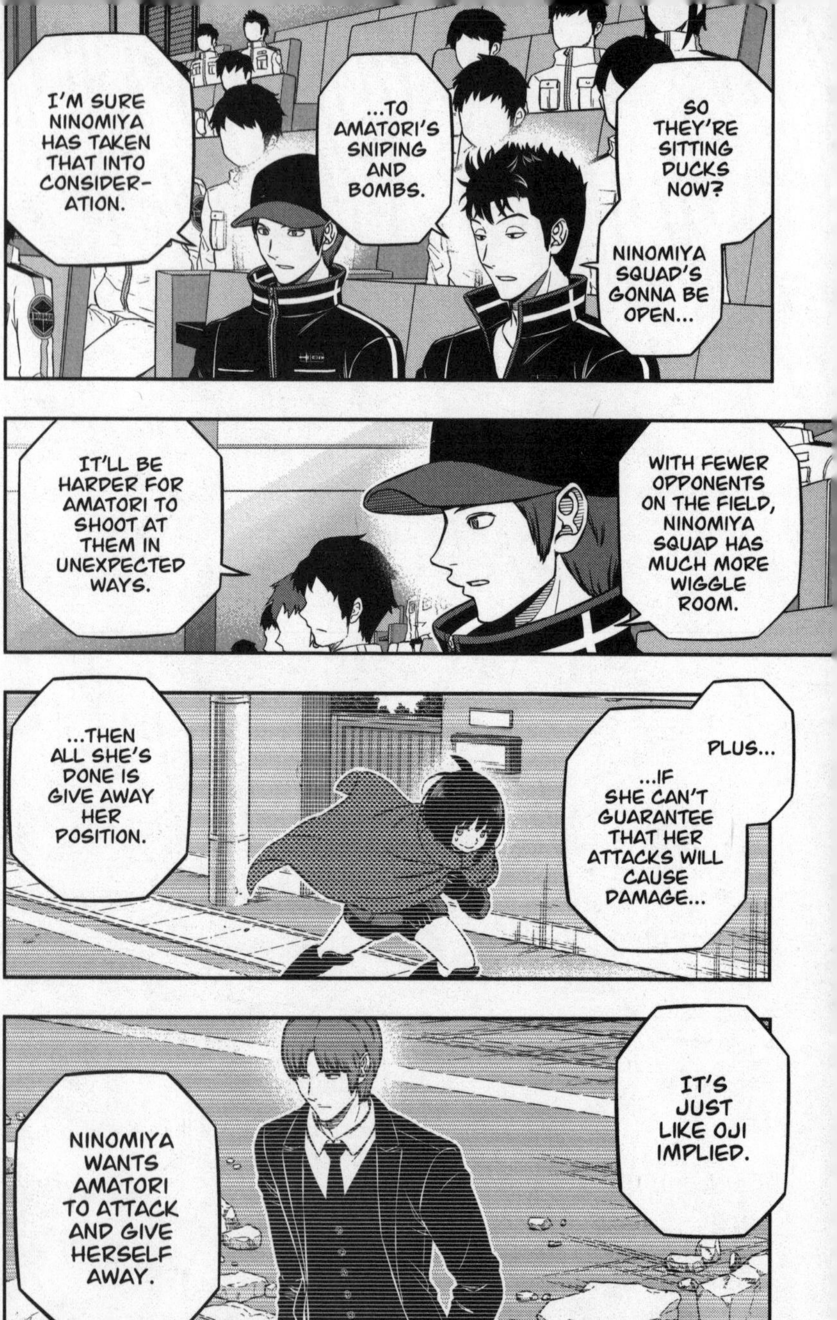
SO THEY'RE SITTING DUCKS NOW?
NINOMIYA SQUAD'S GONNA BE OPEN...
...TO AMATORI'S SNIPING AND BOMBS.
I'M SURE NINOMIYA HAS TAKEN THAT INTO CONSIDER-ATION.
WITH FEWER OPPONENTS ON THE FIELD, NINOMIYA SQUAD HAS MUCH MORE WIGGLE ROOM.
IT'LL BE HARDER FOR AMATORI TO SHOOT AT THEM IN UNEXPECTED WAYS.
PLUS...
...IF SHE CAN'T GUARANTEE THAT HER ATTACKS WILL CAUSE DAMAGE...
...THEN ALL SHE'S DONE IS GIVE AWAY HER POSITION.
IT'S JUST LIKE OJI IMPLIED.
NINOMIYA WANTS AMATORI TO ATTACK AND GIVE HERSELF AWAY.

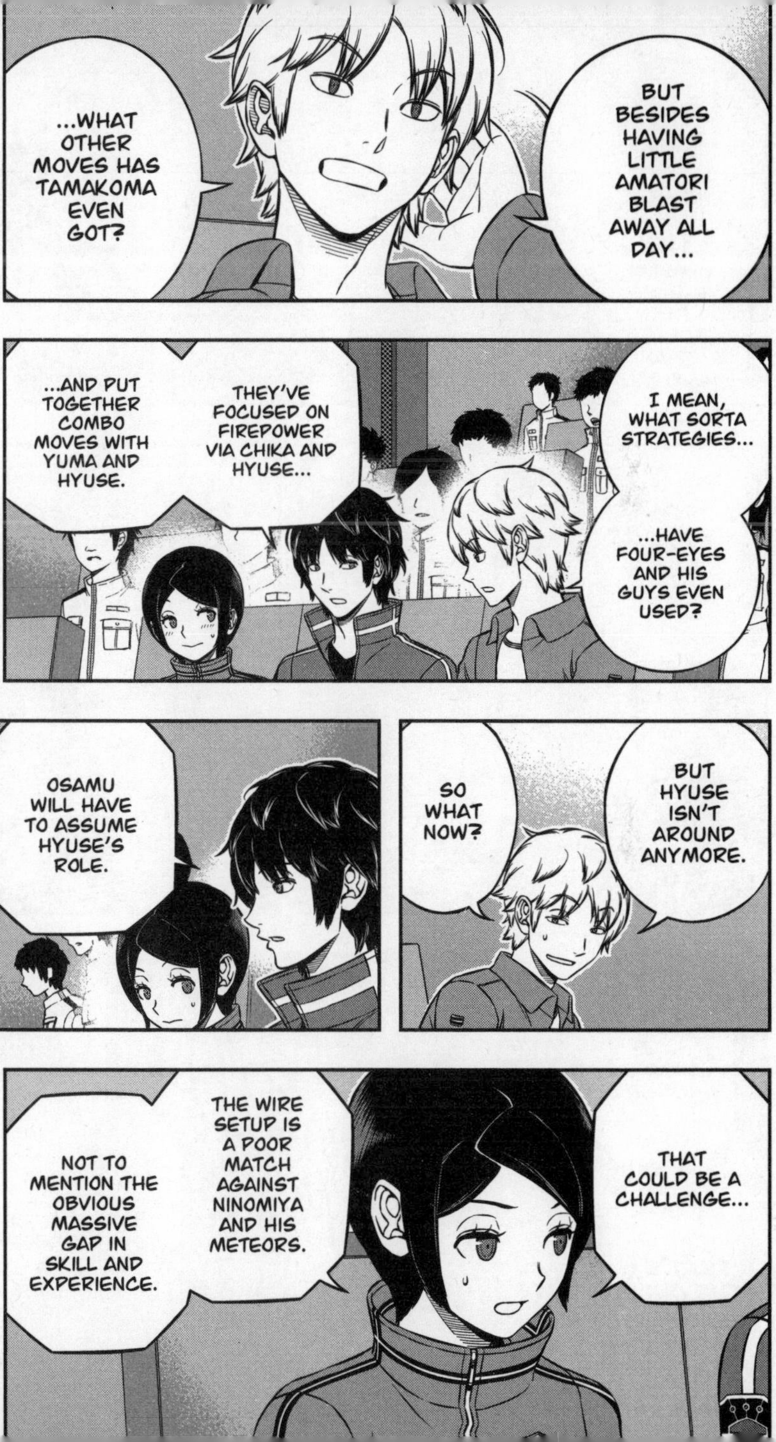
BUT BESIDES HAVING LITTLE AMATORI BLAST AWAY ALL DAY...
...WHAT OTHER MOVES HAS TAMAKOMA EVEN GOT?
I MEAN, WHAT SORTA STRATEGIES...
...HAVE FOUR-EYES AND HIS GUYS EVEN USED?
THEY'VE FOCUSED ON FIREPOWER VIA CHIKA AND HYUSE...
...AND PUT TOGETHER COMBO MOVES WITH YUMA AND HYUSE.
BUT HYUSE ISN'T AROUND ANYMORE.
SO WHAT NOW?
OSAMU WILL HAVE TO ASSUME HYUSE'S ROLE.
THAT COULD BE A CHALLENGE...
THE WIRE SETUP IS A POOR MATCH AGAINST NINOMIYA AND HIS METEORS.
NOT TO MENTION THE OBVIOUS MASSIVE GAP IN SKILL AND EXPERIENCE.

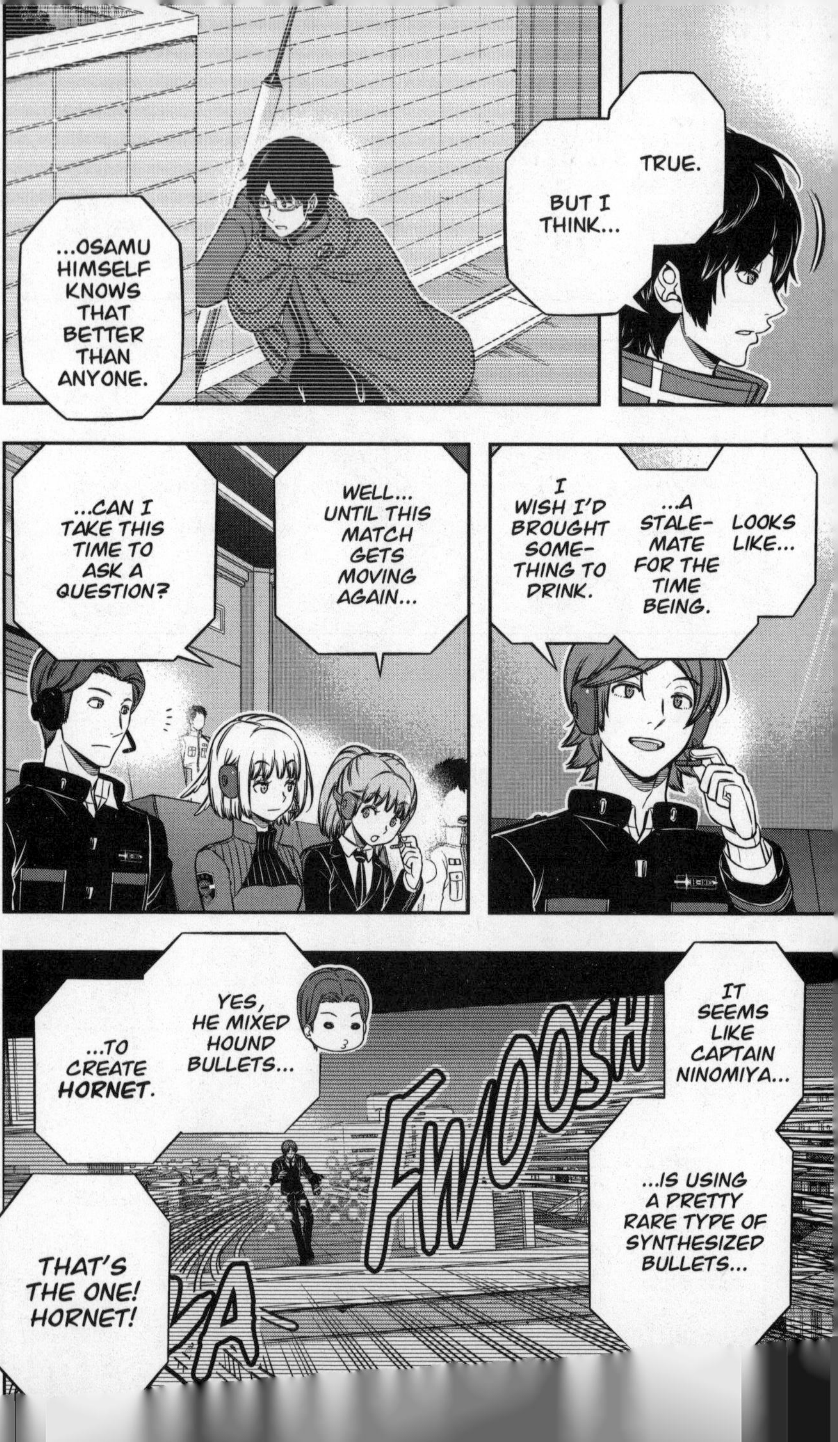
TRUE.
BUT I THINK...
...OSAMU HIMSELF KNOWS THAT BETTER THAN ANYONE.
LOOKS LIKE...
...A STALEMATE FOR THE TIME BEING.
I WISH I'D BROUGHT SOMETHING TO DRINK.
WELL... UNTIL THIS MATCH GETS MOVING AGAIN...
...CAN I TAKE THIS TIME TO ASK A QUESTION?
IT SEEMS LIKE CAPTAIN NINOMIYA...
...IS USING A PRETTY RARE TYPE OF SYNTHESIZED BULLETS...
FWOOSH
YES, HE MIXED HOUND BULLETS...
...TO CREATE HORNET.
THAT'S THE ONE! HORNET!

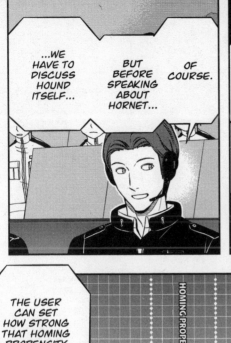

AS I'M SURE MANY OF US ARE ONLY SEEING HORNET FOR THE FIRST TIME...
...WOULD YOU MIND BREAKING IT DOWN FOR US, AGENT KURAUCHI...?
OF COURSE.
BUT BEFORE SPEAKING ABOUT HORNET...
...WE HAVE TO DISCUSS HOUND ITSELF...
TO START WITH...
...HOUND BULLETS DON'T ALWAYS HOME IN ON THE OPPONENT.
HOMING PROPENSITY
NONE
STRONG
WEAK
THE USER CAN SET HOW STRONG THAT HOMING PROPENSITY IS WITH EACH ATTACK.
BY FIDDLING WITH THOSE SETTINGS...
HOMING PROPENSITY
NONE
STRONG
WEAK
...ONE CAN ACHIEVE THAT MOUNTAIN-LIKE ARC WE WITNESSED EARLIER.

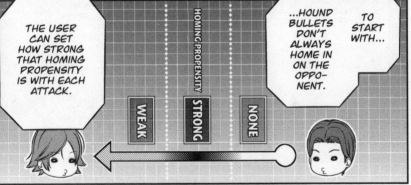

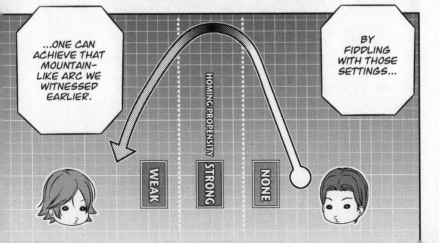

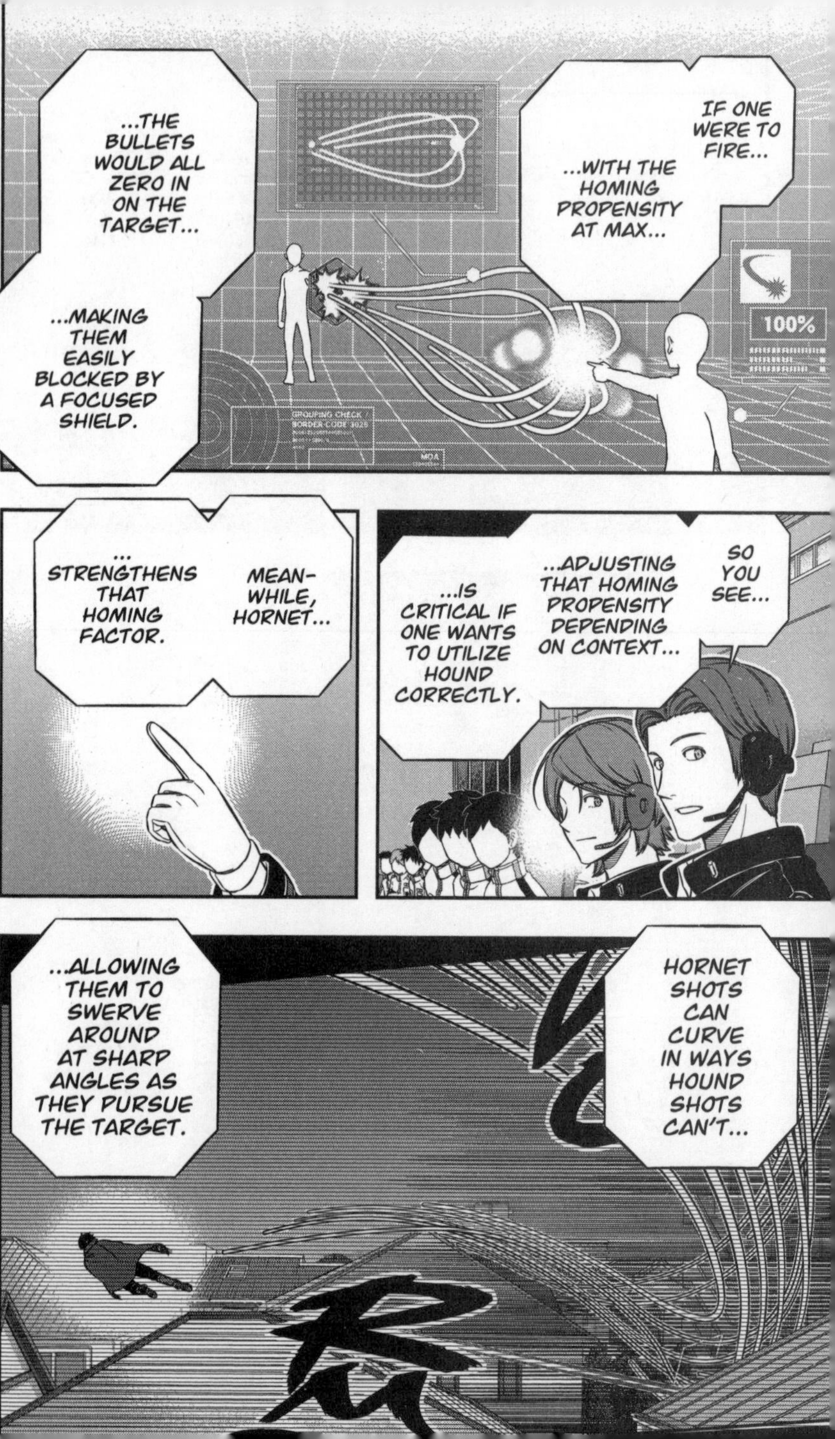
IF ONE WERE TO FIRE...
...WITH THE HOMING PROPENSITY AT MAX...
100%
...THE BULLETS WOULD ALL ZERO IN ON THE TARGET...
...MAKING THEM EASILY BLOCKED BY A FOCUSED SHIELD.
GROUPING CHECK /
BORDER-CODE 3025
SO YOU SEE...
...ADJUSTING THAT HOMING PROPENSITY DEPENDING ON CONTEXT...
...IS CRITICAL IF ONE WANTS TO UTILIZE HOUND CORRECTLY.
MEAN-WHILE, HORNET...
...STRENGTHENS THAT HOMING FACTOR.
HORNET SHOTS CAN CURVE IN WAYS HOUND SHOTS CAN'T...
...ALLOWING THEM TO SWERVE AROUND AT SHARP ANGLES AS THEY PURSUE THE TARGET.

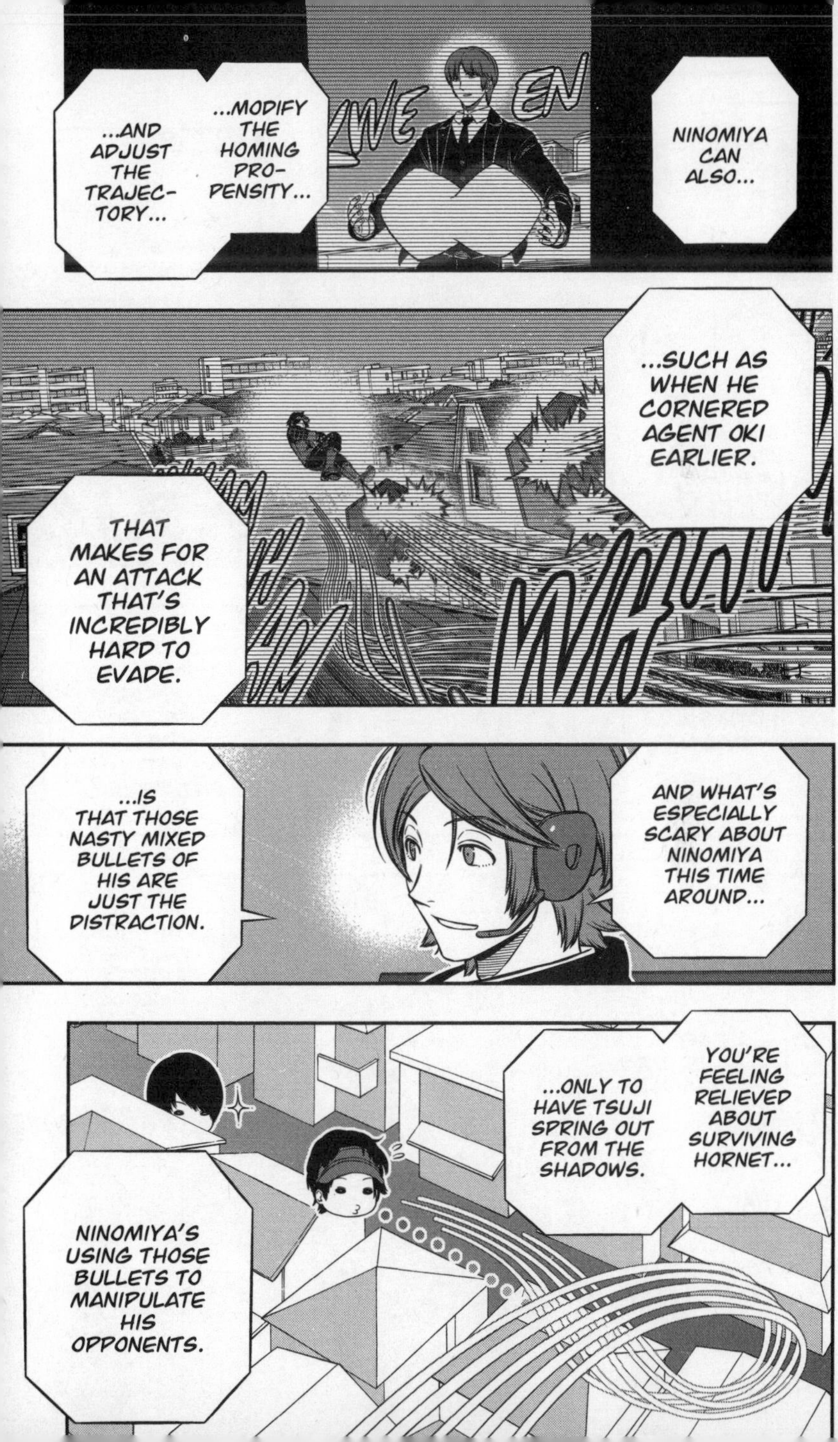
NINOMIYA CAN ALSO...
...MODIFY THE HOMING PRO-PENSITY...
...AND ADJUST THE TRAJEC-TORY...
...SUCH AS WHEN HE CORNERED AGENT OKI EARLIER.
THAT MAKES FOR AN ATTACK THAT'S INCREDIBLY HARD TO EVADE.
AND WHAT'S ESPECIALLY SCARY ABOUT NINOMIYA THIS TIME AROUND...
...IS THAT THOSE NASTY MIXED BULLETS OF HIS ARE JUST THE DISTRACTION.
YOU'RE FEELING RELIEVED ABOUT SURVIVING HORNET...
...ONLY TO HAVE TSUJI SPRING OUT FROM THE SHADOWS.
NINOMIYA'S USING THOSE BULLETS TO MANIPULATE HIS OPPONENTS.

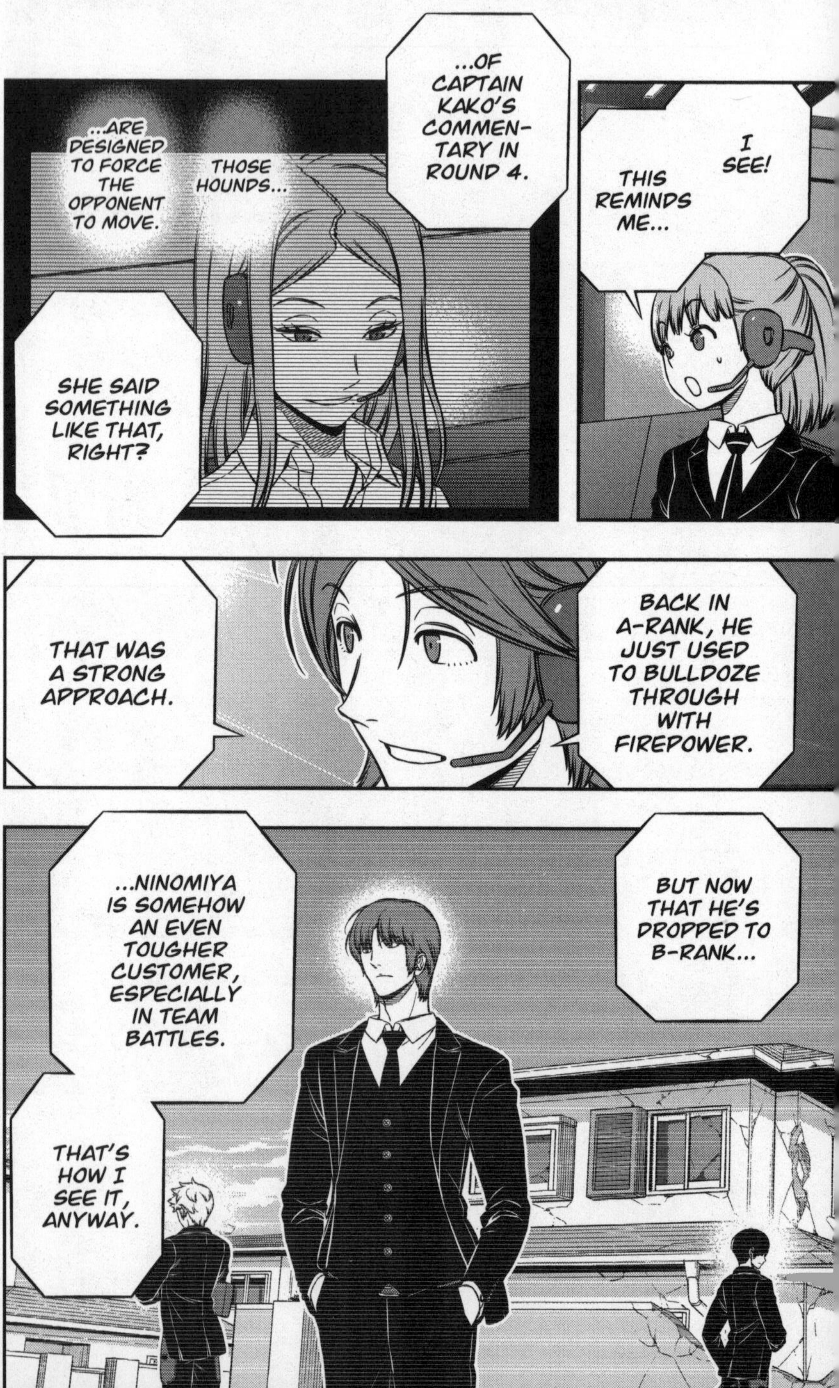
I SEE!
THIS REMINDS ME...
...OF CAPTAIN KAKO'S COMMENTARY IN ROUND 4.
THOSE HOUNDS...
...ARE DESIGNED TO FORCE THE OPPONENT TO MOVE.
SHE SAID SOMETHING LIKE THAT, RIGHT?
BACK IN A-RANK, HE JUST USED TO BULLDOZE THROUGH WITH FIREPOWER.
THAT WAS A STRONG APPROACH.
BUT NOW THAT HE'S DROPPED TO B-RANK...
...NINOMIYA IS SOMEHOW AN EVEN TOUGHER CUSTOMER, ESPECIALLY IN TEAM BATTLES.
THAT'S HOW I SEE IT, ANYWAY.

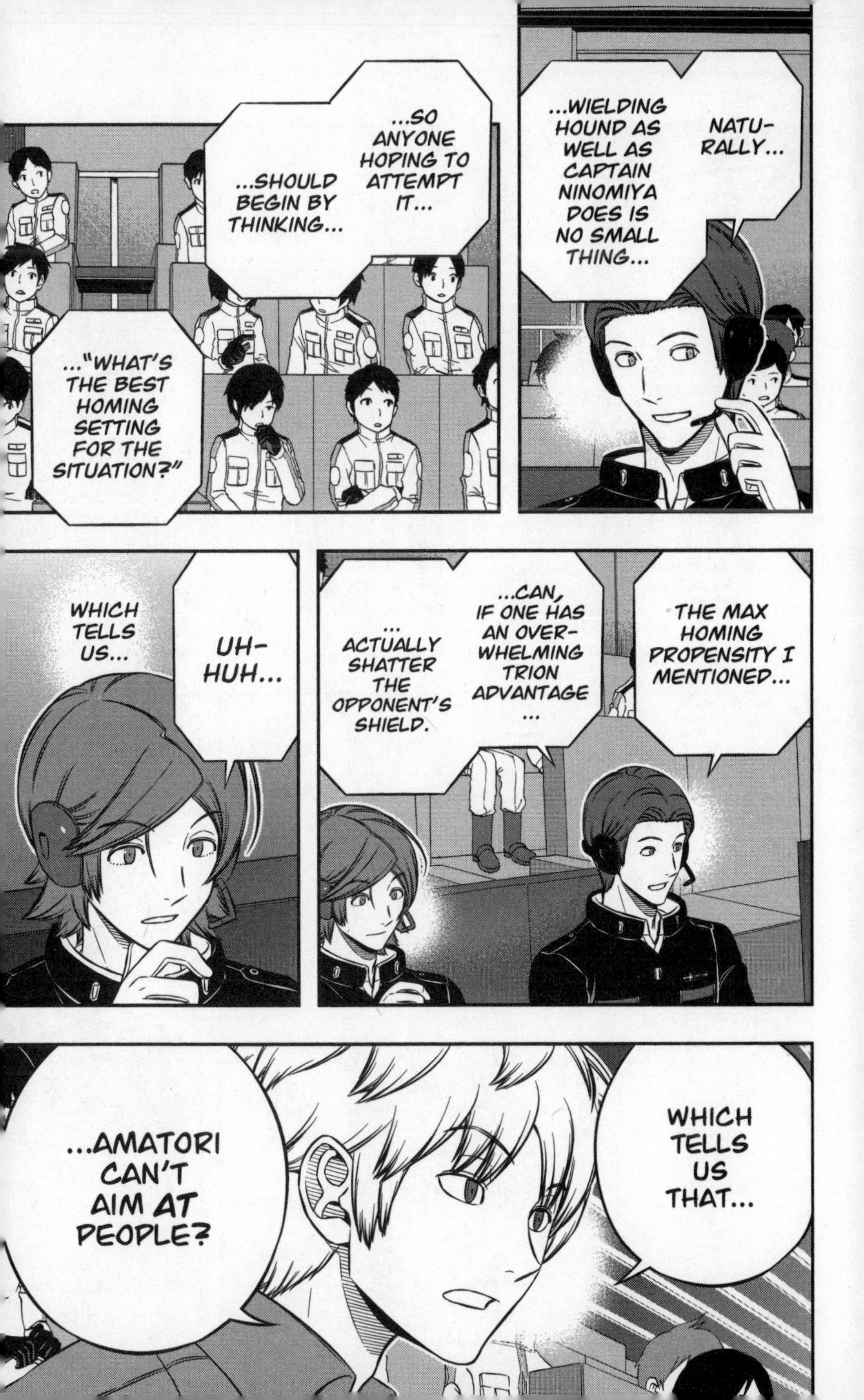
NATURALLY...
...WIELDING HOUND AS WELL AS CAPTAIN NINOMIYA DOES IS NO SMALL THING...
...SO ANYONE HOPING TO ATTEMPT IT...
...SHOULD BEGIN BY THINKING...
..."WHAT'S THE BEST HOMING SETTING FOR THE SITUATION?"
THE MAX HOMING PROPENSITY I MENTIONED...
...CAN, IF ONE HAS AN OVERWHELMING TRION ADVANTAGE...
...ACTUALLY SHATTER THE OPPONENT'S SHIELD.
UH-HUH...
WHICH TELLS US...
WHICH TELLS US THAT...
...AMATORI CAN'T AIM AT PEOPLE?

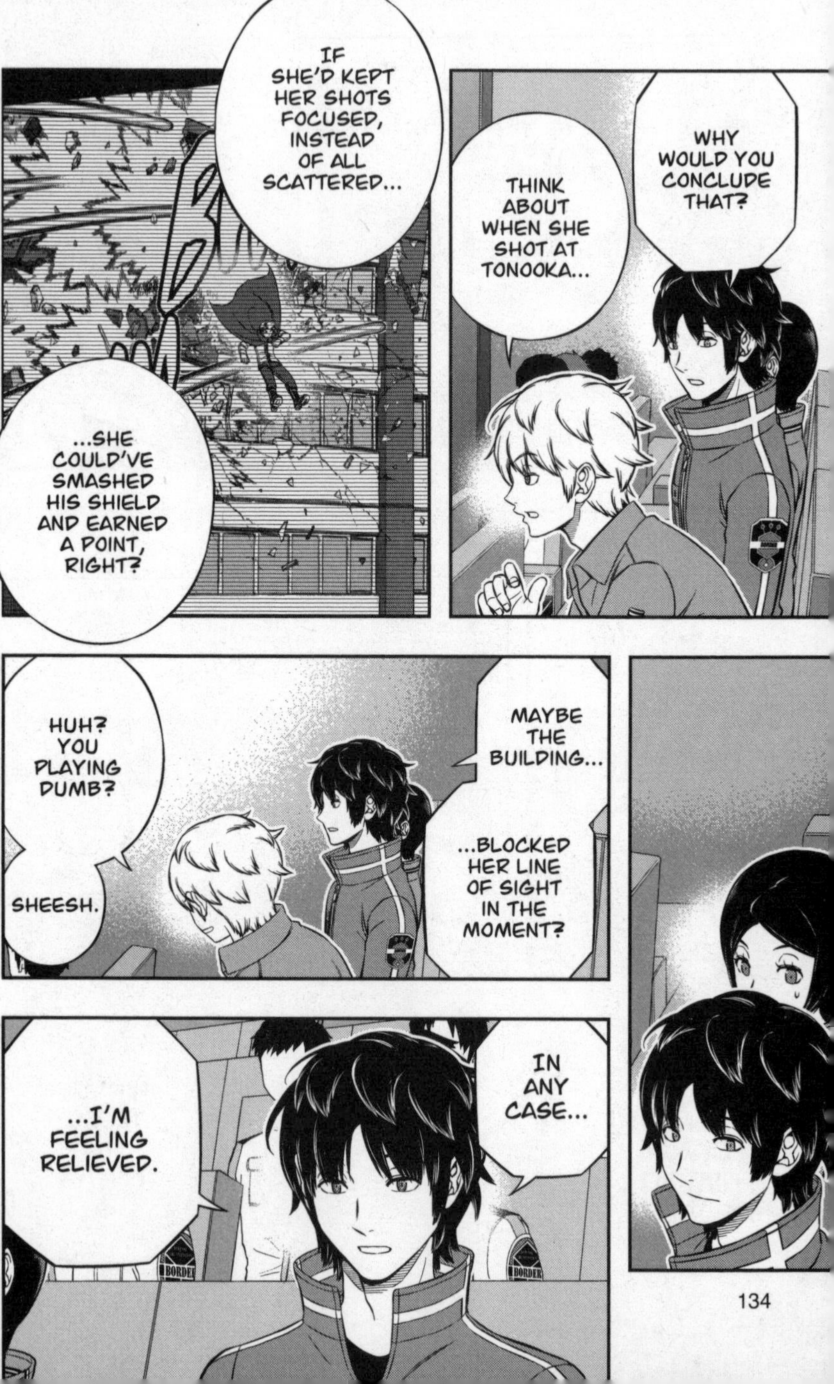
WHY WOULD YOU CONCLUDE THAT?
THINK ABOUT WHEN SHE SHOT AT TONOOKA...
IF SHE'D KEPT HER SHOTS FOCUSED, INSTEAD OF ALL SCATTERED...
...SHE COULD'VE SMASHED HIS SHIELD AND EARNED A POINT, RIGHT?
MAYBE THE BUILDING...
...BLOCKED HER LINE OF SIGHT IN THE MOMENT?
HUH? YOU PLAYING DUMB?
SHEESH.
IN ANY CASE...
...I'M FEELING RELIEVED.

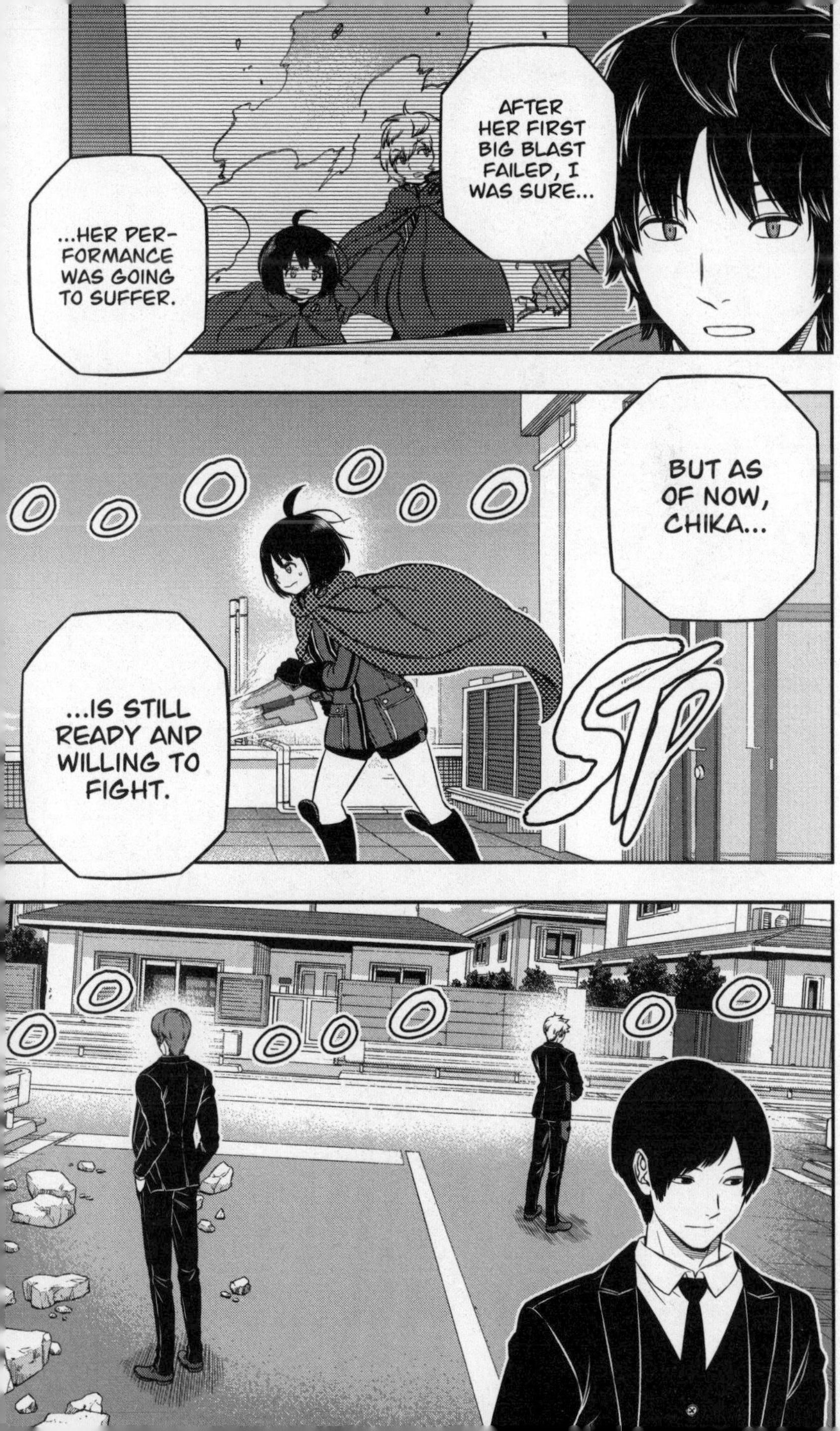
AFTER HER FIRST BIG BLAST FAILED, I WAS SURE...
...HER PER-FORMANCE WAS GOING TO SUFFER.
BUT AS OF NOW, CHIKA...
STP
...IS STILL READY AND WILLING TO FIGHT.

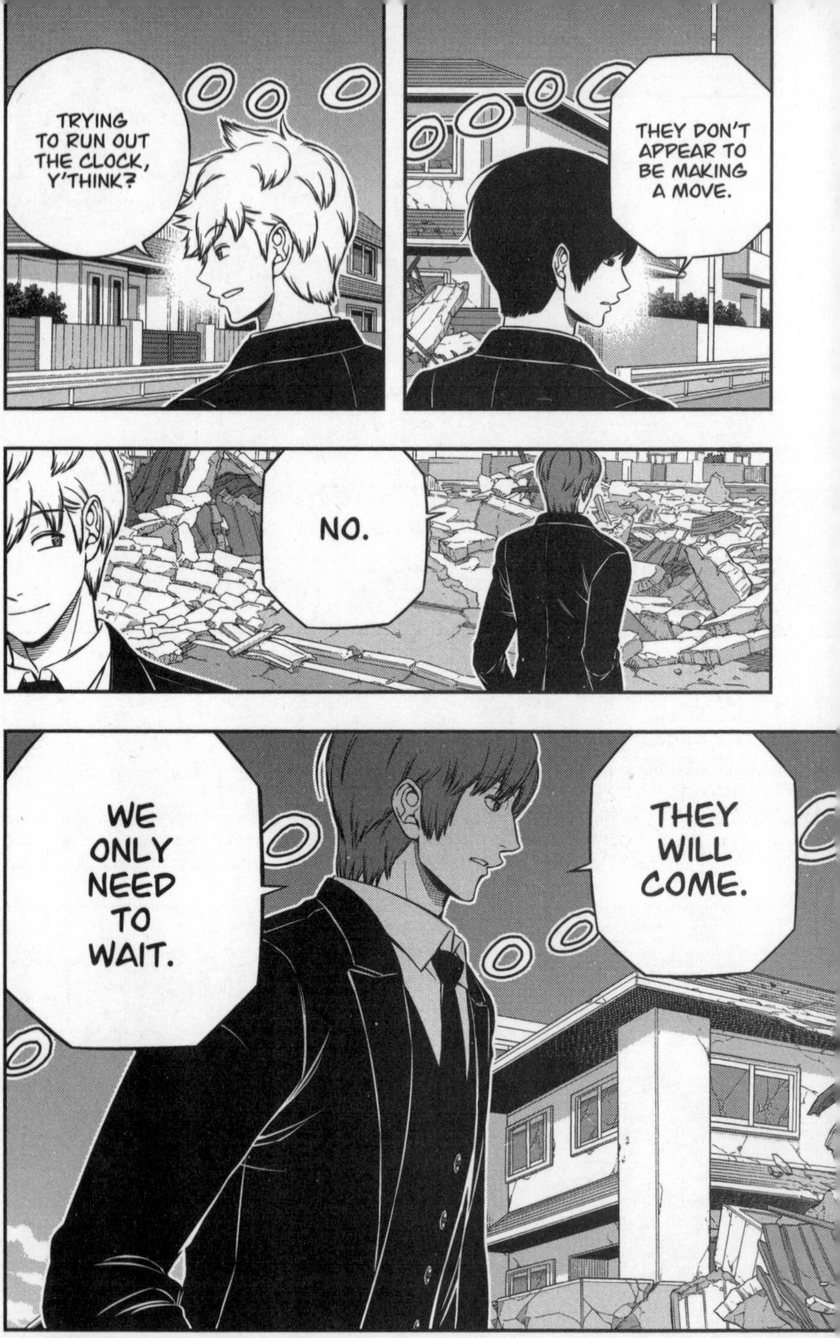
THEY DON'T APPEAR TO BE MAKING A MOVE.
TRYING TO RUN OUT THE CLOCK, Y'THINK?
NO.
THEY WILL COME.
WE ONLY NEED TO WAIT.

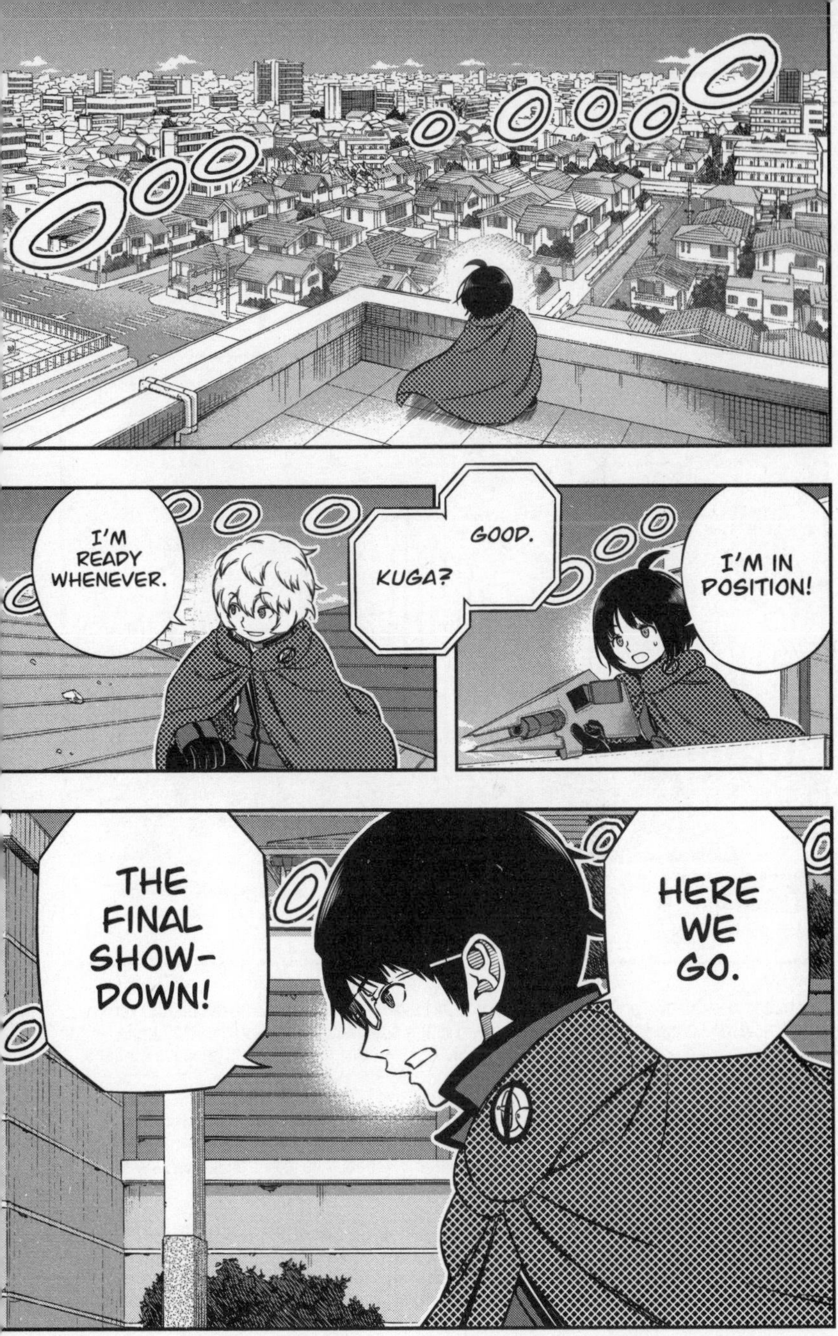
I'M IN POSITION!
GOOD.
KUGA?
I'M READY WHENEVER.
HERE WE GO.
THE FINAL SHOW-DOWN!

The Final: The Schools of Mikado City (Part 5)

Mikado Public College

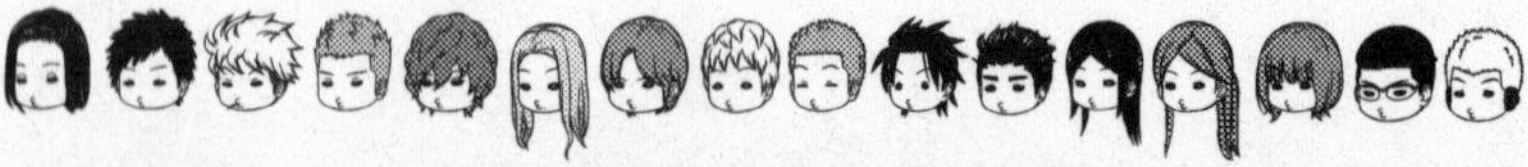

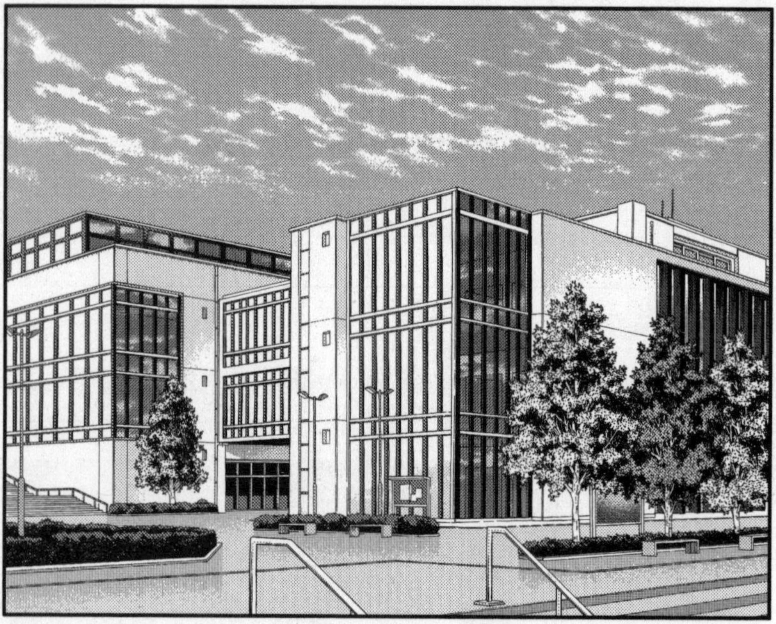

This building is relatively new, having been built almost four years prior. The old building (in what's now the Forbidden Zone) was destroyed rather spectacularly during the Ranbanein fight in volume 7. Rumor has it that the new building was completed quickly because Border's trigger technology was used in the process.

Students and faculty from the old Mikado College automatically switched over to the new campus. The college has a trigger-research facility for long-term research and experiments concerning trion. It's used as tantalizing bait when the school tries to recruit students with an interest in Border.

Using Mikado City itself as a conduit, the college receives kickbacks from Border in the form of relocation funds and working capital, creating a shady pipeline for people like Tachikawa to become college students based on a recommendation from Border. Border personnel who get admitted to the college are almost automatically given access to the trigger research lab, and they get college credits for assisting with that research. Engineers from HQ pop by the lab from time to time to request analyses, experiments, or what have you.

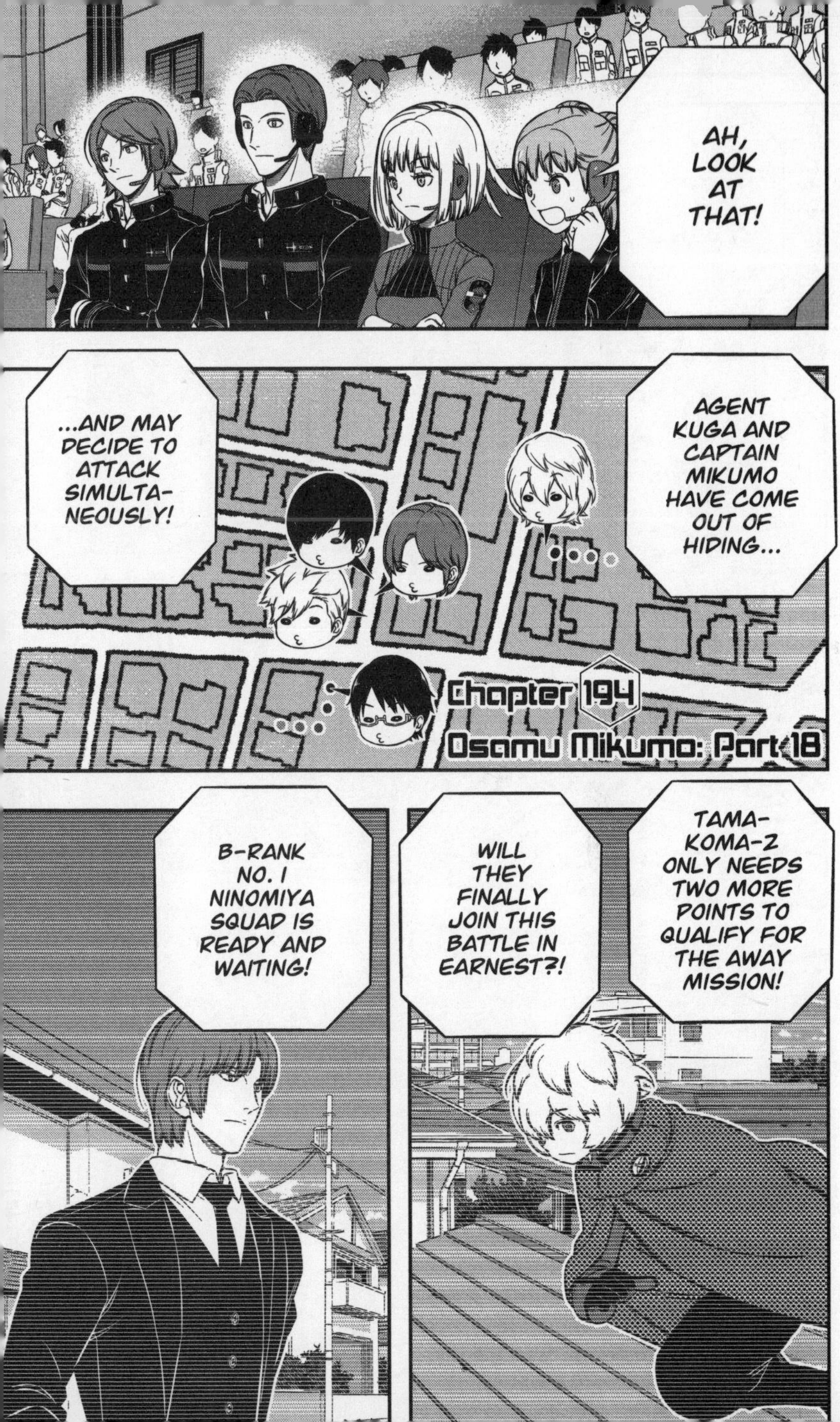
AH, LOOK AT THAT!
AGENT KUGA AND CAPTAIN MIKUMO HAVE COME OUT OF HIDING...
...AND MAY DECIDE TO ATTACK SIMULTA-NEOUSLY!
Chapter 194
Osamu Mikumo: Part 18
TAMA-KOMA-2 ONLY NEEDS TWO MORE POINTS TO QUALIFY FOR THE AWAY MISSION!
WILL THEY FINALLY JOIN THIS BATTLE IN EARNEST?!
B-RANK NO. 1 NINOMIYA SQUAD IS READY AND WAITING!

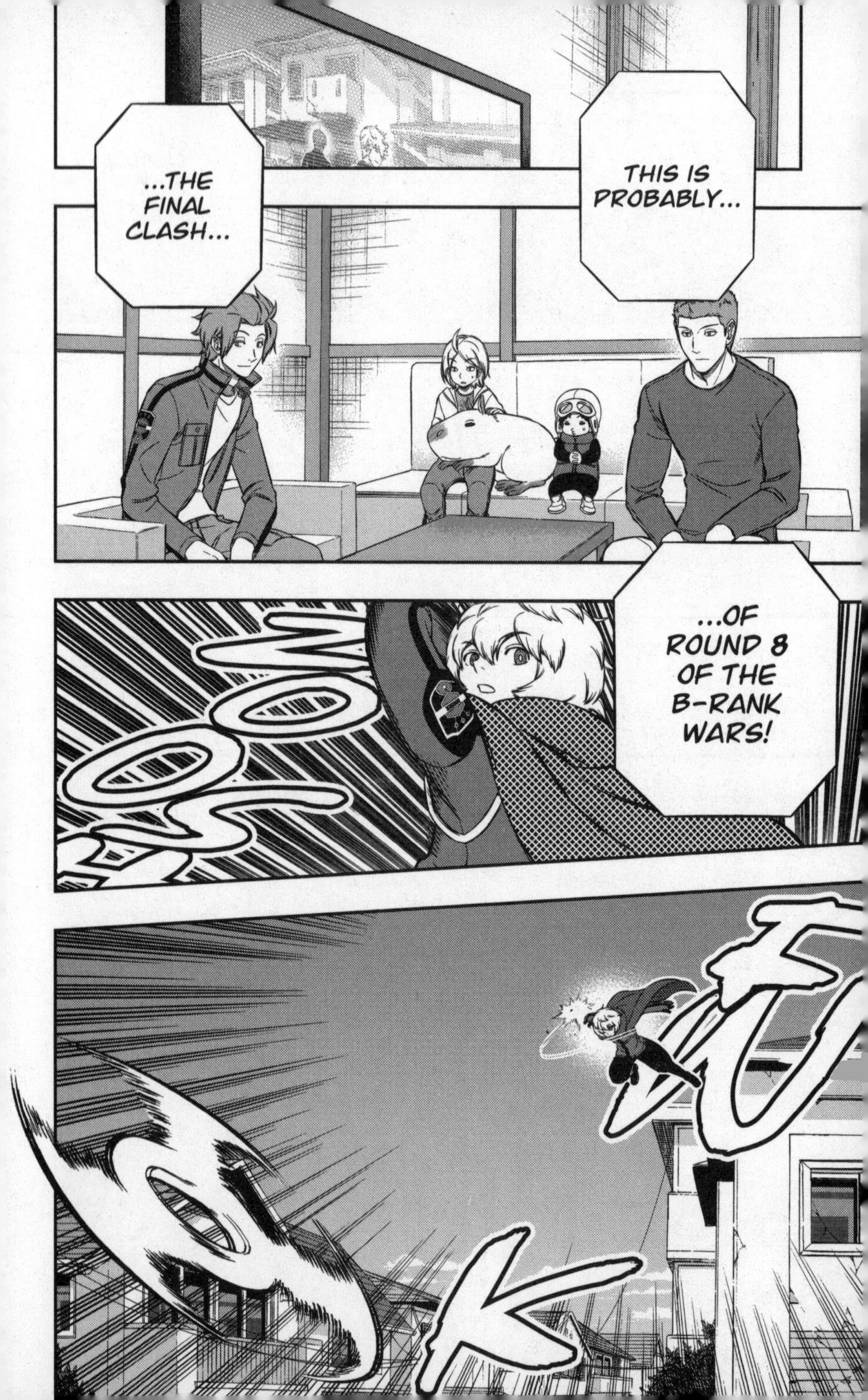
THIS IS PROBABLY...
...THE FINAL CLASH...
...OF ROUND 8 OF THE B-RANK WARS!

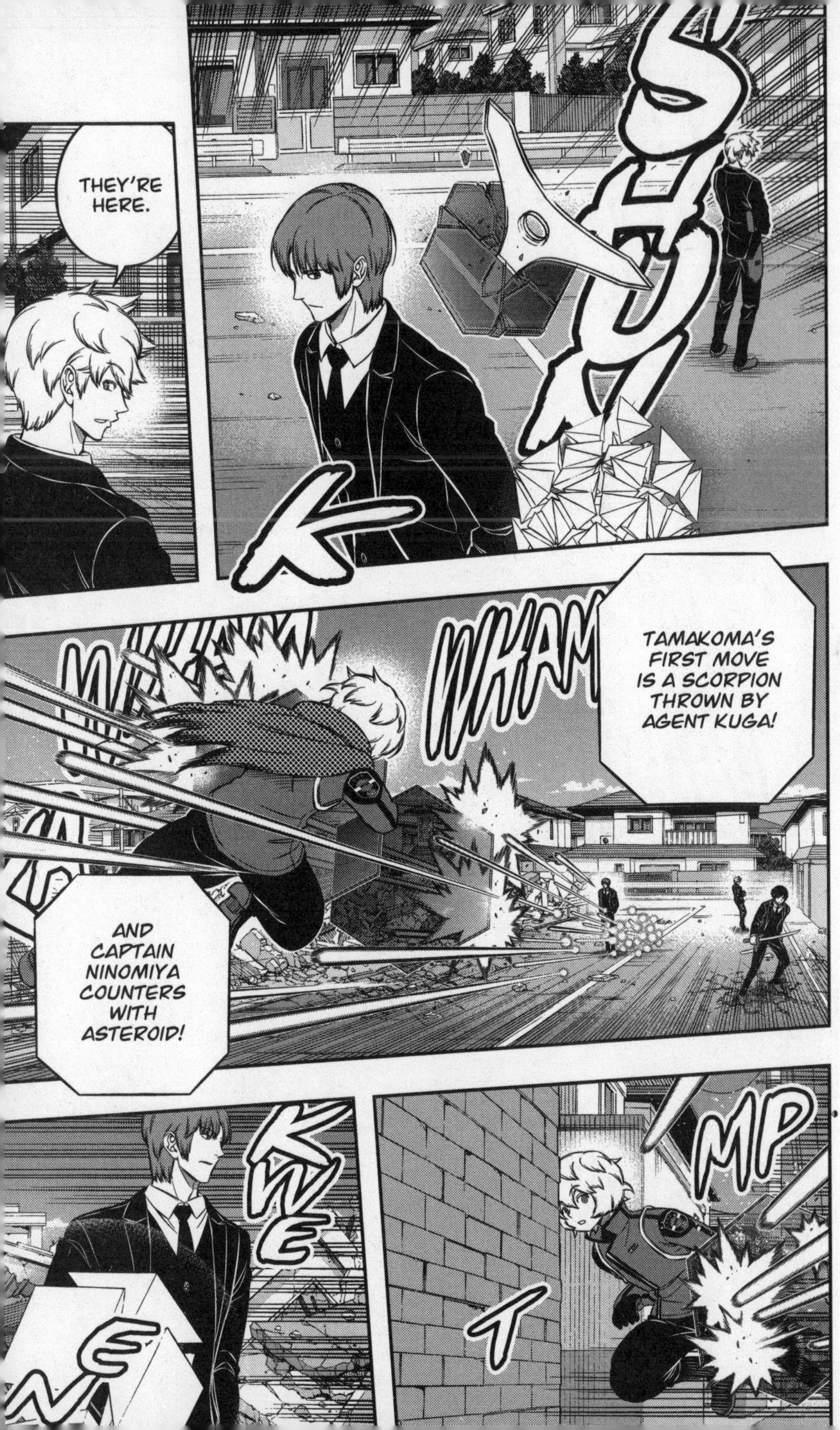
THEY'RE HERE.
TAMAKOMA'S FIRST MOVE IS A SCORPION THROWN BY AGENT KUGA!
AND CAPTAIN NINOMIYA COUNTERS WITH ASTEROID!

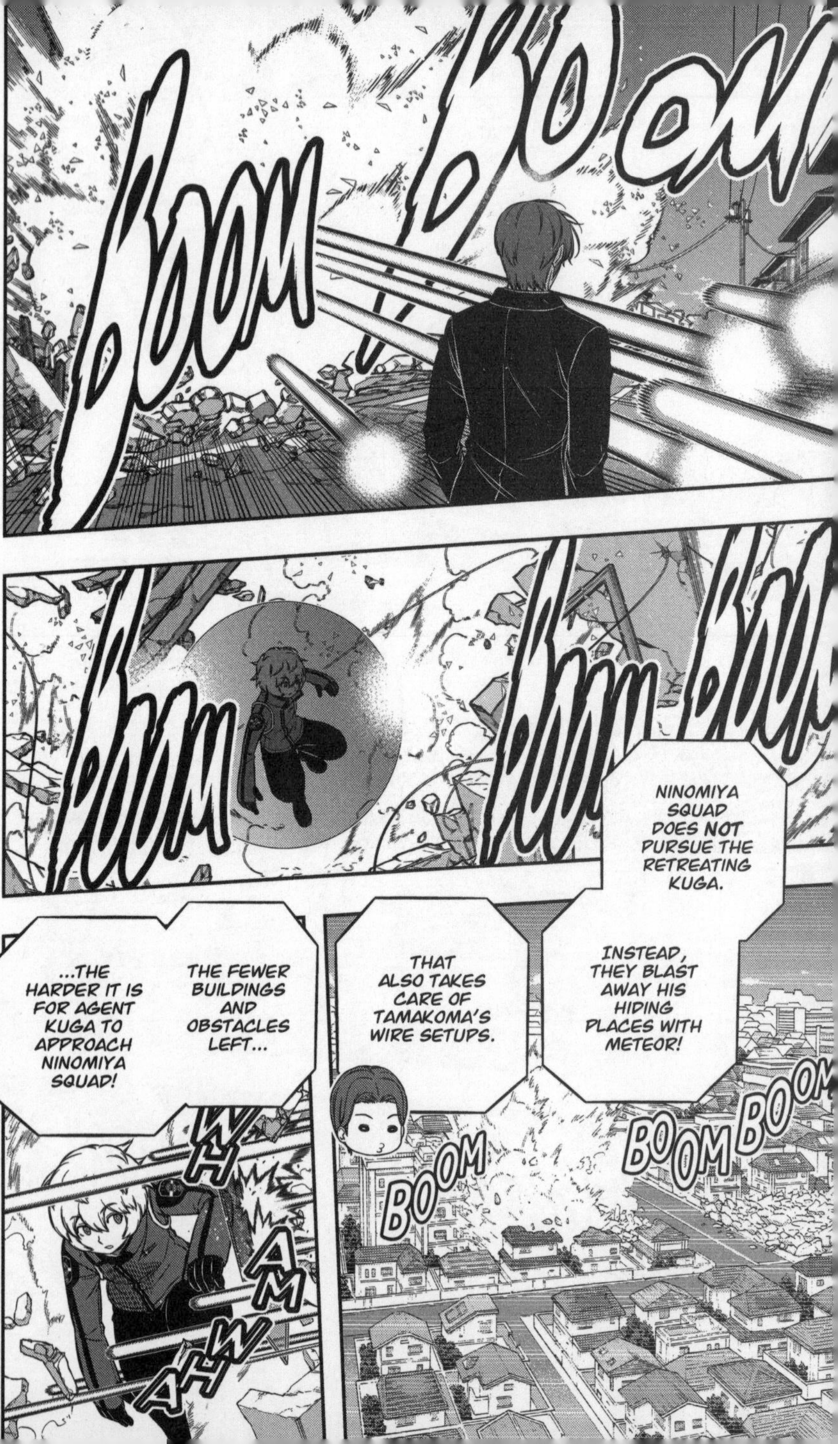
NINOMIYA SQUAD DOES NOT PURSUE THE RETREATING KUGA.
INSTEAD, THEY BLAST AWAY HIS HIDING PLACES WITH METEOR!
BOOM BOOM
THAT ALSO TAKES CARE OF TAMAKOMA'S WIRE SETUPS.
BOOM
THE FEWER BUILDINGS AND OBSTACLES LEFT...
...THE HARDER IT IS FOR AGENT KUGA TO APPROACH NINOMIYA SQUAD!

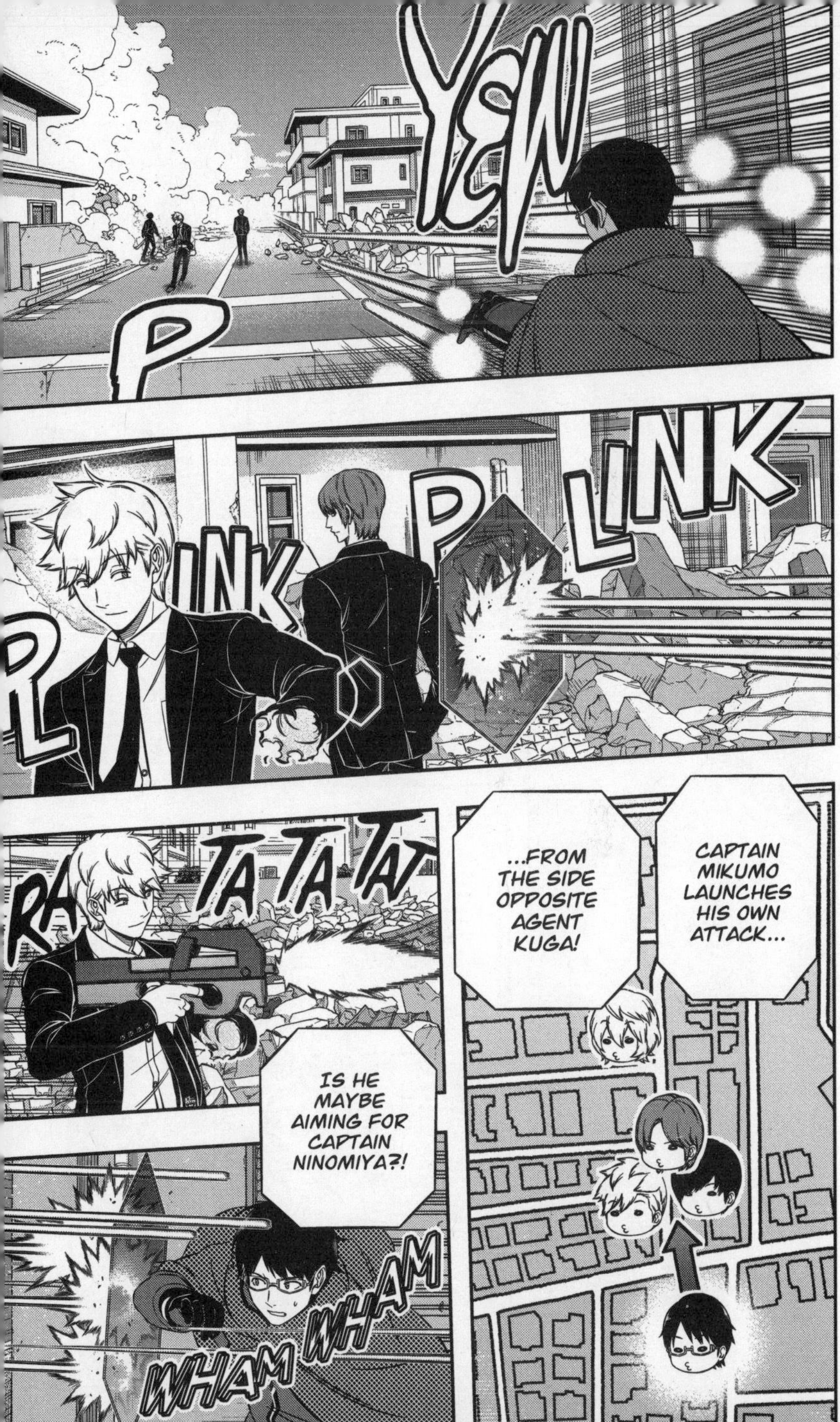
YEW
P
PLINK
PLINK
CAPTAIN MIKUMO LAUNCHES HIS OWN ATTACK...
...FROM THE SIDE OPPOSITE AGENT KUGA!
RA TA TA TAT
IS HE MAYBE AIMING FOR CAPTAIN NINOMIYA?!
WHAM WHAM

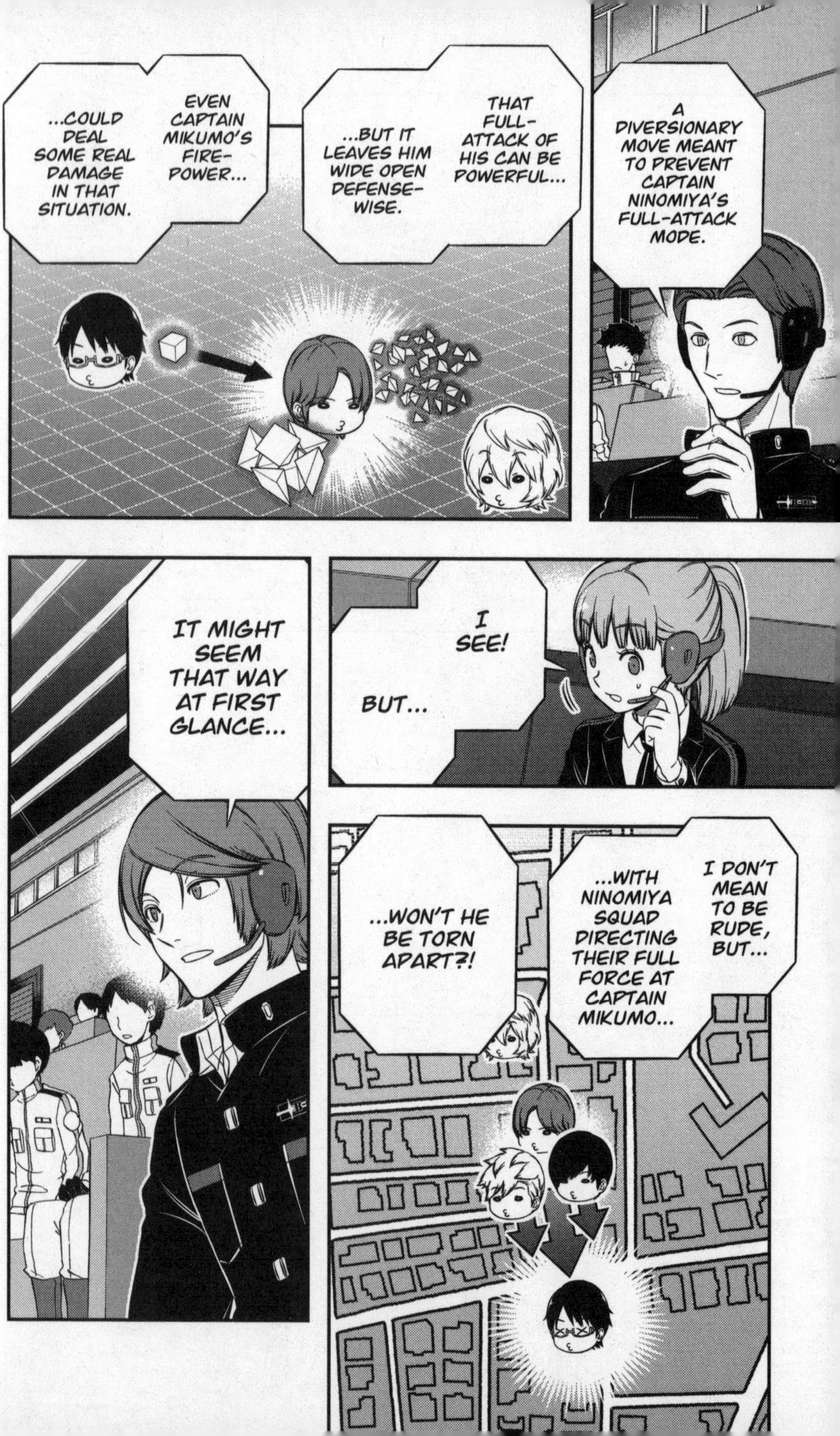
A DIVERSIONARY MOVE MEANT TO PREVENT CAPTAIN NINOMIYA'S FULL-ATTACK MODE.
THAT FULL-ATTACK OF HIS CAN BE POWERFUL...
...BUT IT LEAVES HIM WIDE OPEN DEFENSE-WISE.
EVEN CAPTAIN MIKUMO'S FIRE-POWER...
...COULD DEAL SOME REAL DAMAGE IN THAT SITUATION.
I SEE!
BUT...
I DON'T MEAN TO BE RUDE, BUT...
...WITH NINOMIYA SQUAD DIRECTING THEIR FULL FORCE AT CAPTAIN MIKUMO...
...WON'T HE BE TORN APART?!
IT MIGHT SEEM THAT WAY AT FIRST GLANCE...

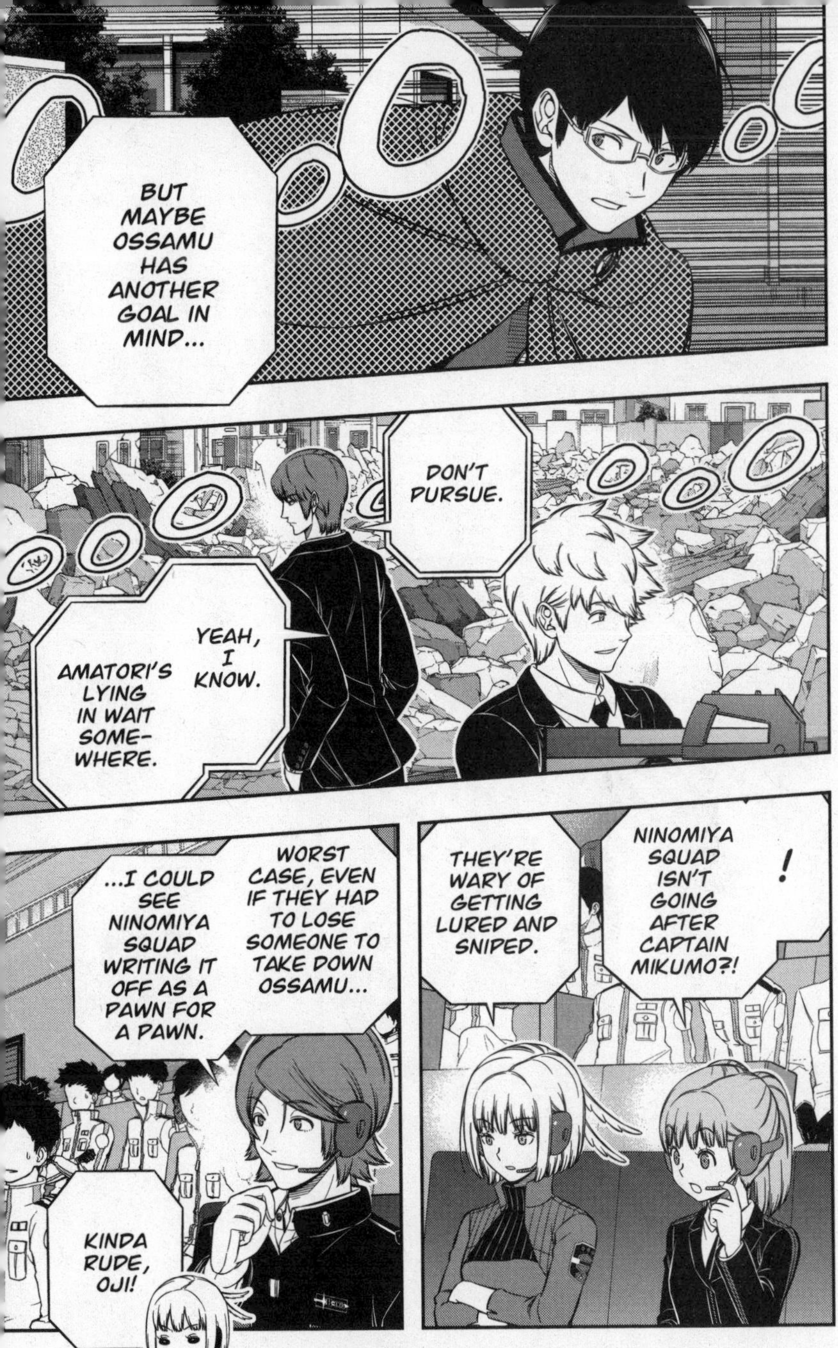
BUT MAYBE OSSAMU HAS ANOTHER GOAL IN MIND...
DON'T PURSUE.
YEAH, I KNOW.
AMATORI'S LYING IN WAIT SOME-WHERE.
!
NINOMIYA SQUAD ISN'T GOING AFTER CAPTAIN MIKUMO?!
THEY'RE WARY OF GETTING LURED AND SNIPED.
WORST CASE, EVEN IF THEY HAD TO LOSE SOMEONE TO TAKE DOWN OSSAMU...
...I COULD SEE NINOMIYA SQUAD WRITING IT OFF AS A PAWN FOR A PAWN.
KINDA RUDE, OJI!

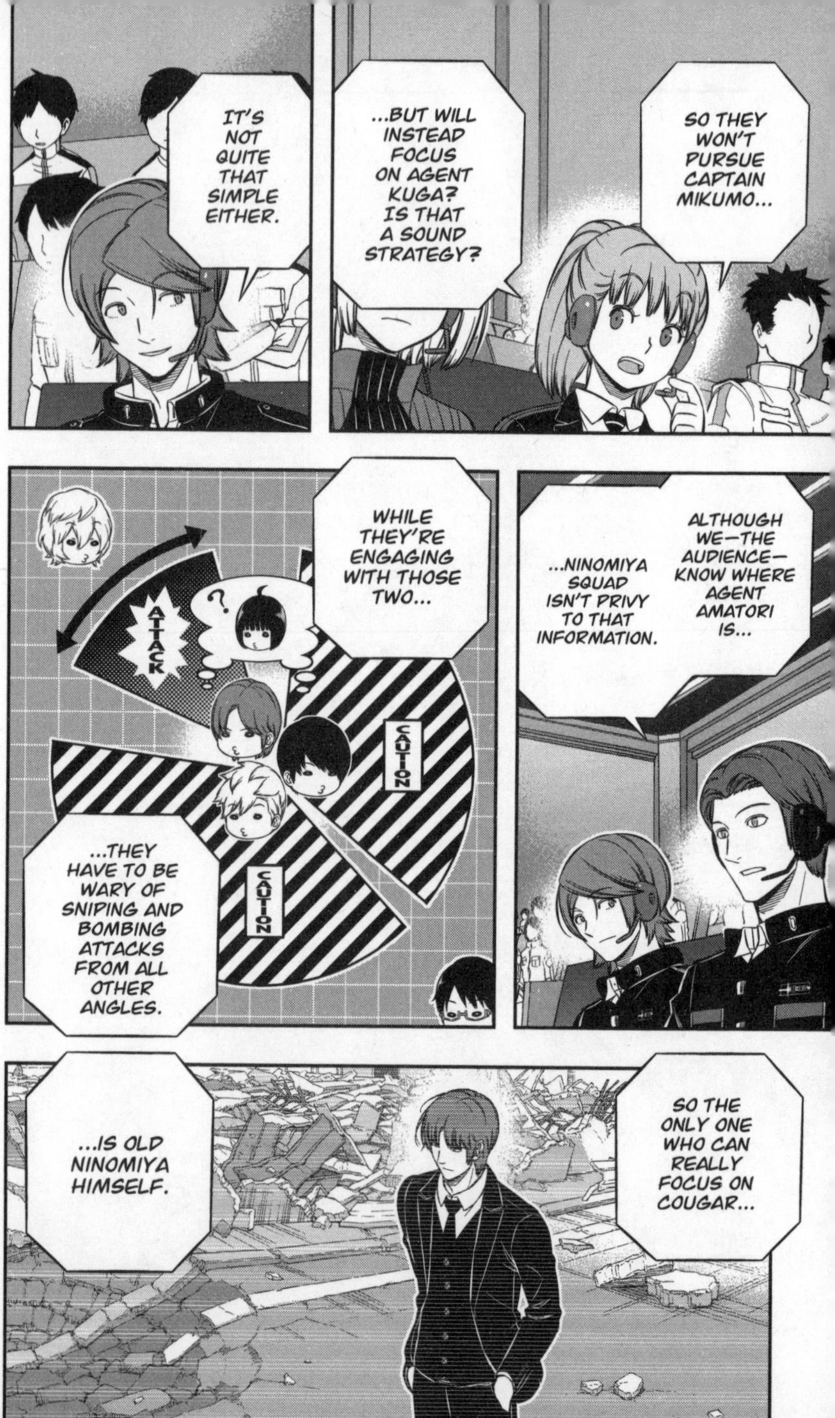
SO THEY WON'T PURSUE CAPTAIN MIKUMO...
...BUT WILL INSTEAD FOCUS ON AGENT KUGA? IS THAT A SOUND STRATEGY?
IT'S NOT QUITE THAT SIMPLE EITHER.
ALTHOUGH WE—THE AUDIENCE—KNOW WHERE AGENT AMATORI IS...
...NINOMIYA SQUAD ISN'T PRIVY TO THAT INFORMATION.
WHILE THEY'RE ENGAGING WITH THOSE TWO...
ATTACK
?
CAUTION
CAUTION
...THEY HAVE TO BE WARY OF SNIPING AND BOMBING ATTACKS FROM ALL OTHER ANGLES.
SO THE ONLY ONE WHO CAN REALLY FOCUS ON COUGAR...
...IS OLD NINOMIYA HIMSELF.

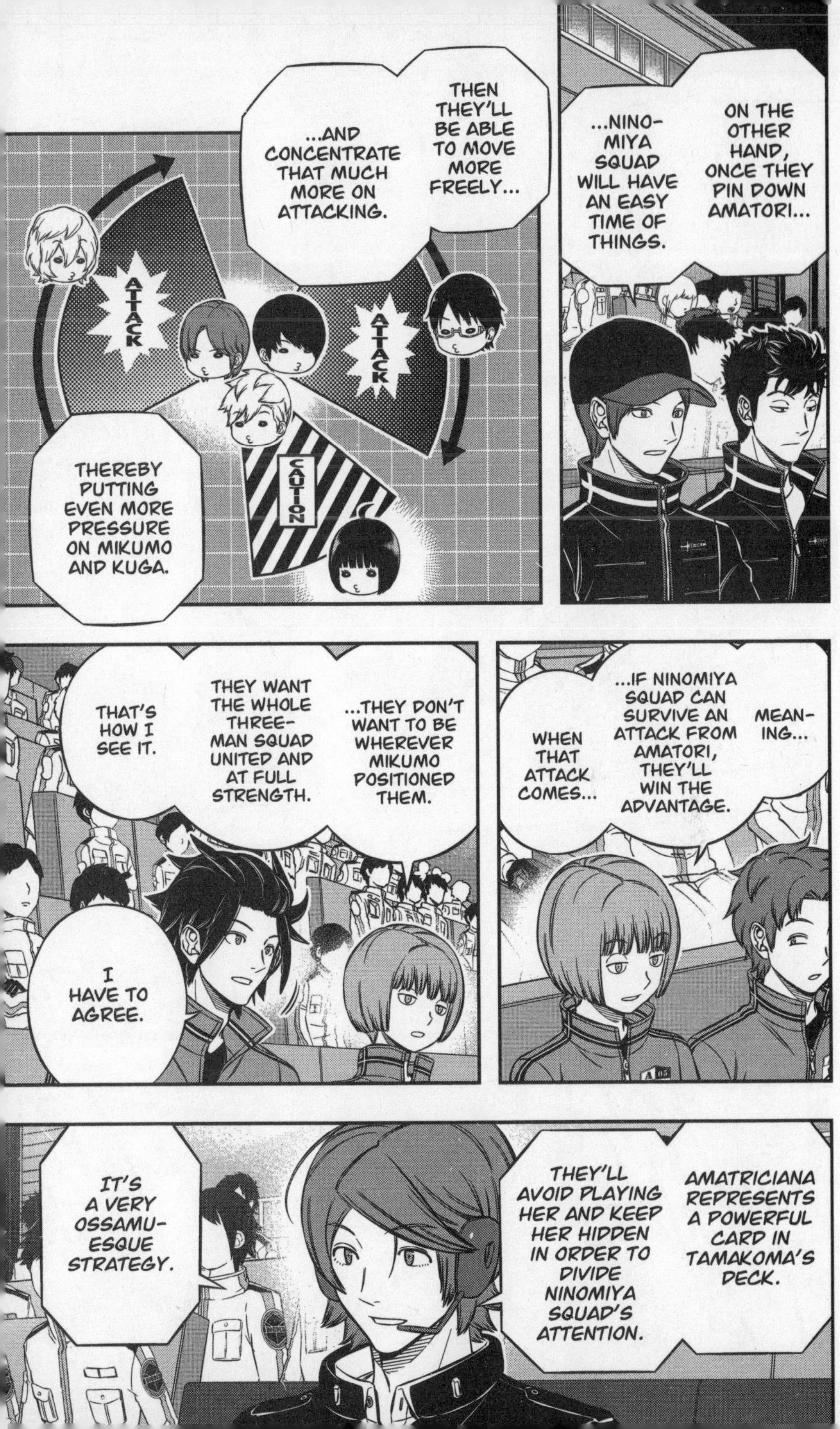
ON THE OTHER HAND, ONCE THEY PIN DOWN AMATORI...
...NINOMIYA SQUAD WILL HAVE AN EASY TIME OF THINGS.
THEN THEY'LL BE ABLE TO MOVE MORE FREELY...
...AND CONCENTRATE THAT MUCH MORE ON ATTACKING.
ATTACK
ATTACK
CAUTION
THEREBY PUTTING EVEN MORE PRESSURE ON MIKUMO AND KUGA.
MEANING...
...IF NINOMIYA SQUAD CAN SURVIVE AN ATTACK FROM AMATORI, THEY'LL WIN THE ADVANTAGE.
WHEN THAT ATTACK COMES...
...THEY DON'T WANT TO BE WHEREVER MIKUMO POSITIONED THEM.
THEY WANT THE WHOLE THREE-MAN SQUAD UNITED AND AT FULL STRENGTH.
THAT'S HOW I SEE IT.
I HAVE TO AGREE.
AMATRICIANA REPRESENTS A POWERFUL CARD IN TAMAKOMA'S DECK.
THEY'LL AVOID PLAYING HER AND KEEP HER HIDDEN IN ORDER TO DIVIDE NINOMIYA SQUAD'S ATTENTION.
IT'S A VERY OSSAMU-ESQUE STRATEGY.

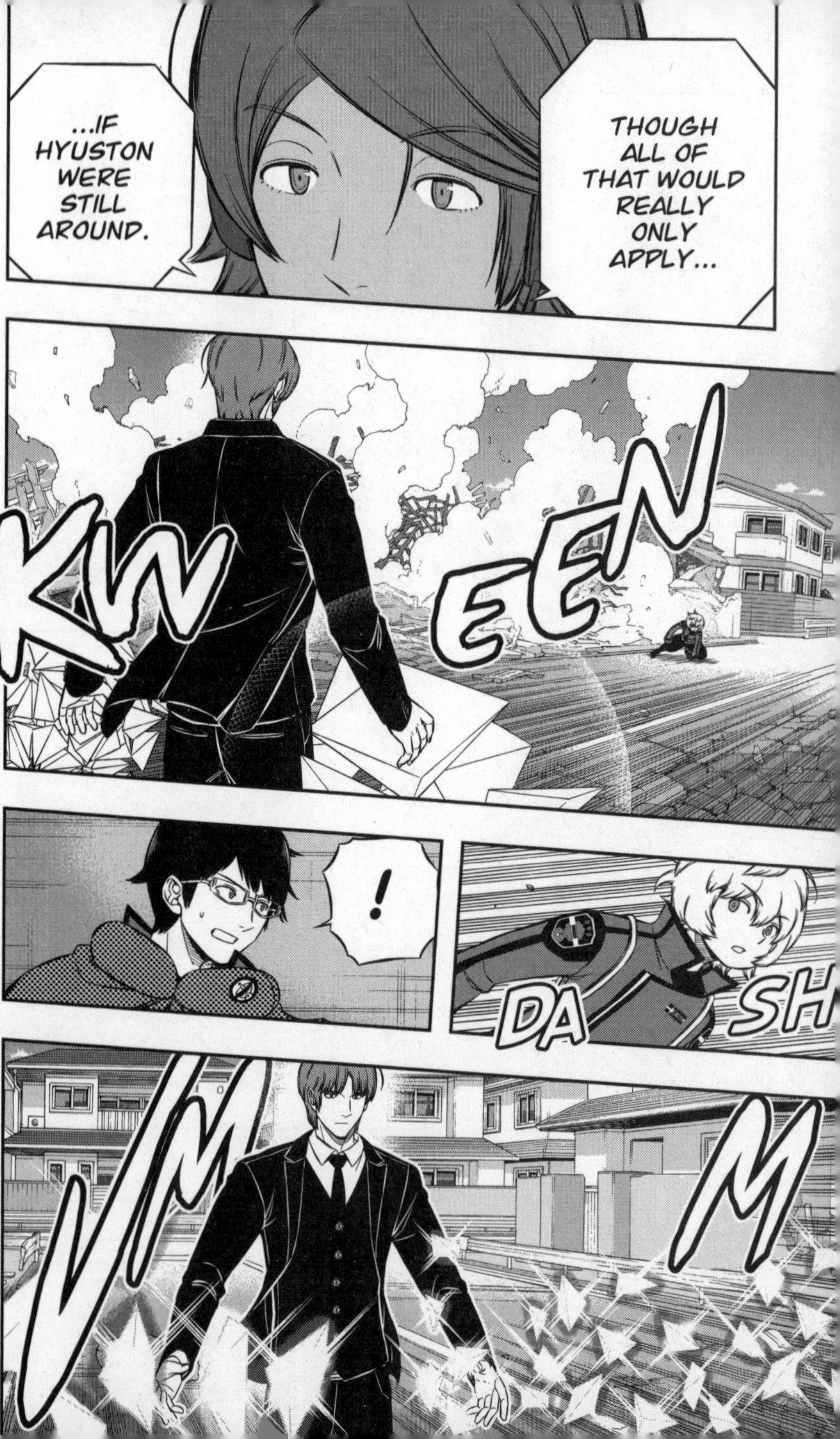
THOUGH ALL OF THAT WOULD REALLY ONLY APPLY...
...IF HYUSTON WERE STILL AROUND.
KWEEN
DASH
!
VMMM

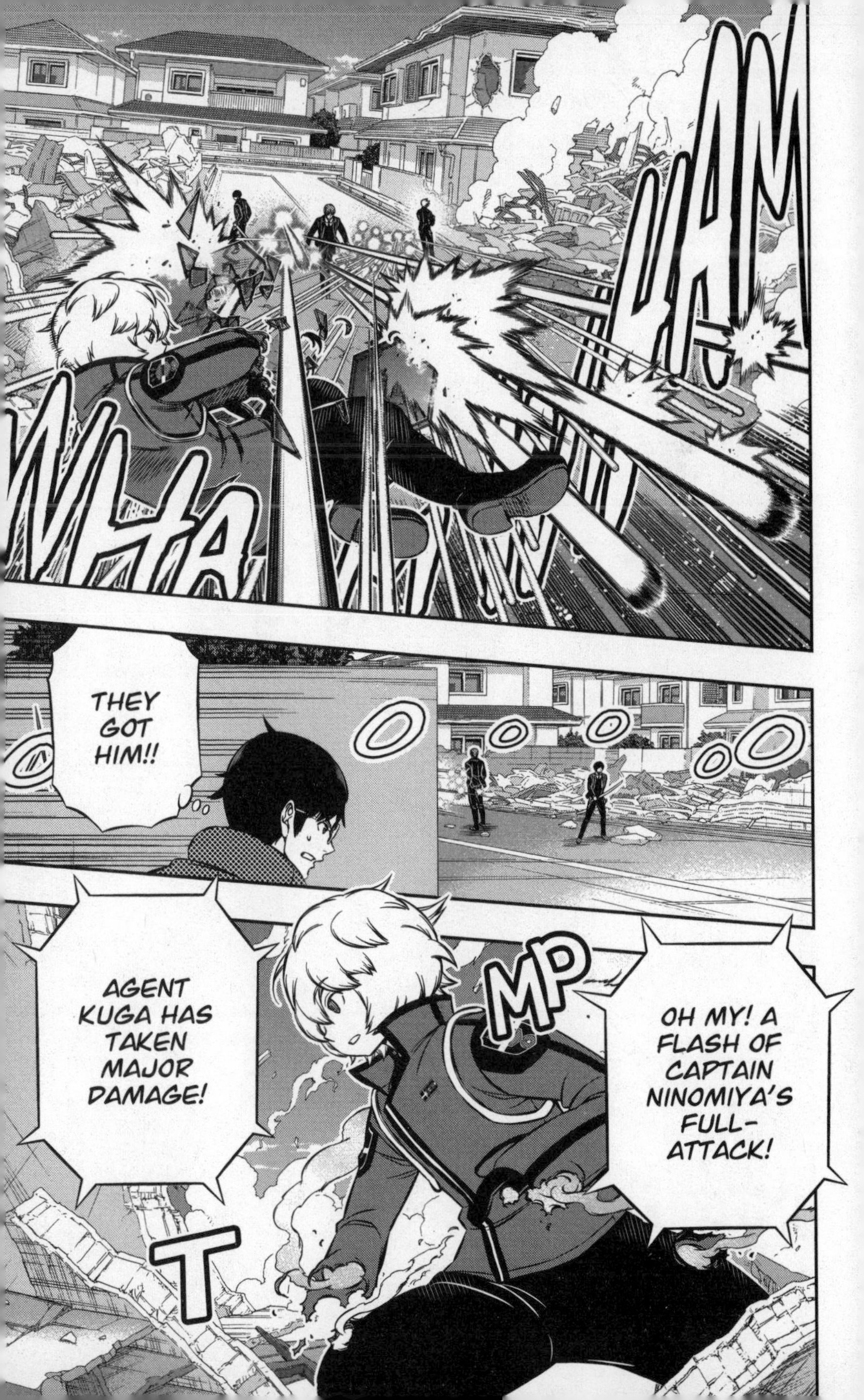
THEY GOT HIM!!
OH MY! A FLASH OF CAPTAIN NINOMIYA'S FULL-ATTACK!
MP
AGENT KUGA HAS TAKEN MAJOR DAMAGE!
T

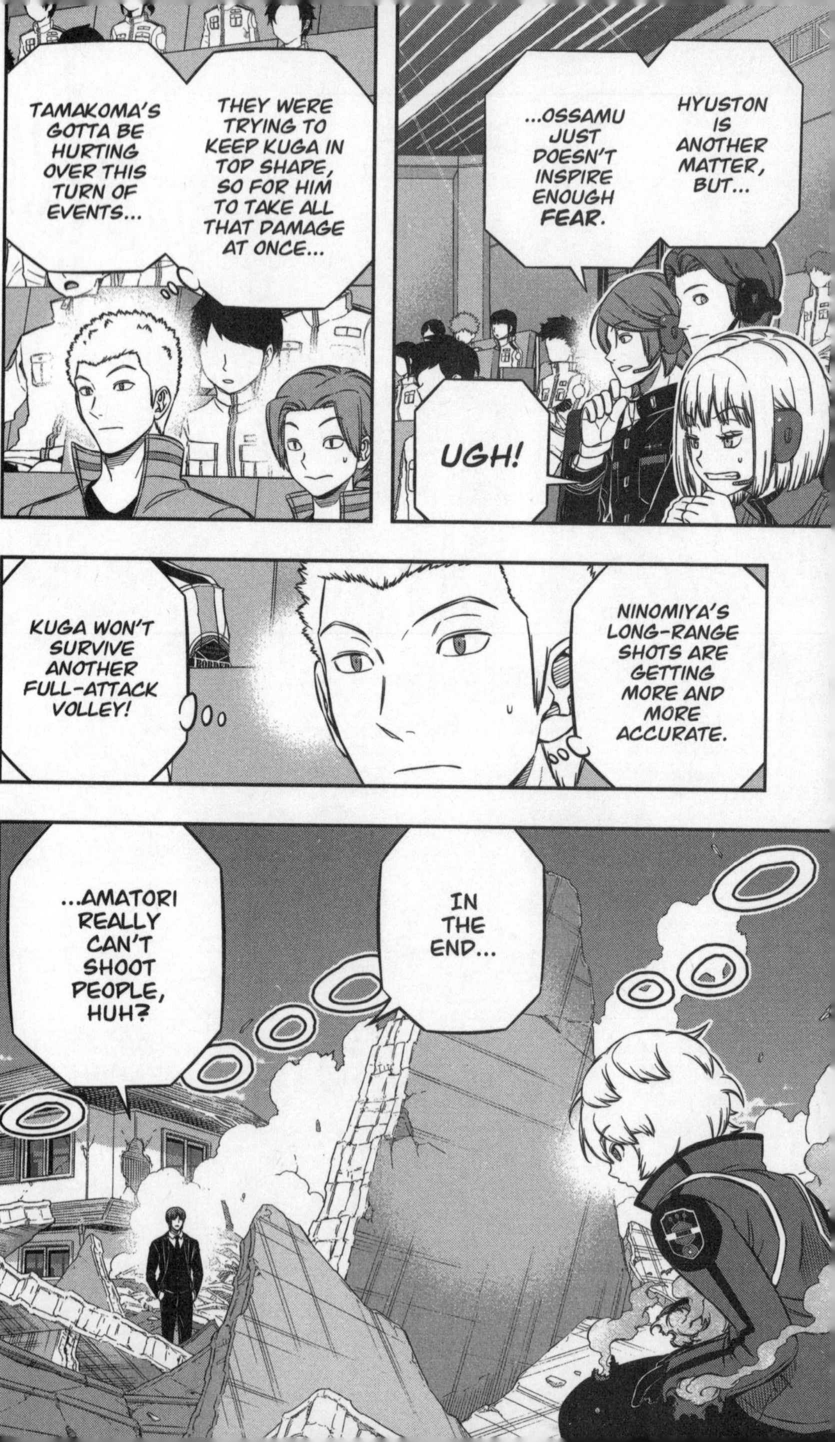
HYUSTON IS ANOTHER MATTER, BUT...
...OSSAMU JUST DOESN'T INSPIRE ENOUGH FEAR.
UGH!
THEY WERE TRYING TO KEEP KUGA IN TOP SHAPE, SO FOR HIM TO TAKE ALL THAT DAMAGE AT ONCE...
TAMAKOMA'S GOTTA BE HURTING OVER THIS TURN OF EVENTS...
NINOMIYA'S LONG-RANGE SHOTS ARE GETTING MORE AND MORE ACCURATE.
KUGA WON'T SURVIVE ANOTHER FULL-ATTACK VOLLEY!
IN THE END...
...AMATORI REALLY CAN'T SHOOT PEOPLE, HUH?

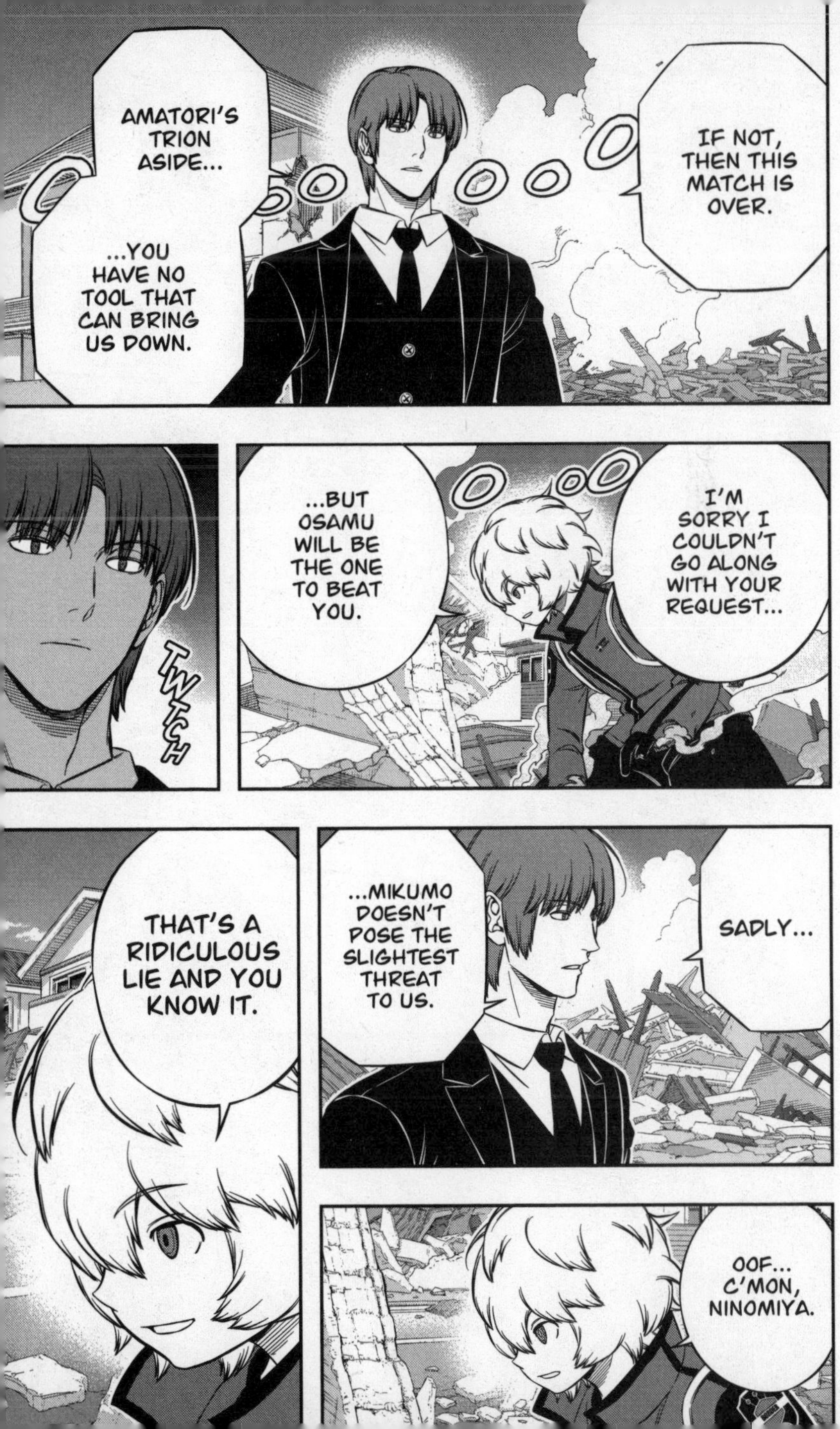
IF NOT, THEN THIS MATCH IS OVER.
AMATORI'S TRION ASIDE...
...YOU HAVE NO TOOL THAT CAN BRING US DOWN.
I'M SORRY I COULDN'T GO ALONG WITH YOUR REQUEST...
...BUT OSAMU WILL BE THE ONE TO BEAT YOU.
TWITCH
SADLY...
...MIKUMO DOESN'T POSE THE SLIGHTEST THREAT TO US.
OOF... C'MON, NINOMIYA.
THAT'S A RIDICULOUS LIE AND YOU KNOW IT.

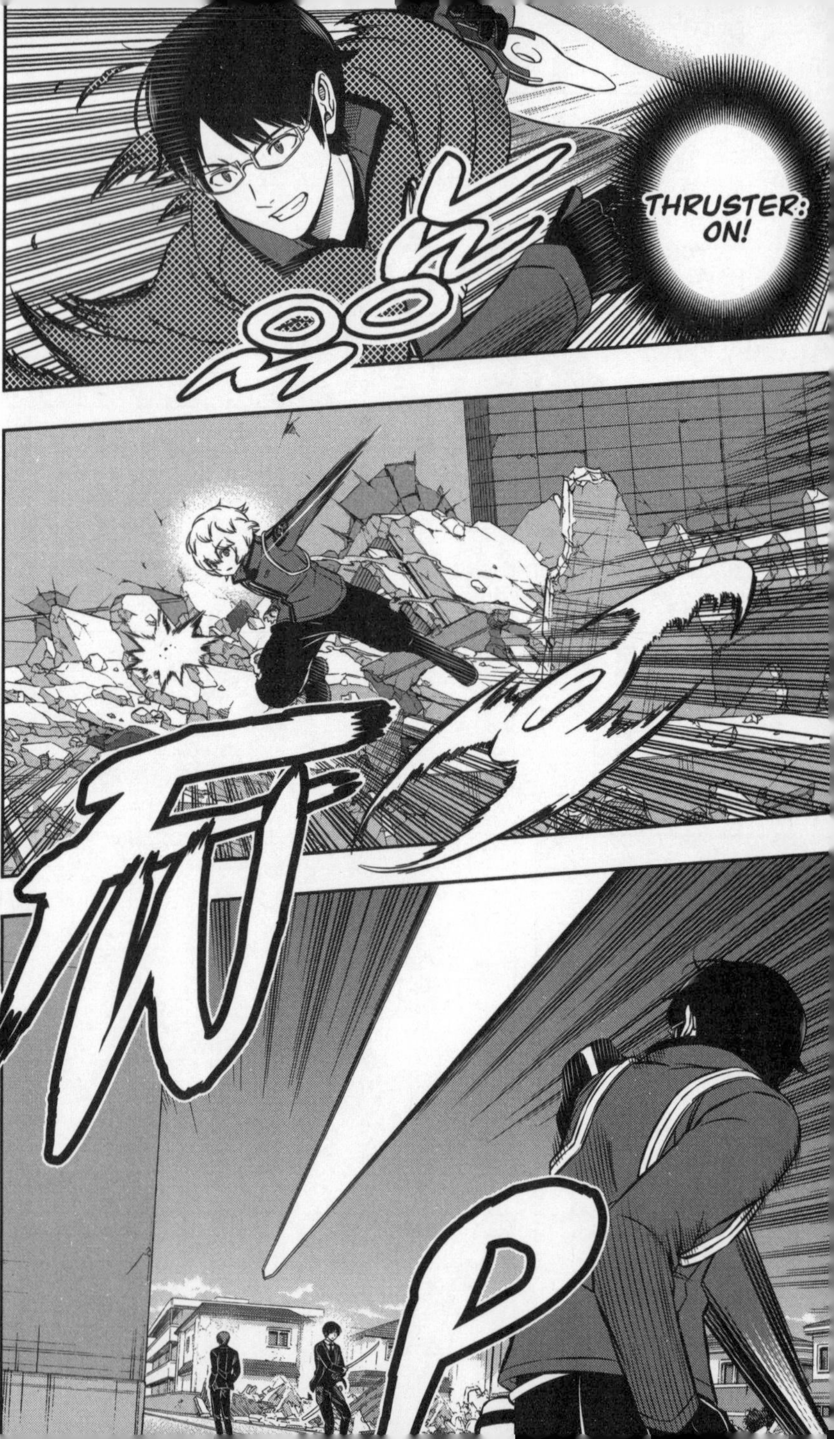
THRUSTER: ON!

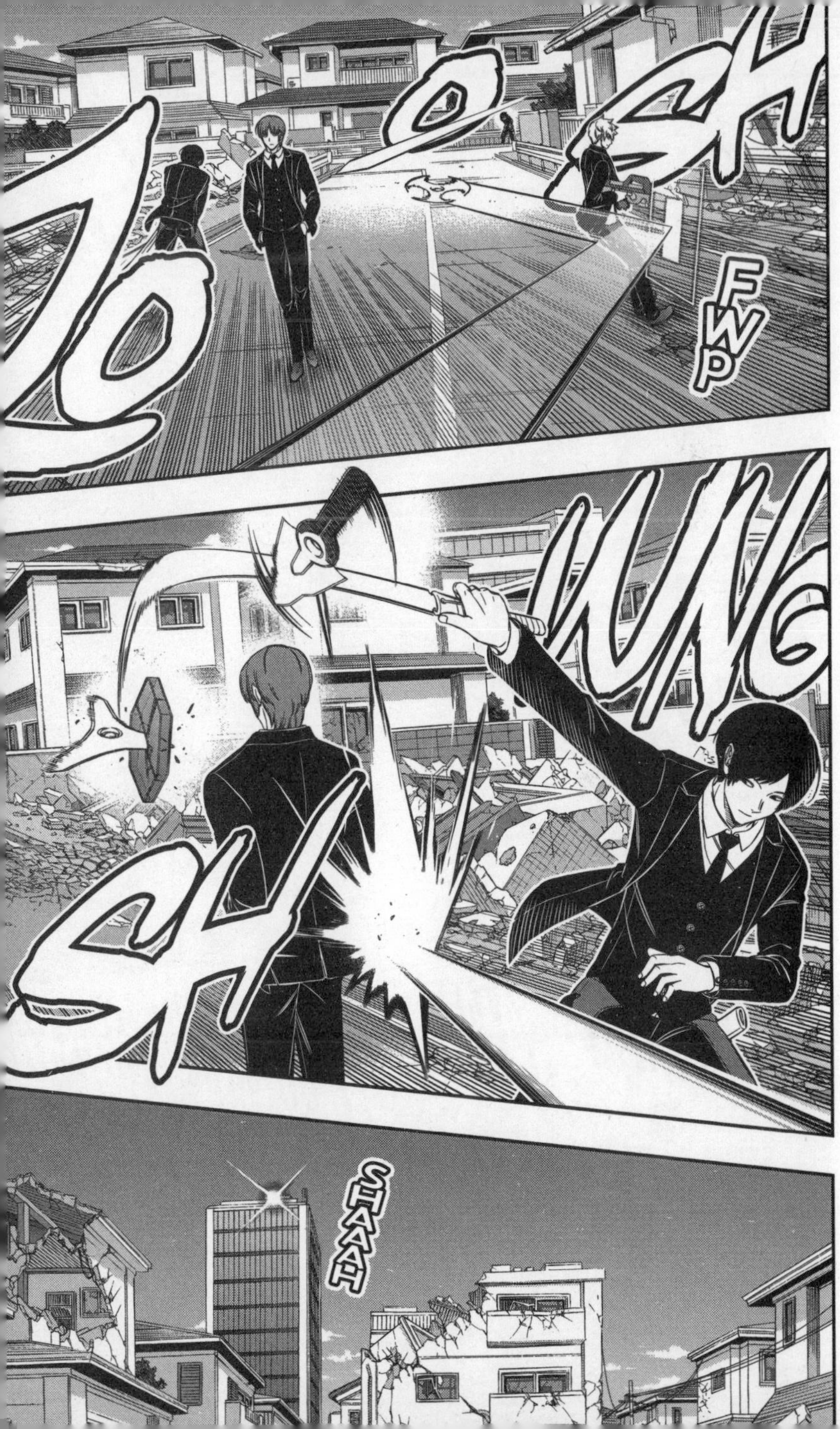
FWP
SHAAAH

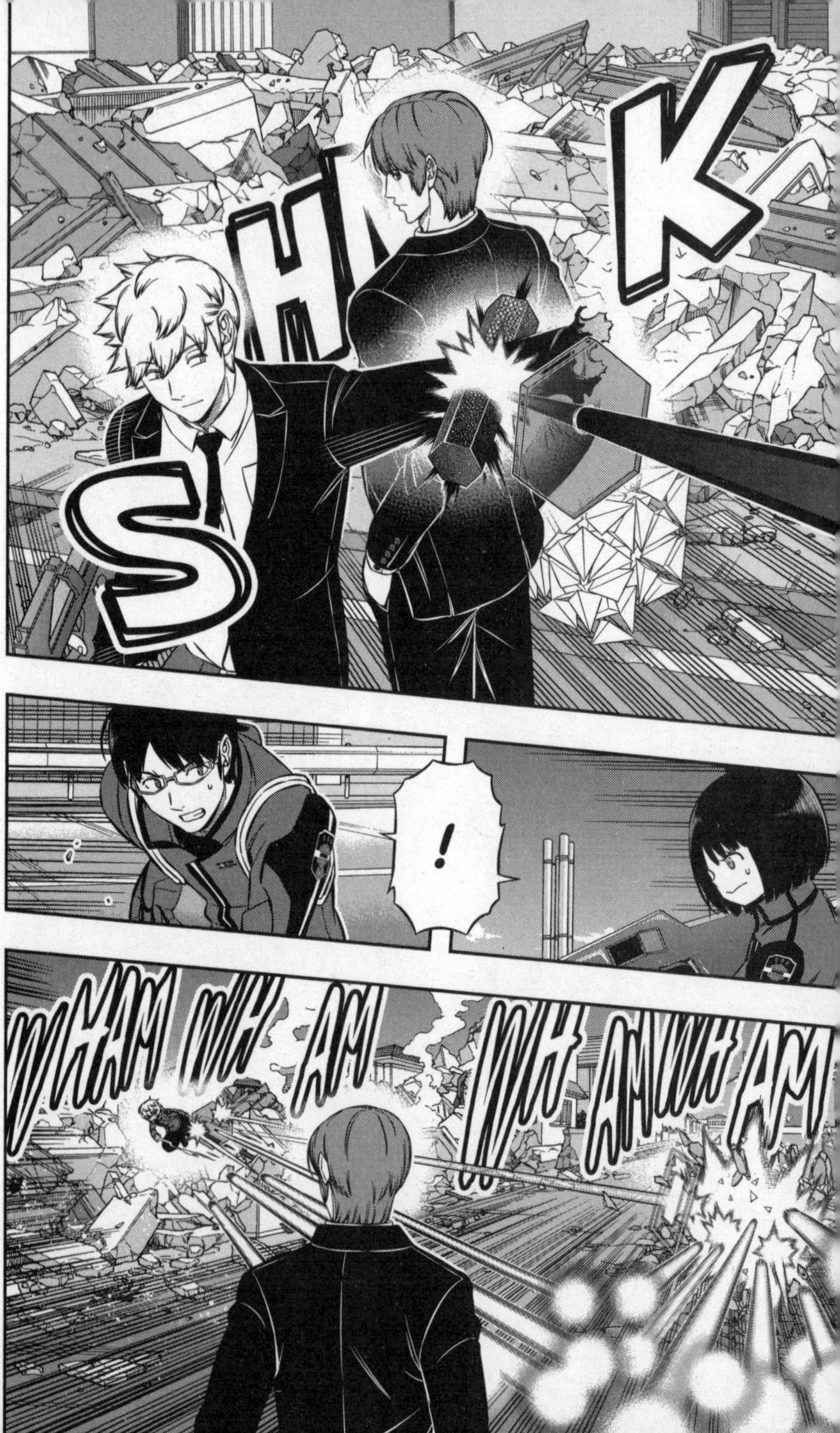
!

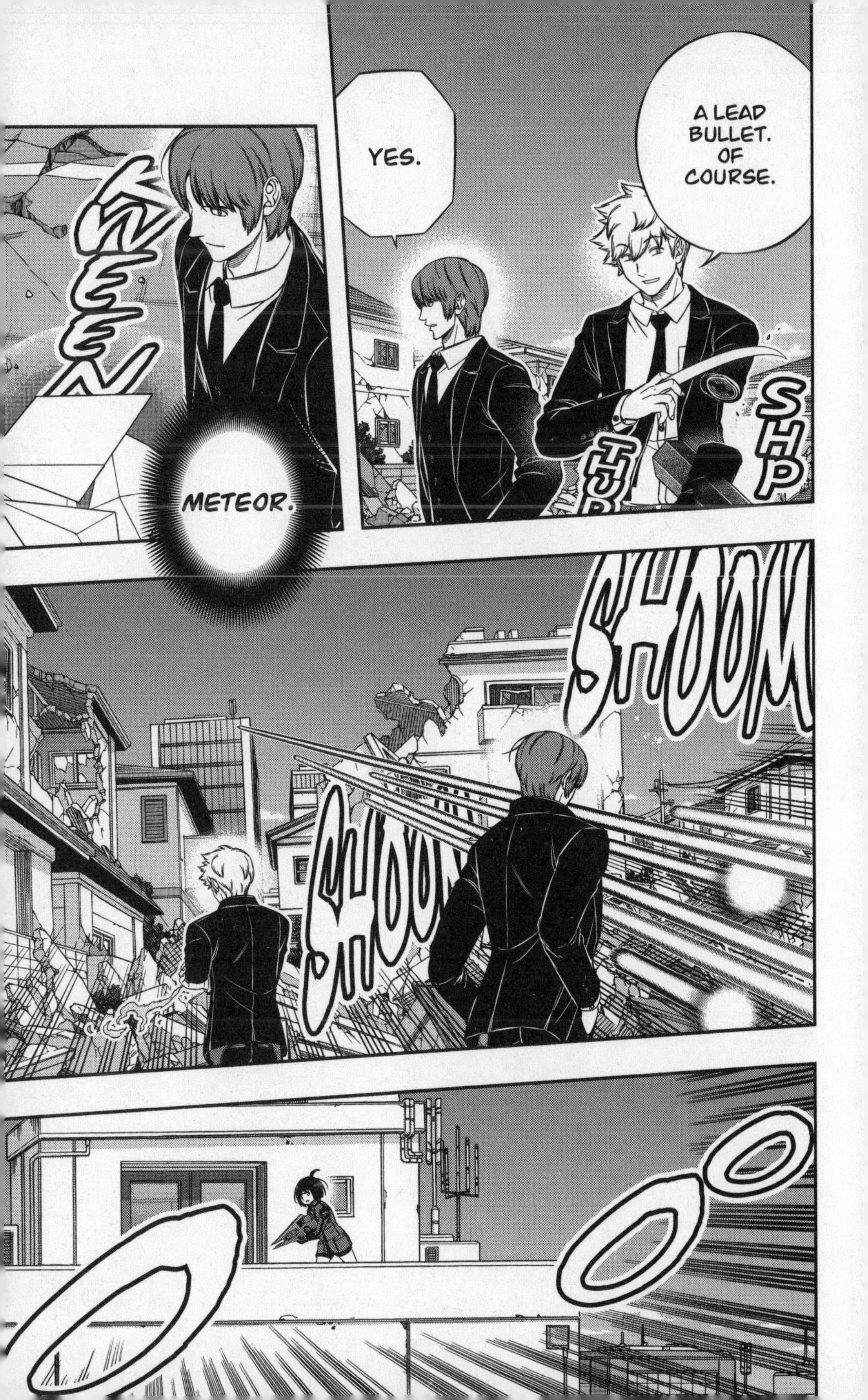
A LEAD BULLET. OF COURSE.
YES.
SHP
KWEEN
METEOR.
SHOOM
SHOOM

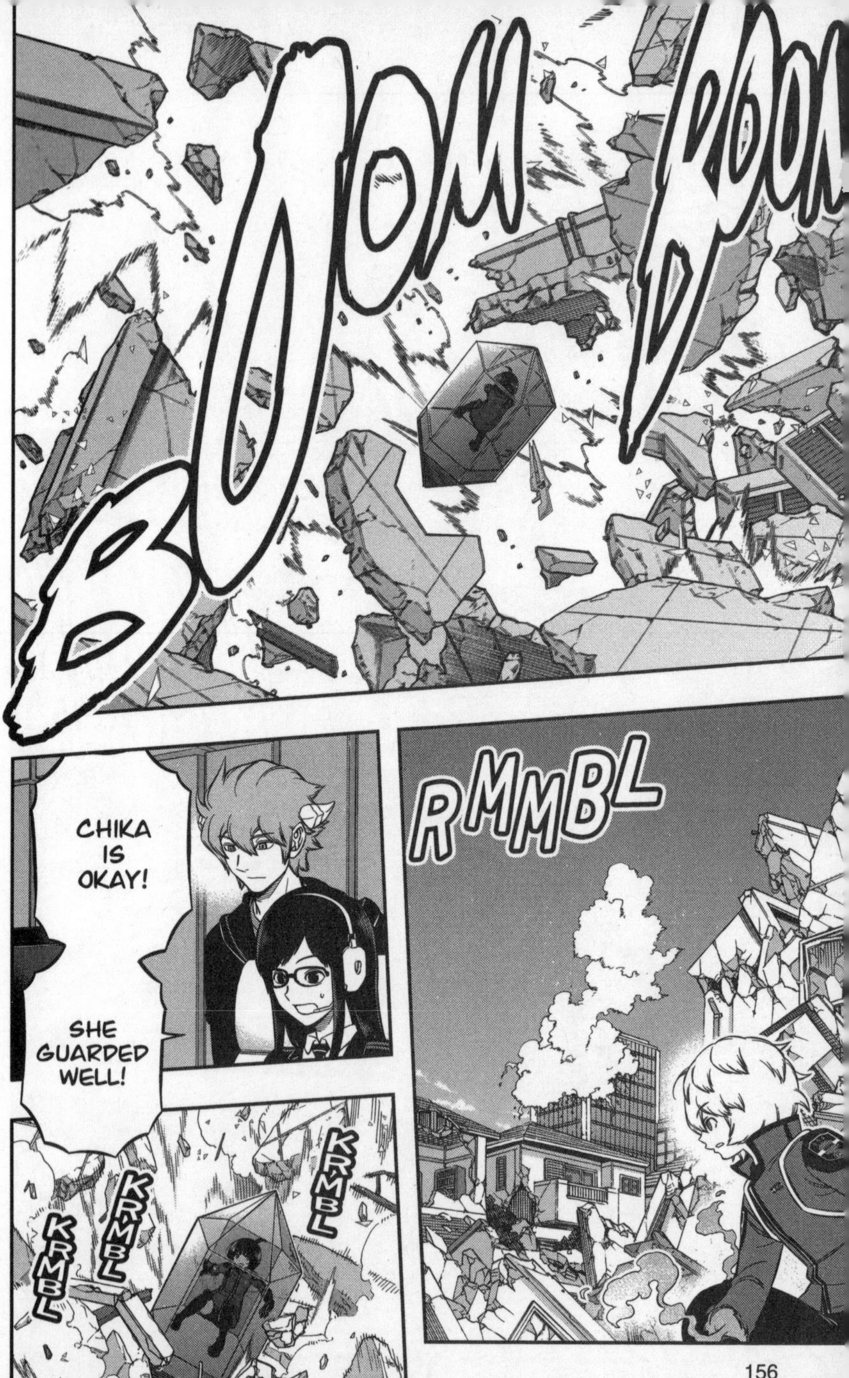
BOOM
BOOM
RMMBL
CHIKA IS OKAY!
SHE GUARDED WELL!
KRMBL
KRMBL
KRMBL

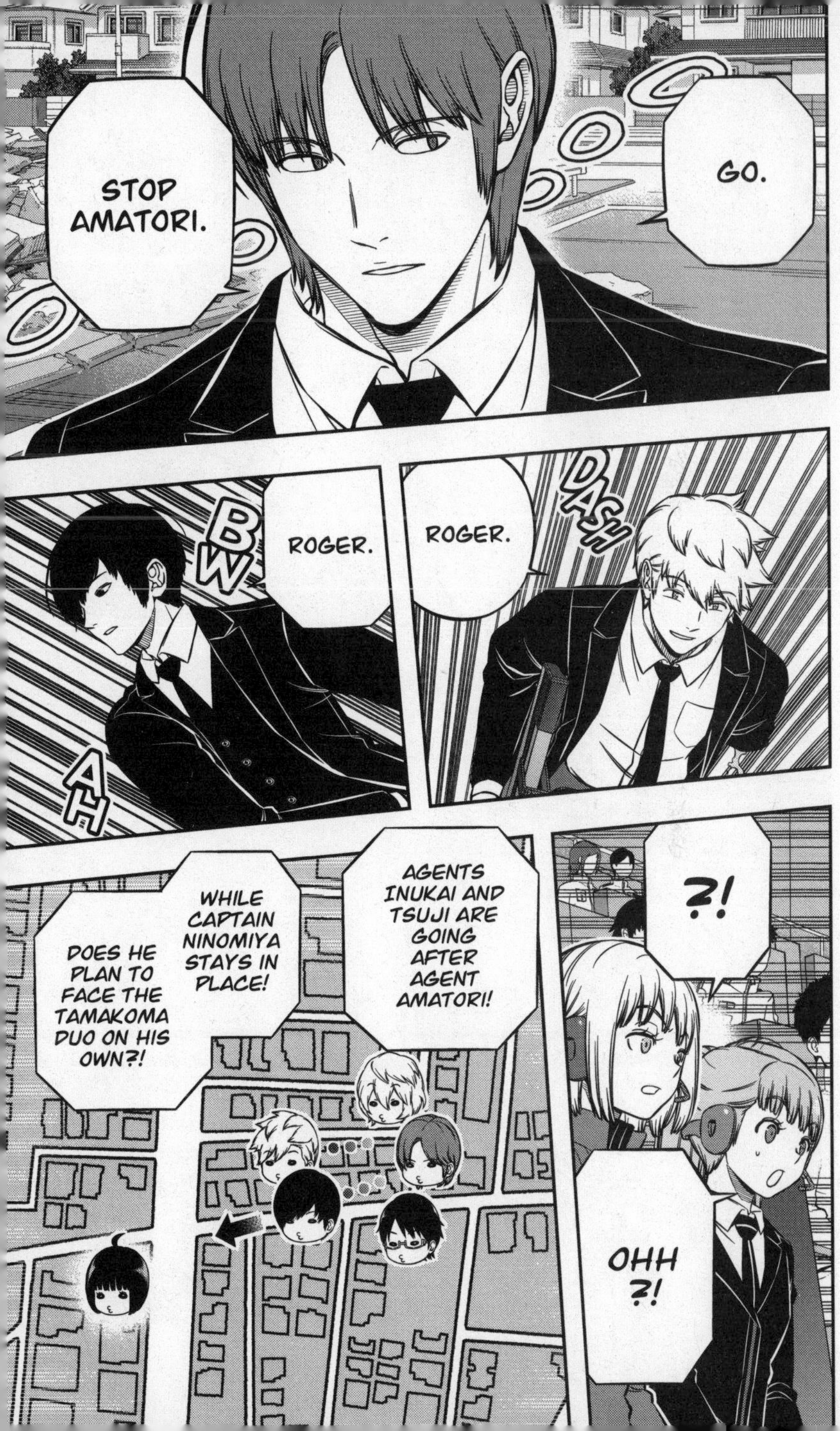
GO.
STOP AMATORI.
DASH
ROGER.
ROGER.
BW
AH
?!
OHH ?!
AGENTS INUKAI AND TSUJI ARE GOING AFTER AGENT AMATORI!
WHILE CAPTAIN NINOMIYA STAYS IN PLACE!
DOES HE PLAN TO FACE THE TAMAKOMA DUO ON HIS OWN?!

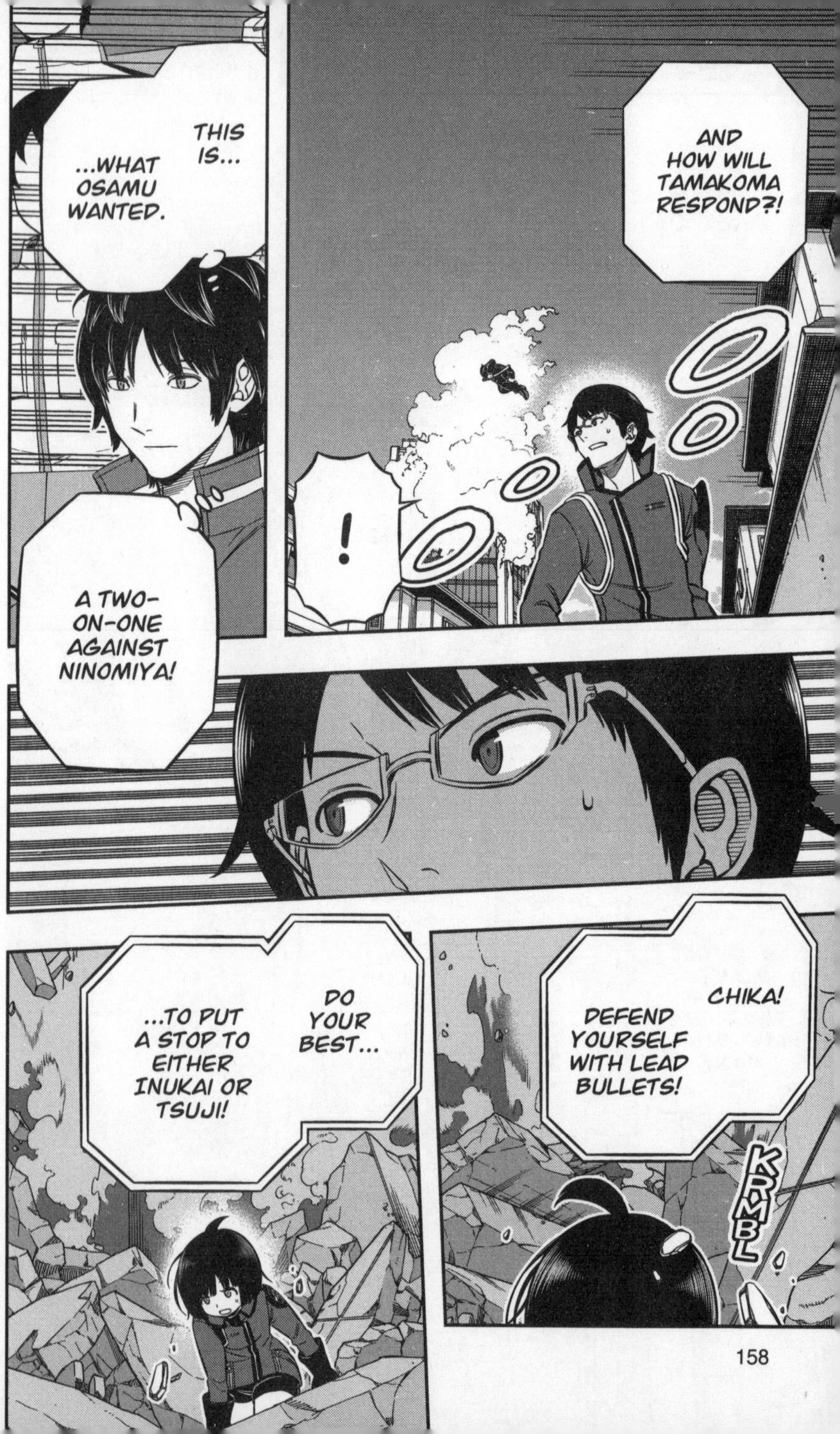
AND HOW WILL TAMAKOMA RESPOND?!
!
THIS IS...
...WHAT OSAMU WANTED.
A TWO-ON-ONE AGAINST NINOMIYA!
CHIKA!
DEFEND YOURSELF WITH LEAD BULLETS!
KRMBL
DO YOUR BEST...
...TO PUT A STOP TO EITHER INUKAI OR TSUJI!

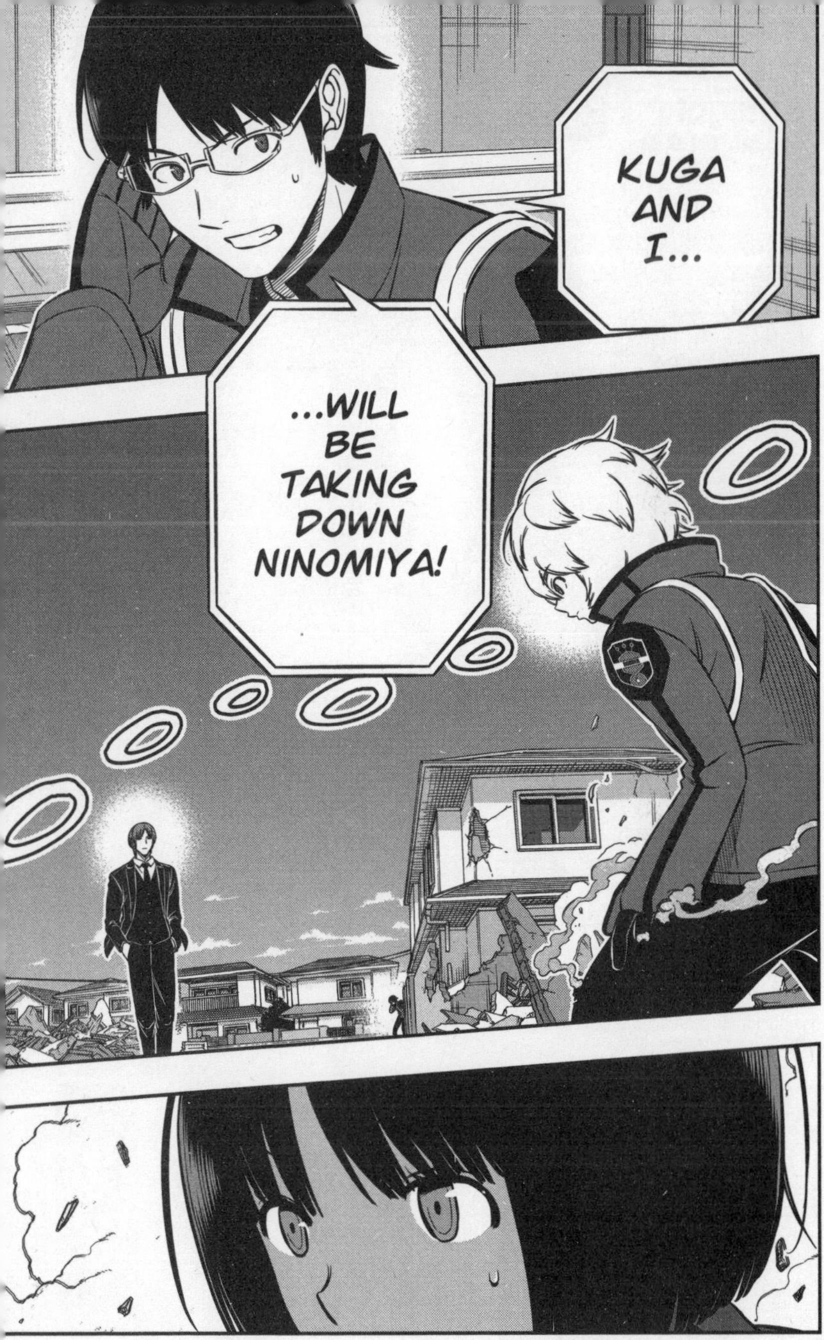
KUGA AND I...
...WILL BE TAKING DOWN NINOMIYA!

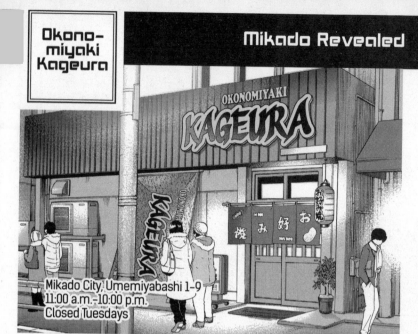

Okonomiyaki Kageura

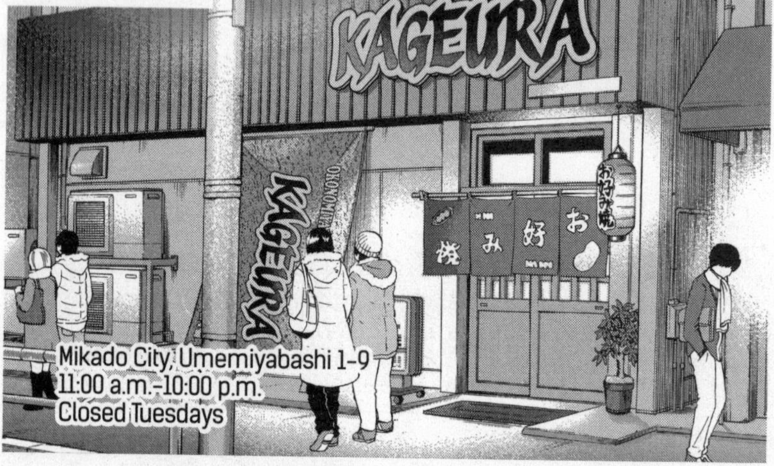
OKONOMIYAKI
KAGEURA
OKONOMIYAKI
KAGEURA
お好み焼
Mikado City, Umemiyabashi 1-9
11:00 a.m.-10:00 p.m.
Closed Tuesdays

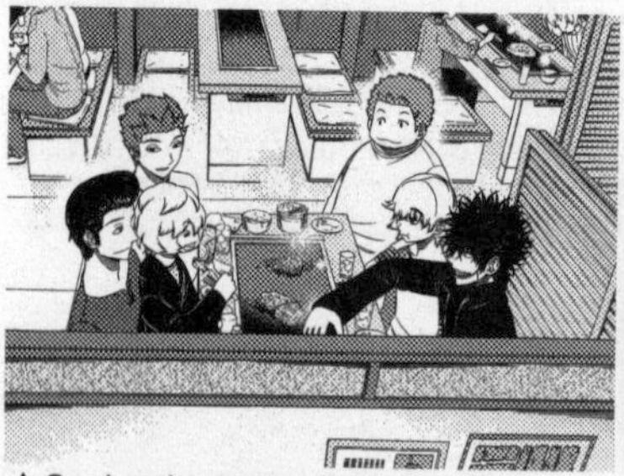

↑ One has the option of having an employee do the cooking, but regulars prefer to do it themselves.

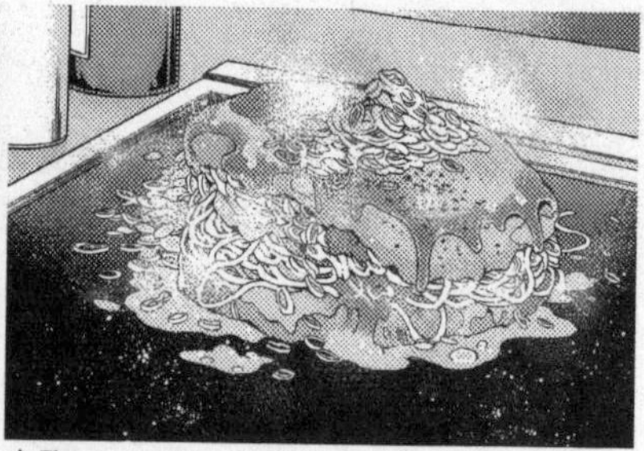

↑ The pork sobayaki option adds pork and egg to the standard modanyaki (1,480 Yen)

This is Kage's family's home and restaurant. His parents and older brother run the place. Yuma shows up just about every week to eat with Zoe, Kage, and those guys.

They're getting close to having tried everything on the menu.

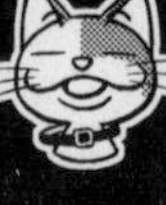

This mom-and-pop shop is beloved by locals.

The restaurant used to be located in East Mikado, but when the Forbidden Zone was expanded one year ago, they moved to their current location.

Border affiliates are frequent customers, perhaps because the family's second son is a Border employee himself.

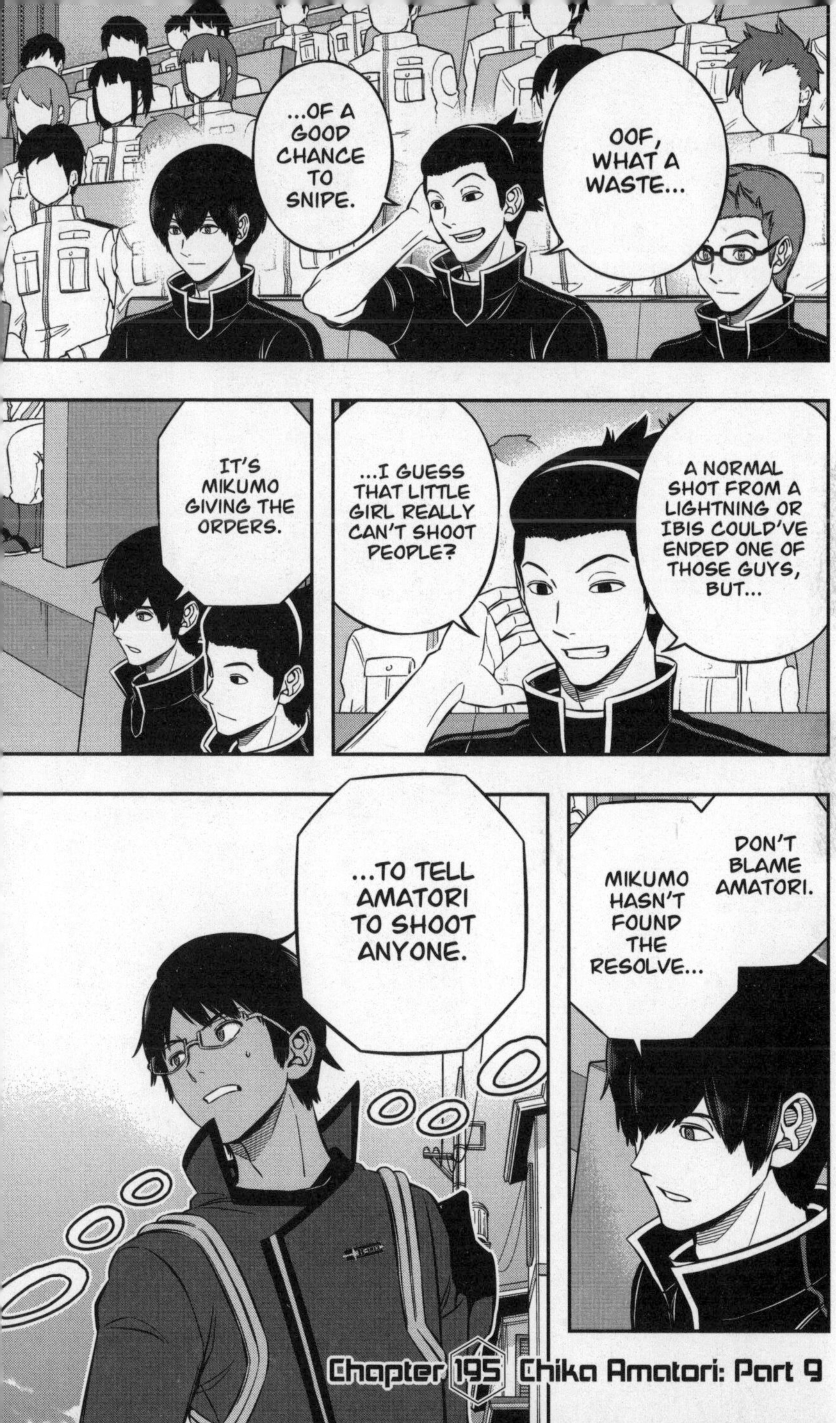
OOF, WHAT A WASTE...
...OF A GOOD CHANCE TO SNIPE.
A NORMAL SHOT FROM A LIGHTNING OR IBIS COULD'VE ENDED ONE OF THOSE GUYS, BUT...
...I GUESS THAT LITTLE GIRL REALLY CAN'T SHOOT PEOPLE?
IT'S MIKUMO GIVING THE ORDERS.
DON'T BLAME AMATORI.
MIKUMO HASN'T FOUND THE RESOLVE...
...TO TELL AMATORI TO SHOOT ANYONE.
Chapter 195 Chika Amatori: Part 9

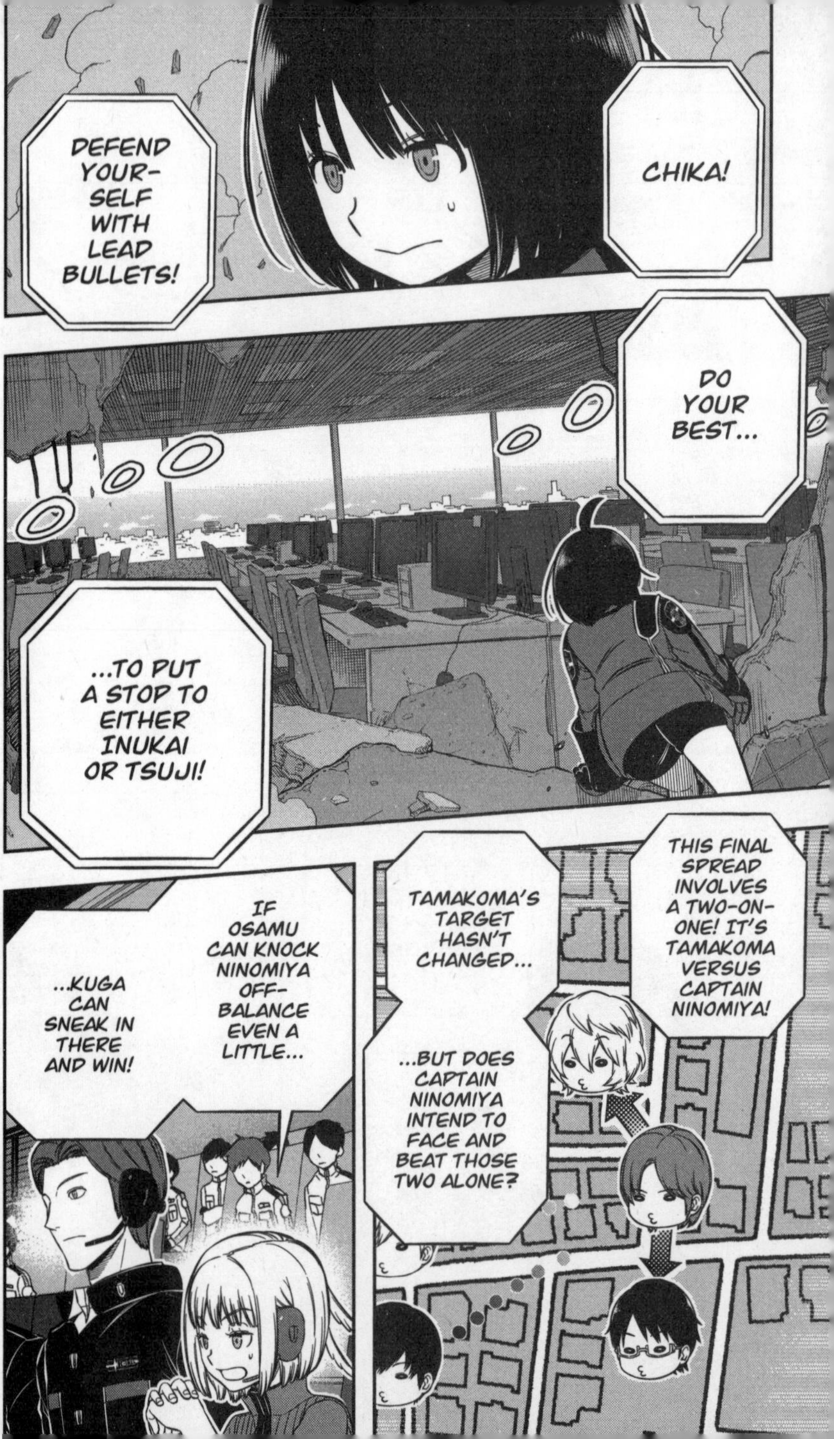

CHIKA!
DEFEND YOURSELF WITH LEAD BULLETS!
DO YOUR BEST...
...TO PUT A STOP TO EITHER INUKAI OR TSUJI!
THIS FINAL SPREAD INVOLVES A TWO-ON-ONE! IT'S TAMAKOMA VERSUS CAPTAIN NINOMIYA!
TAMAKOMA'S TARGET HASN'T CHANGED...
...BUT DOES CAPTAIN NINOMIYA INTEND TO FACE AND BEAT THOSE TWO ALONE?
IF OSAMU CAN KNOCK NINOMIYA OFF-BALANCE EVEN A LITTLE...
...KUGA CAN SNEAK IN THERE AND WIN!

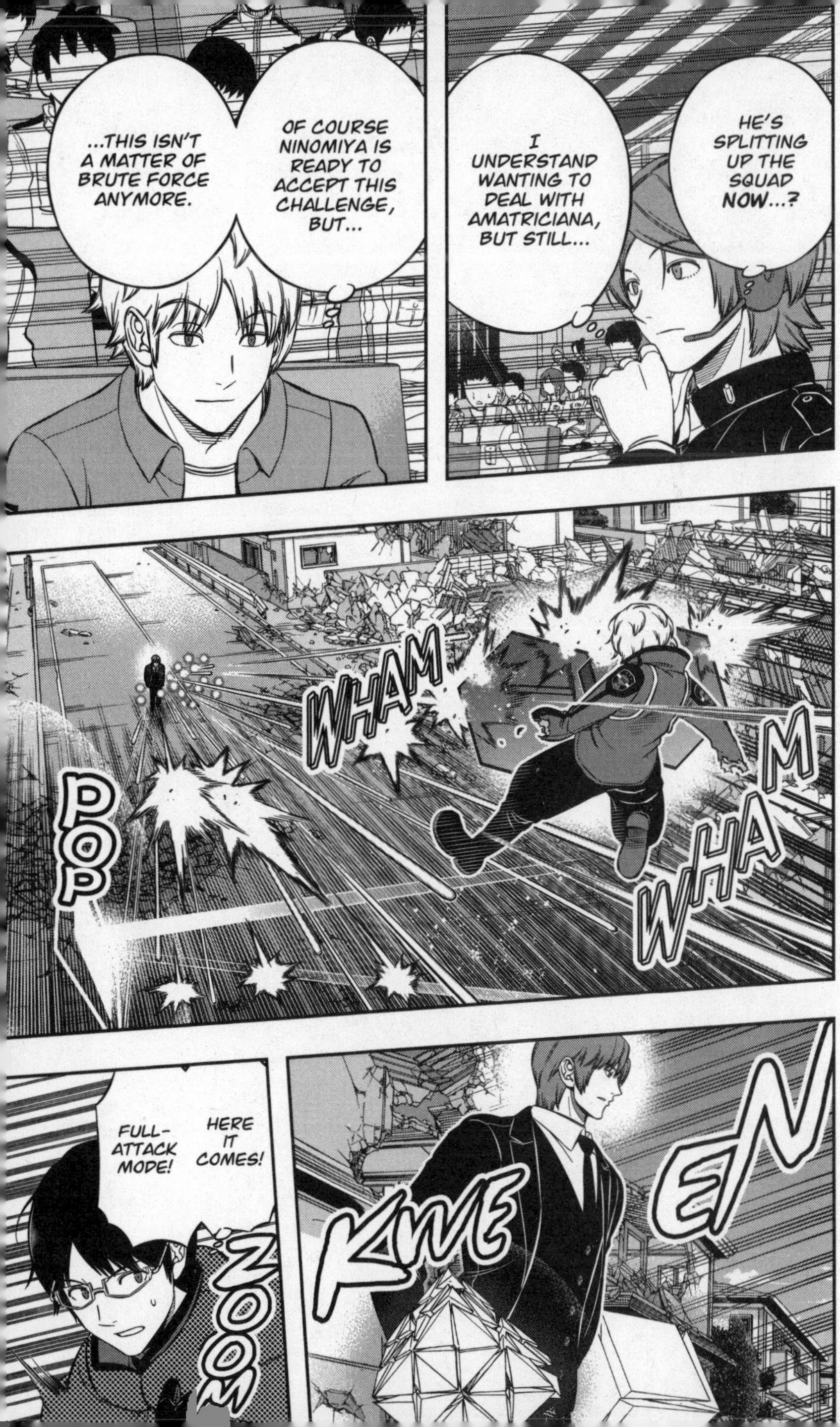
HE'S SPLITTING UP THE SQUAD NOW...?
I UNDERSTAND WANTING TO DEAL WITH AMATRICIANA, BUT STILL...
OF COURSE NINOMIYA IS READY TO ACCEPT THIS CHALLENGE, BUT...
...THIS ISN'T A MATTER OF BRUTE FORCE ANYMORE.
WHAM
WHAM
POP
KWEEN
HERE IT COMES!
FULL-ATTACK MODE!
ZOOOM

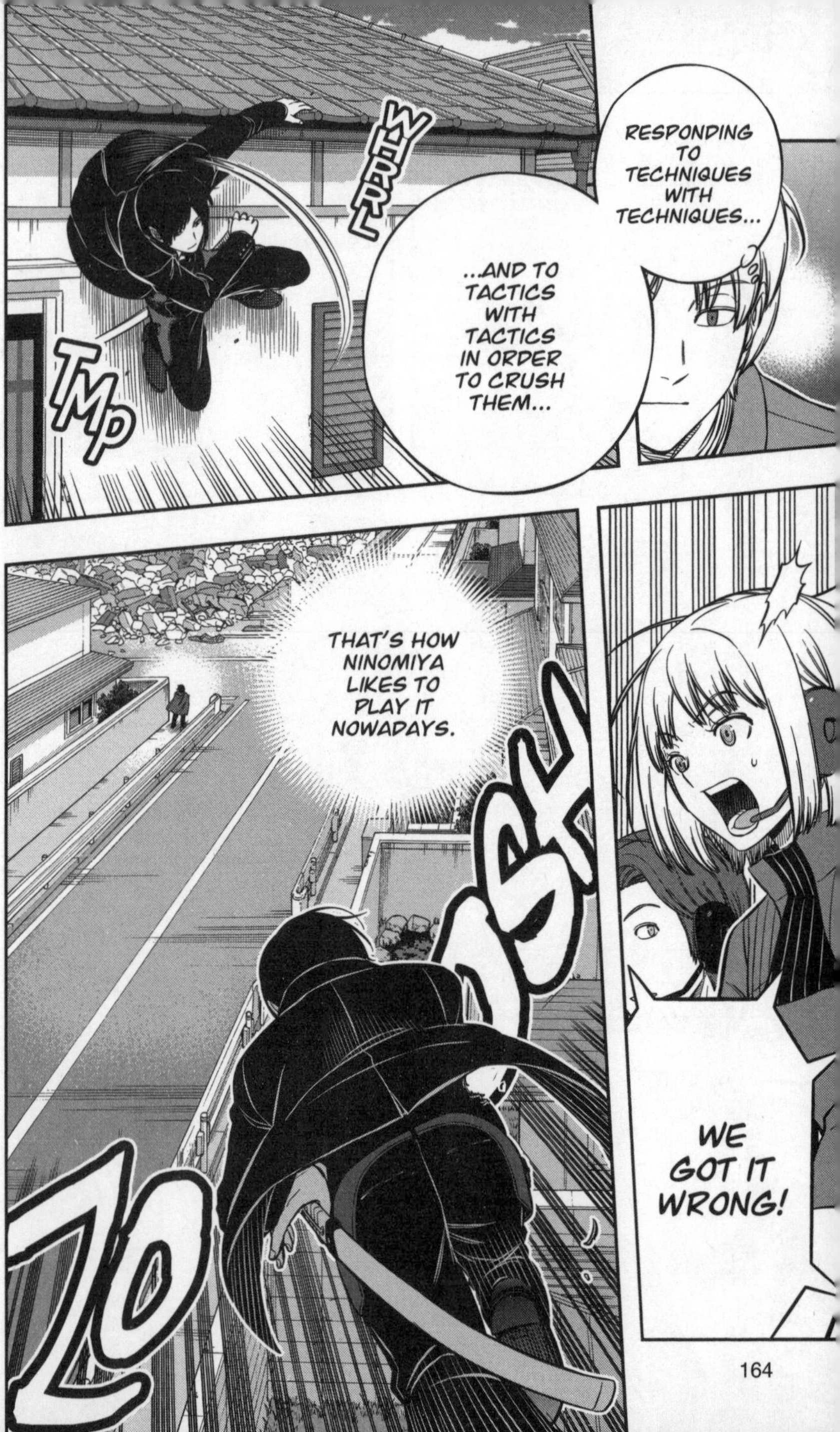
RESPONDING TO TECHNIQUES WITH TECHNIQUES...
...AND TO TACTICS WITH TACTICS IN ORDER TO CRUSH THEM...
WHRRL
TMP
WE GOT IT WRONG!
THAT'S HOW NINOMIYA LIKES TO PLAY IT NOWADAYS.

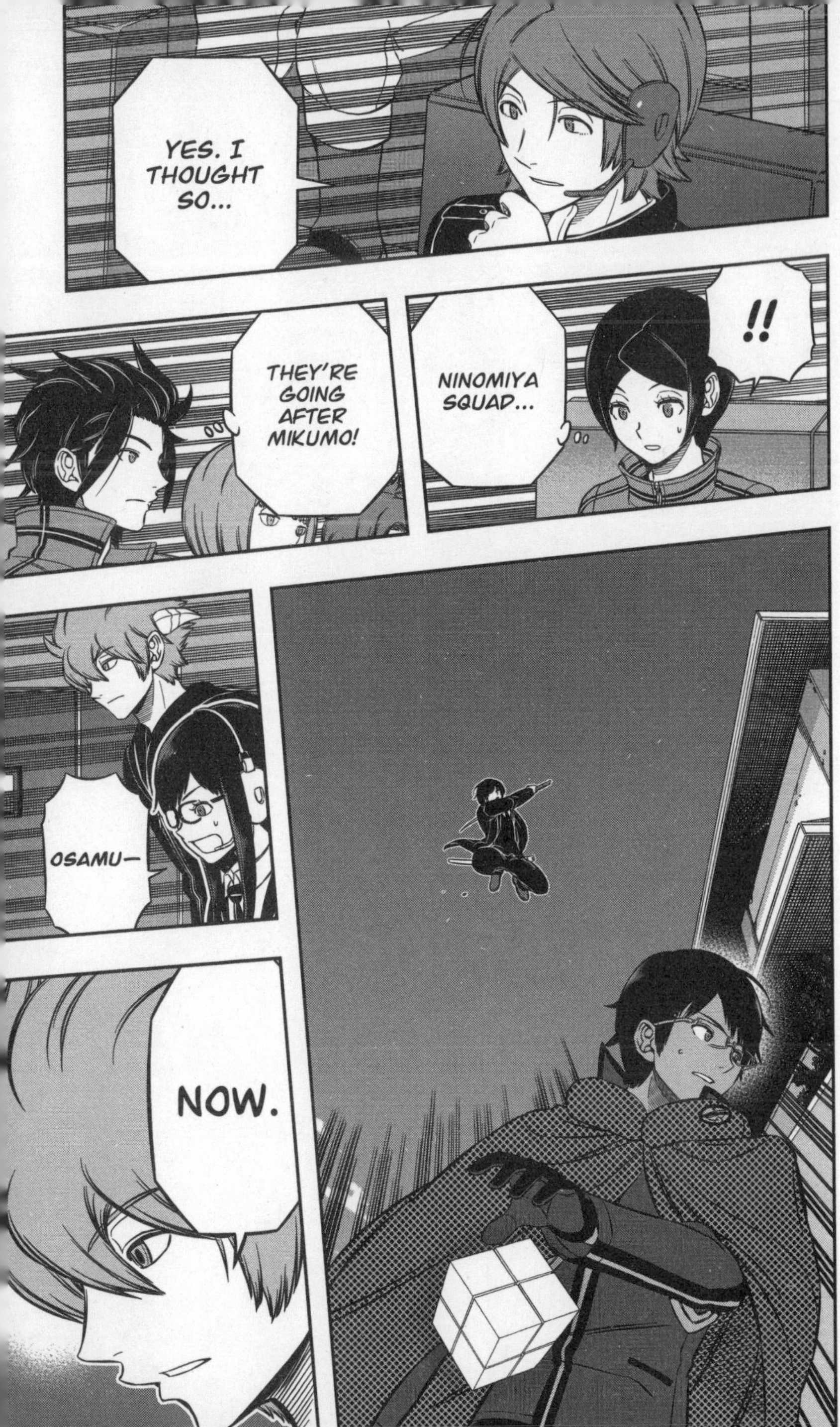
YES. I THOUGHT SO...
!!
NINOMIYA SQUAD...
THEY'RE GOING AFTER MIKUMO!
OSAMU—
NOW.

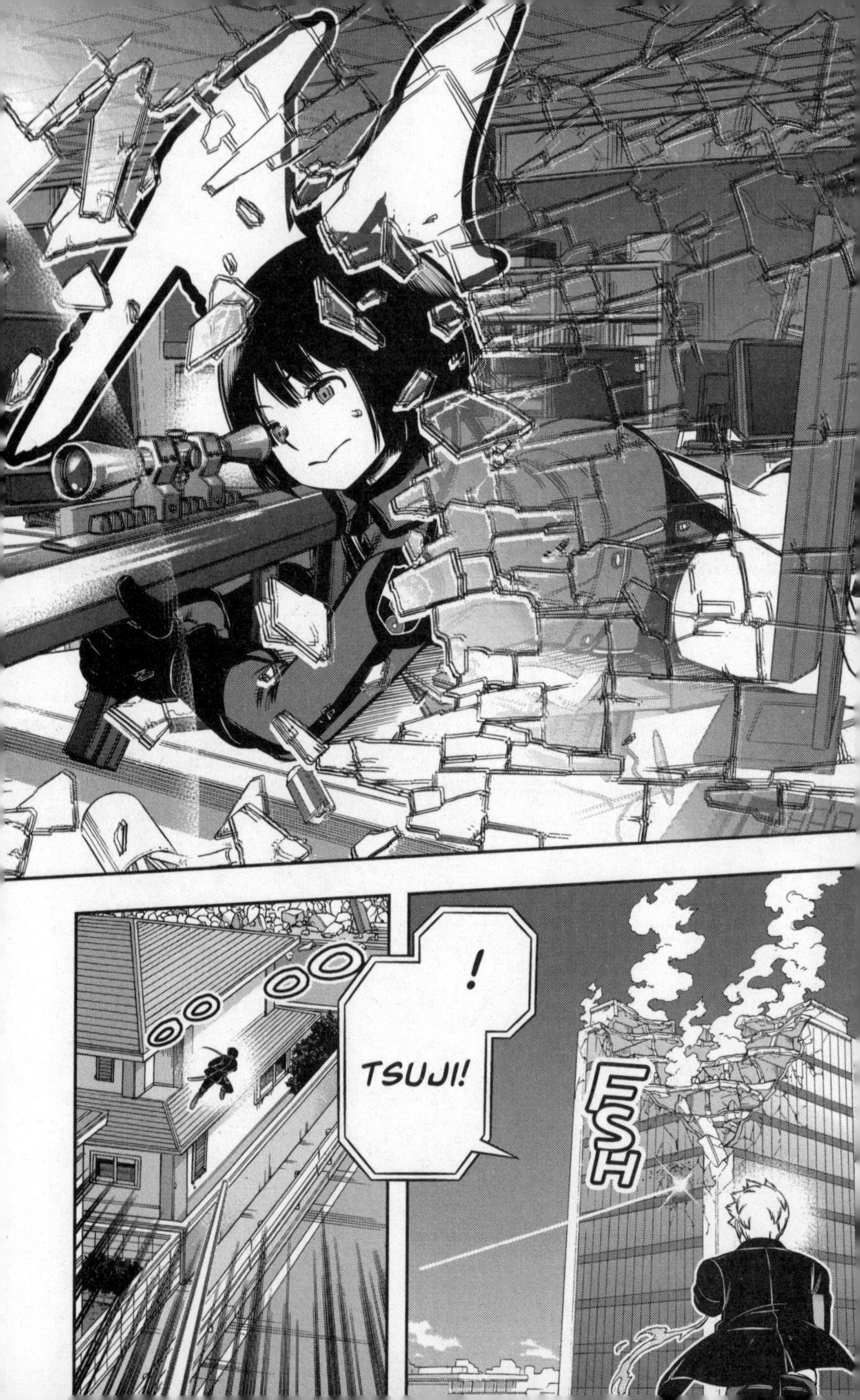
FSH
!
TSUJI!

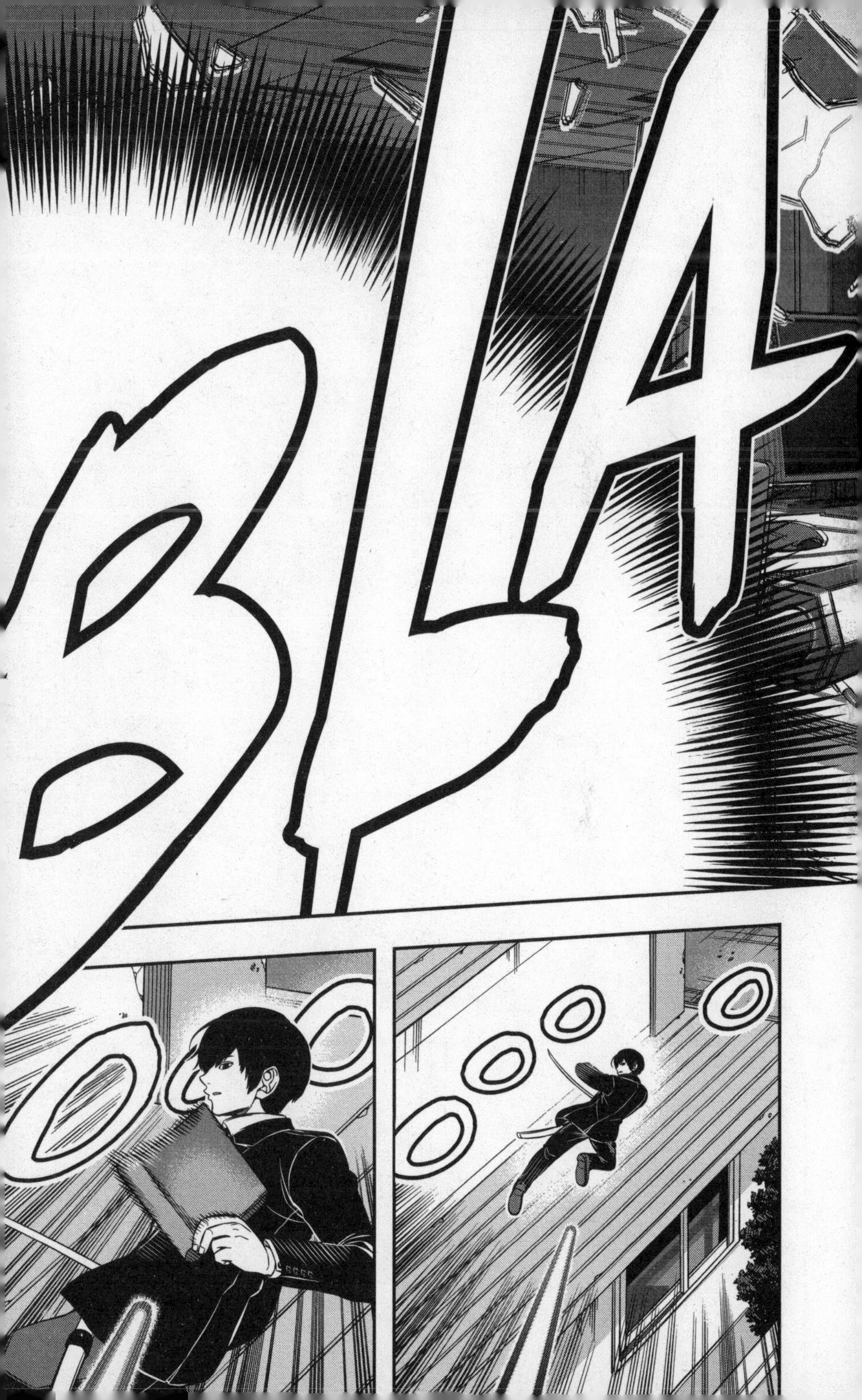
BLA

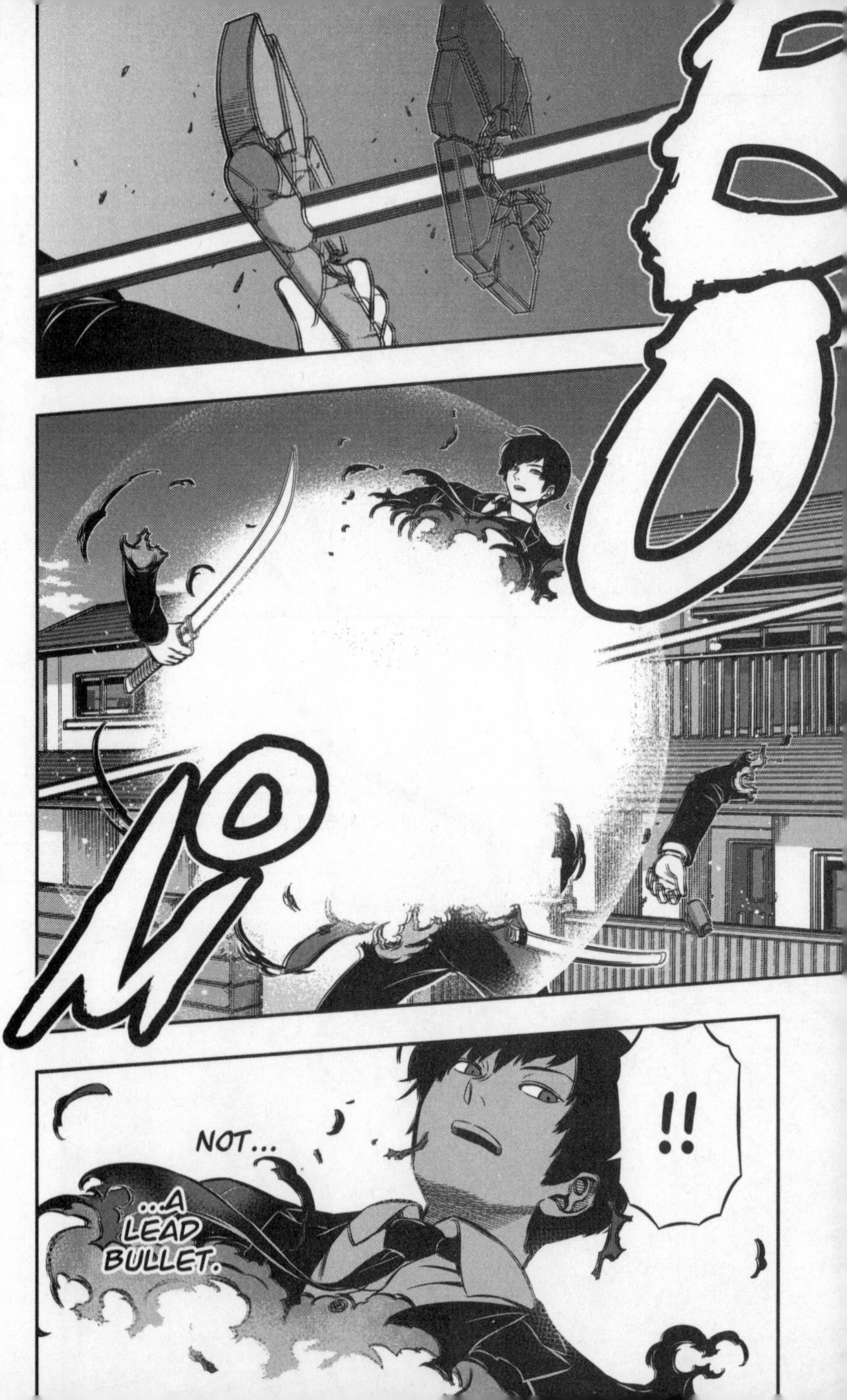
!!
NOT...
...A LEAD BULLET.

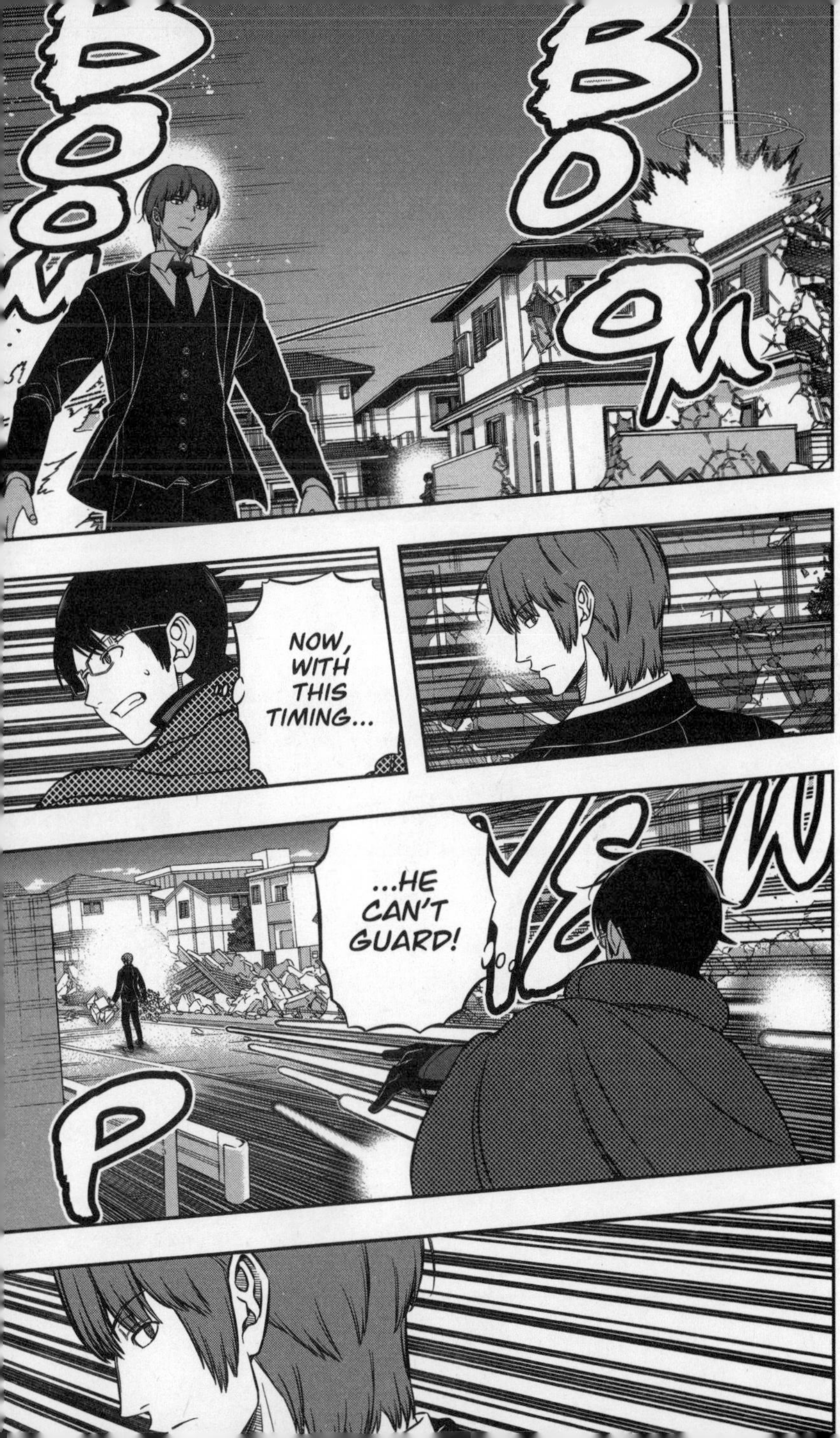
BOOM
BOOM
NOW, WITH THIS TIMING...
...HE CAN'T GUARD!

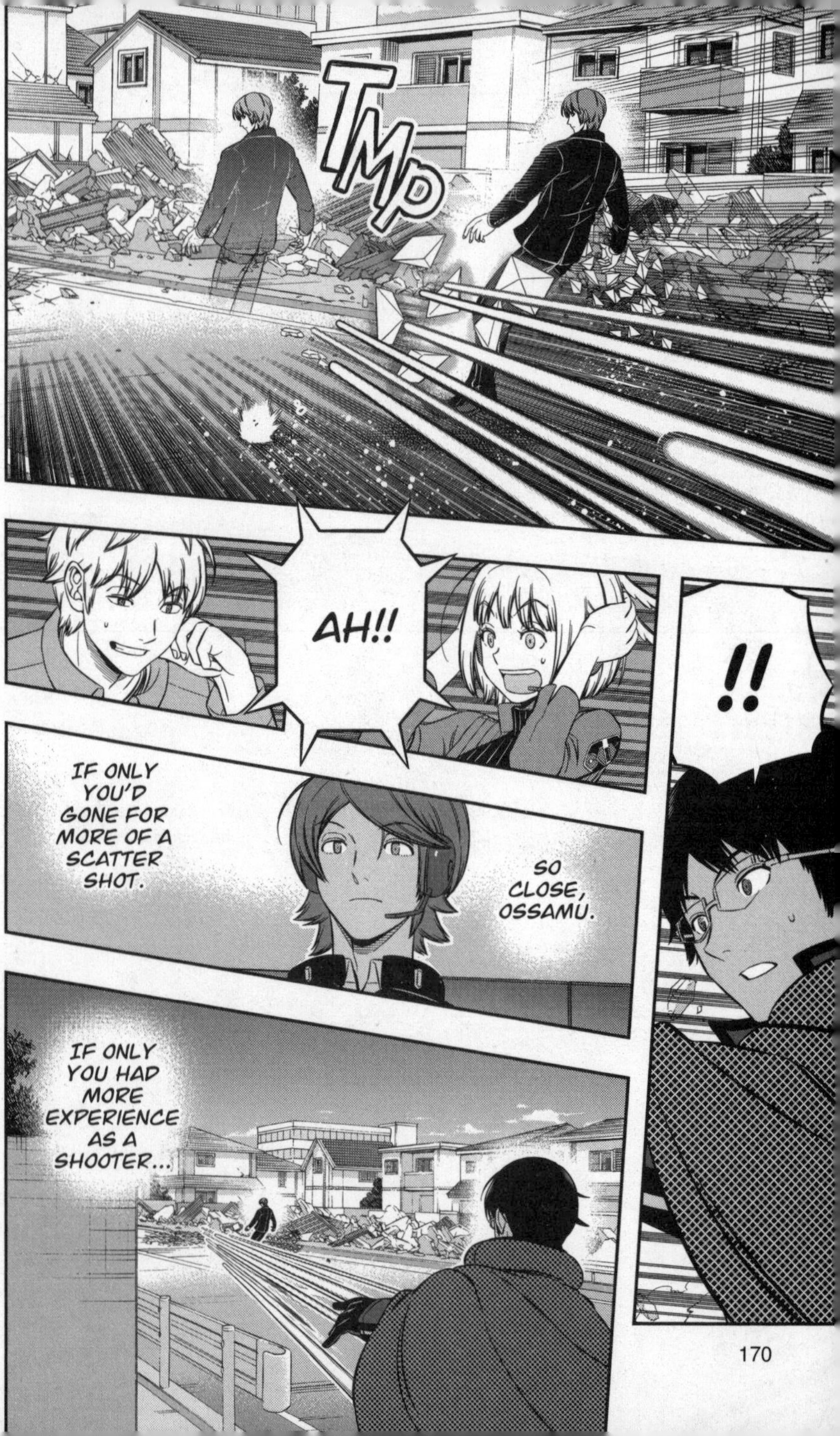
TMP
!!
AH!!
SO CLOSE, OSSAMU.
IF ONLY YOU'D GONE FOR MORE OF A SCATTER SHOT.
IF ONLY YOU HAD MORE EXPERIENCE AS A SHOOTER...

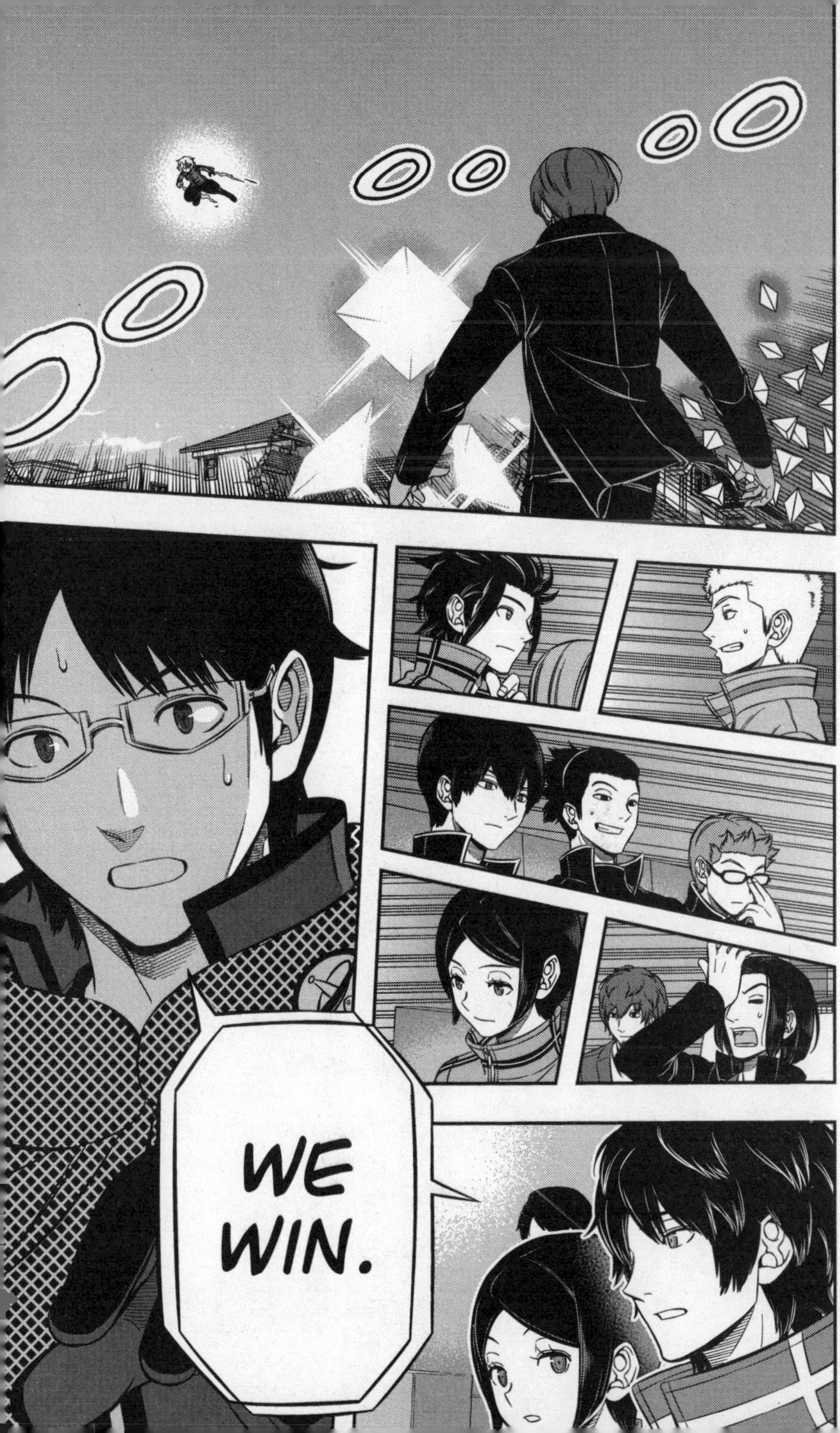
WE WIN.

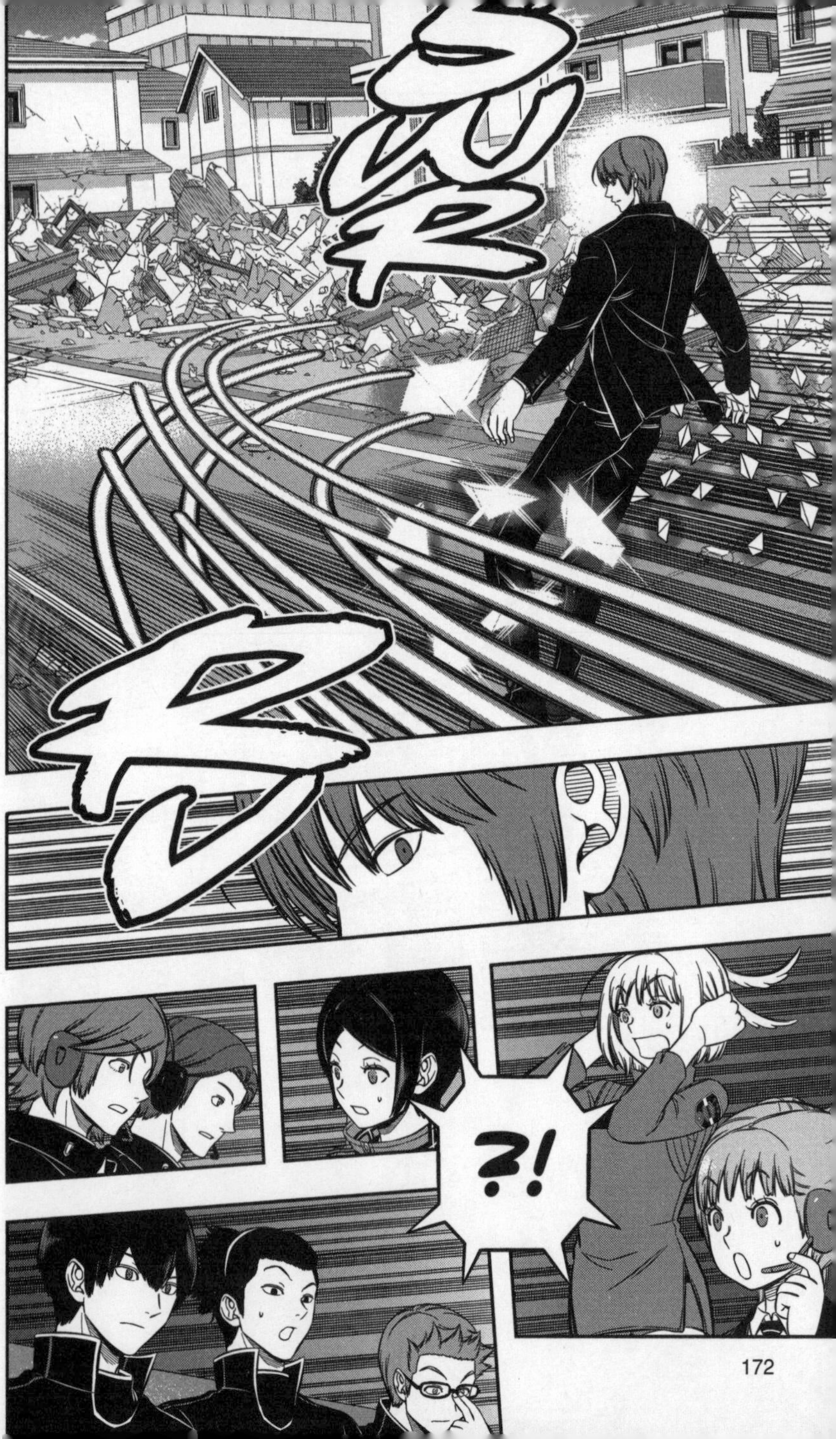
?!

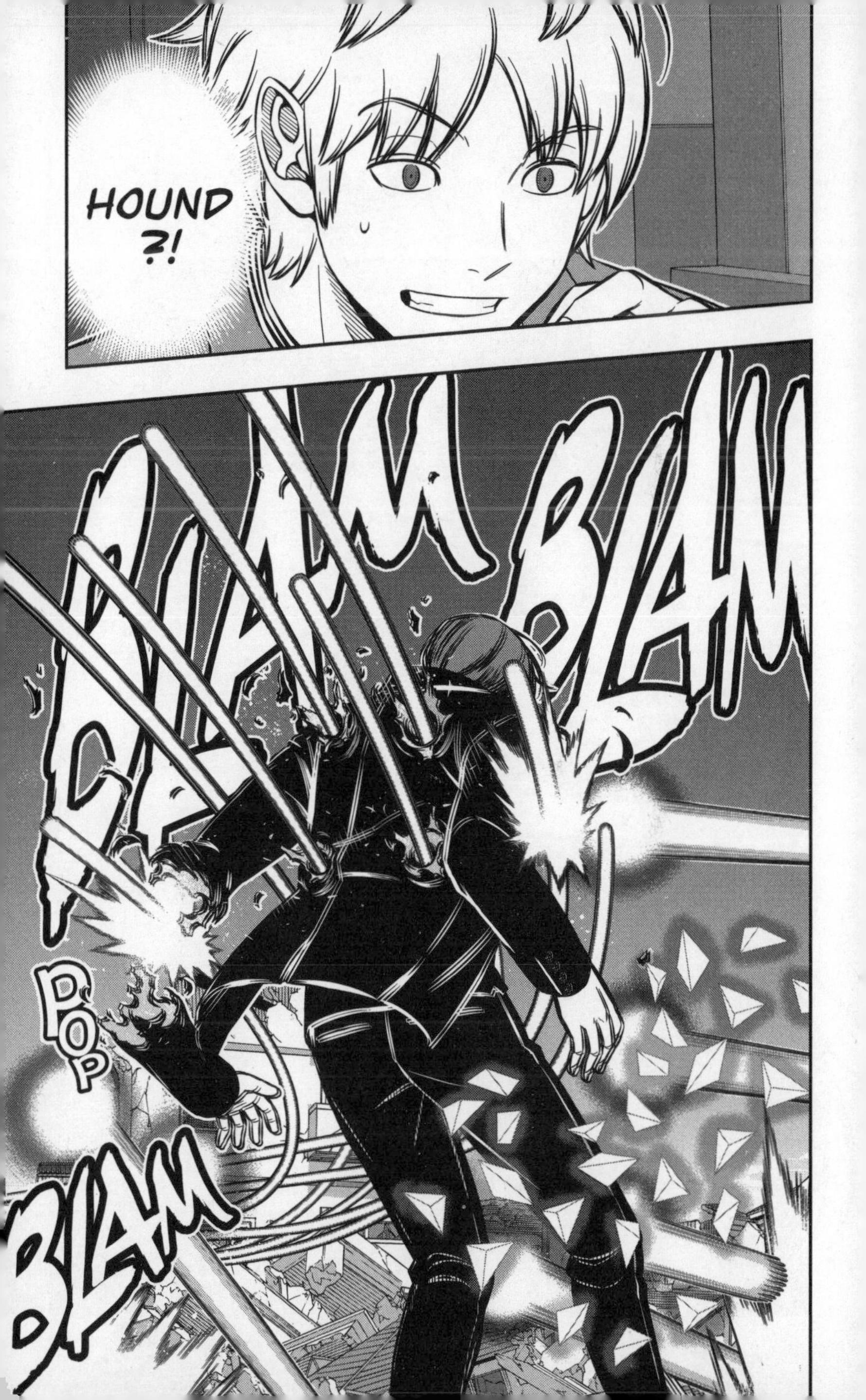
HOUND ?!
BLAM
BLAM
POP
BLAM

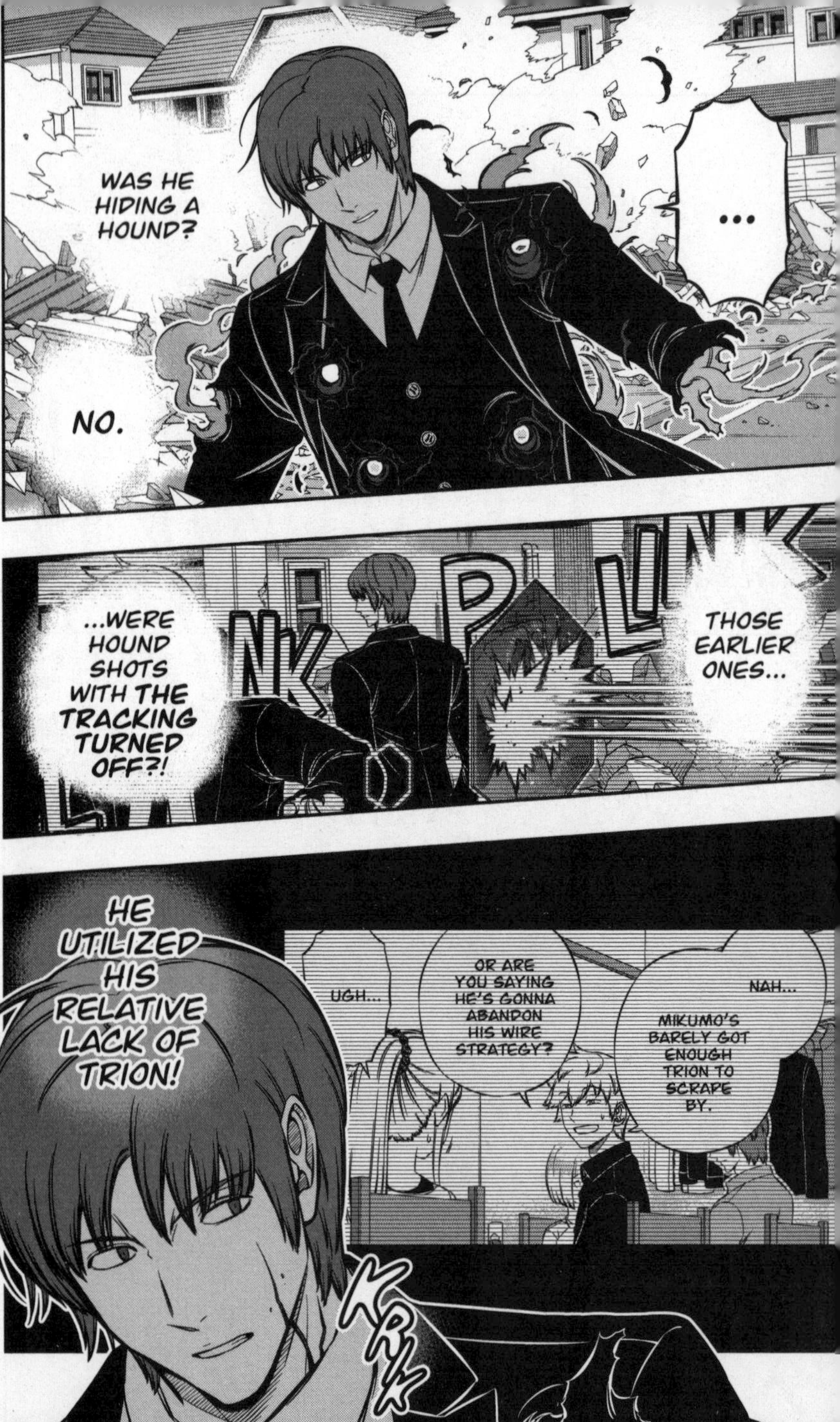
...
WAS HE HIDING A HOUND?
NO.
THOSE EARLIER ONES...
PLINK
...WERE HOUND SHOTS WITH THE TRACKING TURNED OFF?!
NAH...
MIKUMO'S BARELY GOT ENOUGH TRION TO SCRAPE BY.
OR ARE YOU SAYING HE'S GONNA ABANDON HIS WIRE STRATEGY?
UGH...
HE UTILIZED HIS RELATIVE LACK OF TRION!
KRK

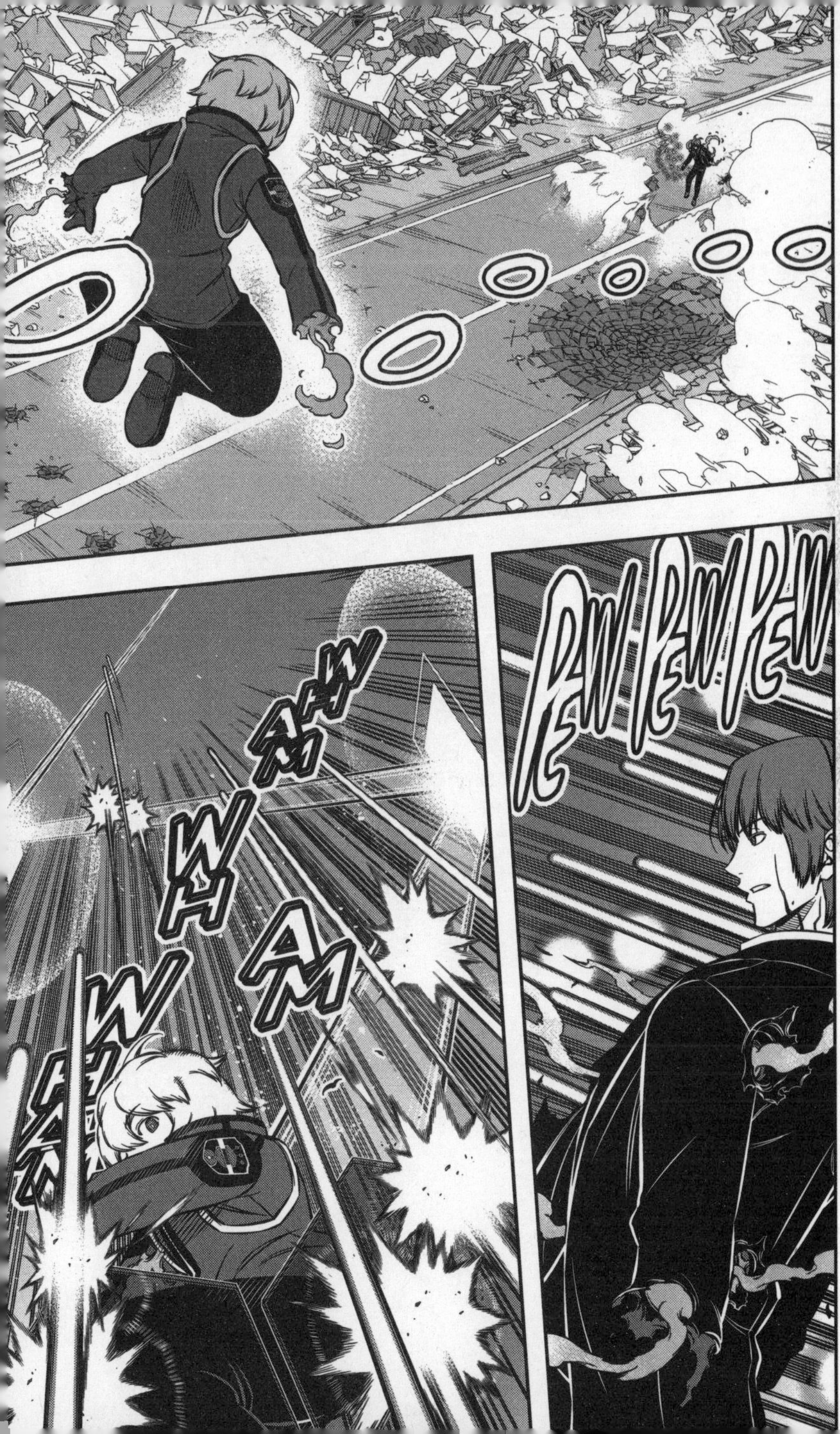
PEW PEW PEW
WHAM
WHAM
WHAM

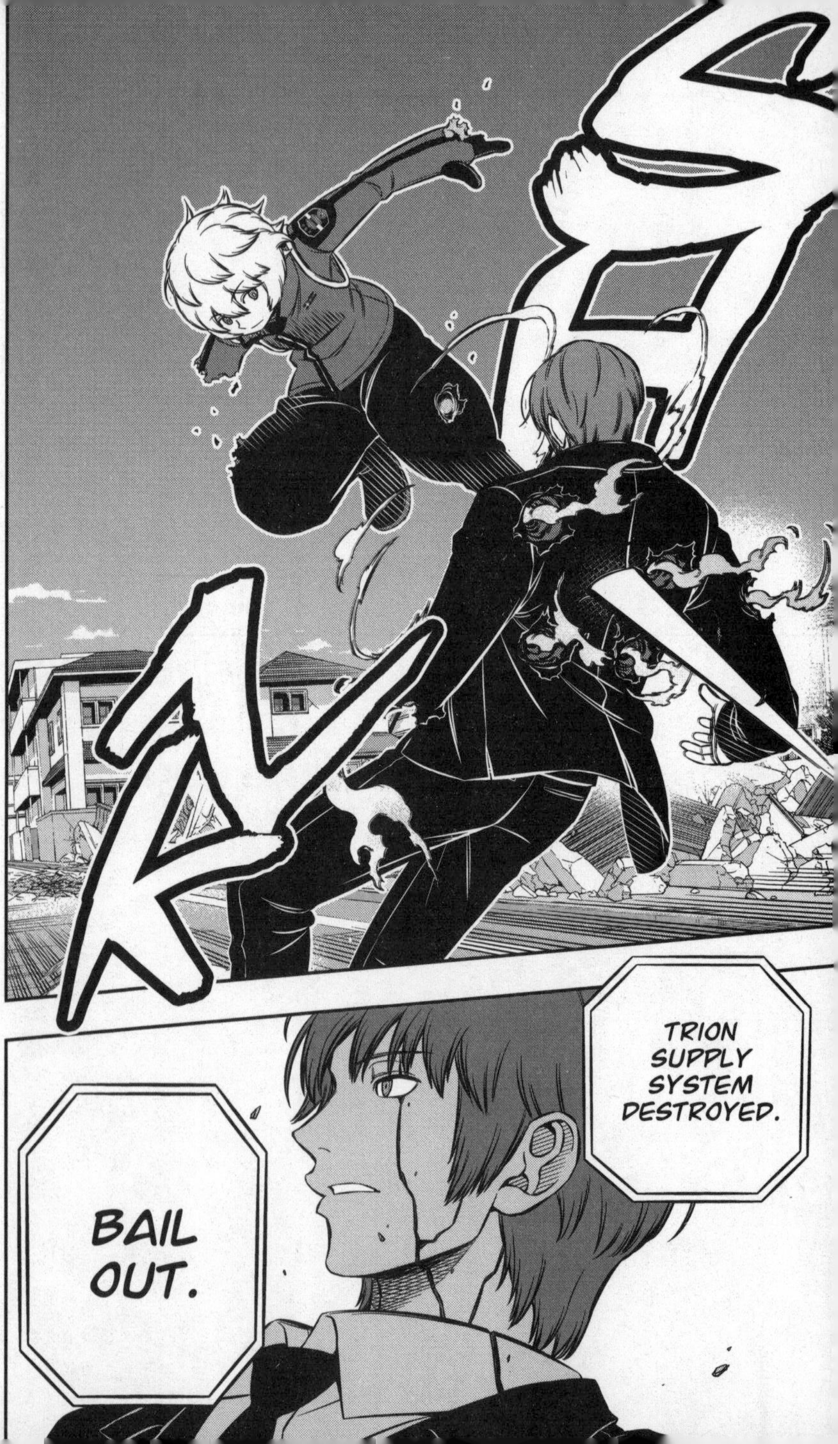
TRION SUPPLY SYSTEM DESTROYED.
BAIL OUT.

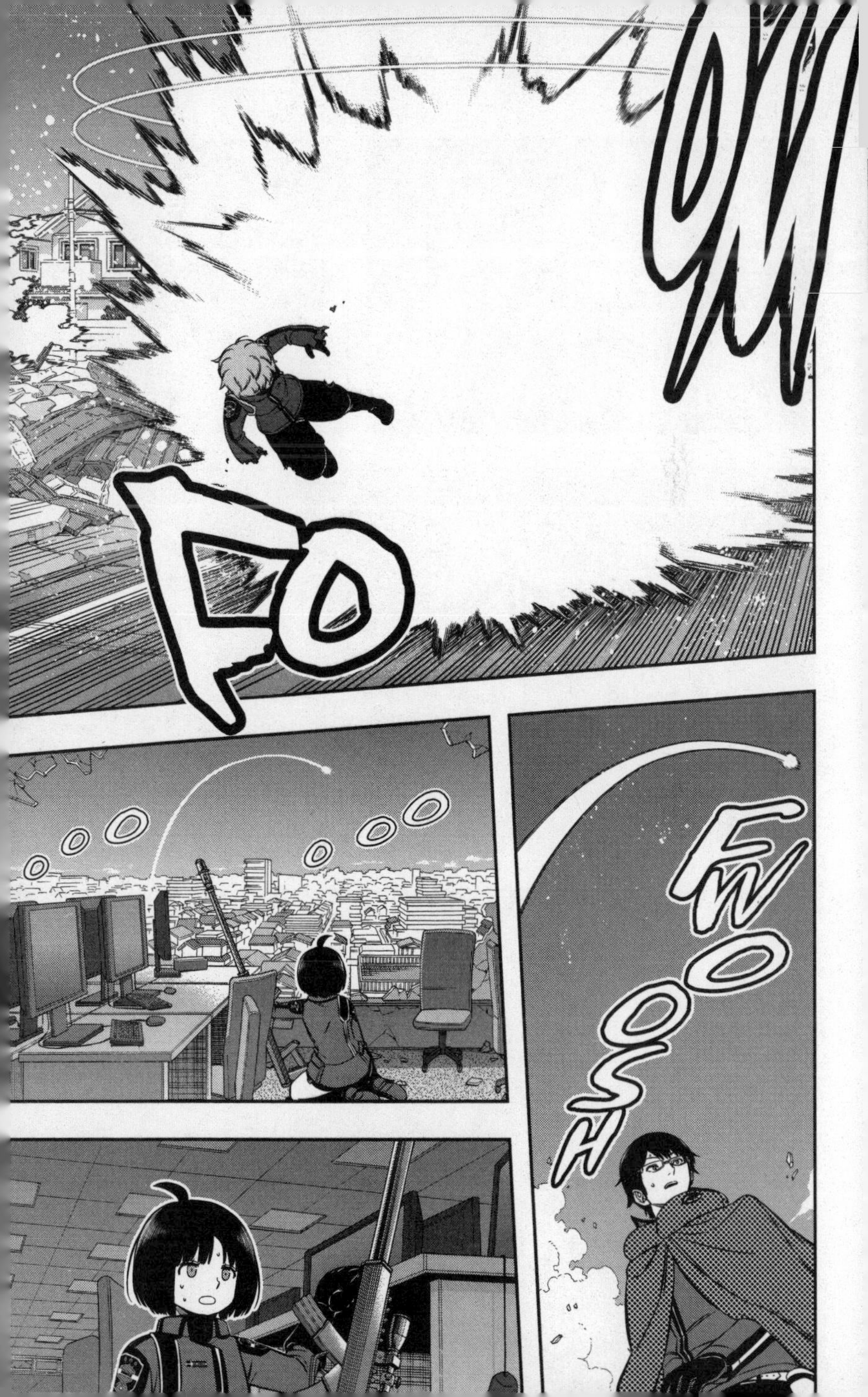
FWOOSH

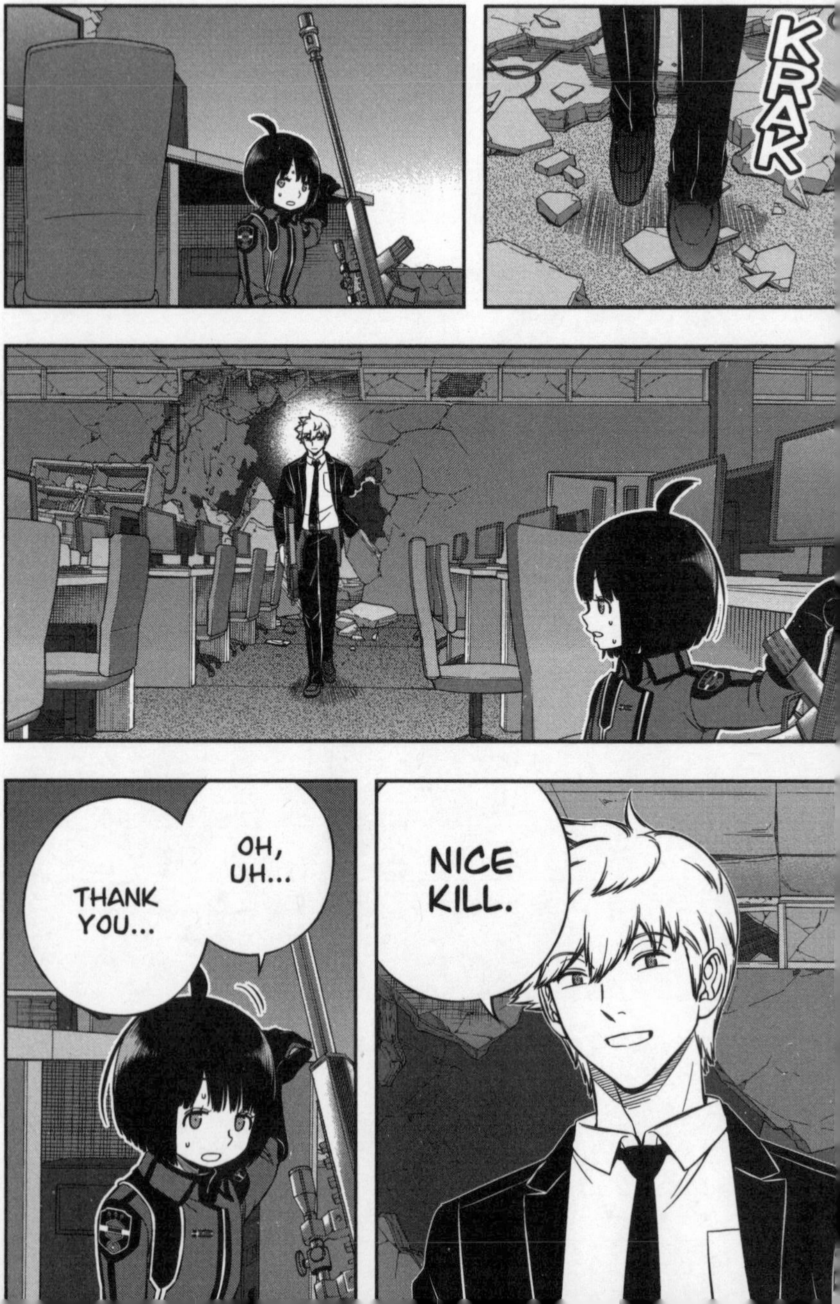
KRAK
NICE KILL.
OH, UH...
THANK YOU...

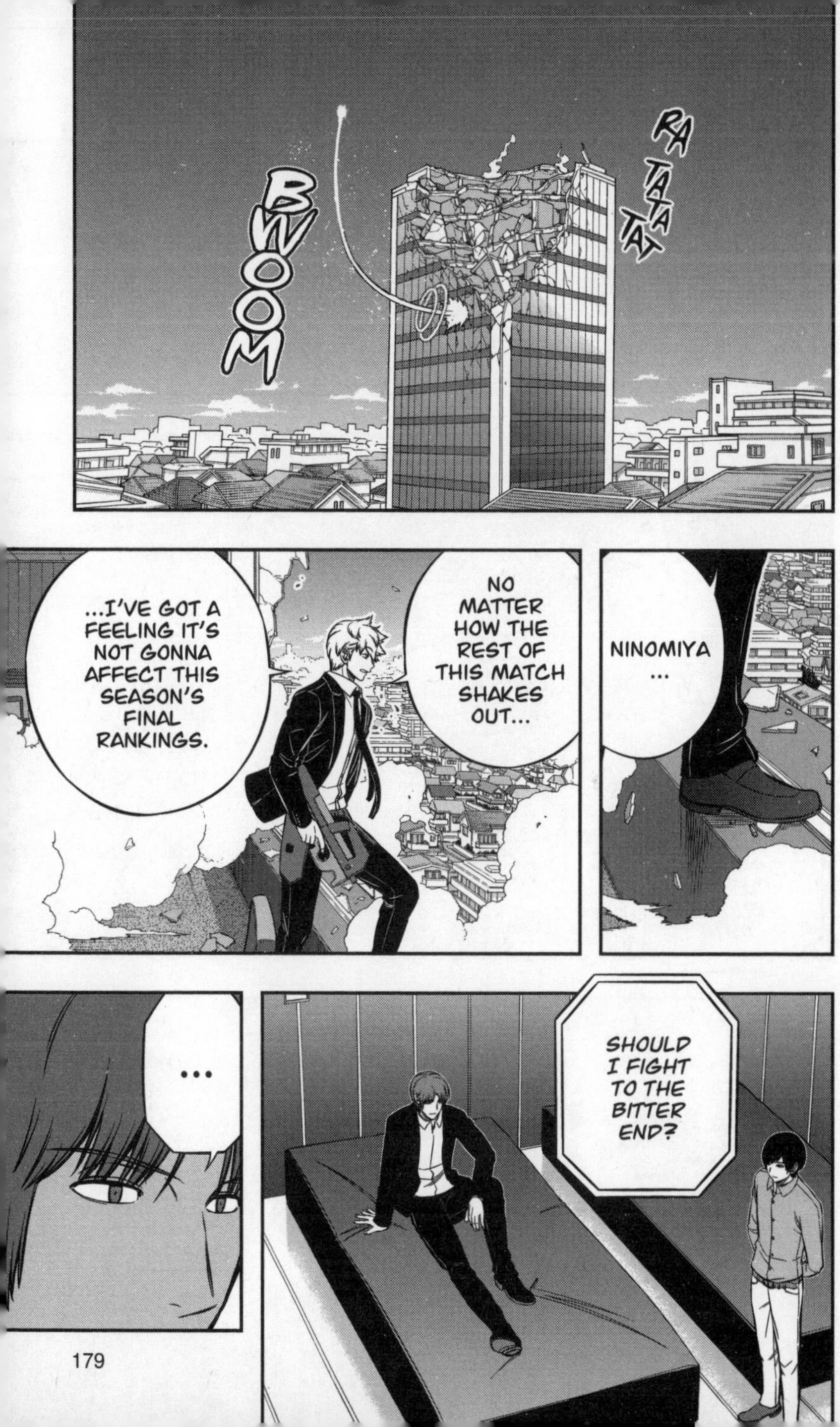
RA TATATAT
BWOOM
NINOMIYA...
NO MATTER HOW THE REST OF THIS MATCH SHAKES OUT...
...I'VE GOT A FEELING IT'S NOT GONNA AFFECT THIS SEASON'S FINAL RANKINGS.
SHOULD I FIGHT TO THE BITTER END?
...

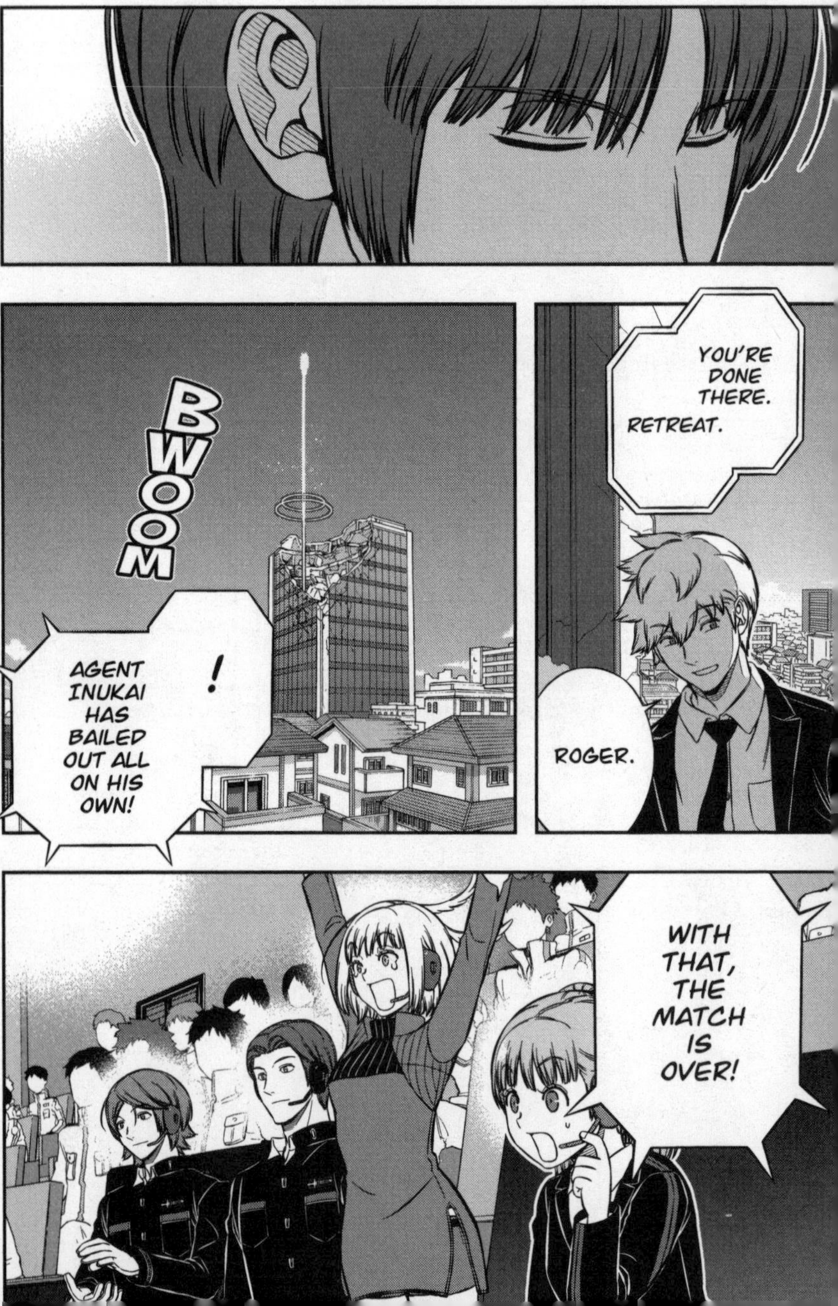
YOU'RE DONE THERE.
RETREAT.
ROGER.
BWOOM
!
AGENT INUKAI HAS BAILED OUT ALL ON HIS OWN!
WITH THAT, THE MATCH IS OVER!

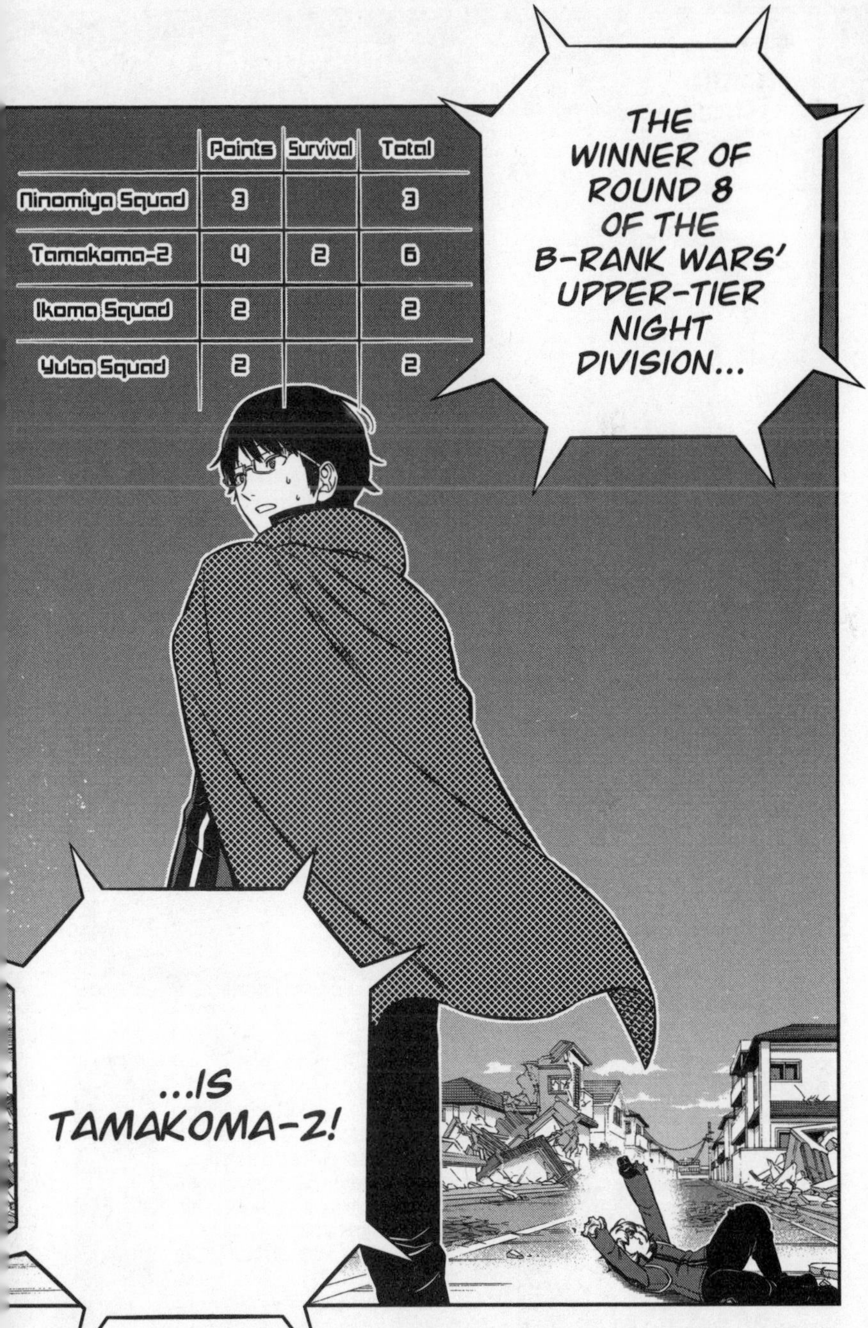
THE WINNER OF ROUND 8 OF THE B-RANK WARS' UPPER-TIER NIGHT DIVISION...
Points Survival Total
Ninomiya Squad 3 3
Tamakoma-2 4 2 6
Ikoma Squad 2 2
Yuba Squad 2 2
...IS TAMAKOMA-2!

Taiyaki Shop: Taian Kichijitsu

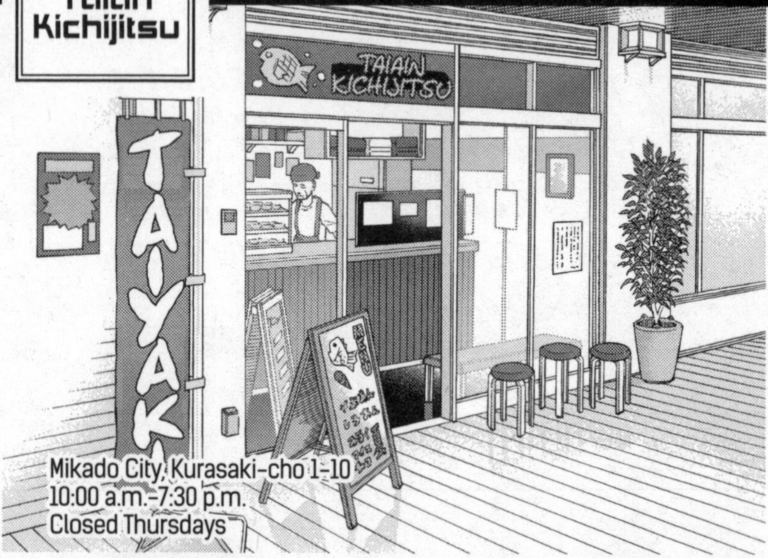
TAIAN KICHIJITSU
TAIYAKI

Mikado City, Kurasaki-cho 1-10
10:00 a.m.-7:30 p.m.
Closed Thursdays

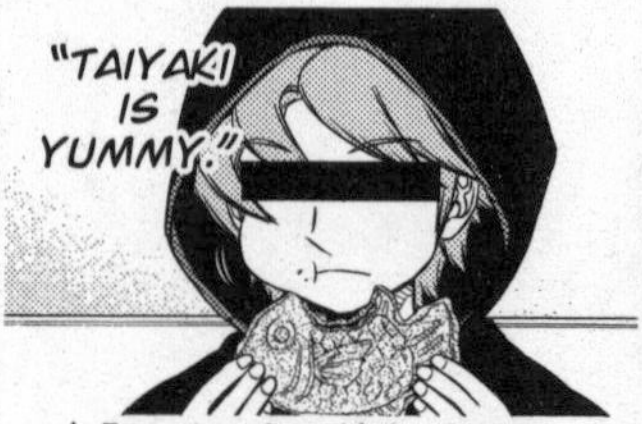
"TAIYAKI IS YUMMY."

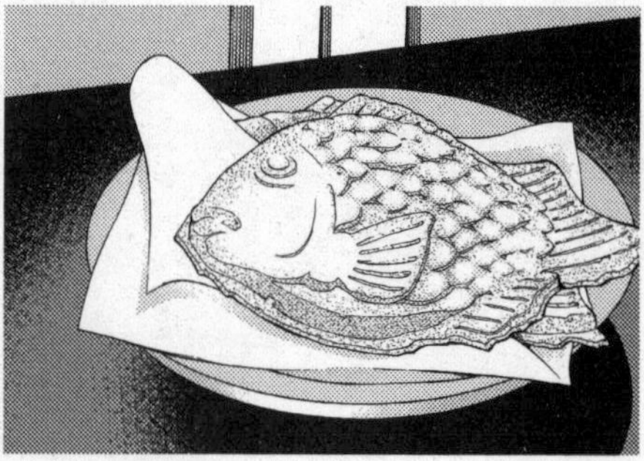

↑ Even popular with foreign exchange students.

→ Beyond the typical anko or cream types, the shop also offers a variety of seasonal fruit cream fillings, and even ice-cream-filled taiyaki during summer.

This is the taiyaki shop involved in Yotaro's wager. Chief Rindo sometimes buys taiyaki from here for the gang, on a whim. It's the perfect walking distance from Tamakoma Branch, so they use it as a convenient destination when they need to take the prisoner out on a walk.

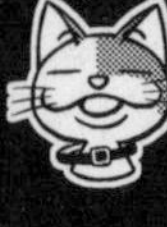

This tiny shop is located a short walk from Tamakoma Branch. Even just watching the skilled workers cook up the taiyaki is a treat on its own. The owner was very pleased with his naming sense when he came up with *Taian Kichijitsu*, so it was a shock to his system when he learned that many other taiyaki shops were already using that name.

**Taian kichijitsu* means "very auspicious day," but this "taian" uses the kanji for "tai" as in taiyaki and "an" as in anko.

Casual Sweets

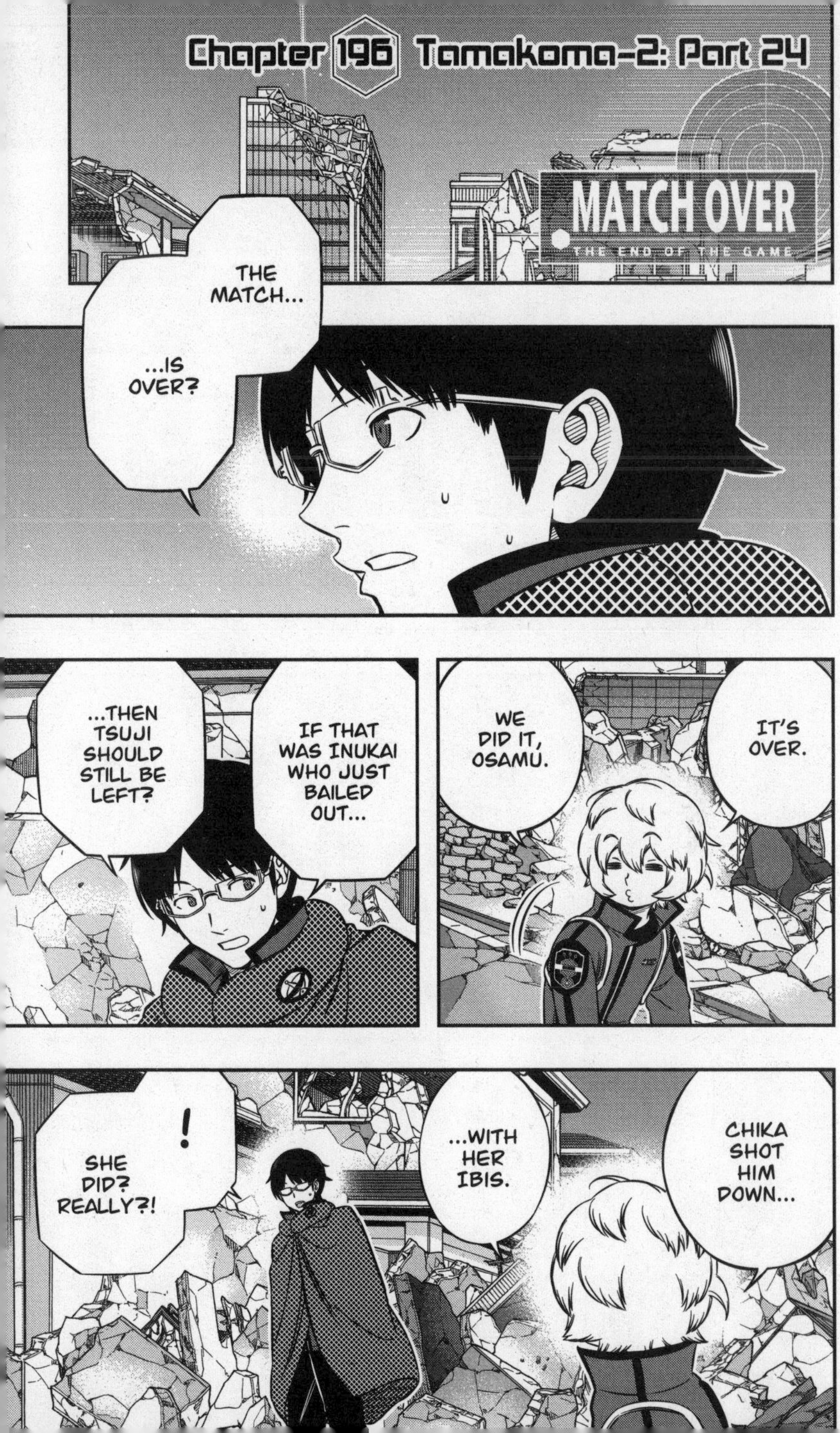
Chapter 196 Tamakoma-2: Part 24
MATCH OVER
THE END OF THE GAME
THE MATCH... ...IS OVER?
IT'S OVER.
WE DID IT, OSAMU.
IF THAT WAS INUKAI WHO JUST BAILED OUT...
...THEN TSUJI SHOULD STILL BE LEFT?
CHIKA SHOT HIM DOWN...
...WITH HER IBIS.
!
SHE DID? REALLY?!

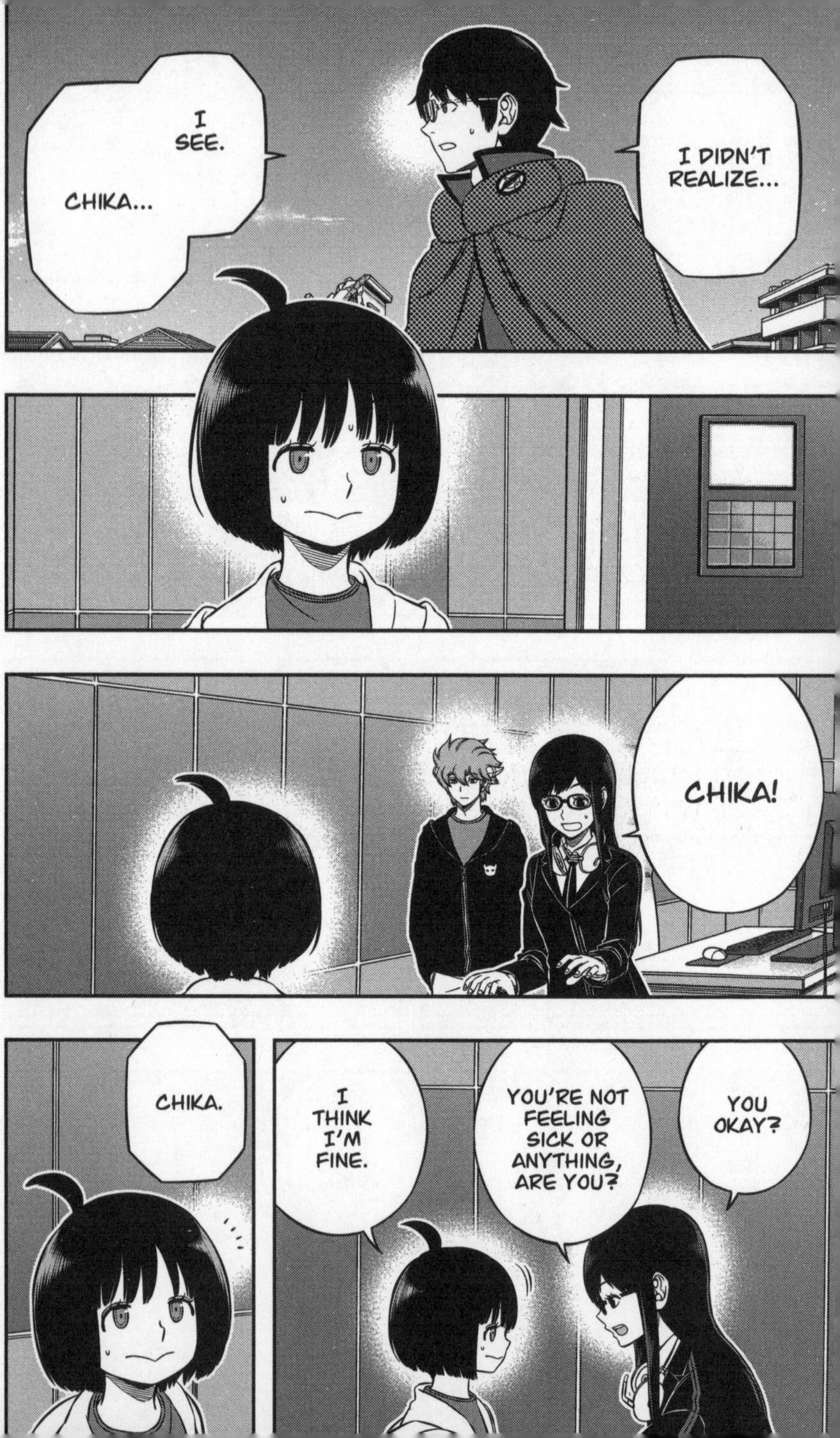
I DIDN'T REALIZE...
I SEE. CHIKA...
CHIKA!
YOU OKAY?
YOU'RE NOT FEELING SICK OR ANYTHING, ARE YOU?
I THINK I'M FINE.
CHIKA.

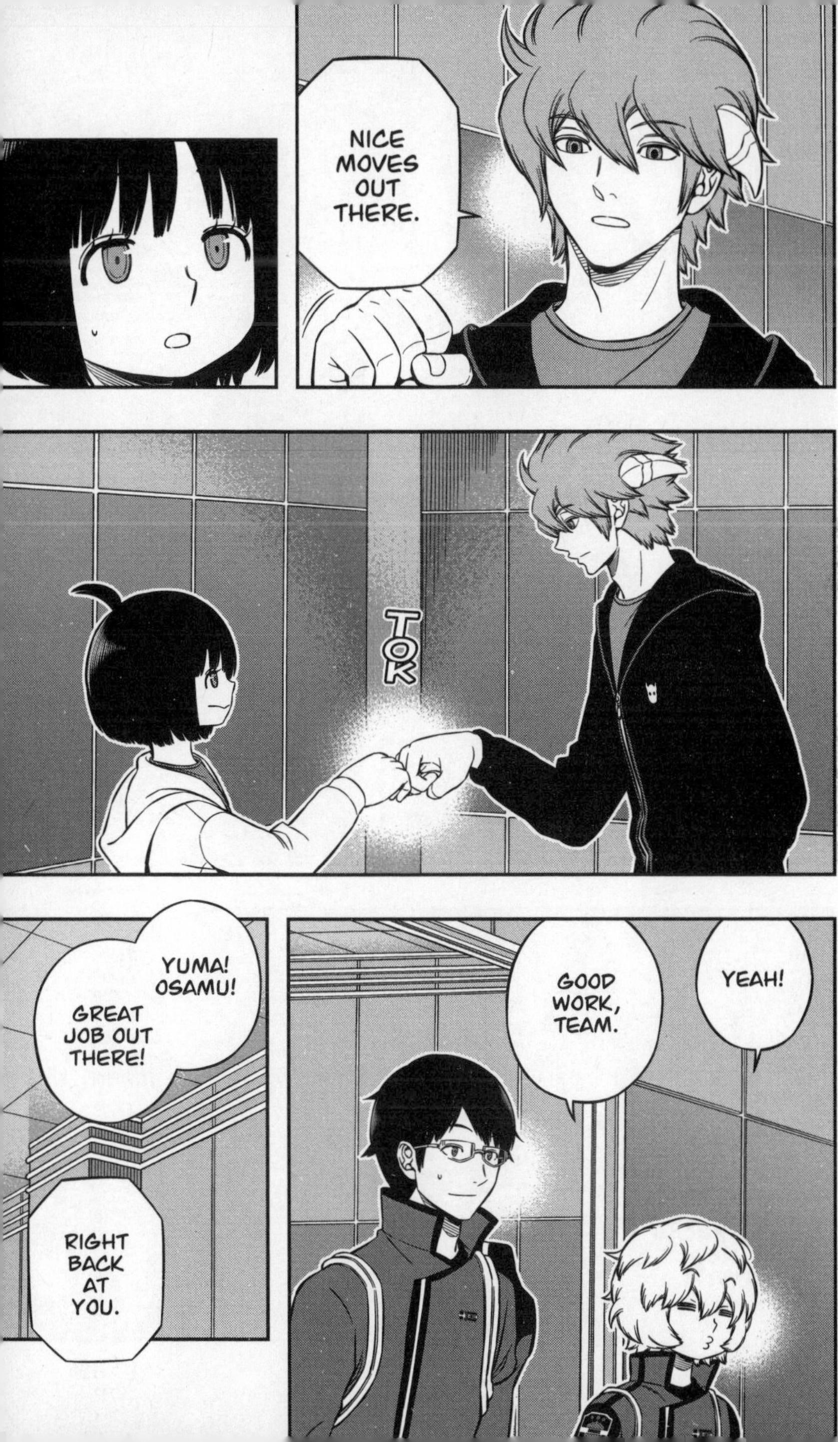
NICE MOVES OUT THERE.
TOK
YEAH!
GOOD WORK, TEAM.
YUMA! OSAMU!
GREAT JOB OUT THERE!
RIGHT BACK AT YOU.

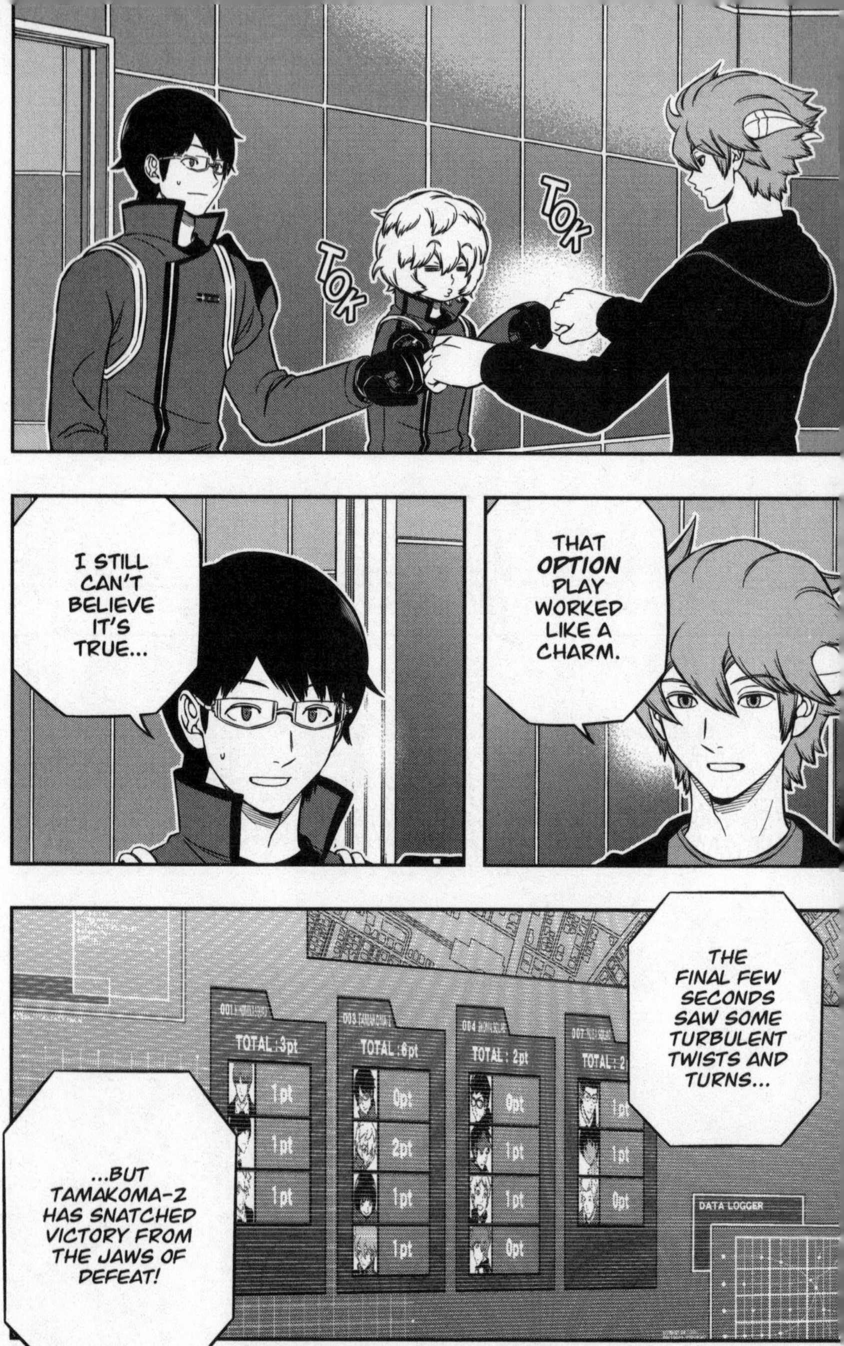
TOK
TOK
THAT OPTION PLAY WORKED LIKE A CHARM.
I STILL CAN'T BELIEVE IT'S TRUE...
THE FINAL FEW SECONDS SAW SOME TURBULENT TWISTS AND TURNS...
...BUT TAMAKOMA-2 HAS SNATCHED VICTORY FROM THE JAWS OF DEFEAT!
TOTAL : 3pt
TOTAL : 6pt
TOTAL : 2pt
DATA LOGGER

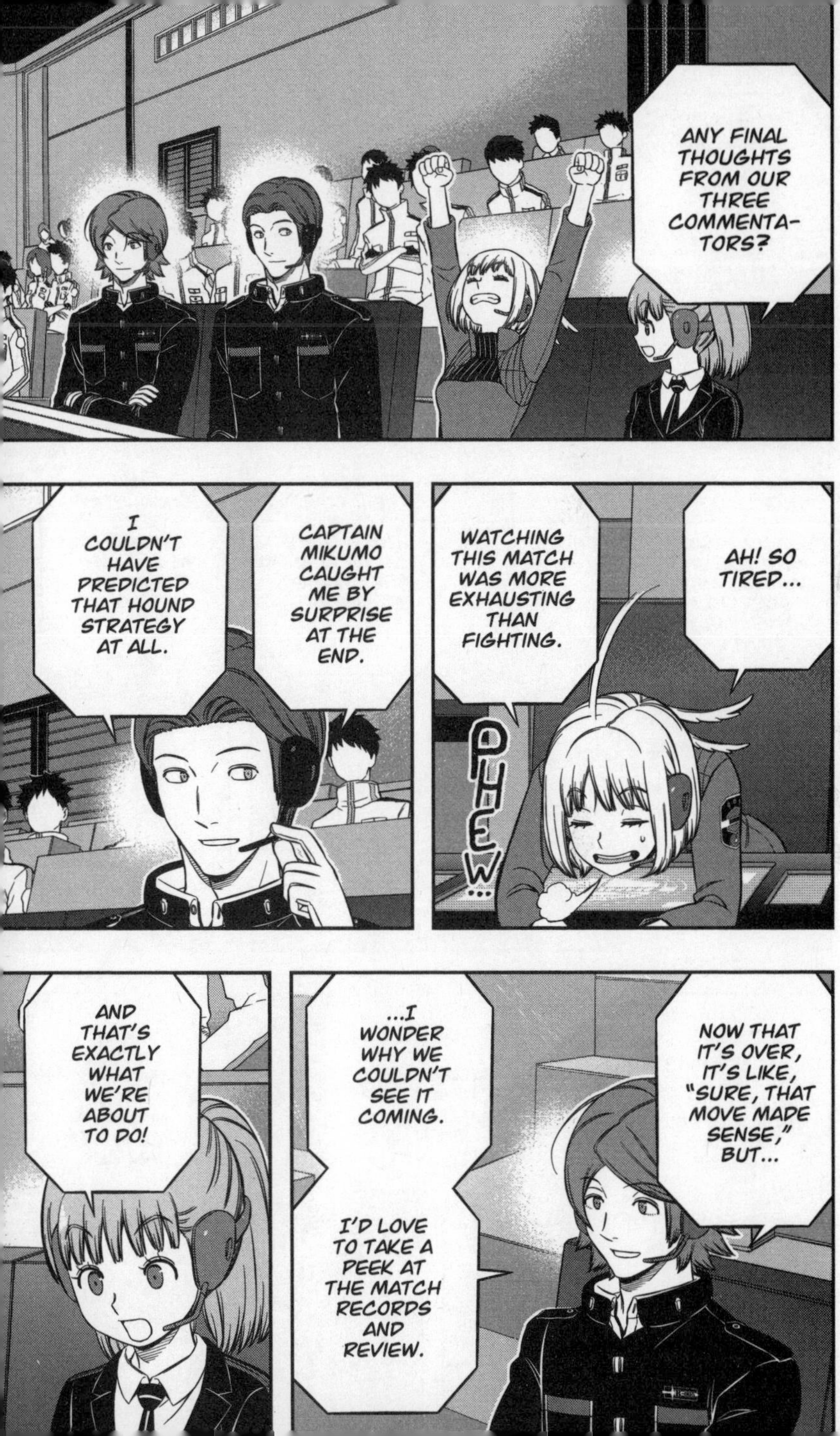
ANY FINAL THOUGHTS FROM OUR THREE COMMENTATORS?
AH! SO TIRED...
WATCHING THIS MATCH WAS MORE EXHAUSTING THAN FIGHTING.
PHEW...
CAPTAIN MIKUMO CAUGHT ME BY SURPRISE AT THE END.
I COULDN'T HAVE PREDICTED THAT HOUND STRATEGY AT ALL.
NOW THAT IT'S OVER, IT'S LIKE, "SURE, THAT MOVE MADE SENSE," BUT...
...I WONDER WHY WE COULDN'T SEE IT COMING.
I'D LOVE TO TAKE A PEEK AT THE MATCH RECORDS AND REVIEW.
AND THAT'S EXACTLY WHAT WE'RE ABOUT TO DO!

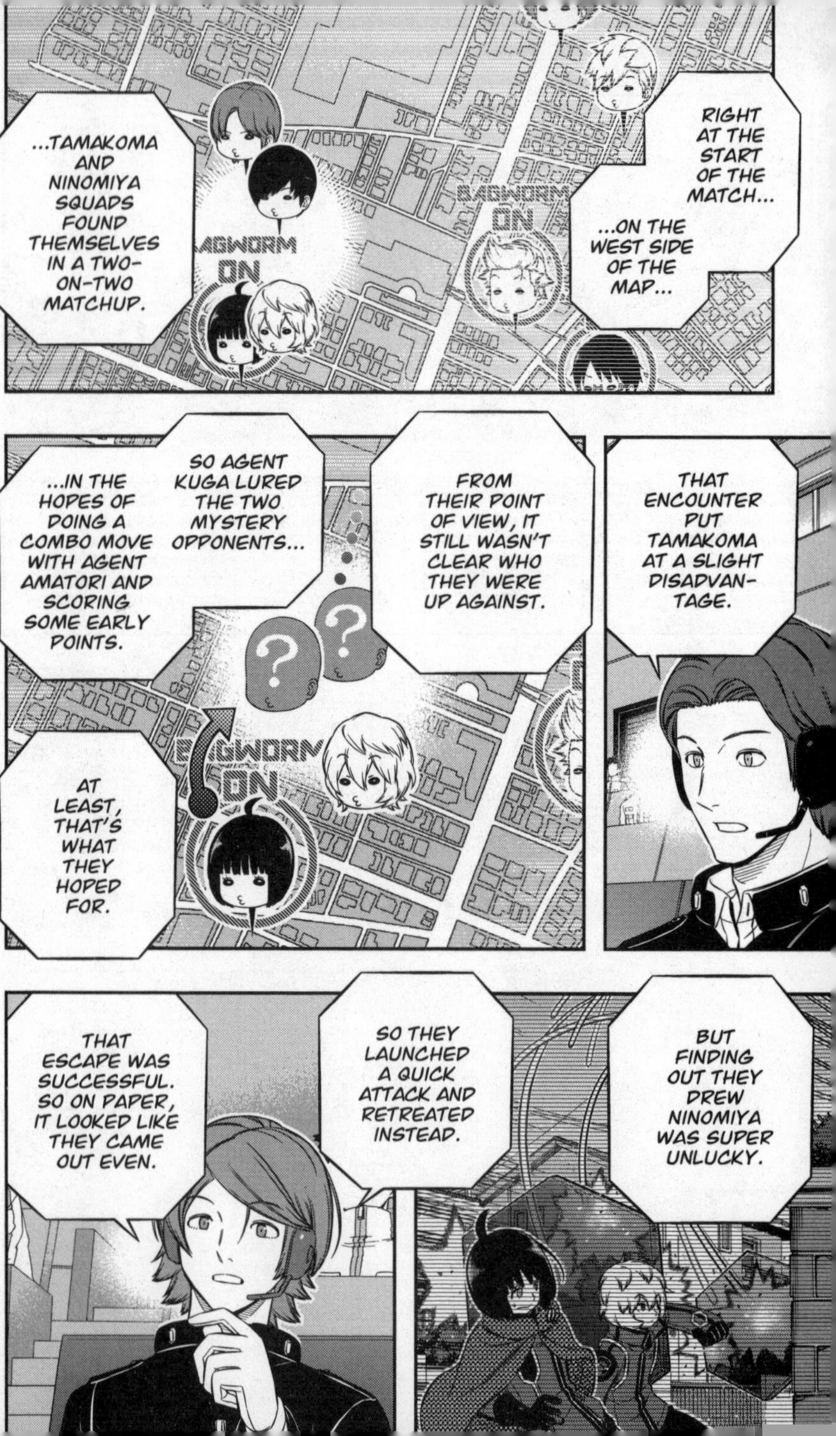
RIGHT AT THE START OF THE MATCH...
...ON THE WEST SIDE OF THE MAP...
BAGWORM ON
...TAMAKOMA AND NINOMIYA SQUADS FOUND THEMSELVES IN A TWO-ON-TWO MATCHUP.
THAT ENCOUNTER PUT TAMAKOMA AT A SLIGHT DISADVANTAGE.
FROM THEIR POINT OF VIEW, IT STILL WASN'T CLEAR WHO THEY WERE UP AGAINST.
SO AGENT KUGA LURED THE TWO MYSTERY OPPONENTS...
...IN THE HOPES OF DOING A COMBO MOVE WITH AGENT AMATORI AND SCORING SOME EARLY POINTS.
AT LEAST, THAT'S WHAT THEY HOPED FOR.
BUT FINDING OUT THEY DREW NINOMIYA WAS SUPER UNLUCKY.
SO THEY LAUNCHED A QUICK ATTACK AND RETREATED INSTEAD.
THAT ESCAPE WAS SUCCESSFUL. SO ON PAPER, IT LOOKED LIKE THEY CAME OUT EVEN.

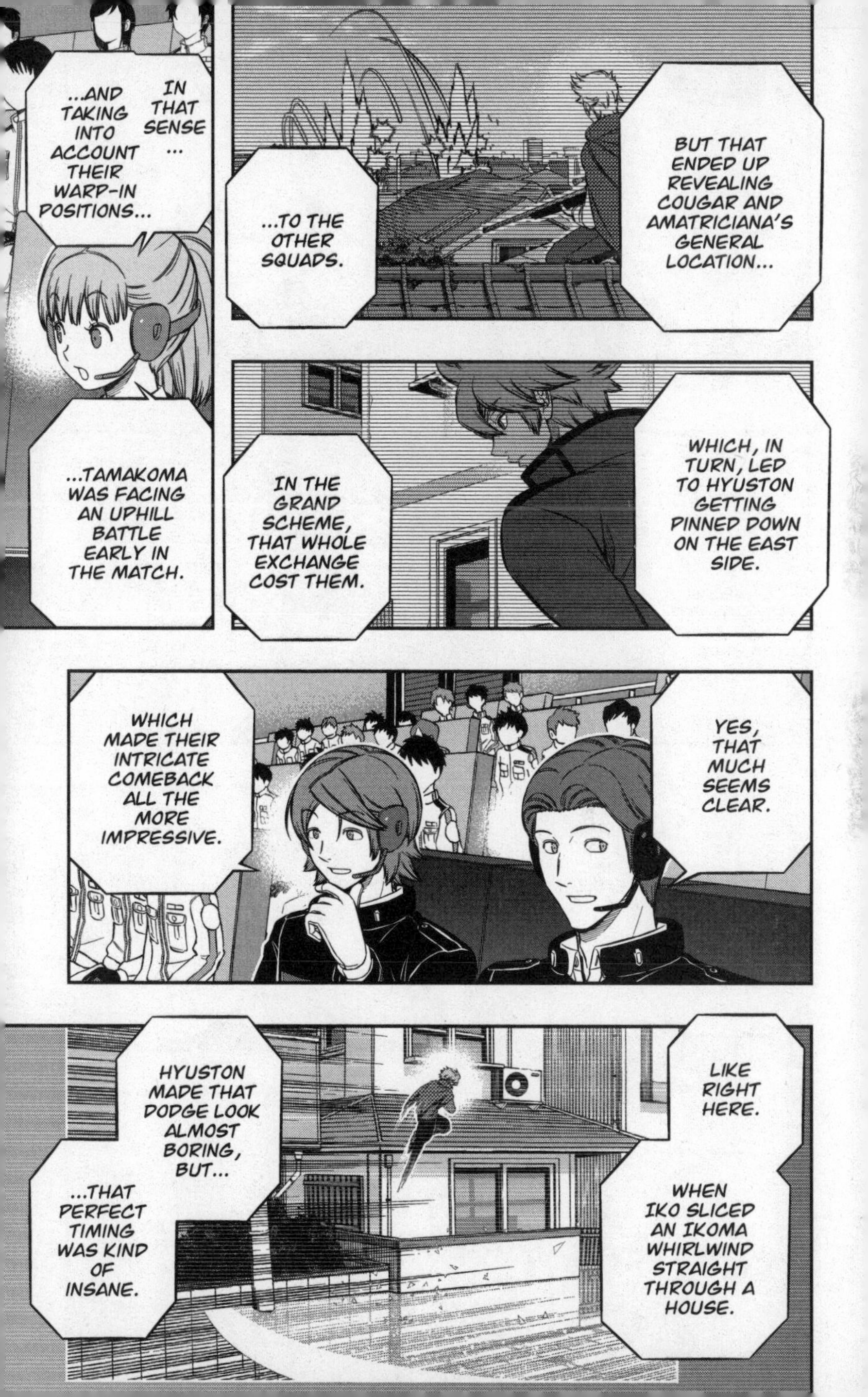
BUT THAT ENDED UP REVEALING COUGAR AND AMATRICIANA'S GENERAL LOCATION...
...TO THE OTHER SQUADS.
WHICH, IN TURN, LED TO HYUSTON GETTING PINNED DOWN ON THE EAST SIDE.
IN THE GRAND SCHEME, THAT WHOLE EXCHANGE COST THEM.
IN THAT SENSE...
...AND TAKING INTO ACCOUNT THEIR WARP-IN POSITIONS...
...TAMAKOMA WAS FACING AN UPHILL BATTLE EARLY IN THE MATCH.
YES, THAT MUCH SEEMS CLEAR.
WHICH MADE THEIR INTRICATE COMEBACK ALL THE MORE IMPRESSIVE.
LIKE RIGHT HERE.
WHEN IKO SLICED AN IKOMA WHIRLWIND STRAIGHT THROUGH A HOUSE.
HYUSTON MADE THAT DODGE LOOK ALMOST BORING, BUT...
...THAT PERFECT TIMING WAS KIND OF INSANE.

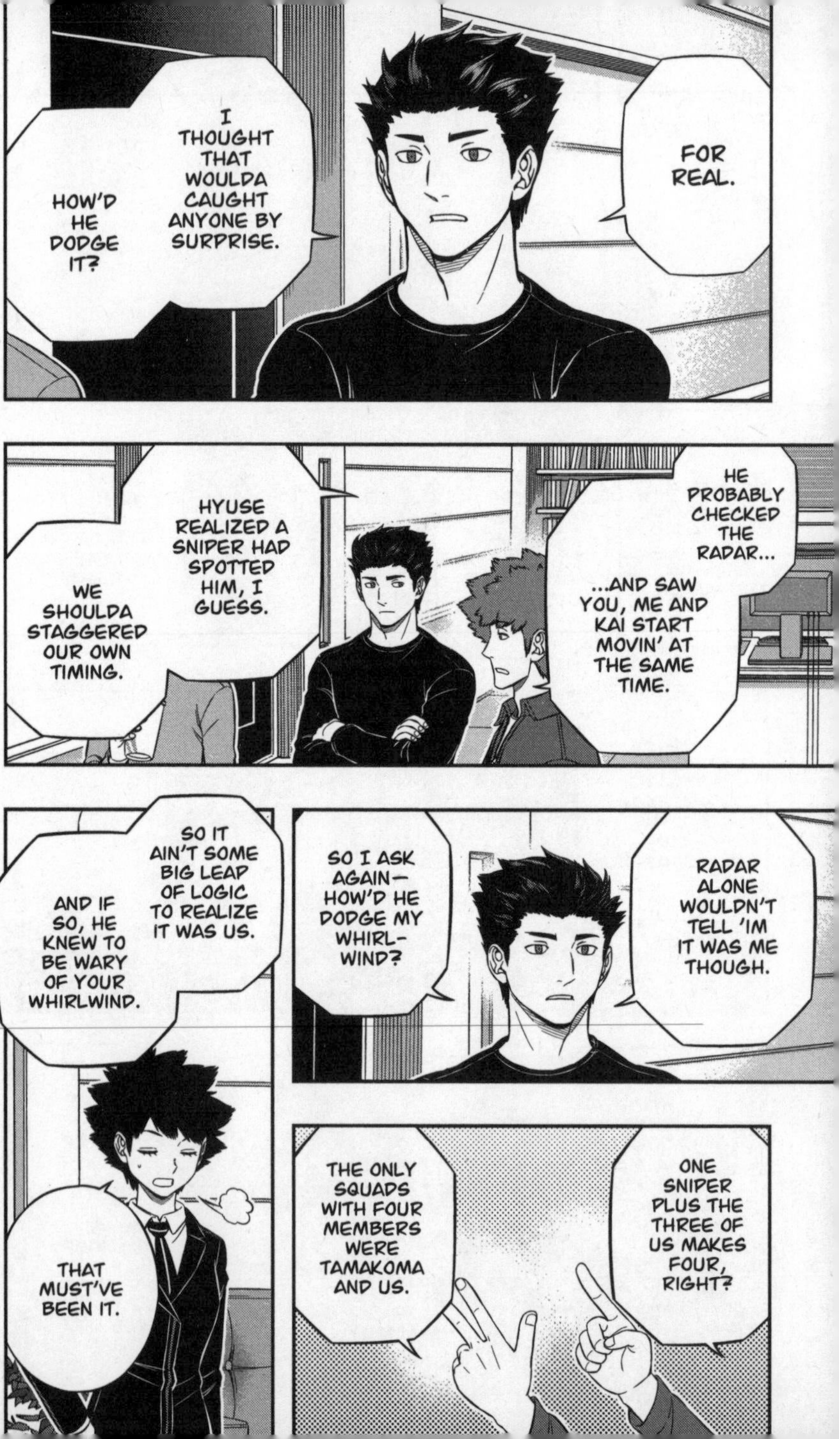
FOR REAL.
I THOUGHT THAT WOULDA CAUGHT ANYONE BY SURPRISE.
HOW'D HE DODGE IT?
HE PROBABLY CHECKED THE RADAR...
...AND SAW YOU, ME AND KAI START MOVIN' AT THE SAME TIME.
HYUSE REALIZED A SNIPER HAD SPOTTED HIM, I GUESS.
WE SHOULDA STAGGERED OUR OWN TIMING.
RADAR ALONE WOULDN'T TELL 'IM IT WAS ME THOUGH.
SO I ASK AGAIN— HOW'D HE DODGE MY WHIRLWIND?
ONE SNIPER PLUS THE THREE OF US MAKES FOUR, RIGHT?
THE ONLY SQUADS WITH FOUR MEMBERS WERE TAMAKOMA AND US.
SO IT AIN'T SOME BIG LEAP OF LOGIC TO REALIZE IT WAS US.
AND IF SO, HE KNEW TO BE WARY OF YOUR WHIRLWIND.
THAT MUST'VE BEEN IT.

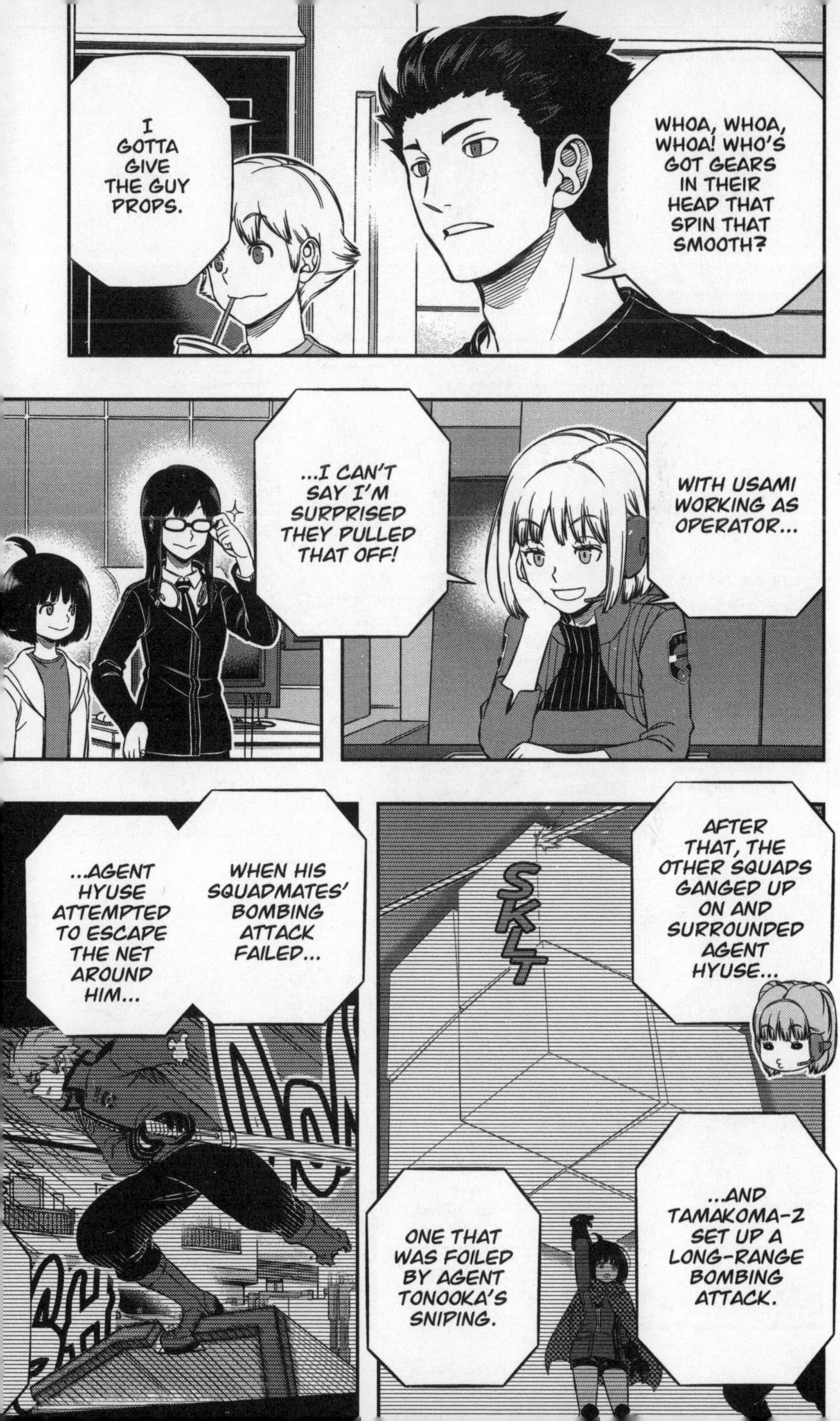
WHOA, WHOA, WHOA! WHO'S GOT GEARS IN THEIR HEAD THAT SPIN THAT SMOOTH?
I GOTTA GIVE THE GUY PROPS.
WITH USAMI WORKING AS OPERATOR...
...I CAN'T SAY I'M SURPRISED THEY PULLED THAT OFF!
AFTER THAT, THE OTHER SQUADS GANGED UP ON AND SURROUNDED AGENT HYUSE...
SKLT
...AND TAMAKOMA-2 SET UP A LONG-RANGE BOMBING ATTACK.
ONE THAT WAS FOILED BY AGENT TONOOKA'S SNIPING.
WHEN HIS SQUADMATES' BOMBING ATTACK FAILED...
...AGENT HYUSE ATTEMPTED TO ESCAPE THE NET AROUND HIM...

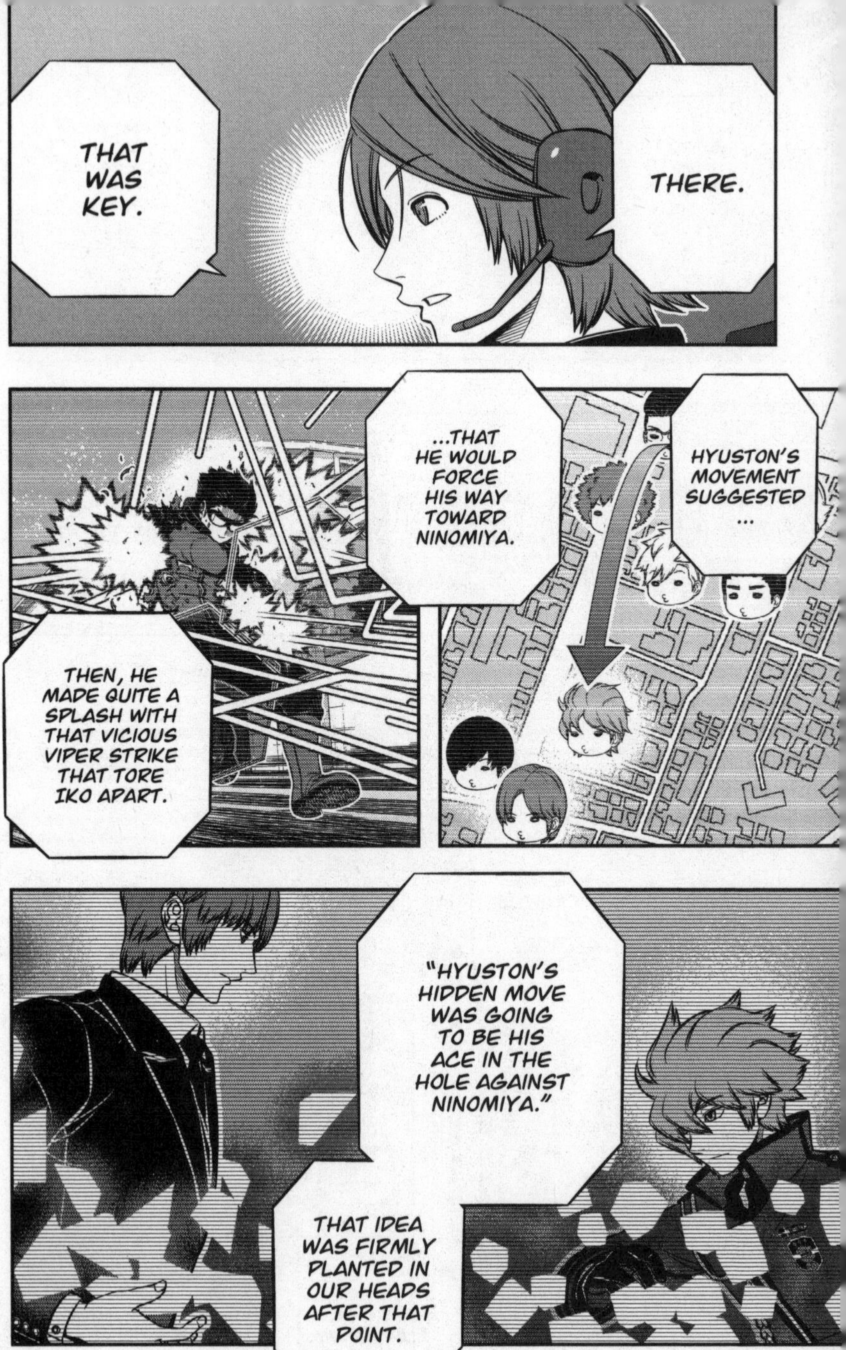
THERE.
THAT WAS KEY.
HYUSTON'S MOVEMENT SUGGESTED...
...THAT HE WOULD FORCE HIS WAY TOWARD NINOMIYA.
THEN, HE MADE QUITE A SPLASH WITH THAT VICIOUS VIPER STRIKE THAT TORE IKO APART.
"HYUSTON'S HIDDEN MOVE WAS GOING TO BE HIS ACE IN THE HOLE AGAINST NINOMIYA."
THAT IDEA WAS FIRMLY PLANTED IN OUR HEADS AFTER THAT POINT.

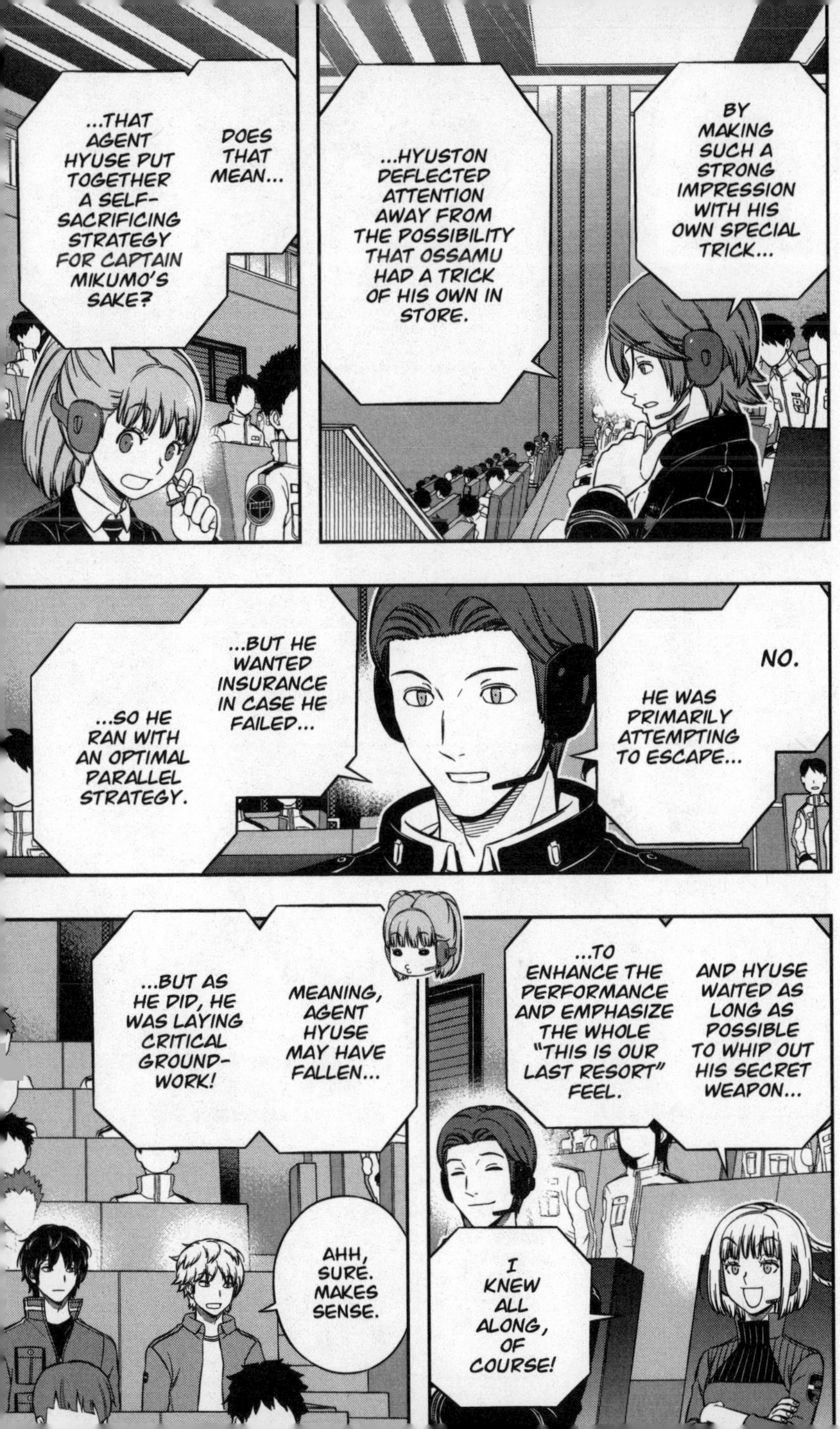
BY MAKING SUCH A STRONG IMPRESSION WITH HIS OWN SPECIAL TRICK...
...HYUSTON DEFLECTED ATTENTION AWAY FROM THE POSSIBILITY THAT OSSAMU HAD A TRICK OF HIS OWN IN STORE.
DOES THAT MEAN...
...THAT AGENT HYUSE PUT TOGETHER A SELF-SACRIFICING STRATEGY FOR CAPTAIN MIKUMO'S SAKE?
NO.
HE WAS PRIMARILY ATTEMPTING TO ESCAPE...
...BUT HE WANTED INSURANCE IN CASE HE FAILED...
...SO HE RAN WITH AN OPTIMAL PARALLEL STRATEGY.
AND HYUSE WAITED AS LONG AS POSSIBLE TO WHIP OUT HIS SECRET WEAPON...
...TO ENHANCE THE PERFORMANCE AND EMPHASIZE THE WHOLE "THIS IS OUR LAST RESORT" FEEL.
I KNEW ALL ALONG, OF COURSE!
MEANING, AGENT HYUSE MAY HAVE FALLEN...
...BUT AS HE DID, HE WAS LAYING CRITICAL GROUNDWORK!
AHH, SURE. MAKES SENSE.

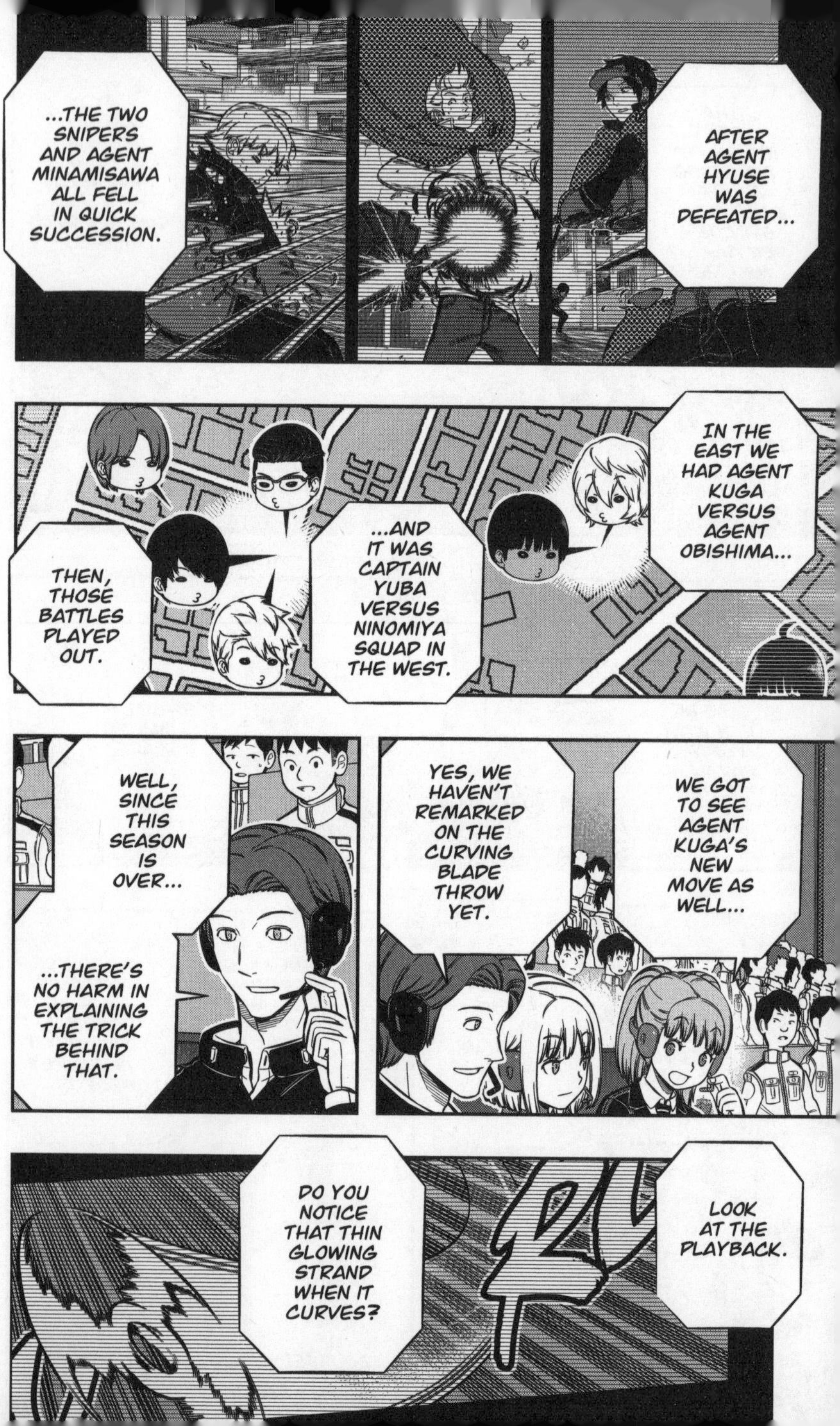
AFTER AGENT HYUSE WAS DEFEATED...
...THE TWO SNIPERS AND AGENT MINAMISAWA ALL FELL IN QUICK SUCCESSION.
IN THE EAST WE HAD AGENT KUGA VERSUS AGENT OBISHIMA...
...AND IT WAS CAPTAIN YUBA VERSUS NINOMIYA SQUAD IN THE WEST.
THEN, THOSE BATTLES PLAYED OUT.
WE GOT TO SEE AGENT KUGA'S NEW MOVE AS WELL...
YES, WE HAVEN'T REMARKED ON THE CURVING BLADE THROW YET.
WELL, SINCE THIS SEASON IS OVER...
...THERE'S NO HARM IN EXPLAINING THE TRICK BEHIND THAT.
LOOK AT THE PLAYBACK.
DO YOU NOTICE THAT THIN GLOWING STRAND WHEN IT CURVES?

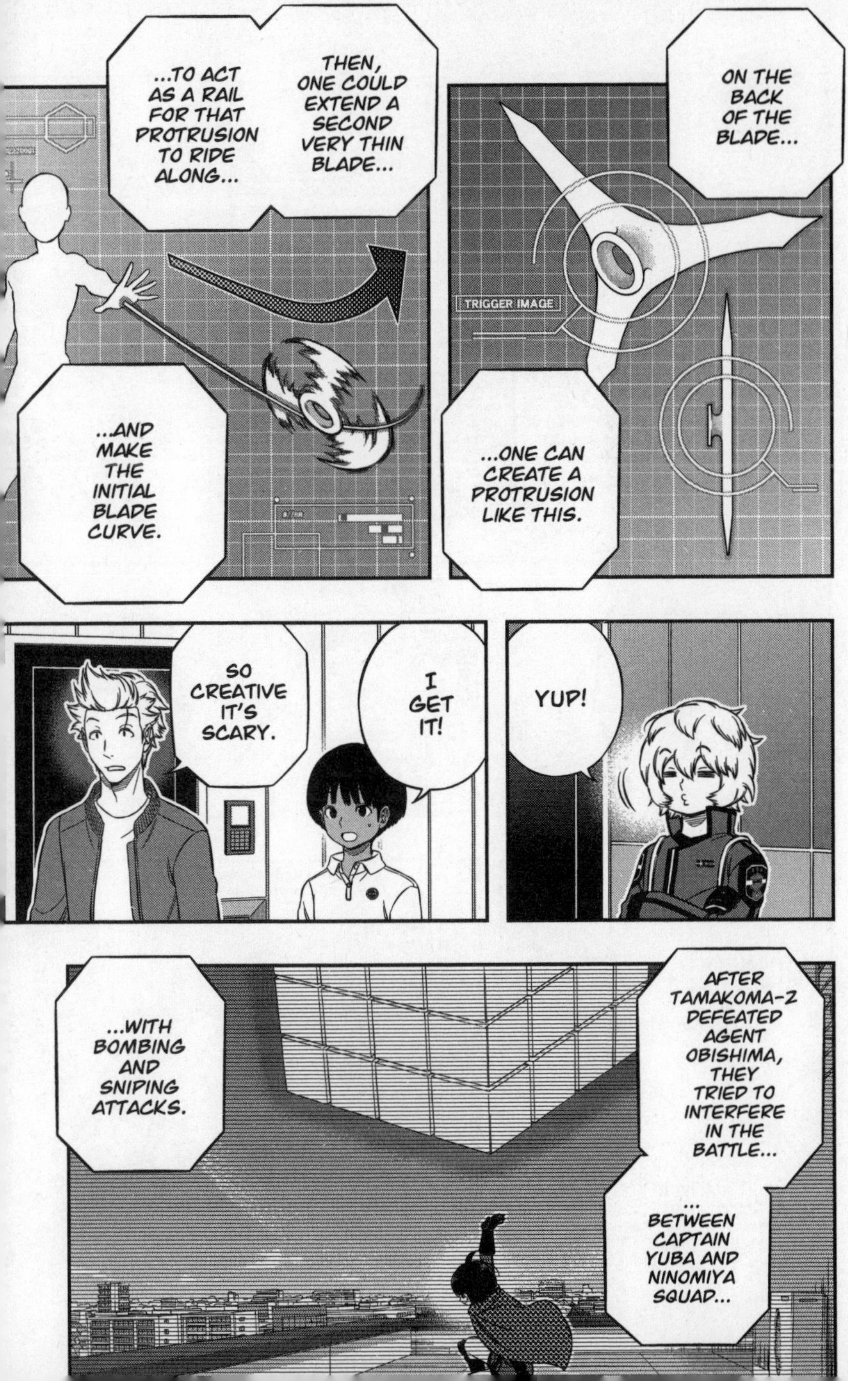
ON THE BACK OF THE BLADE...
TRIGGER IMAGE
...ONE CAN CREATE A PROTRUSION LIKE THIS.
THEN, ONE COULD EXTEND A SECOND VERY THIN BLADE...
...TO ACT AS A RAIL FOR THAT PROTRUSION TO RIDE ALONG...
...AND MAKE THE INITIAL BLADE CURVE.
YUP!
I GET IT!
SO CREATIVE IT'S SCARY.
AFTER TAMAKOMA-2 DEFEATED AGENT OBISHIMA, THEY TRIED TO INTERFERE IN THE BATTLE...
...BETWEEN CAPTAIN YUBA AND NINOMIYA SQUAD...
...WITH BOMBING AND SNIPING ATTACKS.

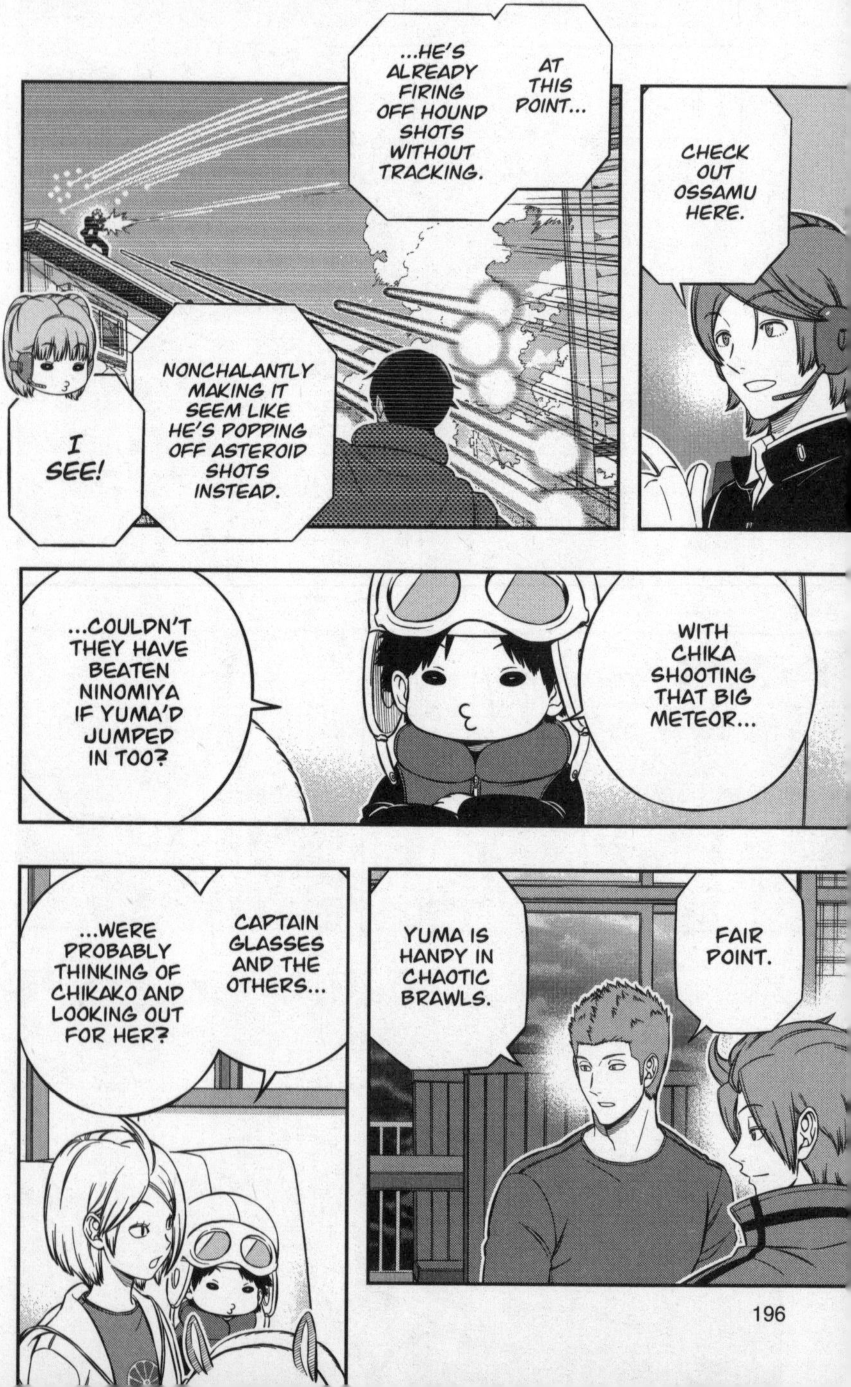
CHECK OUT OSSAMU HERE.
AT THIS POINT...
...HE'S ALREADY FIRING OFF HOUND SHOTS WITHOUT TRACKING.
NONCHALANTLY MAKING IT SEEM LIKE HE'S POPPING OFF ASTEROID SHOTS INSTEAD.
I SEE!
WITH CHIKA SHOOTING THAT BIG METEOR...
...COULDN'T THEY HAVE BEATEN NINOMIYA IF YUMA'D JUMPED IN TOO?
FAIR POINT.
YUMA IS HANDY IN CHAOTIC BRAWLS.
CAPTAIN GLASSES AND THE OTHERS...
...WERE PROBABLY THINKING OF CHIKAKO AND LOOKING OUT FOR HER?

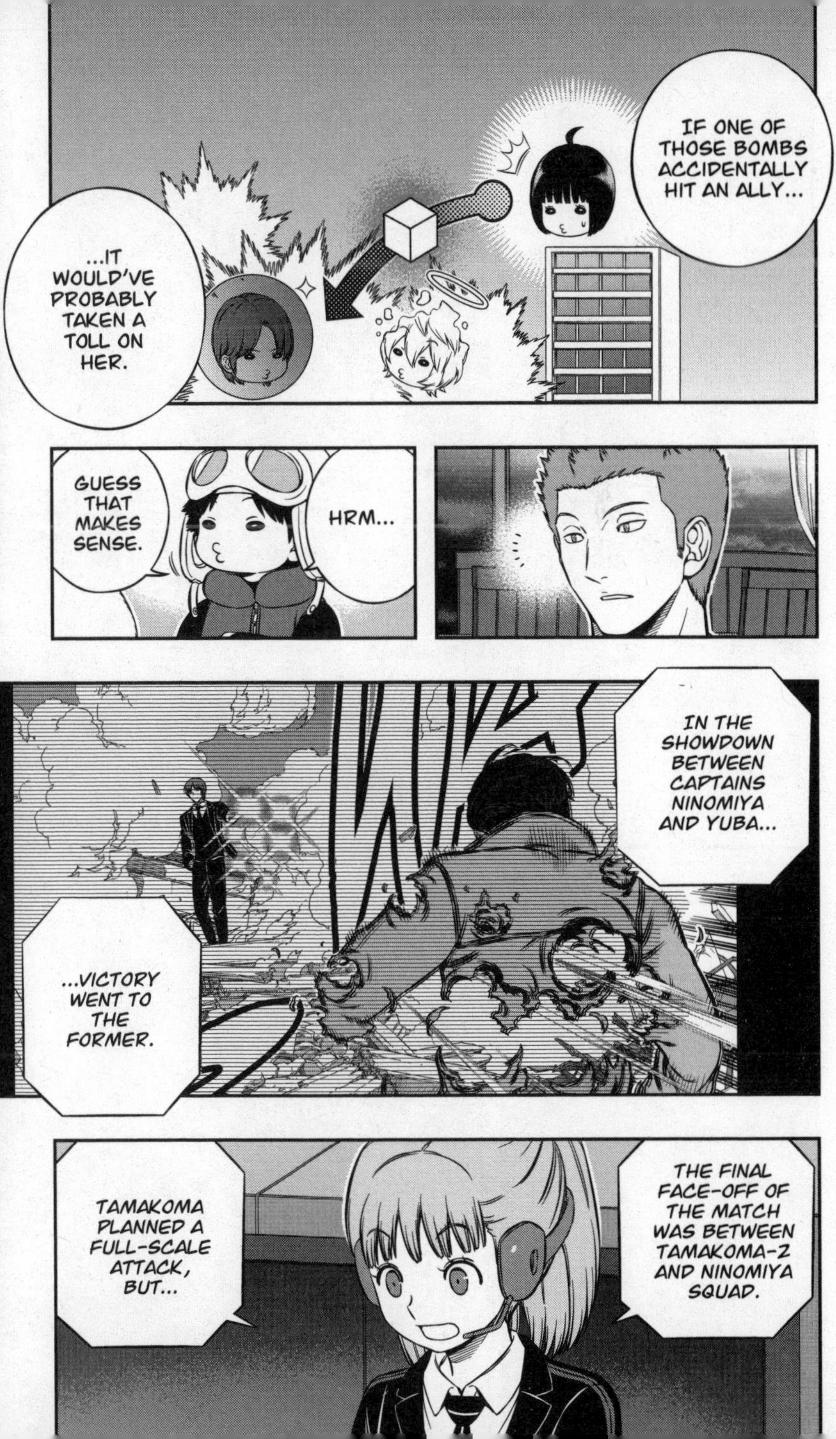
IF ONE OF THOSE BOMBS ACCIDENTALLY HIT AN ALLY...
...IT WOULD'VE PROBABLY TAKEN A TOLL ON HER.
HRM...
GUESS THAT MAKES SENSE.
IN THE SHOWDOWN BETWEEN CAPTAINS NINOMIYA AND YUBA...
...VICTORY WENT TO THE FORMER.
THE FINAL FACE-OFF OF THE MATCH WAS BETWEEN TAMAKOMA-2 AND NINOMIYA SQUAD.
TAMAKOMA PLANNED A FULL-SCALE ATTACK, BUT...

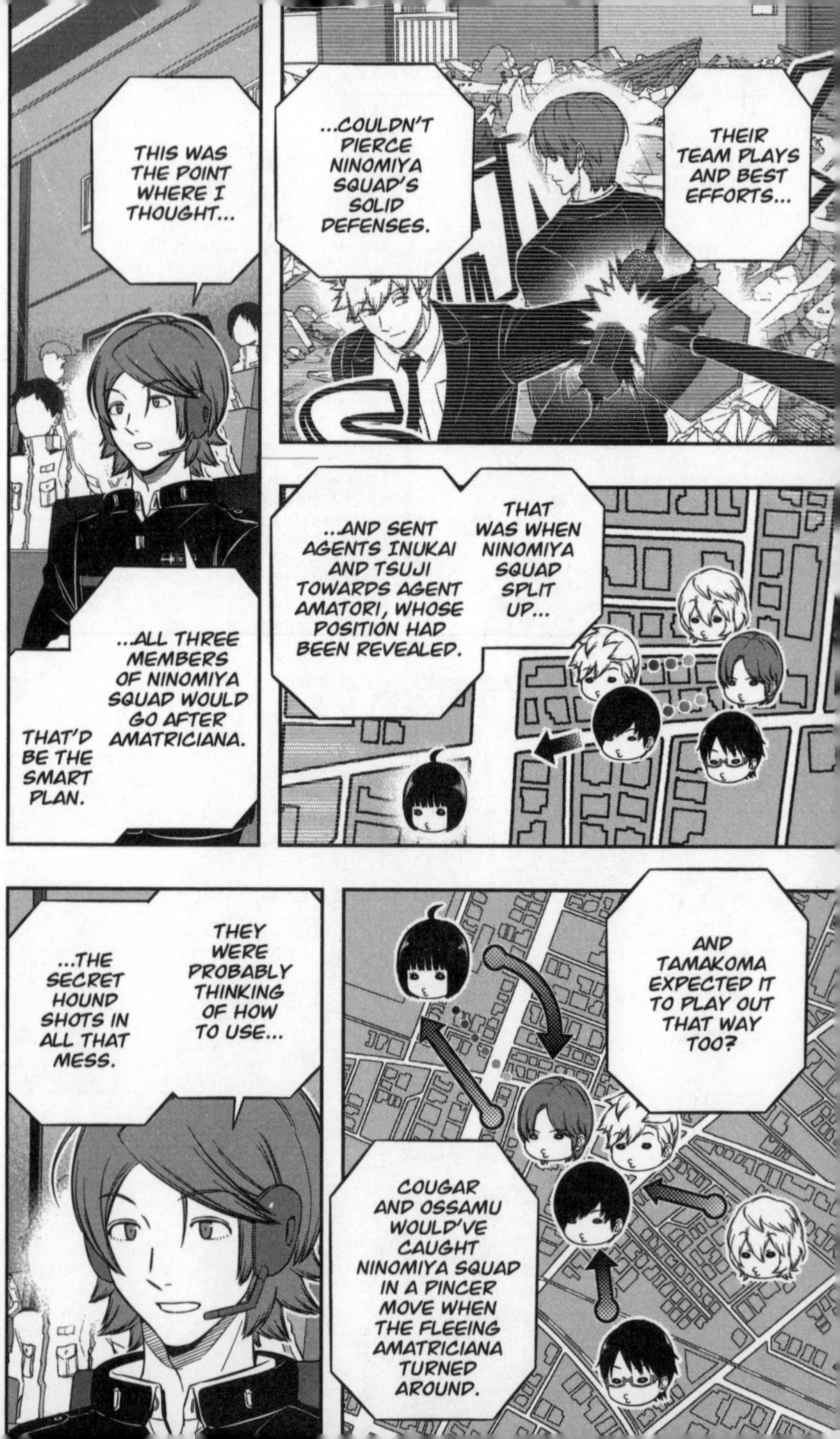
THEIR TEAM PLAYS AND BEST EFFORTS...
...COULDN'T PIERCE NINOMIYA SQUAD'S SOLID DEFENSES.
THAT WAS WHEN NINOMIYA SQUAD SPLIT UP...
...AND SENT AGENTS INUKAI AND TSUJI TOWARDS AGENT AMATORI, WHOSE POSITION HAD BEEN REVEALED.
THIS WAS THE POINT WHERE I THOUGHT...
...ALL THREE MEMBERS OF NINOMIYA SQUAD WOULD GO AFTER AMATRICIANA.
THAT'D BE THE SMART PLAN.
AND TAMAKOMA EXPECTED IT TO PLAY OUT THAT WAY TOO?
COUGAR AND OSSAMU WOULD'VE CAUGHT NINOMIYA SQUAD IN A PINCER MOVE WHEN THE FLEEING AMATRICIANA TURNED AROUND.
THEY WERE PROBABLY THINKING OF HOW TO USE...
...THE SECRET HOUND SHOTS IN ALL THAT MESS.

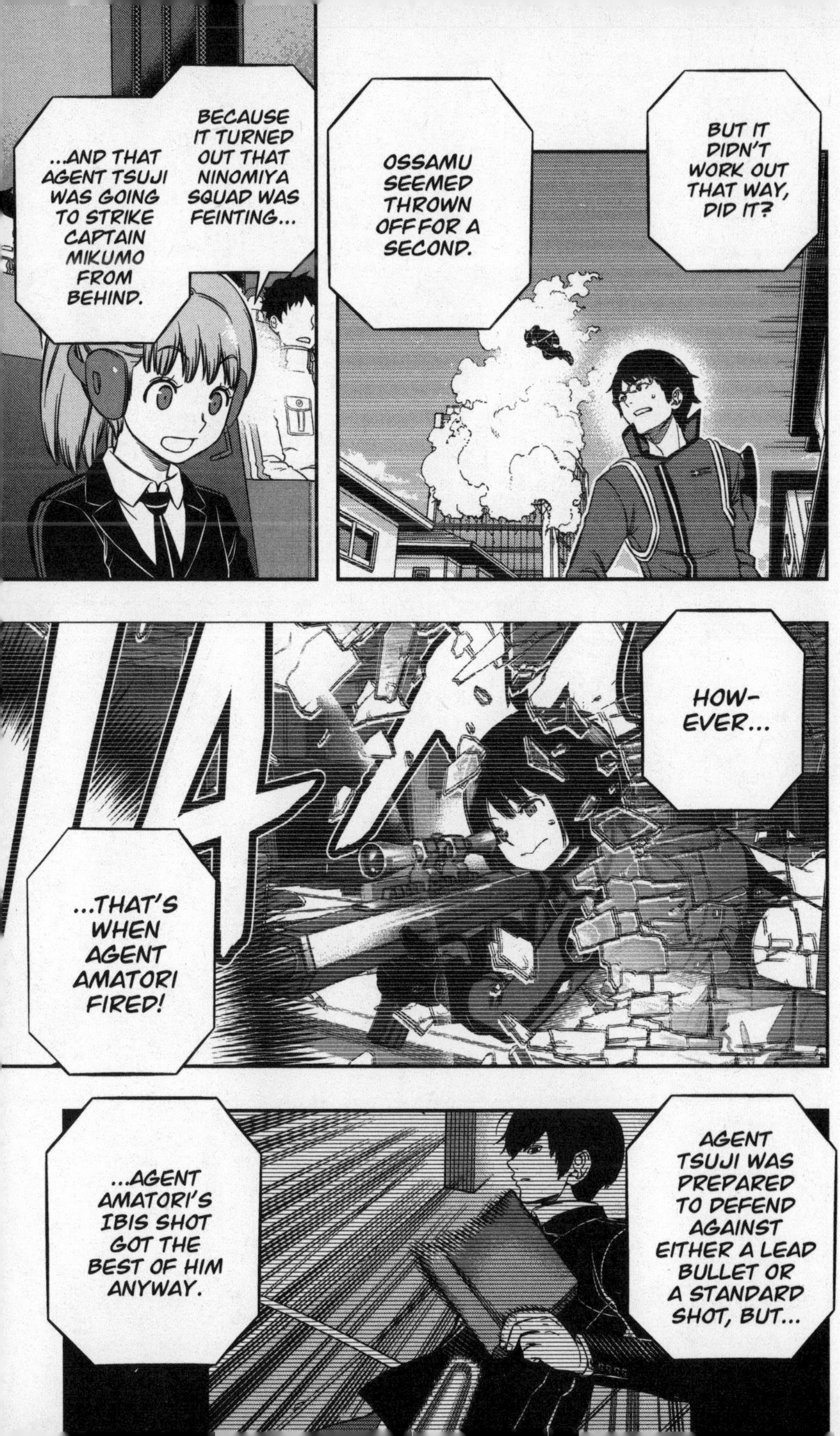
BUT IT DIDN'T WORK OUT THAT WAY, DID IT?
OSSAMU SEEMED THROWN OFF FOR A SECOND.
BECAUSE IT TURNED OUT THAT NINOMIYA SQUAD WAS FEINTING...
...AND THAT AGENT TSUJI WAS GOING TO STRIKE CAPTAIN MIKUMO FROM BEHIND.
HOW-EVER...
...THAT'S WHEN AGENT AMATORI FIRED!
AGENT TSUJI WAS PREPARED TO DEFEND AGAINST EITHER A LEAD BULLET OR A STANDARD SHOT, BUT...
...AGENT AMATORI'S IBIS SHOT GOT THE BEST OF HIM ANYWAY.

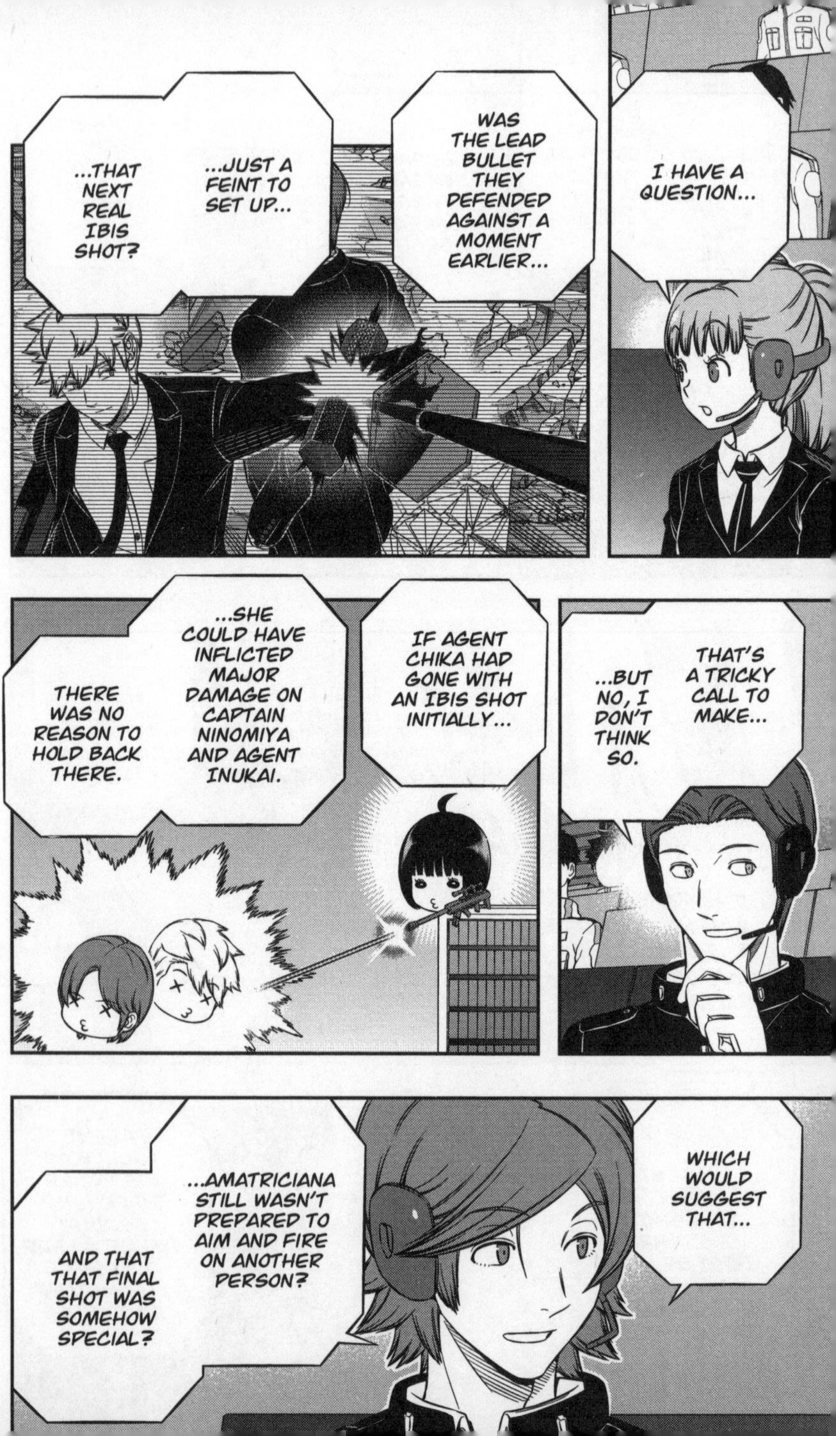
I HAVE A QUESTION...
WAS THE LEAD BULLET THEY DEFENDED AGAINST A MOMENT EARLIER...
...JUST A FEINT TO SET UP...
...THAT NEXT REAL IBIS SHOT?
THAT'S A TRICKY CALL TO MAKE...
...BUT NO, I DON'T THINK SO.
IF AGENT CHIKA HAD GONE WITH AN IBIS SHOT INITIALLY...
...SHE COULD HAVE INFLICTED MAJOR DAMAGE ON CAPTAIN NINOMIYA AND AGENT INUKAI.
THERE WAS NO REASON TO HOLD BACK THERE.
WHICH WOULD SUGGEST THAT...
...AMATRICIANA STILL WASN'T PREPARED TO AIM AND FIRE ON ANOTHER PERSON?
AND THAT THAT FINAL SHOT WAS SOMEHOW SPECIAL?

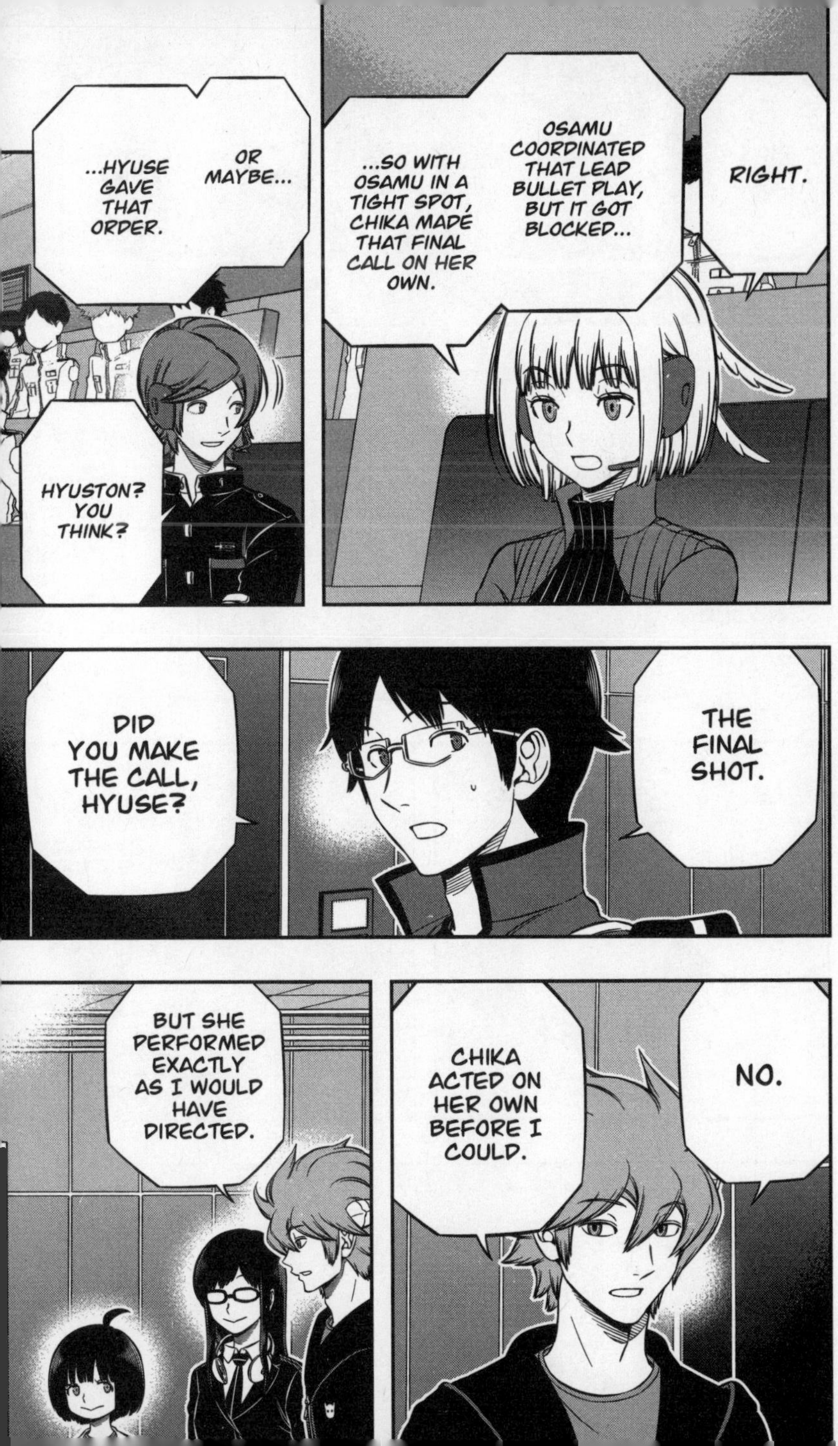
RIGHT.
OSAMU COORDINATED THAT LEAD BULLET PLAY, BUT IT GOT BLOCKED...
...SO WITH OSAMU IN A TIGHT SPOT, CHIKA MADE THAT FINAL CALL ON HER OWN.
OR MAYBE...
...HYUSE GAVE THAT ORDER.
HYUSTON? YOU THINK?
THE FINAL SHOT.
DID YOU MAKE THE CALL, HYUSE?
NO.
CHIKA ACTED ON HER OWN BEFORE I COULD.
BUT SHE PERFORMED EXACTLY AS I WOULD HAVE DIRECTED.

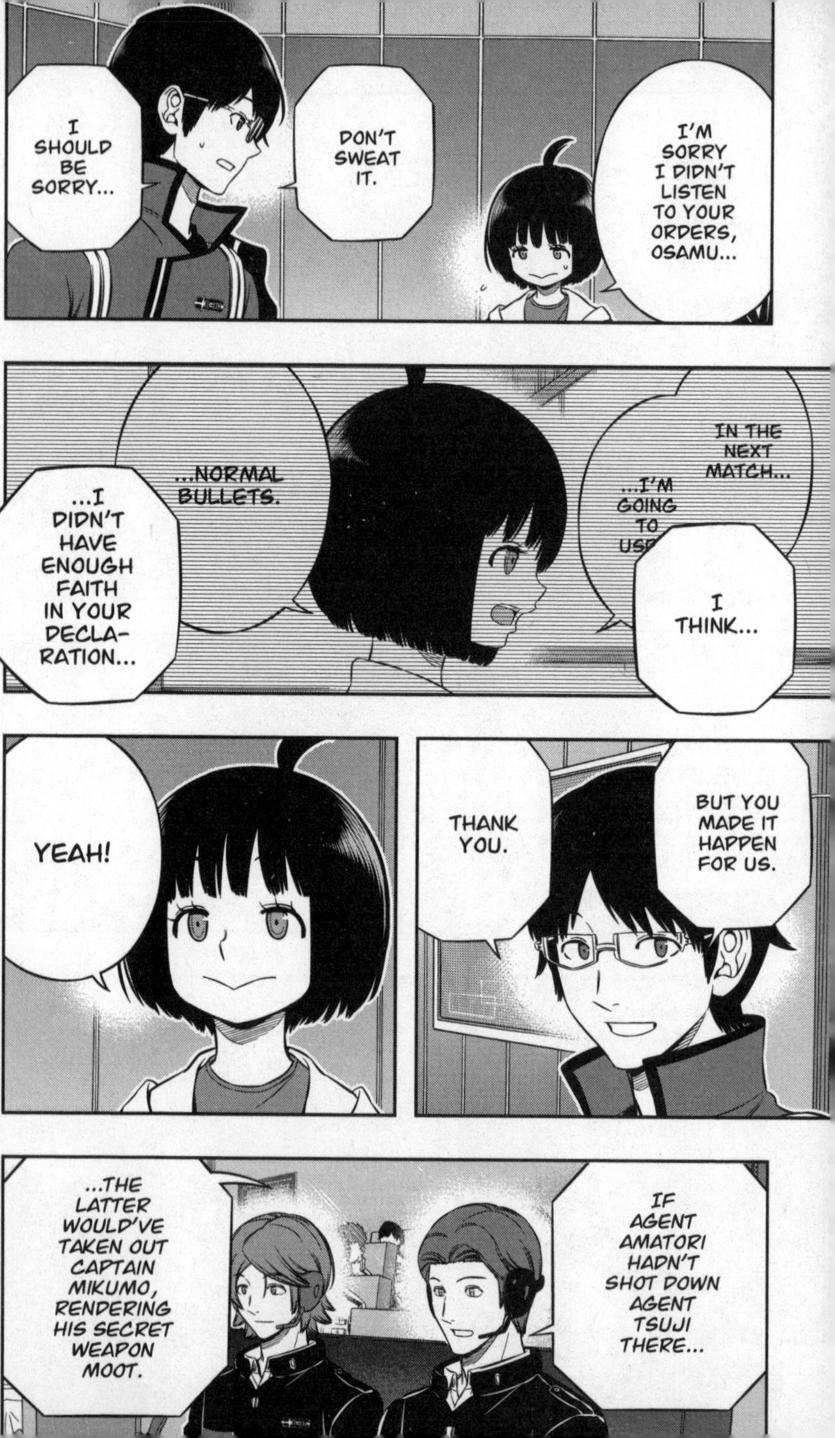
I'M SORRY I DIDN'T LISTEN TO YOUR ORDERS, OSAMU...
DON'T SWEAT IT.
I SHOULD BE SORRY...
IN THE NEXT MATCH...
...I'M GOING TO USE
I THINK...
...NORMAL BULLETS.
...I DIDN'T HAVE ENOUGH FAITH IN YOUR DECLARATION...
BUT YOU MADE IT HAPPEN FOR US.
THANK YOU.
YEAH!
IF AGENT AMATORI HADN'T SHOT DOWN AGENT TSUJI THERE...
...THE LATTER WOULD'VE TAKEN OUT CAPTAIN MIKUMO, RENDERING HIS SECRET WEAPON MOOT.

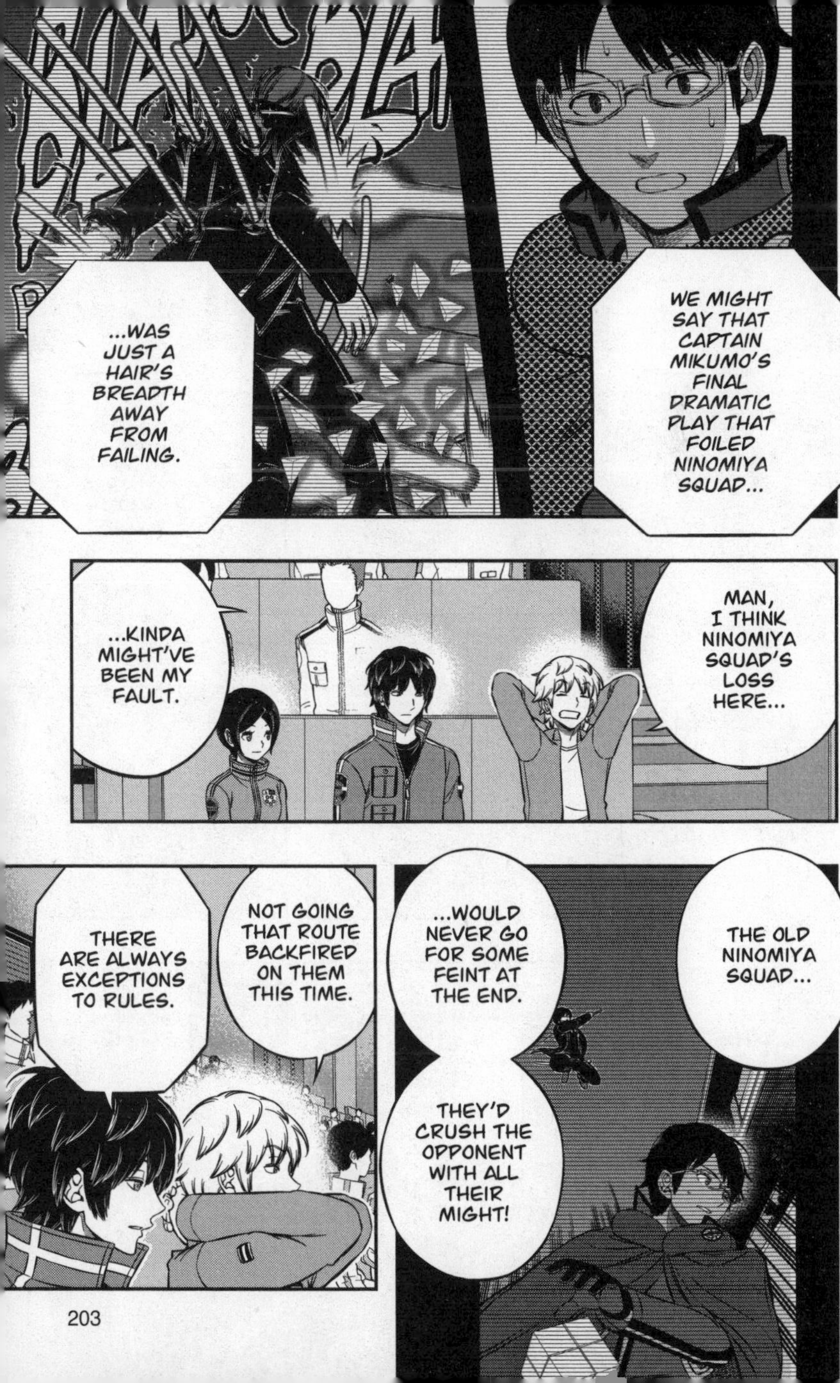
WE MIGHT SAY THAT CAPTAIN MIKUMO'S FINAL DRAMATIC PLAY THAT FOILED NINOMIYA SQUAD...
...WAS JUST A HAIR'S BREADTH AWAY FROM FAILING.
MAN, I THINK NINOMIYA SQUAD'S LOSS HERE...
...KINDA MIGHT'VE BEEN MY FAULT.
THE OLD NINOMIYA SQUAD...
...WOULD NEVER GO FOR SOME FEINT AT THE END.
THEY'D CRUSH THE OPPONENT WITH ALL THEIR MIGHT!
NOT GOING THAT ROUTE BACKFIRED ON THEM THIS TIME.
THERE ARE ALWAYS EXCEPTIONS TO RULES.

...A PERSON CAN PERFORM PERFECTLY EVERY TIME.

AND IT'S NOT AS IF...

001 NINOMIYA SQUAD	44 POINTS
002 TAMAKOMA-2	42 POINTS
003 KAGEURA SQUAD	39 POINTS
004 IKOMA SQUAD	34 POINTS
005 OJI SQUAD	33 POINTS
	30 POINTS
	30 POINTS
	30 POINTS
	MID-MATCH
	MID-MATCH
	30 POINTS

TAMAKOMA-2 HAS SUCCESSFULLY REACHED SECOND PLACE!

ANYWAY, NOW THAT THIS MATCH IS OVER...

...WE HAVE UPDATED RANKING RESULTS!

AMAZINGLY, THEY HAVE QUALIFIED FOR A SPOT ON THE AWAY TEAM!

...WHETHER OR NOT YUBA SQUAD REMAINS IN THE TOP TIER...

AND...

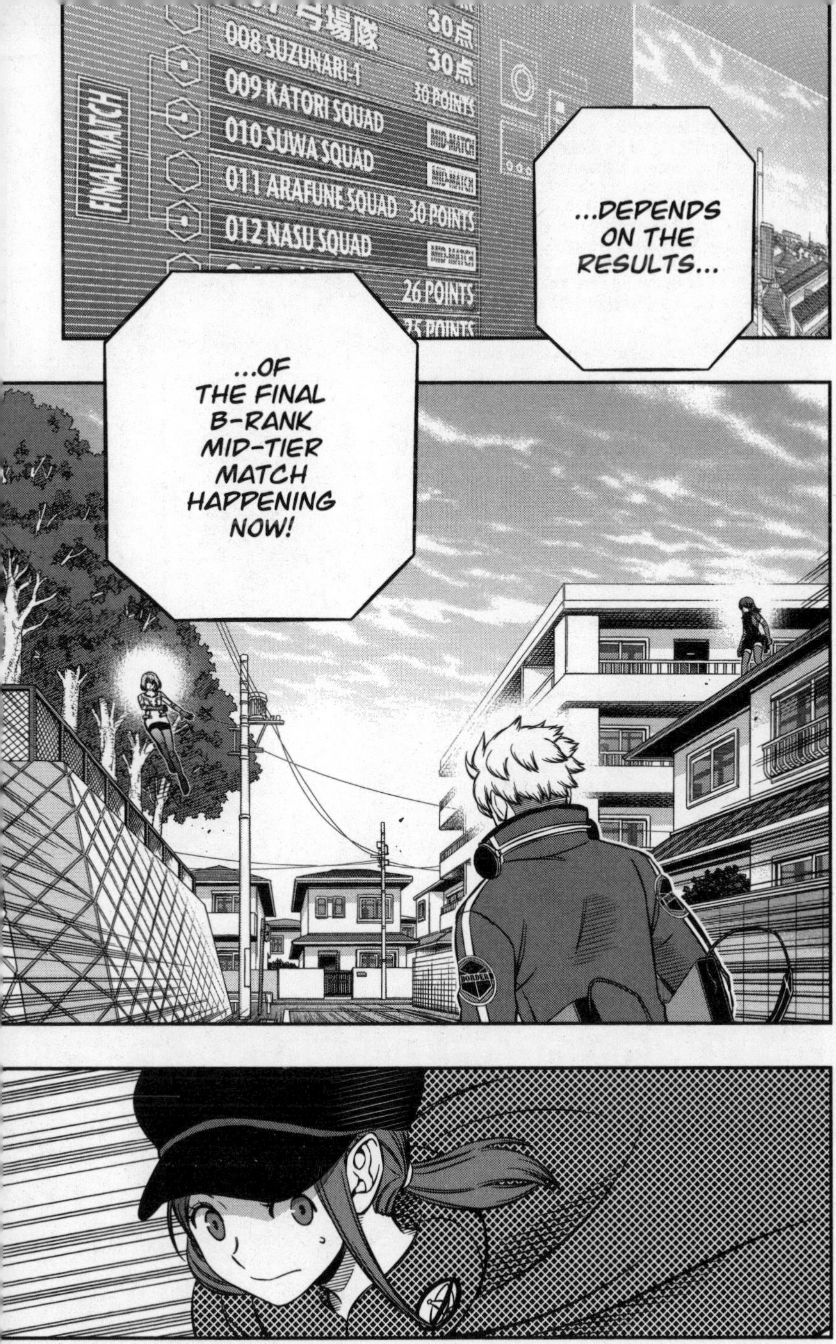
FINAL MATCH
008 SUZUNARI-1 30点
009 KATORI SQUAD 30 POINTS
010 SUWA SQUAD MID-MATCH
011 ARAFUNE SQUAD 30 POINTS
012 NASU SQUAD MID-MATCH
26 POINTS
...DEPENDS ON THE RESULTS...
...OF THE FINAL B-RANK MID-TIER MATCH HAPPENING NOW!

Afterword

Ashihara's Primary Personalities in his Head

*Don't take this seriously

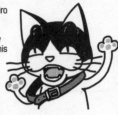

A sunny optimist who believes everything should be fun. He creates characters, writes the overall story, fiddles with the plot and figures out panel arrangements. Sometimes, Terajiro also does inking and finishing touches. He only wants to do something if it's fun, which explains why I was such an abysmal student (since Terajiro was the primary personality during my elementary and middle school years). He loves his own manga, and he frames his terrible memory as a good excuse to go back and reread the series. Terajiro sings his own praises without a shred of shame, prompting forced, uncomfortable smiles from those around him. For better or worse he's a feeler, not a thinker, so most of the careless mistakes you'll find are definitely his fault. His favorite food is sweet-and-sour pork.

Pet Saying: "The fun factor is all that matters."

Terajiro Hayakawa

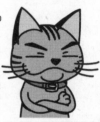

A half-baked craftsman in charge of page layout, rough sketches, inking, instructing the staff and final touches. Ricardo is very fussy and pretty awkward at communicating. He's not the greatest artist, but he's a pointlessly prideful perfectionist whose harsh criticism of everyone (including himself) and generally obnoxious attitude make others see him as a nuisance. Ricardo's got a wicked inferiority complex about his own art, so even when he feels a sense of accomplishment over finishing, before long he'll be overwhelmed by the thought that he sucks big time. At that point, he'll sulk in bed and get drunk on bottled water for days. His favorite food is tempura (specifically, chicken tender and sweet potato).

Pet Saying: "Time off only invites decay."

Ricardo Tennoji

A logical fellow in charge of organization, world building, and data. He loves transforming ambiguous concepts and ideas into coherent explanations, so when Terajiro produces scattered bits of plot, Akashi is the one to edit the content so people will actually understand. He focuses on data and numbers, but on the other hand, he realizes that all those little values are just chopped up pieces of the whole story. Still, Akashi fears that his own biases will bleed into his interpretations of the data, so he doesn't like to consider himself a creator. Instead, he's firmly a background player/assistant. He got along great with the second editor, Saito-san. His favorite food is pasta with meat sauce.

Pet Saying: "Logic is a universally-applicable ointment."

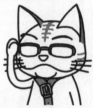

Akashi

be out in Japan December 2020!!

STAFF

Author:
Daisuke Ashihara

Manager/Art Assistant:
Koma

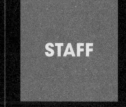

A talkative poser, and the most sociable of my personalities. Gavalier takes over for business meetings and work-related phone calls, but outside of work, his appearances are increasingly limited by the "body weight factor" and "length of bangs factor." He'll pop by the studio whenever he feels like it, start spouting intelligent-sounding things in the middle of work, and demand equally witty repartee from his staff. Something is definitely off about him, but he likes himself best when he's being kind to others. Because no small number of people whisper that I have a black hole where my heart should be, Gavalier is responsible for handling empathy, common sense, and manners. Sure, he'll help out with the work itself, but since he's such a chatterbox, he's only about half as efficient as Ricardo. He loves grapefruit-flavored sweets and drinks.

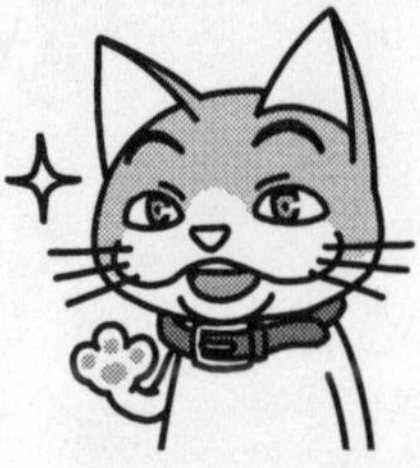

Gavalier Yoshikawa

A guy who prefers solo hobbies. Once the work is finished and I need a cooldown period, Middle takes over to play video games or read books. He usually prefers single-player games, but in recent days, the staff have gotten him interested in Pokémon battling. He couldn't care less about optimal strategies or 100 percent speedruns; it's more his style to play through a game all carefree-like, without even glancing at strategy guides. Seeing his own reflection on the screen has a way of breaking Middle's immersion, so he secretly believes that all games should have a "day mode" setting for loading screens. He can't draw to save his life, and he can barely speak, but he does manage to share with Akashi the tidbits he picks up from games and books. Sometimes Middle even takes over panel arranging for Terajiro, gives instructions to the staff so Ricardo doesn't have to, and contributes to the manga creation process in other unexpected ways. His favorite food is daifuku filled with koshian.

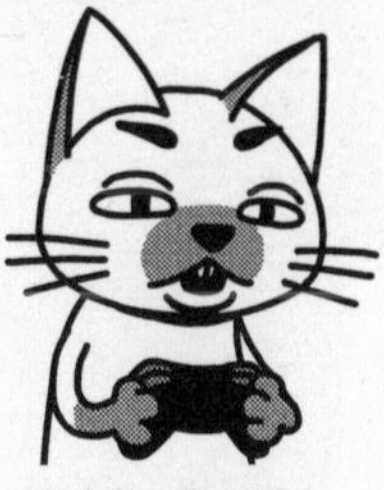

Middle Gorilla

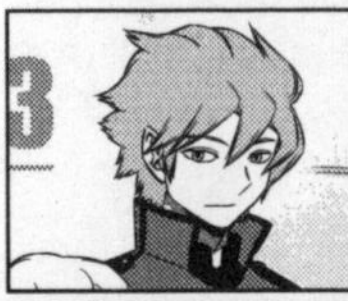

Zenimaru's Art

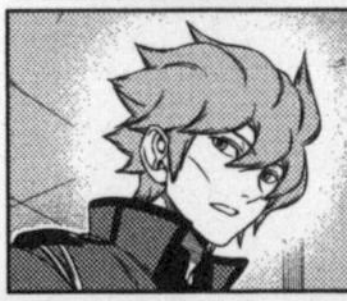

Ricardo's Art

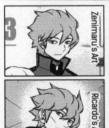

The ever-doubting pessimist. When I get frazzled, this negative bastard crashes the party. Weighed down by narcissism and burdened with a persecution complex, Zenimaru is convinced that the people at the top are all villains and that society is trying to exploit him. This was the guy who was on bad terms with my first editor, Batty-san, for a time. He may be incorrigible, but Zenimaru has surprising stamina and willpower, so when the other personalities are feeling pooped, he'll emerge to finish the draft, grumbling all the while (his art isn't as good as Ricardo's, though). His favorite food is dashi-flavored yakiudon.

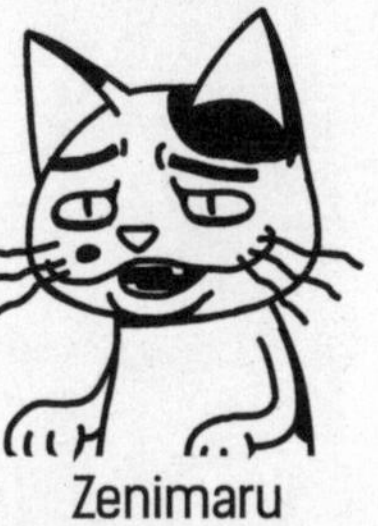

Zenimaru

World Trigger Volume 23 will

Assistants:
Satoshi Watanabe
Haruto Nawashirowaza
Shingo Sasai
Daisuke Kakehi
Issei Odoru

Volume Editor:
Akihiro Katayama

Volume Designer:
Yuta Yuzawa

Magazine Release Editor:
Koji Yoshida

WORLD TRIGGER

Bonus Character Pages

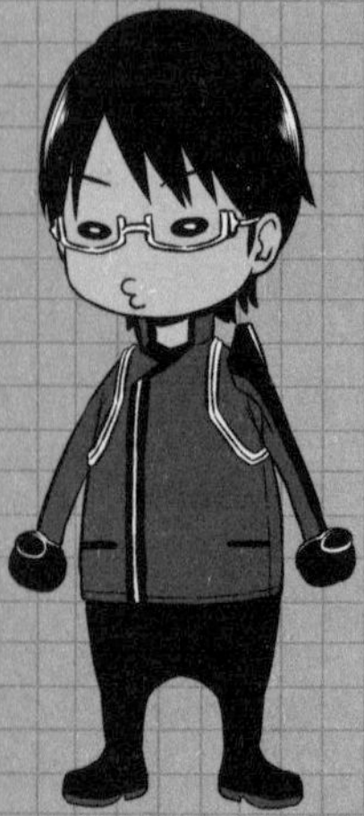

OSAMU

The Four-Eyes With Six Wounds

This glasses guy has survived it all so far. More chapters means more mentor-like characters for Osamu. According to my calculations, at this rate, he'll have had 3,800 mentors by the year 2050. He's still covered in that cold sweat, but now with a glistening sheen of, "I think he'll pull this off somehow," making him more of a protagonist than ever before. Behold, Metal Osamu is always by our side.

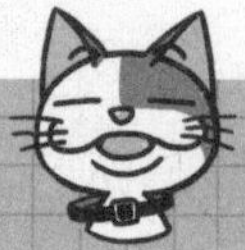

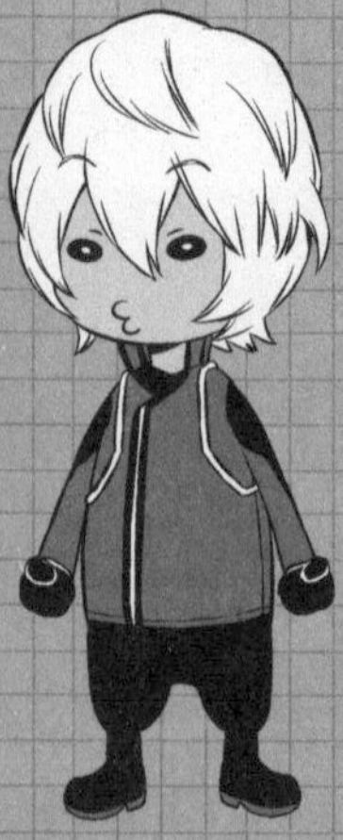

YUMA

Diffuse Reflection Handsome Dude

The feral hunk who won't bite so hard it causes damage. Back in his really wild days, he was into breaking unimportant characters' legs, but ever since Tamakoma gave him a permanent home, Yuma's coat has been looking glossy and healthy. He's grown into the backbone of the family who acts as a go-between for Hyuse and Osamu, provides Chika with plenty of backup and meddles as much as he needs to get the job done. Yuma's been looking almost too good lately, so I use the classic *3*-shaped mouth to neutralize his good looks.

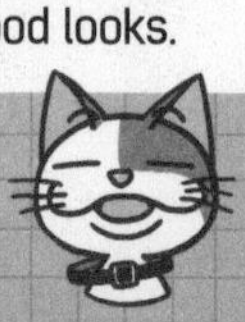

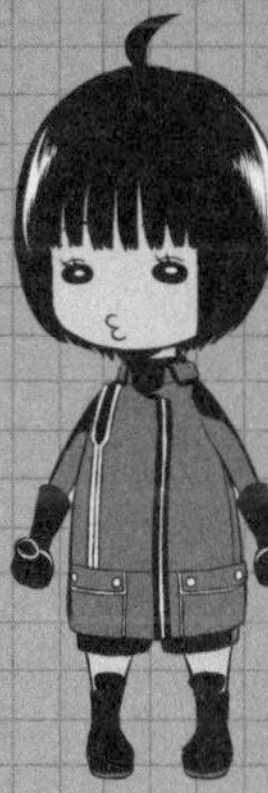

CHIKA

Behold, the Power of White Rice

This human cannon has gone from hunted to hunter. In the world of *Dragon Quest*, Chika would be an ultimate destroyer who unleashes rapid-fire Megaflare attacks, but because she's not actually using hacks, the admins can't ban her. She's gotten a lot easier to draw since chapter 179, and one explanatory theory is that her trion cubes have just gotten bigger and bigger (Lead Bullets used to be small). I might've mentioned this elsewhere, but Chika's head is meant to resemble an apple.

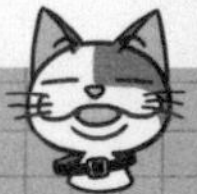

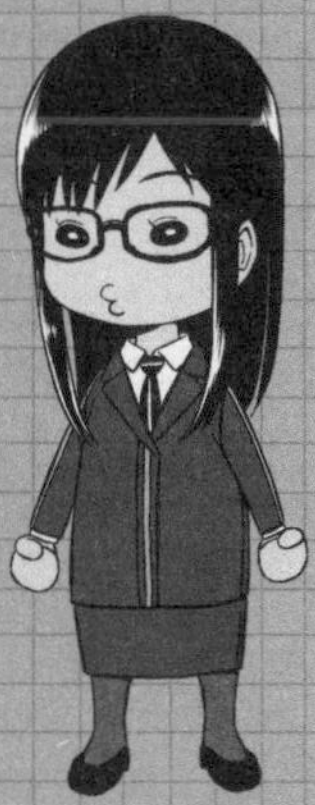

OPERATOR USAMI

Hard Worker, Solid Friend

She used to be a kind four-eyes, but nowadays she's more like bespectacled kindness. That's the general concept for this 17-year-old. Usami probably works harder in the background than anyone, but she never forgets to heap praise on others. How on earth did her parents manage to raise such a perfect angel?! I'd love to bring her parents into the story, but it's not like she has some heavy, dramatic backstory to explore. Usami's weaknesses are heat (weather/temperature) and heat (spicy food).

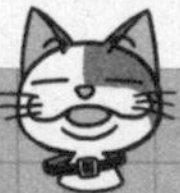

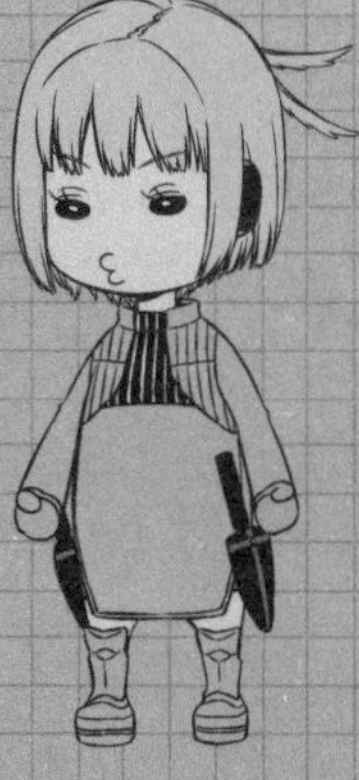

BATTLE KONAMI

Go! Do it!

This awesome senior doesn't even try to hide her obvious favoritism for her allies. Before the match, there was a lot of concern over whether or not Konami could be trusted to give unbiased commentary. Normally those concerns would be warranted. You get the sense that Sakurako (who asked Oji and Kurauchi to participate as well) provided a stabilizing influence as the one in charge. Konami unwittingly supplied some nice assists during the *yakiniku* meal, but once she realized that, she started looking smug, so please don't refer back to check.

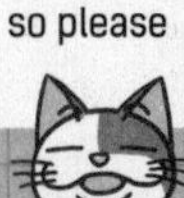

Black ✳ Clover

STORY & ART BY YŪKI TABATA

Asta is a young boy who dreams of becoming the greatest mage in the kingdom. Only one problem—he can't use any magic! Luckily for Asta, he receives the incredibly rare five-leaf clover grimoire that gives him the power of anti-magic. Can someone who can't use magic really become the Wizard King? One thing's for sure—Asta will never give up!

SHONEN JUMP   VIZ media
www.viz.com

Story and Art by
KOYOHARU GOTOUGE

In Taisho-era Japan, kindhearted Tanjiro Kamado makes a living selling charcoal. But his peaceful life is shattered when a demon slaughters his entire family. His little sister Nezuko is the only survivor, but she has been transformed into a demon herself! Tanjiro sets out on a dangerous journey to find a way to return his sister to normal and destroy the demon who ruined his life.

RATED TEEN · VIZ

ASTRA
LOST IN SPACE

CAN EIGHT TEENAGERS FIND THEIR WAY HOME FROM 5,000 LIGHT-YEARS AWAY?

It's the year 2063, and interstellar space travel has become the norm. Eight students from Caird High School and one child set out on a routine planet camp excursion. While there, the students are mysteriously transported 5,000 light-years away to the middle of nowhere! Will they ever make it back home?!

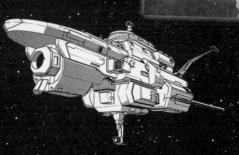

YOU'RE READING THE WRONG WAY!

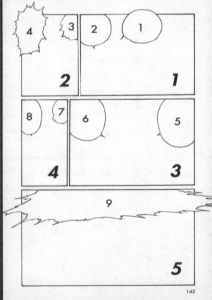

World Trigger reads from right to left, starting in the upper-right corner. Japanese is read from right to left, meaning that action, sound effects, and word-balloon order are completely reversed from the English order.